Praise for *We Are the Nerds*

"This is the untold story of how one of the world's most popular websites was hatched—and how it took on a mind of its own. It's a gripping read, and it's full of lessons for building startups and organizing communities"—**Adam Grant, *New York Times* bestselling author of *Originals, Give and Take* and *Option B* with Sheryl Sandberg**

"Reddit is life. Or at least that's the case for millions upon millions of people on the Internet. Christine Lagorio-Chafkin has done a masterful job of explaining how Reddit became the Internet's dominant cultural force. Fast-paced, packed with insight and, above all, wonderfully entertaining, this is a must read for anyone hoping to make sense of the century ahead"—**Ashlee Vance, *New York Times* bestselling author of *Elon Musk***

"Incisive, witty and brilliantly written. Lagorio-Chafkin gives you a front row seat to the world-altering consequences of sometimes responsible decisions made by a few tiny humans on the front lines of the internet, nerds and all"—**Emily Chang, author of the national bestseller *Brotopia***

"The best, grittiest, most accurate book yet about what it's like to build a startup and a community from scratch (a struggle I know well). And it's a great story; truly fun to read!"—**John Zeratsky, former design partner, Google Ventures, and *New York Times* bestselling author of *Sprint* and *Make Time***

"I've heard every start-up story you can imagine, but Reddit's is as fascinating as it gets. Christine has captured what it really looks like to start a company and turned Reddit's struggle for success into a gripping, entertaining book that is a must-read for every entrepreneur"—**Daymond John, star of ABC's *Shark Tank*, bestselling author of *Rise and Grind***

"A triumph—a business book that reads like a page-turning novel . . . This book captures all the wonder and anxiety we feel about human connection in the social media age"—**James Ledbetter, author of *One Natio***

WE
ARE
THE
NERDS

WE
ARE
THE
NERDS

The Birth and Tumultuous Life of Reddit, the Internet's Culture Laboratory

CHRISTINE LAGORIO-CHAFKIN

piatkus

PIATKUS

First published in the US in 2018 by Hachette Book Group, Inc.
First published in Great Britain in 2018 by Piatkus

1 3 5 7 9 10 8 6 4 2

A CIP catalogue record for this book
is available from the British Library.

ISBN 978-0-349-41636-6

Printed and bound in Great Britain by
Clays Ltd, Elcograf S.p.A.

Papers used by Piatkus are from well-managed forests
and other responsible sources.

Piatkus
An imprint of
Little, Brown Book Group
Carmelite House
50 Victoria Embankment
London EC4Y 0DZ

An Hachette UK Company
www.hachette.co.uk

www.littlebrown.co.uk

CONTENTS

contents

AUTHOR'S NOTE

I woke up in Austin, Texas, on March 13, 2011, to an email from Alexis Ohanian. He explained that I must have swapped business cards with one of his programmer colleagues the prior evening, because mine had been passed on to him "for safekeeping." That was certainly possible; it was my first time navigating the five days of over-the-top marketing stunts and extreme networking known as the South by Southwest Interactive Festival, and as a new reporter for *Inc.*, I'd swapped a lot of cards. Ohanian proposed a coffee. He wanted to introduce me to his business partner, a hacker who had started a new tech company. Hours later, at a café called Halcyon on Lavaca Street, I was seated across from Steve Huffman.

Huffman pitched me on his new travel-search website, Hipmunk, which allowed people to sort flights based on the "agony" their itineraries would induce. Once he'd finished, Ohanian gave me a vinyl luggage tag featuring a chipmunk wearing old-timey aviator goggles.

I didn't want a luggage tag, and, if I'm really being honest, I didn't care a great deal about Hipmunk. I'd jumped on the meeting because I had an inkling these two young men might be remarkable. Huffman and Ohanian had started Reddit back in 2005, a few weeks after they graduated college—long before they started slinging plane tickets.

By this time, in early 2011, if you were working in media you were keenly aware of the "Reddit hug of death." That is to say, when a news story was endorsed ("upvoted," it's called) by enough Reddit users ("Redditors," they're called) to earn a spot on the site's home-page, it would send your website so much lucrative traffic that it could cripple your servers. At the time, Reddit had just exceeded a billion page views, after tripling in traffic over the past year. But Reddit was more interesting than the raw numbers. Huffman and Ohanian had created a Petri dish for discussion and proliferation of the most inter-esting, funny, and awful parts of the Internet. The site was gloriously anarchic, allowing users rather than individual editors to select the stories front-page readers were shown. This led to stunts, memes, nerdy in-jokes, and massive collective acts of charity. It also resulted in lots of limit-pushing, so that you'd often find hate speech and misog-yny smattered in with the derpy dog photos and Star Wars memes. Entire separate forums were dedicated to fat shaming, racist ideolo-gies, and revenge porn.

One currency of Reddit is known as "karma"—points awarded to users for creating popular posts or comments. Another, in-creasingly, seemed to be raw outrage. Users debated everything, but especially the decisions of forums' moderators and Reddit's own policy and enforcement. Watching controversy unfold became known as "munching on popcorn," as if the lurker had a front-row seat to a feature film.

How, I wondered, did something this nutty and sprawling—this mirror of the entire Internet—come out of the brains of these two apparently normal guys?

(• •)

My curiosity about Reddit would not be sated on that day in Austin. Huffman and Ohanian had left Reddit years ago by this point and had measured interest in talking about it. But I was persistent, and back in Brooklyn, Ohanian and I met at a café on Atlantic Avenue halfway between his loft overlooking the Brooklyn waterfront and the apartment I shared with four roommates on noisy Flatbush Avenue. He told me the Reddit origin story.

It was the most improbable startup journey I'd ever heard. I wanted to learn everything. The next time we met, I pitched Ohanian on speaking to me exclusively for a book. I also flew to San Francisco and asked Huffman to give me his time and attention for the same purpose. They both said yes. I knew I'd gotten extremely lucky, but I didn't know that by this time, just months since I'd first met them, squeezed shoulder-to-shoulder in a tiny coffee shop booth, the two men were no longer on speaking terms. There was plenty more I didn't know. An ocean, really.

Over the next few years, I conducted dozens of interviews, racked up introductions to current and former Reddit employees, and pored over leaked chat logs and old photographs. In the meantime, Reddit, as its userbase swelled and its leadership tried to transform it into a profitable company, underwent a series of staffing convulsions and scandals that would have proven the downfall of many startups. A well-regarded Silicon Valley insider was installed as the new CEO, and, in the midst of a massive pornography scandal, raised $50 million. Shortly after, he flamed out under mysterious circumstances.

Silicon Valley feminist hero Ellen Pao, who famously sued a top venture capital firm for gender discrimination, was promoted to chief executive. In 2015, Pao too would be forced out after a user revolt that included sexist attacks, personal threats, and which culminated in a near-site-wide blackout. It appeared as if Reddit's enormous community, by then the seventh most popular site on the American Internet, might snuff itself out.

During Reddit's roller-coaster adolescence, Ohanian's and Huffman's stars had risen. After becoming the face of the tech world's efforts to solve net neutrality, Ohanian wrote a book and became an in-demand speaker at U.S. college campuses and tech conferences.

Huffman followed a less flashy, though no less impressive path; he became one of the startup world's most respected chief technology officers. Life hadn't been all rainbows, though. There was the widening rift in the friendship of the two founders. Also, Ohanian's mother had died of brain cancer, Huffman's marriage was deteriorating, and in early 2013, their onetime friend and business partner, the hacker wunderkind Aaron Swartz, under indictment for wire fraud and computer fraud, had hanged himself in his Brooklyn apartment.

It seemed like a hell of a story: Two nice guys who made it, by crafting something incredible and yet ridiculously unwieldy, with no lack of turbulence along the way. I continued interviewing Huffman and Ohanian, hearing their founding and life stories, through all of it. Then something remarkable happened: Pao dramatically resigned from Reddit, and Huffman made the long-considered and difficult decision to step back in. He would return to the helm of his creation as chief executive. Ohanian would be alongside him, on the board and in an operational role, too, evangelizing for the company's future. The looming question was whether Huffman's leadership could turn the whole misdirected enterprise around. Ohanian called me on my cell that evening.

Now, this, I thought, *this is a book.*

(• •)

Over the years of reporting and researching, I had a close look at three eras of leadership at Reddit. I watched the site's community heave and grow to hundreds of millions of people, who at turns participated in extraordinarily uplifting moments, and at others engaged in hateful, harmful behavior, and even mutinied against the very system that had nurtured them. I was rapt by the hyperpoliticized lead-up to the 2016 election on Reddit, which had already kindled some of the roots of the modern alt-right's digital strategy, and was, we'd later learn, providing a fertile ground for Russian propagandists. Reddit was also where Donald Trump's most vociferous online community had taken root.

When I began working on this book, Reddit had a couple dozen employees spread across several cities; it was a ramshackle operation. In part because Huffman and Ohanian had already let me into their lives, I wound up with a view into the inner workings of the company once they returned in 2015, something extraordinarily rare for a company of its size. Today, Reddit is America's third most popular website, with more than three hundred employees and a valuation of more than $1 billion.

To tell the story of the twelve years of Reddit, I interviewed more than a hundred people—current and former Reddit employees, investors, friends, family, competitors—over the course of six years. I also relied on hundreds of photographs, emails, and documents I obtained. My sources did not always agree with one another, of course. This book's narrative is most heavily influenced by the perspectives of sources whose memories have proven to be both sturdy and rich, and who proved over time to be consistent and reliable. I've done my best to render scenes as they happened. I've reconstructed dialogue very rarely; when I have, I've done it in both the spirit and natural speech pattern of the speaker, usually with consent, and always with assistance, either from the individual, multiple other reliable sources, or documentation. Any dialogue attributed to Huffman or Ohanian was spoken to me, by one of them. I've changed one woman's name out of respect for her privacy. It is marked at first mention with an asterisk.

Avid Redditors may bristle at certain formalities, such as seeing "Reddit" capitalized, which Reddit itself didn't do for many years, and which I've done for consistency. Sorry, guys. When quoting company posts, documents, emails, and comment threads on Reddit, though, I've mostly left typos in place. They, in their own small ways, help tell the story.

As one might say on Reddit, *enjoy your popcorn*.

WE
ARE
THE
NERDS

PART I

THIS GUY HAS NO SHAME

cambridge, massachusetts

(march 2005)

A lexis Ohanian squinted into the silver early evening light, his eyes darting all over Harvard's quad. From the steps of Emerson Hall, he could see spindly trees and an expansive lawn webbed by narrow paved footpaths—but he didn't see a kiosk. What did that even mean, *kiosk*? Ohanian looked at his feet for a moment before taking a breath and locking eyes with Steve Huffman, his best friend for the past four years. Huffman immediately recognized that look. It was Ohanian's "oh shit" face.

Minutes earlier, the pair had left a lecture in a small third-floor auditorium in Harvard's Emerson Hall. To arrive at this auditorium, numbered 304, Huffman and Ohanian had traveled fourteen hours north to Boston on multiple trains; they'd made arrangements to crash for the weekend with distant friends. They had come to see a man little known to the general public. Among a particular niche of programmers, however, Paul Graham was a legend. It was perhaps the nerdiest senior-year spring break in history.

Graham had cofounded Viaweb, an online shopping engine that earned him notoriety once he sold it to Yahoo for almost $50 million. Graham wasn't just a hacker; he was a former artist who'd gone on to write both a programming language and a renowned spam-fighting technology, and he had most recently become known as a prolific online essayist and author. His essays, with titles such as "Why Nerds Are Unpopular" and "Return of the Mac," had become required reading for programmers and aspiring entrepreneurs like Huffman and Ohanian. When Huffman had discovered online that Graham would be speaking at Harvard—and that it would occur during his spring break—he knew he had to be there.

After the speech, Huffman and Ohanian, determined to make the most out of their long journey, had risen from their seats and made their way to the front of room 304. Soon they were standing just inches from their idol. Ohanian knew Huffman was nervous, so he spoke first. He told Graham they were big fans, and then thrust Huffman's soft and worn copy of Graham's book *On Lisp: Advanced Techniques for Common Lisp* into Graham's hands, asking him to autograph it. Graham chuckled. It was the first time anyone had ever asked him to sign his manual for an obscure computer programming language. As Graham scrawled his name, Ohanian blurted that he and Huffman would love to buy Graham a drink if he'd listen to their pitch for a company they were trying to start.

"I guess since you came all the way from Virginia I can't say no," Graham said, figuring he had part of the evening to kill and that the conversation would at least be flattering. "We'll meet at the kiosk," Graham said. He turned away to shake other hands.

The kiosk? Shit. Huffman and Ohanian had been too stunned in Graham's presence to ask what he meant.

"I had no fucking idea what 'the kiosk' was," Ohanian explained later. For a moment, on the steps of Emerson Hall, Ohanian wondered if their quixotic trip north would come to nothing. He tried to calm himself, but frantically scrolled through the rudimentary web browser on his cell phone, attempting to find contact information for Paul Graham. Nothing.

This looked bleak. Senior year had begun winding down at the University of Virginia, where Ohanian had abruptly ceased studying for the LSAT, having decided that being a lawyer required too much faking and bullshit. He vastly preferred smoking weed, hanging out with his friends, and dreaming up ideas for little companies or charities with potential to make a dent in the universe. Ohanian had majored in business, but he'd always had a philanthropic bent. Since high school, he had made a hobby of assisting not-for-profit organizations. Huffman, who had spent time in Silicon Valley and admired successful technology companies, had an infectious zeal for startups, and, recently, Ohanian had caught from him the startup bug. Now they together dreamed of creating a tech company of their own—and they had an idea. So here they were, at this moment in Cambridge, a day's journey from the house they shared with six other college seniors in Charlottesville, with what felt like their entire future hinging on getting advice from Paul Graham.

(• •)

Finally, twenty minutes after the appointed time, Graham appeared in Harvard Square at the tourist information kiosk, which the young men had eventually located. As Graham walked up, they were plain to spot: Huffman, with his thick shock of gold hair, resembled Schroeder from the *Peanuts* comic strip sprung to life and grown tall, and Ohanian, even taller, with warm brown eyes, still beaming as he'd been when he introduced himself earlier.

The trio walked up Brattle Street. Graham—too young to be their father, but rather paternal-looking in khaki shorts and a loose polo, a few grays sneaking into his sandy brown hair—took the lead. Minutes later, the boys were seated across from him at Café Algiers, a Cambridge classic. At the meeting's outset, Graham was tranquil. As Ohanian made small talk with him, Huffman, too socially awkward to know he should order a drink, just slurped down water. But the pair weren't just there to chat. They were there to pitch.

The idea was one Huffman had schemed up, and for which Huffman alone would write the original code. But tonight, he mostly kept his mouth shut. From the moment he had told Ohanian back in the auditorium that they should go up and talk to Graham, he meant—and Ohanian understood—*we* go up and *you* talk to Graham.

As hummus appeared at the table, Ohanian got down to business.

(• •)

Steve Huffman had been both perplexed and thrilled the first time he encountered the name Alexis Ohanian.

It was freshman move-in day at University of Virginia in the fall of 2001. Huffman had just unpacked a couple suitcases into a cramped room on the first floor of a dormitory called Hancock House in the old part of campus. While hauling a load of stuff from his mom's car, he passed doors bearing the names of new occupants. There was ThaiHuu The Nguyen on the first door. Whoa. Huffman couldn't wait to meet *that* guy. Farther down the hall, there was a room with the name Alexis Ohanian. Huffman's mother, who was helping him move in, turned to her son and asked, "Oh, is this a coed floor?" Huffman shrugged. Silently, he thought, *God, that would be fantastic.*

Later that day, a group of freshman girls meandered downstairs from the upper two floors of Hancock—which were in fact occupied by women—to meet the guys who'd moved into the lower two. The ladies popped into Huffman's room, where a few young men were already getting to know each other. "There were girls in my room," Huffman remembers. "And we were talking." This. Was. Epic.

Just then, Huffman heard a rap on his open door, and caught a whiff of melted butter and chocolate. In walked a super-tall guy with a flannel shirt draped over his slouched shoulders. A paper plate was balanced on one of his hands. "Hello, ladies!" he said. "I have this plate of warm cookies."

His name was Alexis, and he most definitely did not possess two X chromosomes. His look seemed modeled after that of Jason

Newsted, the bassist in Metallica: There was the plaid flannel, an oversized, tattered T-shirt, and on his head a stringy, grunge-inspired mop of hair. For some of the year his hair would be dyed green; at times Ohanian also maintained a smattering of lower-chin and upper-neck fuzz, which Huffman would soon refer to as "chin pubes."

As Ohanian handed out his cookies to the young women, Huffman thought, "This guy has no shame."

It wasn't long before Huffman grew to appreciate Ohanian's uninhibited streak. "That's the fun thing about hanging out with Alexis: He will say anything to anybody, either on a dare, or he'll think of it himself first," Huffman said.

As conceited as Ohanian seemed to Huffman that first day, making college friends was something that had put him on edge for months. He worried that he'd be a loner—particularly, that no one would be there to do what he loved: playing video games. Looking back, Ohanian can barely surface a memory of the girls, or the cookies—but what struck him that first week in the dorm was seeing Huffman playing *Gran Turismo*. He thought, "There is hope! There is a gamer in the building."

They became fast friends. Huffman explained, "I was always kind of an asshole, and he always had super-high self-confidence, so we just kind of got along well. I could kind of make fun of him, or we could kind of make fun of other people." Although they communicated differently, Huffman and Ohanian soon realized that they saw the world through similar lenses. Their mutual addiction to video games didn't hurt.

Initially, their joint fixation was *Gran Turismo*, a PlayStation 2 game heralded for its realistic, quick-rendering graphics and accurate—for the era—simulations of the physics involved in auto racing. But *Gran Turismo* was just a gateway fix to a more obscure game called *Wolfenstein: Enemy Territory*. The team-based shooter was still in beta when the guys in Hancock took it up as a collective hobby. For optimal play, the game required many players, each on a computer, to form a team of soldiers in a D-Day-like sea-land battlefield. One team starts in the water and rushes the beach. The other team defending the land is essentially the Nazis. "We used to play that scenario over and over again, just hundreds of times. So we all got very, very good at it," Huffman said.

When the young men of Hancock House took on neighboring old-campus dorm residents in a *Wolfenstein* competition, it was barely a contest: The first floor of Hancock crushed every other team definitively. "It was so epic and funny, we were just screaming and laughing," said Nguyen, who went by Huu, and who bonded with Huffman and Ohanian over video games and blasting heavy metal.

(• •)

Steven Ladd Huffman, born in 1983 in Lansing, Michigan, was always a bright kid, serious and observant. His grandmother called him an old soul. His mother, Jeanette Irby, suspects he was born wired to engineer: His first object of affection as a baby was a vacuum cleaner, which he would investigate and hug. Through his childhood he retained that wrinkled-brow look of skepticism that usually vanishes once a baby reaches toddlerdom.

In school, he was quiet, but excelled easily—that was, when he could focus. Huffman's parents had divorced when he was five, and his mom moved him and his sister to Warrenton, Virginia, a quiet and affluent outer suburb of Washington, D.C. Both his mother and father remarried within a few years and each had two more sons. The resulting family logistics necessitated that Huffman—whose family calls him Steven—and his one-year-younger sister, Amanda, were left largely to their own devices. They were a unit, two bright-blond, saucer-eyed, pale kids, occasionally dressed in matching outfits, often mistaken for twins. Amanda and Steven shuttled between families and states for holidays and long summers in Michigan or Buffalo, New York.

By middle school Huffman was still scrawny, and more outgoing kids pushed him around. His mom stepped in and ushered in a new era of his life that he recalls as a formative change. She transferred the siblings to Wakefield School, a tiny private college-prep school in nearby The Plains, Virginia. Just twenty-six classmates graduated with Huffman, and most were with him from seventh grade through graduation. At Wakefield, the Huffman siblings excelled. They each won Athlete of the Year (he was MVP of cross-country and volleyball; she of soccer), and together they edited the school's literary magazine. They were student body president and vice president. Outside of school, they together took up ballroom dancing.

The one aspect of Huffman's Wakefield years that didn't seem ripped from a Wes Anderson film was his deep love for computers. He'd been dabbling in programming since he was eight years old. His dad encouraged early web browsing by giving young Huffman access to AOL—before the "Eternal September" of 1993 when AOL opened up Usenet access and connected millions of new users to the Internet proper. Summers with his dad were time for offline engineering, too: He would roam the cul-de-sacs with buddies, find discarded appliances such as a lawn mower or a washing machine, and tinker with and repair them.

Back home in Virginia, Steven's stepdad, Jeff Irby, was also into technology and happily supplied Steven and Amanda with Nintendo and assorted gadgetry. Thanks to Steven's tinkering, his mom, an attorney, would sometimes arrive home in the evening to find that he had fried something electronic; sometimes it would be a singed telephone jack, or on one occasion, all three garage-door remotes. In 1994, in an attempt to give him an outlet for his technical explorations, his mom and stepdad gave their then eleven-year-old boy exactly what he wanted for Christmas: a computer. Steven wept tears of joy.

At one point when Steven was in middle school, his stepdad, Irby, took him along on a trip to Silicon Valley, where Irby worked for a startup called CyberCash. It was a short-lived banking startup, with all the early hurdles PayPal faced, but without the funding to clear them. Some of the dynamic in terms of the ongoing dot-com boom was lost on Huffman (he was still an early teenager), but he was smitten by the allure of a super-fast Internet connection. Back in Virginia, he had a snail-paced 2,400-bit-per-second modem. Some of his friends had better 56Ks. CyberCash had a T1 line, approximately 1.5 megabytes per second: epic. Huffman went on a video-game-downloading and -playing tear. He was sold on the awesomeness of the Bay Area.

(• •)

Alexis Kerry Ohanian was born in 1983 in Brooklyn, the only child of doting parents who built their life around his. When he was a toddler, they bought a home in Ridgewood, Queens, not far from Williamsburg, Brooklyn. Within years they deemed it unsafe, and uprooted to lush and affluent Columbia, Maryland, with its lawns and playgrounds and well-rated public schools. Alexis attended high school nearby, in one of America's quintessential large-scale planned communities, Ellicott City. His mom, Anke, a German immigrant, worked as a pharmacy technician during night shifts so she could be home for as many of Alexis's waking hours as possible. His father, Chris, ran a small travel agency that he'd built from scratch while his son was in school. He made a comfortable middle-class living, modest by the standards of one of the nation's most affluent zip codes.

Ohanian was a confident kid, always outgoing and usually pleasant-natured, though a bit of a rascal. When his German-speaking grandmother visited while he was in preschool, he noticed that she eagerly checked the mail. He took to telling her, "Kein Post für du!" (No mail for you!) In grade school he dreamed of playing professional football, but in his spare time he could mostly be found playing Dungeons and Dragons. When asked where he'd like to be in twenty years, the chubby-cheeked kid with chestnut brown bangs and a bowl cut wrote in his grade-school yearbook, "I will probably have rocket-high sales of my comic book, and live the rest of my life in luxury." But his mother's huge heart had already infected his own: "40% of the money I will earn will be used to fight cancer and other deadly sicknesses," he added. (Perhaps his father's business sense had influenced him, too: 40 percent. He wasn't looking to give up the whole farm in fifth grade.)

Ohanian was social, outgoing, and remarkably loyal. His earliest friends, a group of about six guys, all of whom he met before second grade, were by high school still his best buddies. One, Jon Swyers, was hospitalized at age twelve, and recalls that Ohanian came to visit every single day. By high school the guys were still close, and they coached Ohanian through losing a bunch of weight (on top of stubborn baby fat, he'd put on some pounds after a leg injury had resulted in a lot of sitting around playing *GoldenEye 007* and eating Andy Capp's Hot Fries). He was tall already, and after the injury he was a hulking 260 pounds. Rejected by girls, he dealt with the social stigma by making jokes at his own expense. With his friends' encouragement, he ditched the junk food, began working out, and dropped 59 pounds. He also emerged more confident, more willing to stand out.

During high school, to earn spending money, Ohanian cobbled together odd jobs. He took pies and pitchers of soda to tables at Pizza Hut; he worked the counter at a deli for a summer. He answered a newspaper ad placed by a startup called Sidea, and spent a summer hawking software at CompUSA. One of the pieces of software was a children's game based on Ludwig Bemelmans's *Madeline* books. He demonstrated it every thirty minutes, on loop, regardless of whether anyone was watching, his unsteady teenage voice booming through the cavernous big-box store. It was the ultimate, ridiculously mortifying crash course in public speaking. But he was getting paid. "So," he said, "it was wonderful."

(• •)

If Ohanian's early engagement with computers didn't glorify startup life, Huffman's sure did. Coding was Huffman's primary hobby, and he loved reading accounts of startups, such as Jeff Bezos's founding of Amazon. He thought eTrade was super cool. He

watched the skyrocketing share price of eBay, which had gone public in September 1998, during his freshman year of high school.
Why wasn't *he* one of these kids getting rich in Silicon Valley?
Huffman felt cloistered by the rigidity and routine of school. He
dreamed of moving out to San Francisco—or at very least enrolling
in his dream college, MIT. (He ended up applying to UVA after his
mom and stepdad explained they'd only pay tuition if he went to a
state school.)

During summers starting at the end of high school, Huffman
got his first taste of startup life—one in no way connected to the
fast times in the Valley. This first job was with a little government-
contracting company called Image Matters. A local entrepreneur,
John Davidson, whose son also attended Wakefield, led Huffman
up to his attic, pointed to a corner, and said, "See if you can get
this thing working."

It was a hulking computer, a forty-pound tower the size of an
end table. Huffman lit up. He would know that body anywhere: a
Sun Ultra 10. While his classmates used hot rods or nature scenes
as their own screen's background image, Huffman's 386 PC featured a photograph of a Sun Ultra 10. He had never seen one in
person. He giddily hauled it home and got it running. Davidson
gave him the job.

Huffman arrived at Image Matters to find five guys working on
government security and emergency response technology. He later
admitted he didn't fully understand the scope of the work at the
time, but one project helped layer locations of disaster responders
over a map. Another was sort of a web-based assistant like Siri.
What Huffman largely worked on was translating data for the "semantic web," a layer of coding that helps computers understand
and catalog a website's contents. Image Matters didn't behave how
Huffman expected startups should. "It wasn't very glamorous. All
its money was from government contracts, so their projects were
kind of boring," he said. "No users, no scaling problems—none of
that stuff."

In Silicon Valley, he suspected, there were cool, audacious up-

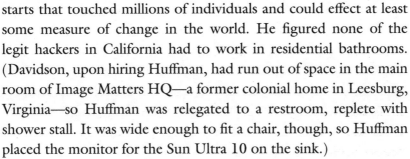

starts that touched millions of individuals and could effect at least some measure of change in the world. He figured none of the legit hackers in California had to work in residential bathrooms. (Davidson, upon hiring Huffman, had run out of space in the main room of Image Matters HQ—a former colonial home in Leesburg, Virginia—so Huffman was relegated to a restroom, replete with shower stall. It was wide enough to fit a chair, though, so Huffman placed the monitor for the Sun Ultra 10 on the sink.)

During his college summers working for Image Matters, Huffman's programming skills metastasized. Ohanian witnessed his buddy becoming a whiz programmer—and realized he wasn't quite as technical. Ohanian decided to major in history and business (or "Commerce," in UVA speak), while Huffman stuck to computer science. Their approaches to coursework also differed. Ohanian spent evenings reading and rereading his textbooks and course notes at university libraries, while Huffman would put off studying all week, then crank through a project the night before turning it in. He usually did well enough to validate that strategy.

Some of the hours spent not studying, Huffman filled with pranking Ohanian. Once, he hacked Ohanian's political website, eyeswide.org, which Huffman thought took itself way too seriously. He wrote a program that made all outgoing emails from the EyesWide domain appear to originate from a website that sold prom dresses. Other pranks were less ephemeral. Once, Huffman sprayed self-hardening foam insulation into Ohanian's trusty L.L. Bean laptop bag. Ohanian was tipped off before the foam solidified—he jammed his right hand into the bag to retrieve his laptop before it became part of a permanent foam brick. The laptop survived. Ohanian's right hand retained small chunks of foam for a week.

HOW TO START A STARTUP

In their junior year at UVA, Huffman and Ohanian moved into an apartment together, a tidy and compact two-bedroom just off campus in a set of buildings called the Preston Square Apartments. Ohanian shared a room with a good friend and fellow student named Jack Thorman, a lifelong resident of Charlottesville. Huffman took the other bedroom.

At Preston Square, Huffman began a subtle mission to inculcate Ohanian with his passion for startups. While they lounged in the two La-Z-Boy recliners Huffman had nabbed from his mom's house, he told Ohanian stories of Intel and Apple and Viaweb. Ohanian had always wanted to study law and assumed he'd use his education for good—maybe be a human rights attorney or work in nonprofits—but slowly Huffman convinced him that creating something cool in the world, even a business, could effect more change. A few months later, Huffman gave Ohanian a copy of *Masters of Doom*.

The 2003 book by David Kushner tells the story of the founding of Id, a scrappy startup that pioneered massive technological innovations in video gaming and went on to create the gaming phenomena *Quake* and *Doom*. The book was an admiring portrait of the company's founders: obsessive and antisocial John Carmack and charismatic "idea guy" John Romero. Ohanian adored it—and he could see something of Huffman and himself in the duo. *Masters of Doom* helped breathe life into what Huffman had laid out.

One gray afternoon, Huffman sank into one of the recliners and launched into a rant. A local gas station he liked, Sheetz, had a touchscreen where customers could order their sandwiches. It was high-tech for the time, and, in theory, pretty efficient. But it was inside near the cashier. Huffman would find himself outside pumping gas, thinking about going inside to order—only to have to wait again for his sandwich. Why not use similar technology to order ahead? Ohanian, fresh off reading *Masters of Doom*, and currently perched on the opposite recliner, sprang into idea mode: "That's brilliant!" he thought, saying, "We could totally make a business out of that."

Lots of their friends had cell phones; it would have to be a cellular-phone-based system. Text messaging, which was catching on with some of their friends, was a possibility. Could people just text their order to restaurants ahead of time? What would that look like? Today, that question is quaint. But mainstream smartphones didn't exist in 2004, nor did today's app ecosystem. Huffman and Ohanian didn't really know how it would work, but they did know what they'd call it if it could: MyMobileMenu. It seemed impossibly clever: MMM, like the soft murmur of satisfaction.

Ohanian followed the playbook he'd learned in his business courses: market research and due diligence. He opened an account at Bank of America and filed papers for Redbrick Solutions, LLC, a name inspired by Charlottesville's architecture that he figured sounded more official than "MMM." Ohanian's "market research," however, mostly involved hoofing around Charlottesville, strutting into local shops and talking to business owners. He'd give them the pitch and shake hands that they'd try it out, someday. Not much came of it.

The following autumn, Huffman, Ohanian, Thorman, and

Nguyen, along with three other guys, moved into a big house at 107A Kent Terrace, which they affectionately dubbed "the Shit Box." It was a dingy, drafty mess of a student house, with what they suspected were layers of old carpeting under the current carpeting. Whatever was going on below their feet, it gave walking around a shiver-inducing, springy sensation. When someone stomped or moved too fast, dust and ants, which seemed to have taken permanent residence, kicked up. Sometimes a few pellets of rabbit poop flew, too—Nguyen, who was now majoring in aerospace engineering, had inherited a bunny named Kichu from a friend, and she often roamed free.

The worst thing about the Shit Box was the basement. Not only was it the epicenter of the ant infestation, but it also occasionally flooded. There was a grimy little bathroom separated from the main room by only a piece of plywood hanging askew. No one wanted to sleep in the basement. Ohanian gamely took it; he knew if his roommates were frightened to venture downstairs, they certainly wouldn't care if he never bothered to clean. Plus, it wasn't like he had a girlfriend to impress.

He did think a lot about one of his classmates, a woman named Amber.* She had diverse, fascinating interests that always seemed to lead her off in new directions. But their relationship was on-again, off-again, and he wasn't holding his breath; she planned to study abroad in Germany soon.

Huffman took a more secluded bedroom, so he could have some privacy with his girlfriend, Katie Babiarz. While Ohanian crammed in all the credits he could his senior year, Huffman's schedule was sparse, which left him plenty of spare time to nurture his hobby of competing in ballroom dancing competitions with his sister, Amanda. (He'd continued lessons in college in part to meet girls, but when it came time to compete, the only partner he considered good enough was Amanda.) He also studied Lisp, the programming language about which Graham wrote the coding manual. At nights, alone in his room, Huffman coded a Lisp calendar application for his senior thesis.

Ohanian, plotting his future, wasn't giving much thought to Redbrick Solutions, a.k.a. MMM, either. He was writing an eighty-page thesis about the firebombing of Dresden, preparing for law school, and cramming in seven courses for twenty-one final college credits. When he and Jack Thorman weren't studying, they were smoking weed. One Saturday morning, the two of them woke up at dawn and plodded to a Kaplan LSAT prep class. It was result-based—more about methods for test taking than actual content learning, which frustrated Ohanian. He and Thorman sat down, were simply presented with a practice test, and told they'd get the results in two weeks. This was what he was paying for, more test taking? Frustrated, Ohanian fidgeted, flipping over the Scantron. There, he saw all the correct answers—those promised in weeks—printed right there on the opposite side of his sheet. They walked out and headed to get breakfast.

Over eggs and hash browns, Ohanian and Thorman talked real talk. They looked past the horizon of their senior year and saw the three looming years of law school. They envisioned daunting piles of debt and career uncertainty. If he'd rather be eating hash browns than taking a test he'd already paid for, Ohanian knew it wasn't worth it. He was not going to be a lawyer. Later, in retelling the story, he would come to call this the "Waffle House Epiphany."

Ohanian had already accepted a summer internship at Ogilvy & Mather, a slick public relations firm in New York, when one of his favorite professors, Mark White, offered him the chance to go to Singapore that summer for a tech-entrepreneurship summit. The words "tech-entrepreneurship" sounded a little like jargon to Ohanian. But he was itching to travel more—White had taken him along on a trip to South Africa the prior year, and he had already studied abroad in London for part of sophomore year. Money was a consideration: The internship was unpaid. The Singapore trip was all expenses paid. Ohanian ditched Ogilvy. Within a couple months, he was on a transatlantic flight with White.

The first evening in Singapore, July 11, 2004, Ohanian felt like a beloved son—and, for one of the first times, a little grown up. He was nestled in that warm and exhilarating feeling of having gone out on a limb—and, for once, wasn't checking his balance for fear of falling. Aside from his own father, White was the man whose judgment Ohanian most trusted. His courses had been the highlight of Ohanian's college education, and his approval had become very important to Ohanian. On this night, White was more like a friend: They decided to go out together and explore Singapore. A couple of drinks into the evening, Ohanian ignited in his belly the courage to explain to White his distinctly nonacademic side project: the mobile food-ordering app. Maybe the Singapore Slings helped. He gave the full spiel, from gas-station inspiration to "MMM."

White loved it. He told Ohanian, "I think you have a chance."

The next morning, in Charlottesville, Huffman woke up to an urgent email from Ohanian:

> hey bro, i'm in Singapore at this technepreneurial seminar, and am basically spending a week learning how to create a tech startup. i spoke to Mark White (a professor in the comm school, the guy who took me to South Africa, and who recruited me to come here, as well as a generally good guy and technophile) over some drinks last nite, and pitched him on our idea...but basically said it was one of the best he's heard, perios [*sic*]. Not only that, but he wants to be on the board of directors, and already knows some people to hit up for starting capital...I've got plenty of more details, but I am seriously considering putting off law school for this, but i need you, and we'll both need to be doing this full time for about a year to get it off the ground...this is the kind of thing that could change our lives...

Ohanian remembers writing that email with a giddy excitement. "I just had to get the message across to Steve that I was so amped up and we just had to do it," he said.

Huffman read the email with an eye roll. He needed no sales pitch. He knew Ohanian had cooled on law school. "I'd already by that point made up my mind to do this thing," he said years later.

The pair had even, Huffman later recalled, plotted out how to work on MMM after graduation while paying for rent and ramen and server costs: Huffman would continue working at Image Matters. Maybe Ohanian would get a job, too, but they'd planned on working together, hustling on nights and weekends, whatever it took.

(• •)

Katie Babiarz, a pretty brunette UVA pre-med student, was sprawled across her bed, half-reading a magazine. It was a blustery winter evening in typically mild Charlottesville, and there wasn't much to do, even if she could tear her boyfriend away from his computer. She'd met Huffman earlier in the year, after he'd spotted her at a party and announced to Ohanian, "I fancy that girl," before approaching her to introduce himself. Now they'd been dating some months, and here he was in her living room, coding a web calendar application for his senior thesis.

Babiarz heard Huffman holler, "Hey, this guy I'm a really big fan of is giving a talk soon." He explained that he'd been reading the website of Paul Graham, one of his programming idols who frequently posted essays online. That day Graham had posted that he'd be delivering a speech soon.

"You should totally go!" Babiarz said.

"Well. It's in Cambridge. At Harvard."

"You should totally go!"

"Well. It's over our spring break."

"Go! What else are you going to do?"

Huffman emailed Ohanian. Two minutes elapsed.

Huffman was still staring at his screen when the reply arrived from Ohanian: "Absolutely, bro!"

(• •)

As Graham, whose hair has a boyish wave and whose shoulders slouch slightly, spoke, he didn't look up much. He didn't gesture.

He didn't boast or tell the sort of seemingly impromptu but actually extremely rehearsed stories the way folks who make a living appearing at college auditoriums like this do. He didn't take questions. He just read, at a lively pace, from sheets of lined yellow paper, into a microphone:

> You need three things to create a successful startup: to start with good people, to make something customers actually want, and to spend as little money as possible. Most startups that fail do it because they fail at one of these. A startup that does all three will probably succeed.

Huffman was in awe. His idol was talking—about the lives of Lisp programmers, about how college buddies should start companies. It was as if Graham's speech was designed with him in mind; everything fit, and each bit of Graham's reasoning seemed sound.

Parts of the speech resonated with Ohanian, too. He latched on to Graham's extraordinarily simple description of how to create a valuable tech startup: Do something better than it's already done, at a lower cost. As Graham read on, describing himself back when he was a young Lisp hacker, Ohanian glanced over at Huffman—it was as if he was describing his best friend. There were glimmers of the inevitability of what they were trying to start back home, from the Shit Box. What Ohanian really loved was the frank, straightforward, indelicate way Graham articulated the basis of a viable business: "I can think of several heuristics for generating ideas for startups, but most reduce to this: Look at something people are trying to do, and figure out how to do it in a way that doesn't suck." Graham described online dating sites as ripe for disruption, because they "suck." He characterized Google's goal at the company's genesis as to "create a search site that didn't suck." The simplicity made Ohanian smile.

In the auditorium, seated not far from Huffman and Ohanian, was a blue-eyed, sandy-haired Harvard physics grad student named Chris Slowe. He'd worked all day in the lab of Danish physicist Lene Hau, which was working on cooling particles down to a micro-kelvin—very close to absolute zero—to conduct experiments on them. (This Harvard lab had already performed an incredible feat: slowing and then stopping a beam of light in these temperatures, a first, for which many suspected Hau would win a Nobel Prize.)

Slowe hadn't heard of Graham until his buddy from the lab, Zak Stone, a Harvard physics undergrad four years Slowe's junior, urged him to attend the talk. Stone, who possessed a contagious enthusiasm for big ideas, had already convinced Slowe to join a loose cohort of mostly undergrads who met weekly in a campus cafeteria to discuss digital information systems management. Back in 2004, if you'd saved a PowerPoint, article, or Word document you'd downloaded, but you didn't recall where, or what specifically you'd named it, finding it again could be a major pain. Something akin to desktop search—which did not yet exist in any mainstream capacity—they realized, would fix that. They named the code base "Kenny," which was a play on *ken*, the range of knowledge, and would also allow them, should they foul up the code at any point, to shout the nerd-zeitgeist zinger from *South Park*: "Oh my God, I killed Kenny!"

Within months, the after-hours brainstorming and diagramming became a welcome creative outlet for Slowe after his long days at the fluid dynamics lab. Even as Slowe began writing a structure for a program, Stone and his ragtag group of physics researchers didn't consider their project a startup—it was simply, in their physics-major vernacular, an extracurricular "research project." But that afternoon in Emerson Hall, Graham's speech allowed Slowe to think about it differently. Graham said, "For a lot of people the conflict is between startups and graduate school. Grad students are just the age, and just the sort of people, to start software startups." Graham explained that starting a company while studying was not insane; it was ideal, for if the company actually took off, it might just provide you a life path that reduced your burning desire to be an assistant professor.

"Huh," Slowe thought, for the first time in years seeing an option for his future that didn't necessitate a life of near-complete social isolation collecting unending data sets. Nor did this alternate future necessitate securing a tenure-track job, publishing research, and running a lab full of machines that needed constant upkeep. He found himself smiling at the possibility.

A few rows away, Huffman and Ohanian soaked it all in, occasionally whispering to each other notes of approval.

(• •)

That same evening, on the other edge of the continent, a pale eighteen-year-old named Aaron Swartz sat in front of a computer in his dorm room at Stanford University. Harvard was on his mind, too. Swartz was pondering crafting an essay about Harvard president Larry Summers's recent comments about women's representation in tenured university positions in science and engineering. He'd been researching the history of fraud in scientific research, shunning both the California sunshine and his fellow students—whom he'd deemed just weeks into college as insufficiently academically serious. Instead, he locked his door and worked on his writing. When he wasn't blogging, he was sharpening his Python coding skills. He, too, followed Paul Graham's blog—and recently they'd been emailing. Within days, once it got posted online, Swartz would encounter Graham's speech, "How to Start a Startup." And soon he would make his own pilgrimage out to Cambridge to see Graham.

(• •)

In the Harvard auditorium, Graham glanced up from his sheaf of yellow papers to see his audience full of youthful faces, and delivered the final lines of his speech:

> If you want to do it, *do it*. Starting a startup is not the great mystery it seems from outside. It's not something you have to know about "business" to do. Build something users love, and spend less than you make.
>
> How hard is that?

(• •)

At Café Algiers that evening, Ohanian dipped a pita triangle in the hummus and set it down on his small white plate. He took a breath, and began his pitch. He explained to Graham the startup idea he'd been tossing around with Huffman, from its genesis at Sheetz to its incorporation as Redbrick Solutions, to its startup-y name, MMM.

Huffman sat silently, and noticed a portrait of a young man about their age, but from a past era, staring down at them. He fixated on the painting hanging behind their table while Ohanian spoke.

Some minutes elapsed, probably five, but to Ohanian it felt like an hour, him prattling away, hoping he was doing his buddy's idea justice. Graham suddenly became enthused. Perhaps he was beginning to feel the pulse of a good idea, a technically smart solution behind the silly name and hyperlocal concept. There was a pain point: waiting in lines. There was a massive audience: everyone who ate out, or, hell, anyone who shopped. There might just be a software-based solution. And these kids could be—and this would be awesome—the first to bring that solution to market.

Graham grabbed the reins of the conversation, transforming into an enthusiastic peer, explaining to the undergrads recent innovations in mobile communications and the history of developments in individual messaging. He explained that Charlottesville might be a fine place to start, but it should never stall their vision to end lines everywhere, all over the United States. "This will be the end of lines," Huffman later recalled Graham said. "No one will ever have to wait in line again!"

Ever since Graham had sold Viaweb to Yahoo—his code would over the years become the technological backbone of Yahoo Shopping—he'd been dabbling in early-stage startup investing. These kids were starting to look like they might fit the bill. They were young and enthusiastic classmates, with wildly different personalities, like Larry Page and Sergey Brin. They were a hacker and a computer-competent salesman, like Steve Wozniak and Steve

Jobs. They were tight friends, like Bill Gates and Paul Allen. They were awkward, and smart. Enthusiastic—and almost too young for him to relate to. Maybe they were perfect.

Huffman piped up suddenly, interrupting Graham's monologue about disrupting the act of line-waiting. "No no no! We just want to solve this problem that's huge in, like, fast-food restaurants."

Still, by the time the three got up to leave, Huffman was feeling inspired, looped into the hyperaware state that seems to tag along with incredible opportunity or vast change. Happy and starstruck from speaking with Graham for the past hour, he said goodbye to the host of the restaurant. Returning the pleasantry was an old man Huffman recognized. He was the man from the painting Huffman had been staring at, a few decades aged.

Huffman leaned over and whispered his observation to Graham. Graham had eaten at Algiers dozens of times but had never noticed the painting, likely of the owner as a young man. Who was this kid?

Graham opened the door and they stepped one by one down onto Brattle Street.

"Startups are hard," Graham said. "But I think you guys have a shot."

NOT YOUR STANDARD
FIXED-POINT COMBINATOR

Paul Graham was satisfied with the praise he'd received for his Harvard speech and essay of the same name. But one thing he'd said the evening he first met Steve Huffman and Alexis Ohanian was still gnawing at him days later. An attendee had shaken his hand and asked for advice on searching for startup funding. Graham had told him to seek out wealthy people, particularly those experienced in technology. The young man stared at Graham, who fit that bill precisely. Graham realized it, and blurted out, "Just don't come to me!"

Graham knew that his recoil was selfish, but he really didn't want a hundred computer science students bugging him with pitches. The lingering guilt allowed him to reconsider. He'd been wanting to invest more—why shouldn't he put his money where his mouth was?

Around this time, he and his girlfriend, Jessica Livingston, would take long walks from dinner in Harvard Square to his home, talking for hours through evenings as they schemed up grand plans for their lives. Livingston, a thirty-four-year-old with a radiantly blonde bob and easy smile, was a marketing executive at the Boston investment bank Adams, Harkness & Hill. She had recently embarked on a new project, a book of interviews with company founders, so she was mulling leaving the bank. Together, Livingston and Graham conceived of an experiment, just for the summer, that would give Livingston a new part-time job and allow Graham to dabble in angel investing.

Graham had more than a few conceptual hang-ups about investing. He firmly believed that Silicon Valley's massive and entrenched venture capital firms were to blame for the age of irrational exuberance that had led to hundreds of frivolous websites and tech companies being overfunded, and then bursting into thin air around the turn of the century, in what became known as the dot-com bubble. He saw venture firms as greedy, due to their tendency to bloat well-tracking upstarts with money, eventually overburdening and crippling them with outsized profit requirements. If Graham was truly going to enter this world officially, he wanted not just to tread lightly, but rather to create an entirely different funding system for upstarts.

The premise he had already laid out in his speech was simple: Young people with few life burdens, few resources, and lots of gall were the ideal candidates to embark on a startup. Heck, Michael Dell and Bill Gates were each just nineteen when they'd set out to create their now-iconic corporations. Graham himself had started Viaweb on $10,000, and he had every expectation that his experience could be replicated with even less funding now, a decade later, with faster, cheaper technology available. In order to find and fund these sorts of individuals without betraying his principles, he would disavow the very language Silicon Valley had adopted around nurturing small companies. His project would be an incubator of sorts, never to be called a "tech incubator," and be funded by money from a group of individuals, never to be called a venture fund. This thing, which he and Livingston dubbed first the "Cambridge Seed" and then the "Summer Founders Program," would only be classified by Graham as an "experiment."

Graham and Livingston hashed out details of the "experiment" in a week. They would try to find a dozen or so of the brightest young hackers, and give them money for pizza and housing for three months. There was no need to choose a precise number of startup teams; they'd accept however many both applied and that they deemed "sufficiently good," starting that very June. By the time they arrived back at his Cambridge home on the evening of March 11, they were both giddy. Graham snapped a photo of Livingston, who was just beaming, to immortalize the moment.

The investment vehicle that would fund the Summer Founders Program soon earned another name: Y Combinator. The name came from an obscure concept in lambda calculus (which uses fixed-point combinators) that allows mathematical equation-writing to achieve something called Curry's paradox. Put into plain English, a Y combinator might help form a sentence such as, "If this sentence is true, mayonnaise is made from peat moss." The same way that sentence defeats itself, a Y combinator can show that lambda calculus is an unsound system, by finding inconsistency in mathematical logic. The concept is referenced in certain computer programming styles, and had become something of a hacker inside joke. Learning what the heck a "Y combinator" is would be a little Easter egg to every applicant who Googled it—so much so that for a while YC's blog included a tagline only a nerd could adore: "Y Combinator: Not your standard fixed-point combinator."

Y Combinator would be not your standard startup incubator. It would start tiny, intended to help a handful of little companies get their legal framework set up, get a product established, and then introduce the founders to bigger, real investors. It would focus on very, very early-stage companies, typically ignored by Sand Hill Road's investment firms, giving them just $6,000 per founder for the summer—enough for rent and pizza, not enough to bloat them or bog them down. It would be a friend and an inspiration, allowing the founders autonomy all week, not chaining them to desks. The founders would gather each Tuesday for a supportive social dinnertime meet-up session. Livingston remembers adoring the little plan, but thinking it so odd that she pondered, "How do we even tell people about this?" Graham had a solution: He stayed up all night building a bare-bones website describing the mission and including a thirty-five-question application. The next day, he linked to it from his popular blog.

Applications—good, legitimate startup ideas—began arriving that week. Dozens arrived each day; 227 had come in by day ten. Clearly the idea had struck many, many nerves. Graham told Livingston, "You better quit your job."

(• •)

Back in Charlottesville, Ohanian paced behind Huffman, who was, as usual, hunched over his computer. After much coaxing by Ohanian, Huffman hit send on an email to Graham, thanking him for the meeting. What he received in return was an appeal to apply to be part of Graham's little summer experiment. They were elated—they'd already spotted mention of it on Graham's website, and now assumed they had an inside track. Still, Huffman and Ohanian agreed they'd have a better chance of getting in if they included another technical founder. Huffman's buddy Andy Barros, one of the smartest guys in Huffman's computer science program, fit the bill. Over a burrito, Ohanian and Huffman convinced Barros to help complete the application. Ohanian emailed around questions and compiled the group's answers.

Most of their answers were standard, if indecisive: To the question "What OS(s) and language(s) will you use?" they wrote, "Steve likes Lisp; Andy likes perl," to "How will you make money?" they wrote that they would charge a commission on every restaurant order placed through the system. One question is illuminating, both for its answer's content and its earnestness:

If you could trade a 100% chance of $1 million for a 10% chance of a larger amount, how large would it have to be? Answer for each founder. (There is no right answer.)

Steve: A million dollars is a lot of money. Considering the paltry amount we need to actually build the system (we need to eat), a million dollars would go a long way. Since we would have only a 10% [chance] of the larger amount, I would expect $1 million to be 10% of the large value (i.e. $10 million).

Andy: The statistician in me wants to say that the expected value of the second item would need to be more than $1 million (so $10 million).

Alexis: See above. I tend to be more risk-adverse [*sic*] (ironic, given how gung-ho I am about this startup despite the pitiful odds of its success), so it would have to be a few million more than $10mil.

Note: Andy and Steve came up with their answers separately. Alexis copied us.

The application also asked, "If you've already started working on it, how long have you been working and how many lines of code (if applicable) have you written?" The trio's answer: "No code written yet."

(• •)

Jessica Livingston had grown to adore Paul Graham's quirks. He refused most days to wear pants, or closed-toed shoes. Shorts and Birkenstocks were his uniform—even when they went out to white-tablecloth dinners. He collected old potato mashers; their undulating wires may have appealed to his inner mathematician. Despite appearances, Graham did possess a sophisticated aesthetic sensibility, and had trained as a visual artist. He had for many months admired on his walks around Cambridge an out-of-place, low-slung industrial building on a residential block of Victorian homes. He inquired about it, and heard it had once been a candy factory, and then a porn studio, and after that, some plumber just used it to store his tools. When one day a For Sale sign appeared out front of 135 Garden Street, Graham promptly paid roughly three-quarters of a million dollars for the property and set in motion renovations.

It would be his own private, sprawling office—Livingston knew Graham well enough to know he was deeply obsessed with his work, his own projects, and that he required both solitude and quiet to truly concentrate. To that end, he ordered the building refitted with double-paned glass windows and two layers of doors, making street noise all but imperceptible. The shell of the bunker was painted bright white, and inside five skylights would usher light down onto oriental rugs topped with a smattering of minimalist-feeling midcentury modern furnishings, courtesy of Graham's architect friend Kate Courteau.

The office was nearly complete when Graham and Livingston schemed up Y Combinator in the spring of 2005. Graham ceded the space to his new project. "The joke was that Paul never got to work there," Livingston said. It would be ideal, with its fascinating little rooftop solarium and stylishly mismatched black wire lounge chairs. They'd agreed to only open it up to the founders one day a week, to still give Graham the run of the space. A few offices were tucked into corners, leaving a broad main room entirely open. It would be filled with custom long folding tables and matching benches, so the space could be transformed easily: tables out for dinner, for speeches or presentations; tables folded away for mingling events.

To bolster the effort of Y Combinator, Graham tapped his former business partners at Viaweb, Robert Tappan Morris and Trevor Blackwell, who were already interested in finding fresh ways to collaborate. Each invested $50,000, to match the $100,000 Graham and Livingston would use to initially fund the experiment. The arrangement was that together Graham and Livingston would run Y Combinator; Blackwell and Morris would read applications and help conduct two days of interviews. Morris was one of Graham's closest friends, and was known to him as RTM. (Graham once wrote a computer language and named it RTML. The language was subsequently used by merchants on Yahoo.) To the rest of the world, Morris was best known as the hacker who created the first computer worm, which he designed at Cornell and unleashed at MIT. For that act, he earned the distinction of being the first person prosecuted under the Computer Fraud and Abuse Act. The other partner, Blackwell, was a Harvard computer science Ph.D. with fluffy white hair who hailed from Saskatoon, Canada. He was fond of building humanoid robots that balance on wheels instead of feet.

As applications arrived in droves, the partners cut off submissions after just ten days. Graham invited twenty groups of young men—there was not a single woman in any group—to Cambridge for interviews the second Saturday and Sunday in April. Livingston tackled logistics.

The applicants who shuffled in and out of Graham's office impressed and fascinated Livingston. One group was composed of three college programmers, each of whom possessed a different severity of Russian accent. Mikhail Gurevich, his cousin Greg Gurevich, and their buddy Mikhail Ledvich pitched an idea for remedying online click fraud, which—theoretically, at least—could boost the effectiveness of online advertising. They called it ClickFacts. Greg Gurevich adeptly and confidently answered Graham's technical questions. (What Graham and Livingston didn't know was that Greg was mostly winging it. He had a talent for mustering confidence; perhaps the shots of vodka chased with Listerine that he, his cousin, and their buddy had just downed helped.)

Nineteen-year-old Sam Altman pitched Loopt, a location-aware social networking application, with two other founders. Only by the time of the interview, Altman's cofounders seemed like they were bailing out. Upon hearing that Altman would be flying solo, Graham emailed him, brushing off a cofounderless endeavor: "You know, Sam, you're only a freshman. You have plenty of time to start a startup. Why don't you just apply later?" Altman responded, "I'm a sophomore, and I'm coming to the interview." In person that day on Garden Street, he impressed Graham immediately.

The same day, Livingston saw a sweaty kid and his out-of-breath father push through the front door of their office. They'd speed-walked there, fearing being a few minutes late. Graham shook their hands and gave them a tour of the space. The kid was Stanford freshman Aaron Swartz, who in certain Internet circles was a minor legend, having at age fourteen cowritten the RSS 1.0 standard, a new way of syndicating web content, and having written a code layer for the online copyright sharing system Creative Commons. Swartz appeared to have all the markings of a bang-up programmer, and his blog had quite a following online—perhaps larger than that of Graham's own. It didn't surprise Livingston when instead of asking Swartz to provide details immediately about his startup idea (Swartz's application proposed creating a website-making tool he'd dubbed Infogami, which rhymes with "pastrami"), Graham pitched Swartz on a different but related idea. They mulled different names for whatever Swartz's creation would be. When the meeting ended, it was already clear that Graham had mentally accepted Aaron Swartz to Y Combinator.

There was Chris Slowe and Zak Stone's group of Harvard grad and undergrad students, whose concept of a desktop search program had already won a Harvard Business School entrepreneurship contest. A group of Yale students who'd been best friends since second grade pitched a universal calendar with a rare four-letter domain name, kiko.com.

Then there was the duo from UVA who wanted to tackle food ordering, and do it through cell phones.

Sitting down across from the four Y Combinator partners was an entirely different experience for Huffman and Ohanian than having coffee alone with Graham. This time, Graham displayed much more skepticism of their market and their ability to enlist restaurants. He may have also raised an eyebrow at the fact that only two of the three applicants showed up (Barros had already bailed). Most of the questions were highly technical, which required Huffman, uncomfortably, to do most of the talking.

Morris asked how the user's phone would take orders, and how it would communicate with the restaurants. It was far-fetched in early

2005 for a brick-and-mortar store or restaurant to employ mobile technology—heck, it was rare they even had a website. The iPhone would not be released for two years. Huffman hadn't fully thought through communications structure, but said, "The phones will just talk to one of our computers," and prattled on at length about the specifics of how a simple Internet server functioned. Later, he was embarrassed: He realized Morris was quite obviously well versed in the ways servers interacted with the World Wide Web. Despite the blunder, when walking out of the office onto Garden Street after forty minutes of grilling, Huffman felt confident.

Graham had told each group to wait for a call around 7 p.m. on Sunday, not long after the interviews wrapped up. The YC partners made quick work of whittling down from twenty interviews the eight they wanted to fund. Livingston wrote a short list on the whiteboard in their Garden Street office, simply listing nicknames she'd made for each group, such as "The Kikos," the Yale group with the great four-letter domain name. They made the cut. Sam Altman, the solo sophomore: yes. The Russians, whom Graham had started to think of as "The 3 Mikhails" (never mind that one of them was named Greg): yes. Aaron Swartz, the Internet phenom: yes. Promptly at 7 p.m., Graham started dialing numbers.

Huffman and Ohanian were crashing that weekend with their friend Felipe Velásquez, who belonged to one of Harvard's elite finals clubs, the Fly Club, and they spent time roaming the clubhouse at Two Holyoke Place near Harvard Square. Huffman and Ohanian toured the trophy room, where taxidermy game heads lined the walls, and which emitted a decades-accumulated hint of stale tobacco. Huffman was told that a Roosevelt had killed some of the trophies. Modern frat-life touches, though, abounded— billiards tables topped with glass, the better for beer pong, and giant mounted speakers to pump hip-hop through keggers.

On Sunday evening at 7 p.m., Ohanian sat on Velásquez's couch and stared at his Palm Treo, an early smartphone. After an excruciatingly long fifteen minutes, it started buzzing. He answered the call, already excited.

"I'm sorry, we're not accepting you," Graham said.

Ohanian was devastated. Huffman, enraged, turned cold. To Ohanian, he appeared indifferent, but inside, he was fuming. He thought Graham had known all there was to know about their idea already when he invited them to come all the way from Virginia. They had traveled six hundred miles on multiple drafty trains, missing classes and sacrificing one of the precious last weekends of their senior year. For this. That was shitty, thought Huffman. He stayed angry all evening, through dinner, and through drinking more Sol beers than he could count at the gaudily festive Border Cafe. He sublimated thoughts of Graham, instead channeling his bitterness toward his surroundings. The dominant thought for Huffman that evening was, "Harvard has no girls."

Ohanian, whose head was swirling from the mix of beer and rejection, was introduced to some soon-to-be Harvard grads who were boasting about their white-shoe finance job offers. He had just experienced the opulence of the Fly Club, which felt a long way from their Shit Box back at UVA. This scene felt like no place for the awkward nerd with a plate of cookies, a late-night video-game player who spent his senior-year spring break seeing a mildly interesting programmer read from an essay aloud. One of the polished seniors asked Ohanian what he was doing with his life.

Between slugs of Sol, Ohanian giddily spun out a story: Well, it just so happened that he'd received backing from a powerful dot-com millionaire for his startup. He would be moving to Boston to be the executive of a company that was destined to make the world a better place. Who knew where it would go, but maybe they'd sell the company for millions; get rich, move on. He lied to their faces.

Uttering that lie is something Ohanian still regretted years later. He would come to think back on that night as the first rejection in a life otherwise filled with trophies. He didn't fit in, and he couldn't accept it.

Huffman, Ohanian, and their new Fly Club pals wandered home very late. Someone was watching Adult Swim on television, and an episode of *Robot Chicken* was playing. Huffman felt like he should be high, but he was not: *Robot Chicken* was the most absurd thing he'd ever seen.

By Monday morning, Huffman and Ohanian were all sour stomachs and lingering bitterness heading to the train station to begin their long schlep back to Virginia.

(• •)

That Monday morning back at 135 Garden, Livingston was over the moon. They'd established a worthy roster of more than a dozen young men who would move to Cambridge for three months that summer, and give up a small fraction of equity in their soon-to-be companies in exchange for $6,000 each.

But Graham was rethinking the list. He told Livingston he was considering adding another team to the eight they had selected, and she immediately nominated Huffman and Ohanian. Their idea would take too long to find a market fit, sure, but as individuals they were upstanding. They were obviously smart and dedicated enough to trek on a long train ride to Cambridge twice, she argued. On top of that, Livingston thought Huffman was so cute she'd called him a "muffin." It was silly, but somehow it stuck. On the whiteboard in the Y Combinator office's conference room, in the list of the top candidates, along with "The 3 Mikhails," she'd written "Cell food muffin" to describe Huffman.

Graham, midday, dialed Ohanian's number.

When Ohanian saw his phone lighting up, he looked out the train window. Where even were they? Maybe somewhere in the middle of Connecticut. He picked up to hear Graham say, "Hey, Alexis. Listen, I'm sorry, we made a mistake. We really liked you guys. We liked you—but not your idea. Let's figure out something else."

Ohanian explained that he and Huffman were already on the train back to school. It was too late.

Huffman thought, "Okay, well at least he's not stupid."

In that moment, Huffman almost at once admitted to himself

that perhaps Graham was correct about their idea. His arrogance didn't subside, despite that he felt validated and redeemed. He was relieved that at least he could go on intellectually respecting Graham: "If we weren't in, that would have just been stupid." The pair conferred, and within minutes, they decided: *What the hell.*

The train pulled to a stop at a platform, and Huffman and Ohanian rushed to the door. With their bags, they hopped down and ran across the active tracks. When the next train heading north to Boston pulled in, they tried to explain their situation to the conductor, who, exasperated by their manic enthusiasm, reluctantly let them on.

Graham got word and emailed Livingston. "Muffins saved."

FRONT PAGE OF THE INTERNET

G raham pulled out a chair at the conference room table and explained where Huffman and Ohanian had gone wrong. It was too early to be focused completely on mobile development. Few people were yet using their cell phones for much Internet browsing. Text messaging and BlackBerry Messenger were still in their infancy. Graham had an entirely different sort of Internet business in mind.

You know who was on to something, Graham mused: Slashdot. He pulled up the site and showed the young men its trove of interesting but somewhat mainstream tech-centric links. There was also, similarly, Delicious (known often by its curious domain name, del.icio.us), a site many people used to bookmark their favorite websites and articles, or find topical content, based on freeform hashtags suggested by users. Co-created by former Morgan Stanley analyst Joshua Schachter, Delicious had earned Graham's esteem after it directed significant traffic to some of his essays, which had been boosted to its "popular" page. Clicking on that particular tab on Delicious yielded a delightful mix of content, from highly technical Linux how-tos to general-interest links to *Saturday Night Live* clips and Roger Ebert's best movie list for the year.

In Graham's mind, the Delicious page was good—but it could be far better. The root of the site's problem was in its utility: Many people used it as a bookmarking site, which meant its content veered toward longer articles and journals and programming guides individuals were saving for later rather than things they simply loved and were currently reading.

It was a "holy shit" moment for Ohanian. "Yes!" he thought. "We need to do exactly this, but for what people want to share at the moment."

Huffman, too, was seeing the wisdom of Graham's thought train. He jotted down a few notes in a graph-paper notebook he'd taken to carrying. The notebook contained some typical college scribbles ("I'm sorry I'll shut up now") and doodles (3-D cubes, a penis) he'd made during class at UVA, and some coursework notes, too, but on this day it transformed into a place where Huffman would document the origins of, and his progress on, their new, as yet unnamed project.

"The site people go to find something new," Huffman wrote in blue pen. "Points for being the first to recommend," he also wrote, likely transcribing Graham's exact words regarding building a recommendation engine before any of their preexisting competitors could.

The recommendation engine was integral to the success of this hypothetical project, Graham thought, because one would need to dangle a carrot for users to entice them to post links in the first place, and then to return again and again to discover and share.

Discover and share. Ohanian immediately considered his own personal use case: He spent a lot of time navigating to the *New York Times*, the *Washington Post*, and a host of blogs every morning. What if the best articles, the ones he'd naturally click on, were all right there for him in one place? That would be awesome.

It was in that moment that Graham said, "Yes. You guys need to build a front page of the Internet."

They liked it. All visions of MMM had been scrubbed from their imagination. They were in: They would build the front page of the Internet. As a measure of congratulation, Graham bought the young men airplane tickets home.

(• •)

Back in Charlottesville, the rest of senior year slipped by, punctuated by keggers and all-night *World of Warcraft* binges. Ohanian turned in his Dresden thesis. The basement of the Shit Box flooded in dramatic fashion, drowning likely thousands of ants and waterlogging Ohanian's few worldly possessions.

Huffman began settling some matters of logistics and emotion. He'd need to quit his job at Image Matters, which he had already committed to join full-time after graduation. He'd have to part ways with his girlfriend, Katie Babiarz, for the summer, and that wouldn't be easy on either of them. He'd also have to tell his mom. Despite multiple conversations, his mom was skeptical of what he and Ohanian were working on, which made sense, because it didn't exist yet. She wanted her son to take the steady job, with health insurance. He overruled her objections. "We were getting $12,000 for me to quit my job and go live in Boston for three months. I guess when you've had a career and you have kids that seems totally outrageous," Huffman said. "But to us, we were just like, 'Who gives a shit?' "

There was an exclamation point at the end of the school year, a trip to Cancun with their closest friends.

Even as the crew of friends sat on towels on the sand, drinking Coronas, the conversation kept turning back to the website Huffman and Ohanian would be building upon moving to Boston. Ohanian showed off possibilities for the site's mascot—he'd doodled a small alien during marketing class, all round edges, beady eyes, and goofy grin. A favorite game was coming up with possible names for the company, which would also have to be taken from available website domain names. The brainstorming—they asked almost everyone they knew—had begun back in April. Ohanian emailed Huffman a running list on April 22, 2005. It included thirty-two names for the domain and company, such as "mysnoo," "hotsnoo," "hotagg," "aggpop," "lexpop," "populoo," and "ripefresh."

Huffman wrote back, "I like poplex still. aggpop isn't bad, neither is hotlex, but i think poplex still takes the cake." As the hour neared 2 a.m., Ohanian replied with a few new ideas, including:

> lol how about poptzar
> hehe get it popTZAR
> like in russia?
> eh?
> -
> damn
> ok i sleep now

Huffman's ideas weren't much better. In his little graph-paper notebook he'd written bufflist.com and a few potential taglines, including "surf in the buff" or "read your news in the buff." Five days later, the email chain was still going, and Ohanian was still coming up with crazy new names, such as perkle.com, oopdoo.com, and aeonpop.com. At noon, he emailed Huffman "more name ideas." A list of seven names included at the bottom Reddit.com, with the note, "I kinda like this one."

Huffman had found a website called Stuckdomains, on which visitors could search for domain names whose owners had allowed them to expire. On it, he typed in "News." One of the many related results that came up was "Newstew," or news stew. He also typed in "Read," and hit enter. A long list of weird portmanteau words appeared, words like "Breadpig." Huffman thought, "Oh man, we *have* to buy breadpig.com. It's so hilarious." Ohanian purchased Newstew and Breadpig.

As he considered words related to "News" and "Read," Ohanian re-added "Reddit" to the running list. Huffman jotted in his graph-paper notebook, "Reddit yet?" But he still liked Poplex and Newstew better. Huffman bet Ohanian, "I'll go ask ten people on the street and no one will know how to spell Reddit properly." Ohanian agreed. The first people they stopped and talked to were a Hispanic-looking couple who spoke little English. Huffman figured he'd gain an early lead in the bet, so he asked them, "How do you spell Reddit?" The man answered: R-E-D-D-I-T.

By the time they were all packed up and ready to move to Boston, Newstew was the front-runner. Over tacos and beers with Katie, along with a few good friends from their freshman-year dorm and their roommate Jack, they hashed it out and took a vote. Newstew won. Everyone drank to the new moniker for the yet-unbuilt site. Ohanian later joked, "I think we liked it...because...alcohol?" The name soon morphed to an abbreviated 'Snew or Snoo, as in "what's new," which Ohanian mocked up as a logo, with the alien perched right next to it.

Graham, however, shared Huffman's skepticism about the name. In an email, he complained to Huffman about the name 'Snew or Snoo. It was likely doomed anyway, as they couldn't easily secure the snoo.com domain, which was owned by a domain squatter. Graham didn't like the name Reddit either. No one really did. When asked years later when he eventually came around to the name, he replied, "I still haven't. I don't think it's a very good name."

Graham wasn't sure about the little alien mascot either. In an email at the time, he wrote Ohanian, "If you're attached to the little bug guy, put him at the bottom instead of the top; then it looks like a joke instead of branding."

Both Huffman and Ohanian felt for the little alien being demeaned. He wasn't a bug. They kept him. And in an act of defiance masquerading as a backup plan, Ohanian purchased Reddit.com.

IT'S ONLINE

In the center of the sunny second-floor room, two desks were
planted back-to-back, so Steve Huffman and Alexis Ohanian
could work all day facing each other. A flimsy unvarnished wood
bookshelf loomed over Huffman's left shoulder, as if daring him to
pile on it yet another programming manual or abandoned beer bottle. Over Ohanian's right shoulder hung a campy centerfold of a
blonde woman in a pink bikini tromping through ankle-high
waves.

This would be their office, and their home, for the next three
months, this summer student sublet in a mint-green duplex at
72 Bristol Road in Medford, Massachusetts. Here, Huffman and
Ohanian spent the bulk of their waking hours—roughly 10 a.m.,
when they'd stumble from their beds to their living room desks
and blast Gwen Stefani's "Hollaback Girl," until midnight, when
they'd wind down by jamming their thumbs on *World of Warcraft*
for a few hours. Their backs to the windows, which were at times
hung with makeshift curtains of towels to prevent screen glare, they
talked and coded and sketched and designed business cards. For
breaks, they sometimes walked to nearby Davis Square to get pizza.

More typically, they simply wheeled their desk chairs over to the PlayStation.

Huffman had arrived in Boston a few days before Ohanian, and brought with him the notebook from college and Cancun, full of potential names, site structures, and concepts. He knew what he wanted: a way for users to submit links, and to give a virtual thumbs-up to content they enjoyed with a single click. That click, or an upvote, would help Reddit rank its homepage—the most interesting, most upvoted stuff would rise to the top. It would be a massively collaborative content popularity contest and key to their model. Their competitors, Delicious and Slashdot, constantly refreshed their "popular" pages; Reddit's homepage would only be a "popular" page.

Also scribbled in Huffman's notebook was the word "karma." Huffman and Ohanian had concocted another secret sauce. They'd give readers feel-good points that would accrue with every activity they partook in on Reddit. Posting a link: karma point. Having your post upvoted by someone else: karma point.

Huffman's notebook also contained a list of four items under the heading "submission." The four items read: "title," "url," "description," and "category." To anyone who's ever submitted an article to Reddit, this list will look familiar. It's a textual mock-up of the site's "Submit" page, which has remarkably remained in nearly this formation since mid-2005.

Now Huffman had to build it. He started out solo, simply learning how to create a system of webpages. PHP, a scripting language for dynamic content of HTML sites, was popular at the time, but Huffman wanted to do something more *Grahamsian*. He had spent a lot of time researching AJAX, a method for organizing the underlying structure of a website that allows data to be retrieved from a server in the background while a user is viewing an apparently static site, and which was becoming more widely used at the time (Gmail, Kayak, and Delicious each employed it). Ruby on Rails, the soon-to-be common back-end framework for sites (Airbnb, Hulu, and Twitter were built on it), would not be released until months later.

One night while working alone, Huffman left his desk and sat with the trusty graph-paper notebook on his bed. In it, he attempted to map out a sample structure of pages for links, and submitting, and the homepage. Despite having coded programs previously, he'd never built a website before, and this night he had gotten stuck on structuring a page with links to different pages, some of which performed a function, others that required continual refreshing. While the homepage of Reddit was to be a list of the most popular links, ranked 1–50, at the top of the page Huffman envisioned tabs that would provide alternative views of the site's content, including by most recent submission, and most popular of all time. These, too, would require constant refreshing, but would need to rely on different versions of a ranking algorithm. His working plan was a cat's cradle of pages and operations, some in AJAX, some in BASIC.

"When I finally had something that made sense, I remember thinking, 'I've been making this way too complicated with all this AJAX shit. They should just be normal pages,'" Huffman said. He ended up creating a Lisp program that would run continually, and that would generate all of Reddit. No more complicated workarounds. No more Googling. He'd just use trusty Lisp, which he'd used a lot during college, and in which he already had written his thesis project at UVA. He pulled some of his old calendar code and got to work.

Ohanian moved in and things got fun: Thinking through big conceptual programming questions was challenging, and was punctuated by rewarding "aha" moments. And Huffman had Ohanian to share them with. While Huffman scoured the few online Lisp directories for inspiration for the site structure, Ohanian worked in a shareware copy of PaintShop Pro 5 on his PC, which ran on Windows XP. He designed static site mock-ups, and perfected the little alien, which had been nicknamed Snoo, a homage to their hopeful but as yet unattained website name. He even designed stickers, with the alien, Reddit.com, and the tagline "what's new online." By July 1, Huffman had added Snoo to the very top left of Reddit.

In early weeks, next to every link and headline was a set of words: "Interesting" and "Boring." For a few days, there were a whole host of different emotions one could select for any given link, but Huffman and Ohanian almost immediately deemed that labeling system overcomplicated. For about twenty-four hours, they tested out a five-star system of rating links. (Huffman determined that the difference between a three-star and a five-star article might not be, well, anything, so they ditched it.) They toyed with a thumbs-up icon, but realized it implied that the link was an inherently positive thing, or that one liked it, when really the action they wanted from users wasn't quite an endorsement of a link; instead it was a click that meant they wanted it to be seen by more people, and to bubble up in popularity (or, of course, the converse, to be pushed down by being downvoted). Huffman and Ohanian wanted to give their users credit for knowing how the site's underlying technology would react to their actions. To that aim, they settled on arrows, one pointing up and one down, to the left of each post.

Those simple arrows fed Huffman's algorithm all the data it needed to sort submissions for the past twenty-four hours by votes per hour, and tally their popularity. That provided the ability to rank the posts on the front page of Reddit. It also provided the extraordinarily simple theoretical framework on which Reddit functions to this day.

(• •)

Every Tuesday evening that summer of 2005, the nineteen Y Combinator batchmates gathered at Graham's Garden Street office. They chowed down on a Crock-Pot full of chili or pasta sauce or whatever "slop," as the guys lovingly referred to it, Graham had dumped from cans into the slow cooker that day. Livingston used the weekly meals to dote upon the young men, shopping for special cheeses for their appetizers at Formaggio Kitchen or brewing her grandmother's secret recipe for iced tea with lemonade and mint.

The doting served as part of a tidy veneer Livingston established early on: to appear as if she was a den mother. She had been mostly silent in the initial interviews, coming across to some of the interview subjects as a secretary, rather than an investment partner. What the young men didn't know was that to a large extent, Livingston was calling the shots. Graham knew her to be a tremendously accurate judge of character, and she made the final call on many applicants, including making that validating push for Ohanian and Huffman. She made other significant judgment calls that summer while running Y Combinator in tandem with Graham. Their lives, home and work, meshed together completely; they were in love (unbeknownst to the young founders) and in love with their new project.

The Tuesday dinners accomplished many aims for Livingston and Graham, the simplest of which was giving the batch of men—who'd spent their weekdays coding alone, headphones on, in front of screens—a chance to meet, collaborate, and commiserate. Before the first dinner, a few of the founders had thoroughly Google searched one another. Huffman knew one he wanted to meet in particular: Aaron Swartz. Huffman had heard he was a hacker prodigy with a libertarian bent and a flair for the dramatic, which was readily on display on his well-read personal blog. "I remember thinking, 'This guy is insufferable. He is so obnoxious.' And the self-righteousness bugged the shit out of me," Huffman said. During the first Tuesday dinner, Swartz was the first person Huffman met. "He was just short, and really shy and quiet, and I just could not believe it was the same guy I had a predisposition to dislike," Huffman said. He came away from that evening thinking Swartz—and his little website company—was really cool.

Other founders shook hands and warned each other of the YC headquarters' most painful "bug": The legs on the benches at the custom-designed long tables in the main room were too close together. If you sat near the end of the bench, the entire other side would fly up in the air like a seesaw, sending you tumbling to the ground. They asked about each other's companies, and some wondered aloud whether Graham and Jessica Livingston were dating.

To several of the other young men, Huffman and Ohanian stood out. Mikhail Gurevich, who had pitched an idea for remedying online click fraud, recalled being impressed immediately by their kind demeanors. Each seemed smart, but neither had an obvious chip on his shoulder. "They were the nicest people I've ever met just in general; the most humble people," he said. Ariel Schwayder, one of the three founders of a company called Simmery Axe (a Gilbert and Sullivan reference; one of the characters lives on St. Mary Axe—say that aloud with a British accent), remembers Huffman and Ohanian being extraordinarily easy to chat with. "They were into other stuff, like video games," Schwader said. "They didn't *only* want to talk about programming or their website."

Huffman made friends easily with the other hackers, but he spent a significant amount of time during those Tuesday meals speaking directly with Graham, asking pointed questions about Lisp programming and website foundations.

Ohanian, an extraordinarily social and courteous guy whose most universal descriptor is "charismatic," had a harder time—not because he wasn't trying. He was trying, perhaps too hard. As the most "nontechnical" cofounder of the batch, he became the subject of a joke among the hackers: "But what does Alexis *do*?"

It didn't help that Graham overtly favored the most talented engineers. He had chosen Huffman and Ohanian in part because they fit a well-observed hacker-slash-business-guy cofounder pair stereotype, but he'd also come dangerously close to calling Ohanian unnecessary. In an interview for a documentary made that summer about incubators, Graham told the camera with a mischievous smile, "The relationship between hackers and business guys, at least in the beginning, is that you need hackers—and you don't need business guys." And despite knowing some web design and HTML, and even having made an attempt to learn Lisp at the summer's outset, Ohanian found that his best defense was to latch on to his identity as a nontechnical founder.

As weeks passed, the answer to the question "What does Alexis *do*?" became clear: He was the charm offensive. He was the guy designing, producing, and plastering Reddit stickers all over Cambridge. While Huffman coded the site's building blocks, Ohanian envisioned the task of building hype, in person and in the press. He'd manage the community that Reddit would develop, answer questions, and keep users happy. But first...they'd need users. In the meantime, he'd do whatever he could do, even if some days that entailed just ordering the pizzas and keeping track of them on a budget spreadsheet.

Tuesday dinners also served as a weekly progress report for each of the teams. They were held accountable there not just to Graham and Livingston, but also to one another. This was also the opportunity for PG, his old Viaweb nickname, to extend his influence over the companies, and the education of these nineteen founders, whose average age was twenty-three.

While eating, they'd listen to a talk by one of Graham's friends, colleagues, or fellow tech luminaries. This first summer, speakers included Stephen Wolfram, the computer scientist known for his controversial tome on applying computational systems to the broader world, *A New Kind of Science*, and Boston-area startup wunderkind Langley Steinert, who'd founded CarGurus and TripAdvisor. Graham's lawyer, Mark Macenka, delivered a talk about patents and copyright, and perhaps, due to his jovial demeanor and ponytail, convinced the young men to drop their fear of lawyers.

The talks offered practical lessons about scaling a company, hiring, and finding customers. They also corroborated the anti-establishment gospel of Paul Graham. Cautionary tales illustrated the ills of the venture capital ecosystem, which Graham thought still entailed too much money chasing too few deals. Venture firms had no lack of interested backing, even from the sorts of pension funds that had suffered so dearly just five years earlier during the dot-com bust. Olin Shivers, a computer scientist at Boston's Northeastern University, included a PowerPoint slide in his presentation that is still legendary. It read: "VCs: soulless agents of Satan, or just clumsy rapists?"

Graham wanted his charges to be wary of investors who, if given the chance, would wrest control of their board of directors and boot them as executives. More important, he wanted the men to know that the system was not designed to help them. There was a recent law, Sarbanes-Oxley, that levied tighter compliance standards on public companies; Graham had already heard whispers from private companies that they'd avoid going public at all costs due to the new burdens. Graham could envision a cruel world in which startups stayed private longer, continuing their funding cycles longer than ever before, despite what they'd learned from the recent crash. (A scrappy website popular among certain college kids called TheFacebook had just received a whopping-for-that-time $13 million investment from Accel Partners that May. It would not go public for seven years.)

Graham's thumb-nosing of the big Silicon Valley firms permeated everything at YC, its vernacular—Graham would for years implore journalists to not describe his project as a "tech incubator"—and even its aesthetic. For YC's logo and signature color, Graham looked to the finance world, whose logos contained swaths of welcoming teal blues and secure deep greens—and went in the opposite direction. He had the front door to 135 Garden Street painted a glaring persimmon orange. That abrasive hue would become YC's signature color, the color of many cups and plates and the Eames shell chairs in the YC kitchen, and the orange-red that PG often chose for his standard dress of polo shirt.

What was left when Graham removed from startup funding all the things he disliked was very close to the concept that was becoming known as "the lean startup." It entails using existing technologies to iterate fast, initially ignoring certain "best practices" commonly associated with running a functional company, such as scalability, internationalization, and heavy-duty security. He advised the founders, instead of being thorough, to release early versions of their work that were lightweight enough to evolve. Graham later wrote on his blog that "best practices . . . interfere with the primary function of software in a startup: to be a vehicle for experimenting with its own design."

Later, he would clarify this idea of what would soon become

known as "minimum viable product." He said, "The sooner you get it out there, users can start telling you what they want instead of you guessing. If you sit down and think of the perfect implementation, the problem is you're thinking of the perfect implementation of the wrong thing."

Graham's philosophy is counterintuitive for perfectionists, compliance junkies, or straight-A types who thrive within rigorous institutions. It means constantly editing your workflow to favor only the most important tasks, and not getting caught up in the details. Slowe and Stone, the Harvard physicists, spent the summer puzzling over the theoretical organizational structure that would underpin their desktop search tool. They wanted to be inclusive of a variety of individuals' search strategies, because the way a programmer might look for a code file on his hard drive would be very different from how an artist might find a photograph. In other words, they got caught up in building something sturdy that would scale broadly and smoothly. They never launched a product.

Huffman, by contrast, was very good at following the lean-startup doctrine. Stone described Huffman's practical approach as: "Okay, what's the most important thing that we can do right now?" Huffman wrote to-do lists, from which he'd methodically start at the top, most important item, and work his way down. Other lists were titled "where do I spend time?" and "what is the problem I'm trying to solve?"

By the middle of the summer, Graham had added a new catch-phrase to his litany of advice. "Make something people want." It stuck, and became a mainstay of Graham's future speeches and a Y Combinator mantra. By the end of summer, the nineteen guys were so accustomed to hearing Graham say, "Make something people want," that they put it on a T-shirt. Well, sort of. The shirt's front bore a Y Combinator logo. On the back were screenprinted the words "Make Something Paul Graham Wants."

(• •)

By about three weeks into the summer of 2005, Huffman had become accustomed to panicking roughly twice each day, when the name Paul Graham would appear at the top of his Gmail in-box. This was the same man who'd pledged them thousands of dollars of his own money to let them experiment with code all summer, the same man who'd expressed so much enthusiasm for their startup pitch months earlier. The same paternal figure they felt comfortable enough around to start calling PG. But this was a different side of PG. These were curt notes with feature suggestions (users should email each other!), feedback on the name (he hated it), the alien mascot (what about an octopus?), and, mostly, the dreaded "check-in" email. "Paul in one person is his own good cop and his own bad cop," Ohanian said later that summer. "And there's this amazing dichotomy between the Paul Graham that we often get emails from and the Paul Graham we know in person."

This third week in June, it finally got to Huffman. One note was particularly harsh. It didn't just ask for a progress report; it ranted. Graham wrote, in essence, "I don't know why you haven't launched yet; either you can't do it or you are waiting for it to be perfect, and I don't know which is worse." It deeply irked Huffman. He thought Graham was being a huge dick.

Huffman stewed. He also thought, "Well, *what if*?" He had been writing the back-end code of the site for just twenty days, along with building the architecture that would determine the site's external functionality. It was bare-bones, and far from perfect—Ohanian didn't have the mascot or logo ready yet—but for the most part, it worked. So, *fuck it*, thought Huffman. He put Reddit.com live on the Internet.

Sure, it was passive-aggressive to play his hand silently. But Huffman knew Graham would be proud. Their site was live. Huffman told Ohanian what he'd done, but he knew no one else would notice. Well, maybe Graham would notice, Huffman thought, knowing full well he'd first be pissed to not have been in the loop. After getting over that, he'd be ecstatic. So Huffman waited. All weekend he obsessively checked his in-box for the glorious, "Well, shit, you did it!" email from Graham. It never came. Whatever. He would see Paul Tuesday.

Tuesday afternoon, Ohanian and Huffman walked into the Y Combinator office, less than two miles from their Medford sublet, and where they were scheduled to see Graham and the others for dinner. Huffman was still fuming. As Graham walked up, the first words out of his mouth were, "Where is Reddit?"

"It's online," Huffman said.

"Really?" Graham's eyes grew wide.

"Yes," Huffman said flatly. He was a little bitter that Graham hadn't bothered to check the URL over the past three long days. "It's online."

Sure enough, when Graham typed www.reddit.com into his browser, he found an actual website with a blue toolbar at the top that read "Reddit" in white, alongside four navigation links, which read "profile," "browse," "submit," and "help." A handful of headlines and hotlinks dribbled down the white page below. It was simple, programmed to display just a default sans serif font, which materialized as Verdana on most browsers. There were no flourishes. To Graham, that was perfect, a truly minimum viable product, live, online. Graham was satisfied to know Huffman and Ohanian *could* do it. It was immediately apparent that they hadn't committed the other sin he'd mentioned, waiting to be perfect. The links were just hyperlinked headlines, though each provided some context: They displayed the user who'd submitted them—at this point either Ohanian or Huffman. More important, perhaps, was that the site had an intangible vibrancy to it; built in were several visual cues to recent activity that had happened on the site, including time of posting, a ranking system, and small "hotness" meters below each link.

For Graham, it was a validation. His persistence at urging Reddit to launch—or "ship" a product, in Silicon Valley parlance—had worked. It was the first of his little funding experiments to yield a real, tangible thing.

Over the following weeks, Graham continued to give Huffman

significant feedback. Reddit was his pet; Huffman suspected Graham was giving extra attention to him and Ohanian because they were earnest people. Other batchmates suspected Graham felt more responsible to "the Reddits," as they were sometimes known, because he'd supplied their idea. He not only stayed in regular contact with Huffman about his progress, but also created a Reddit account, u/bugbear.

As June, the first month of Y Combinator, wrapped, Reddit had something none of the other companies had: a working website. Huffman and Ohanian's batchmates, this class of young men whose ages precisely spanned the tidy demographic of eighteen to twenty-eight, were Reddit's first users. They'd been casually enlisted through Tuesday dinners and over AIM chat, though Graham's primary account, u/bugbear, usually trumped them all in activity. As other founders tinkered with their prototypes and rewrote code, Reddit was another browser window on their screen, one that refreshed regularly with new, interesting links. "Reddit changed every day, so you could see it improving over the summer," said Justin Kan, one of the founders of Kiko.

To say they were the first users is not entirely true. They were the first users aside from Huffman and Ohanian, whose initial, primary—and now long-standing—usernames, respectively, were spez and kn0thing (spez being an abbreviation of another username Huffman favored online, Spengler, as in Egon Spengler, the character who provided the brains of the *Ghostbusters* operation; kn0thing being Ohanian's high school gaming handle, an abbreviation of the title of his favorite song, Metallica's "King Nothing"). A favorite story of Ohanian's is that his first ever post to Reddit on June 23, 2005, was a link to the Downing Street memo, the meeting minutes that exposed the origins of the Iraq War. Huffman, from the desk facing Ohanian's, immediately downvoted Ohanian's post. U/kn0thing's first karma was −1. "Because Steve is a dick," Ohanian said.

Now that the site was live on the Internet, though, spez and kn0thing were not Huffman and Ohanian's *only* usernames. They each created several, or rather several dozen, in order to make the site appear more vibrant—like it had actual users instead of just two nerds posting news from other websites to the little thing they'd built in their living room. Graham, u/bugbear, did too. It's a concept now known as "growth hacking," the usually not so technical act of actually turning a product into a vibrant business, or, in this case, making it look like their website had early traction. "The first hundred or so Reddit users were video-game characters, or pieces of furniture in our apartment. Lampshade was a big user," Huffman later joked.

Reddit, in its early days, and thanks to the interests of its early users—these young hackers along with their friends and mentors—was a narrow trove of technology news and liberal-leaning politics links. "Move to a new planet, says Hawking" linked to the BBC's report on speculation from physicist Stephen Hawking that an asteroid or nuclear attack could wipe out civilization on Earth. "Top 10 Web Fads" was a link to a CNET report. "Students Combat Click Fraud" was a link to a blog post about the company Mikhail Gurevich and his two friends were building. Huffman took to telling friends, family, and press about this list of headlines they'd built by explaining that its posts were "the best of the web."

With each clumsy attempt to explain this new little company, this new social news hub, more users found Reddit.com. Perhaps a few people even signed up after seeing black-and-white 8½-by-11-inch computer-printer flyers around Boston with an alien mascot dressed as Uncle Sam, reading, "I want YOU for Reddit.com." Slowly, Reddit grew.

Over the next four weeks, Huffman slept with his laptop in order to wake every two hours to ensure the site was still online. During days, he solidified the basic structure of the site, making small tweaks to it and its functionality. Now that it was populated regularly with links, Graham was satisfied, even though Huffman and Ohanian had refused to turn their alien into an octopus, per Graham's suggestion, or change its name. Then one day in July, four weeks after Huffman had put the site live, traffic surged. Huffman watched Reddit's site error log, which he kept visible at most times, speed up. The uptick in errors wasn't a bad thing in Huffman's mind—because one thing it meant was there were more users. It was apparent: Suddenly, Reddit had lots of visitors.

It didn't take Huffman long to figure out the source of the traffic to their single web server in Medford. Graham had posted a link to it at the bottom of his personal site, where he'd usually link to his latest essay. "New: Reddit is written in Common Lisp." This was Reddit's first real debut to the Internet: It was a launch. Within another month, there were a couple hundred registered users, some of whom were not Graham, Huffman, Ohanian, or their friends. They were like-minded readers of Graham's blog or frequent users of other similar sites, such as Delicious. "Everybody always says this about every early community," said Stone, who was building the desktop search tool, "but in the early days, the people who were using Reddit were literally the Internet's top power users, and every link was awesome."

One day in August, Huffman was away from his computer for most of the day; he'd self-consciously decided to take a mini-vacation from submitting links and attempting to populate the homepage, which only listed the twenty-five most popular posts from the previous twenty-four hours. He expected the page to be mostly blank when he checked back that evening. To his surprise, there were many new posts, some by usernames he hadn't previously seen. He was awed. Reddit was really working. Other people were really making its popularity engine churn. Reddit was truly alive.

HELL SUMMER

One hot midsummer night after a long day of working together, Ohanian and Huffman cracked open beers and fired up *World of Warcraft*. When Ohanian looked at the clock it was after 3 a.m. He strode to his room, threw his clothes on the floor, and thumped down onto his mattress, also on the floor. At least he was now exhausted enough to ignore the heat, and the nagging thought that they should cave in and get an air conditioner.

At 6 a.m., his BlackBerry started ringing. Foggy-headed and damp, he heard an older woman's unfamiliar voice say, "Alexis?" As Ohanian rubbed his eyes, the woman introduced herself as Amber's mother. Amber and Ohanian had been dating on and off for a year. She'd been studying in Germany, and despite their long phone calls, their relationship was rocky. Amber's mom didn't seem to know, or care, at the moment. She blurted through the phone that her daughter was in the hospital. She'd had an accident and was in a coma.

Ohanian sat up and started pummeling his pillow with his fists. He cursed. Once he calmed down enough to speak, he called his dad. He explained the situation: The night before, Amber had tumbled approximately five stories from a window of the apartment she'd rented while doing a summer abroad in Germany. She'd suffered extreme head trauma and a multitude of other injuries. Improbably, miraculously even, she was alive. He knew he needed to see her—even if she couldn't see or speak to him.

Amber was one of the most exciting people Ohanian had ever met. She was exuberant and curious, and wildly passionate about nearly every new thing she encountered. She was the type who'd strike up a conversation with a stranger and walk away with a newfound interest in fifteenth-century German poetry, or, say, the physics of bumblebee flight. Ohanian relished their wide-ranging phone conversations that summer, in which she educated him about Goethe, and he told her about building a tiny web company. He'd started to think of her as his girlfriend, "even though she probably wasn't," he said.

But now it appeared something awful had happened. A fall seemed unlikely. Had she attempted suicide? Amber was in critical condition, an ocean away.

Chris Ohanian booked his son a flight for the next day. Alexis flew to Baltimore that morning, picked up his passport, and boarded a flight to Germany. He stayed in the hospital with Amber, sitting alongside her mother, for the next ten days. Amber didn't wake from her coma during his trip.

(• •)

Amber's initial recovery took roughly six months; once she awoke from the coma, her memory of Ohanian and their relationship was patchy. Still, Ohanian visited again toward the end of summer, and when in Medford took to calling her every day at noon, so he could talk with her while she ate dinner. When not on the phone, Ohanian attempted to return to regular life, but it was hard. Still, he had Huffman. And Reddit, which had turned a corner.

New users, who'd found Reddit through Graham's site or by word of mouth via Ohanian and Huffman's college friends and their Y Combinator batchmates, or maybe even through the posters and stickers Ohanian plastered around Cambridge and Medford, were becoming regulars.

As summer drew to an end, Huffman observed a flow of content from disparate IP addresses every day. Huffman and Ohanian's goals shifted to nurturing that audience. "Let's not let the users down" became their new mantra. They used their multiple accounts to upvote submissions they loved and spent hours responding to user email. They schemed up new features, and Huffman's patrol of the error log continued. Within months, twelve thousand people would be navigating to Reddit every day.

(• •)

Ohanian had much of his heart torn by Amber's accident, and in the waning weeks of summer he called his parents often. One evening in September, before Chris and Anke left for Norway to celebrate their twenty-first wedding anniversary, they had a particularly lengthy, emotional talk with Alexis. He knew life had been a struggle for his mom since her only child had left for college four years earlier, and he was glad for his parents to be able to celebrate now, together, with this vacation.

The following morning, Ohanian was surprised to see his mom's phone number show up on his vibrating BlackBerry. Her voice quivered. It sounded like she was holding back tears. "Alexis, I'm sorry," Anke Ohanian said. "We put Max down."

Max, the Ohanian family's dog, adopted when Alexis was a kid, had for the past two years been sick with Cushing's disease, which is usually caused by a base-of-brain tumor and results in a host of nasty symptoms, such as thinning skin, sagging abdomen, and nervous system malfunction. Max had been a stand-up dog, a living, wagging symbol of Alexis's relationship with his mother. That summer morning, Anke and Chris had dropped Max off at a kennel, where he had a final, terrible seizure. After ten years with the Ohanian family, Max was gone.

Three hours later, Anke Ohanian fell to the floor of a Lane Bryant dressing room in the throes of a grand mal seizure. Within weeks, she was diagnosed with grade IV glioblastoma multiforme. Brain cancer.   .

(• •)

Ask Ohanian about his mother, her diagnosis, or her death two years later, and he's likely to recite a few lines that he has down pat. They are as follows:

> Three months into Reddit she was diagnosed with terminal brain cancer. The first day that we learned of it I flew to Boston to be with her at the hospital. When I got there, literally the first words out of her mouth were, "I'm sorry." That was the type of selfless person she was.

There are the lines he's decided it's okay to say, lines he has repeated over and over down the course of years, so they don't make him cry. He has grown comfortable with the lines, and with her death, through repeating them over the years like a mantra.

There are more lines. Lines that explain, in nerd vernacular, what Ohanian took away from his mother's terminal illness:

> Having that kind of grounding was the cheat code I was gifted by her. It gave me perspective I carry to this day. On the worst day I have at Reddit, it's a reminder that it's not that bad. There's a limit to how bad it can get. I felt like I got all the wisdom someone usually gets later in their life when I was twenty-two.

This period, the "hell summer" in which Reddit was born, has become an enduring ball bearing in the mechanism of Ohanian's public-speaking career and part of the Reddit company legend.

By turning even these most painful moments into part of the

story, Ohanian has helped build scar tissue on his emotional wounds. But his personal issues that summer and over the following years necessitated his absence from Reddit for significant chunks of the site's formative days. There were weeks away in Germany, and weekends in Maryland to be with his mother. Ohanian knows his response to these moments affected Huffman—and Reddit.

What Ohanian doesn't say in his public speeches is that making the decision to go to Germany immediately after receiving the phone call from Amber's mother has become a sticking point for him: It was the first day of so many he'd leave Huffman alone with Reddit—and has become to him a turning point that has taken on outsized importance in his memory.

While Ohanian was away, there was an empty desk in the sunny central room in Medford; there was no longer any point in Huffman blasting "Hollaback Girl" by himself, or wheeling over to the PlayStation. Occasionally they'd talk on the phone, but mostly, Reddit was on Huffman toward the end of the summer of Y Combinator, through the last Tuesday dinner, in which the young men flipped over one of the tip-happy benches and etched their names in ballpoint pen.

Ohanian recalls being on the phone with Huffman while on another trip to Germany after Demo Day, the final presentation day for the scrappy companies, in which they sought investment from Graham's friends. None of the investor friends bit, but Graham offered Reddit another round of funding, $70,000, in exchange for additional equity, which became known as the "Paul Graham special." It was both a show of continued support in what they were building and a plea not to give up and move home with their parents.

Fund-raising was supposed to fall under Ohanian's duties, but "Steve had to drive that whole thing," Ohanian recalled. Years later, he would feel guilty about this. For his part, Huffman, despite not being the overly warm friend—not the one to pass a tissue—never once complained about his additional duties shepherding Reddit during this time. He did what he thought was right. When he needed to, he scrounged for the piece of paper Ohanian had left him with all the passwords and logins for their credit cards and bank accounts.

"These awful horrible things that happened to us—this stuff beyond our control—this could not break us," Huffman said later, channeling his thoughts from 2006. "So if we have, like, an employee that doesn't want to work anymore? We will figure it out. That will not be the thing that destroys Reddit."

HOW TO ACT LIKE A REAL ADULT

Kanye West's "Gold Digger" bumped from the tinny speakers at Chris Slowe's third-floor walk-up apartment at 368 Washington Street in Somerville. Only a few of the dozens of mostly guys present bopped their heads awkwardly, and their Halloween costumes—some floppy ears, some lightsabers—bopped, too. When the first bare beat of the next song was immediately pierced by Gwen Stefani's voice—"Uhhhh-huh this my shit"—Ohanian cracked a smile, searching for Huffman above the crowd. It was their summer anthem, the song that had gotten them out of bed so many mornings just months earlier, before so much had unfolded in their lives. Before Reddit.com existed.

His Y Combinator friends, and some of their college buddies, huddled in groups. Chris Slowe's physics labmates mulled about. There was one woman he didn't recognize, though. Short, with a dark, nearly black bob, she didn't seem self-conscious—and talked a mile a minute. "This is Jenny 8," Zak Stone said to Ohanian. Jenny Lee shook Ohanian's hand, and explained that "8." was her middle name, and part of her *New York Times* byline: Jennifer 8. Lee.

Lee had met Stone just months earlier; she'd introduced herself after seeing him perform Chinese yo-yo at an unconventional wedding and learned he was a Harvard physics major raised in Hawaii. Lee was drawn to intense quirks, and extremes of talent and intellect. She herself was a study in outlying: a native New Yorker born to Chinese immigrants who'd graduated from Harvard with degrees in economics and applied mathematics, now a reporter for the *New York Times* who specialized in capturing moments in the zeitgeist.

Lee had accompanied Stone to this Halloween party on a whim, and found it impressive that it didn't have a keg; it had a table with a bar setup, and even snacks. Classy, she thought, by student-housing-in-Cambridge standards. Despite her eagle eye for the interesting, Lee had no way of knowing that among these lanky, awkward young men were several who within the decade would change the world—or at least the Internet. In the mix was Justin Kan, the cofounder of Kiko, who would go on to found a live-streaming company that transformed into Twitch, which more than one hundred million people watch per month (Amazon acquired the company in 2014 for nearly $1 billion). There was Trip Adler, the founder of Scribd, an online library and document-sharing platform with more than three hundred thousand titles. There was Aaron Swartz, who would become renowned for his prodigal work on open-Internet projects, and who would become an activist against government regulation of the web. And there were Steve Huffman and Alexis Ohanian.

As Lee shook the hand of the man wearing the floppy brown tricorn hat and fake dreadlocks, her head craned. Ohanian, tonight dressed as Captain Jack Sparrow, was more than a foot taller than Lee. He was gregarious and enthusiastic, and struck her as a showman, especially amid all these engineering and mathematics majors. And, considering that he kept introducing her to new people around the room throughout the evening, he had a dash of social grace that made him seem very mature for twenty-two. Well, maybe not that mature: Later that night, Kan passed out on the couch, and by morning, Ohanian had drawn a mustache in Sharpie on his upper lip.

Over the following year, Lee invited Ohanian to crash on her couch in her Harlem brownstone whenever he traveled to New York on the no-frills Fung Wah Bus for business meetings. In exchange, he'd bring her take-out dinner during her night shifts reporting for the *Times* metropolitan desk on the third floor at 229 West 43rd Street. There, on slow news nights, in Lee's beige cubicle decorated with just a dried-out houseplant, she taught Ohanian how to act like a real adult.

"If it weren't for her, I still wouldn't know how to write a proper email to someone," Ohanian said. Lee also helped Ohanian navigate the world of New York City journalism and publishing. Over the years, she introduced him to dozens of journalists, editors, publishers, agents, and writers. At one party in her brownstone, Ohanian met Liz Nagle, a literary editor for Little, Brown whom he'd date for the next four years, with whom he'd travel extensively and live with in both Brooklyn and San Francisco. Lee also introduced Ohanian to Rachel Metz, a reporter who'd worked with Kourosh Karimkhany, who'd just been hired by Condé Nast with a mandate to infuse the old-media brand with fresh digital life by way of acquisitions.

(• •)

By the autumn of 2005, as fresh packs of college students once again began roaming Cambridge and Medford, Reddit was growing so much that it sometimes struggled to stay online. For Huffman, this was both a rush and a chore. The site crashed frequently, and the maintenance of posting new articles and rebooting the server exhausted a lot of his day-to-day energy. Reddit had been built and launched quickly—so quickly that both Huffman and Graham knew the site would soon outgrow some of its original programming infrastructure. This fact, now daunting, had been by design: Launch fast, with a minimum viable product—and save perfection and scalability for later. In startup vernacular, this is known as incurring "technical debt." And Reddit's hulking loan was coming due.

Graham urged Huffman and Ohanian to have dinner with Chris Slowe, their batchmate from Y Combinator. Slowe spent his days writing software and attempting to freeze light, and looked the part, with his T-shirts tucked into his high-waisted, belted lightwash jeans. But he drove a cool car—a white Mustang—and always seemed to possess an easy gravitas.

The startup Slowe and his cofounder, Zak Stone, were building stalled at the prototype phase when summer ended. Apple had launched Spotlight, bringing to market the desktop search tool they'd barely built. Still, Slowe had one foot firmly in startup land and did not want to extract it. He'd developed a daily routine of waking early and working all day in the lab, only taking a break to train for a half-marathon over lunch. In the evening, he'd put in another five or six hours brainstorming about natural-language processing for his startup. He lived on caffeine and adrenaline, and he loved it.

For Slowe, by year four of his graduate work, physics had become a *job* in the most *meh* sense of the word. He wasn't dissatisfied, and he still assumed that his lab life—stuck in windowless rooms modeling out hypotheses on stodgy computers, experimenting only a tiny fraction of the time—resembled his future postdoctoral life. But his little evening endeavors in tech projects were a chance to exhale.

Over dinner with Ohanian and Huffman, Slowe learned that they needed a place to stay that fall as their summer sublet expired. Stone was moving out, back to a Harvard dorm that fall. Dinner was a blast, and he invited Huffman and Ohanian to move into his third-floor walk-up apartment on Washington Street. He figured they'd help pay the $1,650 monthly rent and wouldn't trash the place. He didn't figure their presence would shift the entire trajectory of his life.

(• •)

Huffman and Ohanian decided to face the windows this time. They plunked their desks there in the living room, backs to each other. The only view from Huffman's window was the brick-colored siding of the house next door, a few feet away. With Chris's desk, too, there wasn't room for a couch or TV, and one had to shimmy between wheeled desk chairs through the living room to get to the kitchen.

For sleeping, Ohanian claimed the big sunny room in the front of the apartment overlooking the stoplights of the bleak Somerville corner, and Huffman took the other back room. Slowe—congenial and quiet and smart—was a fantastic roommate, they quickly learned. He was unflappable and, bonus, he could cook. He made chicken and rice and even assembled pizza from scratch. He woke up early, around 6 a.m., and, like a rooster for the Internet, would knock on Huffman's door and let him know whenever Reddit's site was down.

Slowe had been a Reddit user from the start. He'd been outed as one of the first posters on the site that past summer at a get-together at Graham's place in Cambridge. While chatting with some friends there, he overheard Graham raise his voice from the other room. "And who is this KeyserSosa?!" Slowe popped his head into the room and sheepishly raised his hand, admitting that the username KeyserSosa, an unintentional misspelling of the name of the notorious (and perhaps nonexistent) crime lord Keyser Söze in *The Usual Suspects*, was him.

One week that fall, the jolly Internet rooster's job became increasingly intense. A few days in a row, Reddit had been offline at dawn, and Huffman, a night owl, was sick of being woken so early. He demonstrated to Slowe how to connect to Reddit's server and restart it.

At the time, Slowe still held out the dream of his own startup; he and Stone were halfheartedly trying to turn the code they'd written into a dating site called Cryptomatch. Now—restarting the server here, reviewing some code there—he was increasingly devoting his out-of-lab hours to helping solidify Reddit. It was a bittersweet slide.

Speaking about it many years later, Slowe still has mixed feelings over effectively leaving Stone for Huffman and Ohanian. "It was the same kind of feeling as you have when someone's cheating on you. We didn't talk a lot after that, and he went off and did his own thing, and I did my thing." Stone had over that past summer become the closest friend Slowe had ever had. Now they were both, separately but in unison, letting their dream project stagnate. One afternoon they together moved out Stone's final boxes, and they had a hug goodbye that felt oddly final. Slowe, who is rarely inarticulate, struggled to find words to describe the parting, offering up only "sad" and "awkward," and saying, "I guess we talk about it at therapy now."

After Stone walked away with his boxes, Slowe took a deep breath and walked back up the two long flights of stairs to the apartment, to find Huffman and Ohanian, feet up, letting their wheeled desk chairs slowly drift across the slightly slanted wood floor. He laughed. He'd long ago become accustomed to the sloping floor. He grabbed a roll of duct tape, with which he'd stabilized his own chair's wheels by wrapping them, so he could work without rolling away from his computer. He tossed it to Huffman.

(• •)

The Washington Street apartment was on a desolate block, had slanted floors and a rickety back stairwell that led to a dirt-floor basement with a single bare light bulb and, mysteriously, a grave-sized pit dug into the dirt. But the apartment was bright and just a ten-minute walk from Harvard's campus. Not all the Y Combinator guys were so lucky. Aaron Swartz had spent the past summer awkwardly cohabitating in a tiny MIT dorm room with a foreign stranger he'd met on the Internet, whom he'd lured with the promise of 10 percent equity in his not-yet-launched company. But the cofounder of Infogami, Simon Carstensen, had thrown up his hands by summer's end—Swartz seemed to not trust his code and rewrote it frequently. Carstensen flew home to Denmark.

Swartz had no desire to return to Stanford for sophomore year and more sociology classes. He'd found a calling—and it didn't involve what he called the "fake world of school doing some silly assignment that has no real purpose." But to continue making something "real," he'd need a roof over his head.

Graham and Livingston agreed to take him in. They had plenty of room in their home in Cambridge, and after all, Swartz was only eighteen years old—a boy, really. His company, Infogami, had impressed all his colleagues by late summer, but Swartz had failed to put it online or secure additional investment. Despite his connections, nothing panned out. "I found myself stuck without any money, any partners, or any place to live. The whole experience was incredibly trying. There were many days when I felt like my head was going to literally explode," Swartz wrote on Infogami.

He brought his concerns to Graham over dinner the first week of November, saying he would be giving up on Infogami if he hadn't found funding, a new partner, or an apartment by the end of the week, he later wrote. The subject of his birthday—the following day—came up. He was asked what he wanted as a gift. "A cofounder," he joked. He wrote:

> The next morning was [November 8] my birthday and I was awakened by a knock on the door from Paul. "I thought of a solution to your problem," he exclaimed with his inimitable energy. "Merge with Reddit!" "That's an interesting idea," I said, still picking the sleep out of my eyes. As we discussed it, we just got more and more excited—it seemed like such a perfect fit. I still can't even imagine a better solution.

ROUNDING ERROR

Huffman and Ohanian were listening to the mix CD they'd compiled specifically for this November 2005 trip to San Francisco when they pulled up to the Googleplex in Mountain View. After locating their designated parking space, they were greeted by Chris Sacca, who had been hired at Google as corporate counsel in 2003 but had already amassed a wide range of responsibilities, including helping to create the company's New Business Development organization. Sacca, with his auburn hair and a signature uniform of cowboy boots, jeans, and a vintage-looking Western-style shirt, had confidence to rival Ohanian's, which was evident from his saunter as he led them inside a glass building.

Ohanian expected scooters and Ping-Pong tables and plentiful snacks; still, what he saw awed him. There were, among the many sprawling lawns and all-the-lobster-bisque-you-can-eat cafeterias, some true marks of luxury: a row of miniature swimming pools with jets that allowed their user to swim in place; a full-size replica of a dinosaur skeleton.

Sacca had invited the duo out to California after being introduced to them by Graham—and after seeing a small but noticeable bump in traffic to his site following a link being posted on Reddit. He had set up a day packed with impressive meetings, including with a minor idol of theirs, Evan Williams, whose startup, Blogger (an early tool for letting anyone easily post online), had just been purchased by Google. They also sat down with a bunch of Google engineers, who joked with Huffman and asked him mind-expanding questions like "Give us three different ways you could scale Reddit" and "What would you do with unlimited resources?" Huffman loved shooting the shit with the group of talented engineers. "It just felt awesome," he said. He'd initially missed the entire point of the exercise, which would have been apparent to anyone with more experience in the workings of Silicon Valley: This was a formal "tech interview." Reddit was being sized up for acquisition.

After leaving the Googleplex, Huffman and Ohanian visited Yahoo—also thanks to Graham's connections. Huffman felt dread upon entering Yahoo's campus, which, after Google, struck him as very quiet. His view was perhaps colored by a meeting he'd had with a couple Yahoo business development executives back in Cambridge. They'd questioned the efficacy of usernames and suggested Reddit scrap them, because they didn't correspond to real human identity—something that felt at the time a little privacy-intrusive but that Facebook, then just a year old and exclusive to college campuses, was making inroads on. Huffman took offense.

"They were just the biggest bunch of pricks," he said. A vice president of Advanced Development scoffed at Reddit's total traffic, which was indeed meager, muttering that it amounted to a "rounding error" to Yahoo. "Which it was," Huffman admits. "But you don't need to be a jerk about it."

Still, thanks to Google, by the time Huffman and Ohanian returned home to Somerville, they were feeling incredible. Traffic on Reddit had risen while they were gone. It was now steadily growing week by week. They were the sort of company Google might just be interested in buying. Indeed, within days and several emails exchanged with Sacca, he was asking whether they'd be interested in coming to work for Google.

It was an offer to begin acquisition talks—but the phrasing, Ohanian knew, meant what Sacca had in mind was an "acqui-hire," or an acquisition common for Google at the time, a small deal that technically absorbed a startup, but with the primary aim of hiring its talented engineers rather than developing its technology. There wasn't a figure attached, but it didn't take much sleuthing for the young men to assume that it would be a salary, bonus, and a couple hundred thousand dollars in Google stock. They called it $800,000.

It wasn't enough. Graham and Y Combinator had invested a to-tal of $82,000 in Reddit—even if they had a 10 percent stake, it wouldn't be a significant payday. But the hint of an offer was affirm-ing: Ohanian and Huffman came away with the sentiment Ohanian later characterized as, "We're doing well enough that they think we're not going to screw this up."

Huffman wasn't ready to give up building Reddit and work for Google. He came to agree with what had already become Graham's sentiment: If Reddit wouldn't sell, it would have to grow. That meant bringing on at least one other full-time developer.

Graham pitched Huffman on taking Aaron Swartz. Huffman ad-mired young Swartz, and despite Infogami's stagnation, Swartz was already a legend among certain programmers, an Internet wun-derkind whose online clout could only bolster Reddit's. Ohanian remembers Huffman coming home and pitching him on the idea. Huffman knew that Google had also interviewed Swartz—and was sniffing around at Slowe's YC company, Memamp, too, though it didn't seem to be biting. Together, Huffman posited, the four of them could create a dream team. Ohanian was skeptical. He and Swartz had never clicked. But he knew Huffman desperately needed programming help, and so deferred to him on the decision.

Swartz was in, with little hesitation. The wild card was Slowe—his schedule was already overloaded. He likely wouldn't want to give up his doctoral work. Still, Huffman was optimistic about turning Reddit into a band of four and immediately called Slowe's cell phone.

Slowe remembers the moment with the clarity of mountain air.

He was standing in a Peet's coffee shop in Harvard Square, taking a break from his lab work. "I didn't even have to think about it," he said. "I was like, 'Yes, absolutely yes! One thousand times *yes*!!!'"

The foursome started work in earnest the very next day. Swartz later wrote, "Together, we felt unstoppable."

(• •)

While Reddit and Infogami bore a surface-level similarity—both were sites empowering users to post what was on their mind—their core DNA structures were incompatible: They'd been programmed using different languages. To merge, they'd need to speak the same language. Reddit had been written in Lisp, the obscure language favored by Graham. It lacked the extensive online code libraries other languages already possessed, which meant that Huffman spent a lot of time engineering unique solutions to wide-ranging problems, and writing simple functions out himself. Swartz insisted that Reddit would function better if they rewrote it in Python, a general-purpose, highly readable programming language. Huffman agreed.

The pair went heads-down and rewrote most of Reddit over a single weekend. Huffman and Swartz didn't just rebuild the functions that made Reddit tick, they also built an entirely new foundation on which the site—and others—could rest. (It was called web.py, and wasn't widely adopted, but several companies and websites were built on it, most notably Russia's answer to Google, Yandex.) The rewrite of the code gave the founders significantly more ability to do future database migrations, and to add future features or elements, such as messaging between users, into the site. It also allowed the capacity for certain structural elements of Infogami, which was essentially a blogging platform, to conceptually exist within Reddit.

The transition to Python permitted Huffman and Swartz to nix a number of deep-rooted glitches in Huffman's early design of Reddit. His post announcing the move ended with a textual wink: "I can't wait to introduce some of the new bugs we've been working on as well."

(• •)

Swartz and Huffman became inseparable. They even shared a computer most days, swapping Huffman's Mac iBook G4 laptop back and forth, tandem programming. Several times a week they'd take two-mile walks together between Huffman's home on Washington Street and Graham's home in Cambridge where Swartz lived, or to the Y Combinator office on Garden Street. They'd theorize about the future, about the real integration of their ideas. One theory they talked out was that the Internet could be seen as being comprised of three elements: search engines, such as Google; applications, such as Yahoo Mail; and lists of things, such as Wikipedia, news sites, and blogs. Under this theory, Infogami and Reddit were both lists.

Huffman and Swartz knew that within Reddit, they could also allow users to have their own page, and power their own blog or publishing site, right there—thus integrating Infogami. Everyone seemed sold on the idea of a multipurpose publishing platform, from Graham to Slowe, who said, "Together, you kind of have this whole platform. You can build content, you can make content, this whole thing." None of them could have foreseen what they were getting into.

Slightly more than a month later, the arrangement became lawyer-official. Infogami, or Oubliable.com Corporation, the name it had been registered under as a Delaware corporation, merged with Reddit, a.k.a. Redbrick Solutions, Inc. The surviving company would be renamed Not A Bug, Inc. The name was both a joke on a common programmer refrain, "It's a feature, not a bug," and a response to Graham's quip from the past summer in which he referred to Reddit's mascot alien as a "bug." Huffman and Ohanian signed the board resolution, in lieu of actually having a board.

Huffman, Ohanian, and Swartz were named new directors of

Not A Bug, Inc. in January 2006, and given the respective titles of president, secretary, and treasurer. Each was issued equal shares of the company, roughly 24 percent. Graham and Y Combinator likely retained about 7 percent each, and a percentage remained for future options. Swartz had convinced his former partner, Simon Carstensen, to hand over his meager shares of Oubliable, so he didn't require a cut. None of the shares required the passage of time to vest. Swartz, nineteen years old, was now nearly one-third owner of Reddit.

Chris Slowe was brought on as first employee, with some stock and a salary. He wasn't treated on paper like a cofounder, because he simply couldn't put in the hours. He'd be working on his Ph.D. for at least the next year. Ohanian described the arrangement as casual, satisfying everyone involved. "We said, 'Okay, we'll just take as much of your time as we can writing code.'"

(• •)

Forks clinked against the china at UpStairs on the Square, a Baroque masterpiece in fuchsia, lavender, and gold paint two blocks from Harvard. Huffman and Ohanian once again sat at dinner across from one of Huffman's idols: Joel Spolsky, founder of Fog Creek Software and something of New York City's answer to Boston's Paul Graham.

Spolsky, known as much for his popular tech blog *Joel on Software* as for founding New York City–based Fog Creek Software, was intrigued by Reddit, at least for its caches of programming news. Huffman and he talked programming; Ohanian gregariously joked, as had become his standard line, to Spolsky, "I only make the little alien." Spolsky, unlike so many other coders, was impressed by that statement—and not just for its humility. Spolsky had noticed that the alien mascot at the upper left-hand corner of Reddit.com would be on some days embellished with varying costumes in nods to minor holidays or sporting events. Occasionally Snoo the alien would be shown over the course of a week partaking in a series of events. To Spolsky, the subtle changes to Snoo gave users an addictive little story to follow and another reason to love the site. Visually, Reddit was chalk-dry. Snoo was warm and friendly; Spolsky loved its "big baby eyes."

Spolsky, who has bushy eyebrows and a sly, friendly smile, told Ohanian to keep it up. "It makes the site friendlier," he said. He likened Snoo's shenanigans to miniature marginalia cartoons from decades-past *Mad* magazines.

Huffman asked Spolsky his opinion about a feature he was ready to add to Reddit: comments. Up to this point, Reddit's site consisted of headline links whose original submitters received karma points to their username when their post was upvoted. Beyond amassing karma, usernames weren't good for much—though they did serve to differentiate Reddit from message boards like 4chan and 8chan, on which all posters were strictly anonymous.

Huffman had the distinct impression that Graham disliked the way comments worked on competing sites, such as Slashdot, and wouldn't welcome them on Reddit. Spolsky joined that camp, telling Huffman that he didn't think comments worked well *anywhere* on the Internet; they were a write-only medium, meaning, individuals loved to type in their thoughts the same way they loved to hear themselves speak. His conclusion: "Comments are going to ruin Reddit."

Huffman, though, had already made up his mind. At the time, Slashdot's comments relied on an intricate moderator-based system for ranking and displaying comments, in order from best to worst. "That dynamic, I totally just copied right from them. Except I didn't want to implement the moderation system," Huffman explained. "We already had this voting system, so I decided just to put voting on the comments, too."

Ohanian designed multiple ways comments could appear when visible on the site. Huffman launched the whole feature suddenly on December 12, 2005. He posted to Reddit's blog, "We added a commenting system today for your enjoyment. The comments are votable and can be sorted just as all the other links on reddit."

Many users were livid: A lack of comments had differentiated Reddit from Slashdot, where lots of the most frequent Reddit visitors were also contributors. But for Huffman, comments, which were initially powered by Blogger, were instantly validating. All of a sudden, links to articles elsewhere online became their own dynamic pages, containing discussions between real people. Huffman immediately witnessed something online that he'd only seen before in his onscreen chat logs: the real-time flow of information and opinion. Before comments, his primary way to monitor Reddit's growth and traffic was to examine its error log or its "new" page, which displayed the twenty-five most recent entries at a time.

Before long, Reddit's commenting system would be seen as visionary. Its unique combination of displaying comments by popularity and threading them together, which kept all responses to a comment or question in one movable block of text, served a few important purposes. One of the major problems with comments online—on news sites, blogs, and social media alike—was that they displayed chronologically, allowing trolls and spammers an equal voice to informed critics and enthusiasts. "To me, that's the dumbest thing ever," Huffman said. With his approach of letting users' votes power the ranking of comments, and simply not displaying the most downvoted ones, Reddit deftly hid dull, promotional, harassing, or simply idiotic comments (all of which Huffman simply called "shitty comments"). Negative 5 points, and a comment turned gray and became collapsed, so a user would need to click, or opt in, to read specific threads of unpopular comments. Well, except for those that were gloriously atrocious, Huffman later explained with a sly smile. "If it had fewer than negative 100 points we would show it again, because it was either so offensive or so stupid that it was probably worth reading."

As dinner at UpStairs on the Square wrapped up with coffees and dessert, one subtle comment from Spolsky illuminated that he was already a true Reddit believer. He told Huffman, "You will never write a résumé again." Huffman thought, *That sounds nice, and is something worth chasing.* It stuck in his mind for years, as highly complimentary—if at the time more than a little unbelievable.

Sure, most nights the Reddit foursome ate leftover pizza for dinner; Huffman worked day in, day out staring out a window at a wall of brick-colored siding. He didn't even have a salary. But Spolsky had been correct: Huffman would never have to write a résumé again.

THE ALGORITHM AND THE CUPBOARD

S lowe's working hours were unorthodox, but they allowed a measure of independence that resulted in extraordinarily meaningful contributions to Reddit's growth. He typically joined the rest of the team in the evenings, once he came home from the lab and cooked dinner, for just a few hours before everyone was bleary-eyed and shuffled off to bed. To fit that workflow, Huffman handed him discrete tasks involving algorithmic equations or big, conceptual questions. One of the first was to create a reliable source of site analytics, denoting traffic and tracking it. This was before Google Analytics was available to little companies like Reddit; Slowe adeptly tackled the challenge by rendering graphs for easy viewing of the site's access logs. A few other minor projects also went well. Then he was handed the algorithms. A set of three managed on-site spam, algorithms that Huffman created in part inspired by Graham's work on categorizing certain types of incoming email. Reddit's versions at the time detected likely spam user patterns, such as when a newly registered user immediately posted to the site.

Then there was the elusive hotness algorithm. As Slowe, ever humble, remembers it, he helped Huffman recraft the hotness algorithm so that it could "scale nicely." As Huffman remembers it, Slowe tinkered and learned, and within a month delivered a seriously improved hotness ranking system that was both simple in its code structure and sophisticated in its output; it was difficult to game and accurate in its effect. Previously, the algorithm Huffman had deployed performed a ranking of posts based on their upvotes per hour, roughly every ten minutes. More upvotes on a post equaled more "hotness," and thus a higher ranking on the popular homepage. Slowe's formula did this constantly, in real time and in the site's background. More important, perhaps, it also accounted for time. It created a total score for each submitted post based on upvotes and downvotes, but that total score would be more valuable in the present than in the past. That ensured that newer posts, or newly popular posts, gained momentum quickly, and older ones could keep their rankings only if their popularity kept up. In short, it foresaw the nature of virality that would emerge online over the next decade, and allowed it to exist on Reddit. Huffman said, "That was 100 percent Chris."

What Slowe wrote was exceedingly effective and in fact did scale along with Reddit. For the next decade of Reddit's life, this algorithm served as the foundation for the site's front page and the popularity ranking of posts on every page throughout the site.

One midwinter evening, instead of tromping back to the Washington Street walk-up after lab, Slowe ventured out across the Charles River to drinks at a pub called Clerys in Boston's Back Bay neighborhood. It was an outing organized by friends, and they'd brought friends, one of whom had enormous twinkly brown eyes and shiny hair. She was effervescent—Greek, confident, funny, and just so different from anyone he knew. She talked a mile a minute. Slowe chatted with Kristen Sakillaris all night. She worked in fashion but could hold her own when the conversation turned to his lab work, due to her social grace and a familiarity with it; her father was a chemical engineer.

After a couple weeks of chatting on Gmail (the first time a message from Slowe popped up on her screen, Sakillaris, who had never used Google Talk, a.k.a. Gchat, said she thought, "Oh my God, he is so smart, he is *in* my computer!"), they decided to go out. Awkwardly—it was Valentine's Day *and* a terrible snowstorm was under way. Still, Sakillaris scrubbed her nails and put on heels and told her girlfriends she was going out to a movie at the AMC Loews in Boston Common.

"Wait, with who?!" two of her friends demanded. She told them they'd met that night at Clerys. "Oh my God, the nerdy one? No!" They cracked up.

Slowe was beaming as he got home a bit after 11 p.m. from his Valentine's date, even though it was just a mediocre Steve Martin film and all they'd had for dinner was popcorn. It'd been a long time since he'd had a good date, with someone he wanted to see again. He definitely wanted to see Kristen again. Suddenly Slowe's phone rang. It was Swartz calling.

"Hey, can you come get me right away? I'm moving, I just need some help with some things," Swartz said. Slowe sighed; he was going to put in a couple of hours on his Reddit work anyway, so what was the difference? He agreed to help Swartz and drove his 2001 white Mustang over to Cambridge, to Graham's house, which was otherwise deserted. Graham and Livingston had moved out to the Bay Area to run a winter program of Y Combinator, leaving Swartz alone in their massive home for the past couple months. What had once been a fantastic arrangement for Swartz—a free room in a spacious home, with free food and plenty of dinners out with Livingston and Graham and their tech luminary friends—must have become somehow unbearable. Slowe hauled Swartz's twin mattress out to the driveway and shoved it into the backseat of the little sports car. On the way back to Washington Street, Swartz rode shotgun with a couple of cardboard boxes on his lap.

Swartz moving in had been discussed—*floated*, Slowe thought—and like the rest of the Reddit crew, he assumed they would have more convincing to do before getting Swartz out of his free, exceedingly nice Cambridge home. Whether something had come to a head with Graham and Livingston, Slowe wasn't going to question it.

Swartz crashed on the living room couch that night. In the morning there was the matter of what, physically, to do with him. There wasn't an extra room. Huffman was willing to share, but his was the smallest bedroom. Swartz joked, "Oh, I won't take up any room. I'll just stay in the cupboard." Over beers, it made everyone laugh, and they played along. But then Swartz removed dishes and cereal from a lower set of kitchen cupboards and equipped it with a pillow and a bare light bulb. He crawled in.

Quickly, Swartz's little cubby hideout became more of an annoyance than a joke. Sakillaris came over to visit Slowe and was bewildered by seeing a man popping his head out of the cupboard. She later recalled the bizarre imposition of what Swartz assumed was the opposite, an act of shirking away, making himself meek and unimposing. "It was like, *What are you doing? I'm trying to make some tea and you're sleeping in the cupboard and I'm probably going to burn you because you're in . . . a . . . cupboard.*"

Swartz possessed a combination of youthful frailty and the pale puffiness of a formerly chunky kid. He was small and doe-eyed, and people, particularly older people, doted on him like the child he almost still was. (Right after he arrived in Boston, having been dropped off by his father, Livingston delivered an air conditioner straight to his dorm room at MIT. This was months before taking him into her home, where she had to force him to cut his fingernails when one in particular grew an inch beyond reasonably long.) Swartz had the habit of wearing dark, oversized T-shirts, his favorite being one from Foo Camp, an annual hacker gathering, and although he could argue fervently for his beliefs in a conversation, to the point of offense, he generally attempted to cut an unimposing figure. He worked tucked in corners, or with his legs pulled under his body in the corner of a couch, with his laptop and his Sidekick phone in front of him—together they formed a shield, a technological invisibility cloak.

Swartz loved making things. He loved producing small bits of writing on his blog and solving problems with code, and some of the awkwardness of daily interactions also reinforced the behavior of hiding behind a device. He disdained authority, and disliked the feeling of being in any sort of position of perceived superiority—down to asking for help from librarians or asking for a beverage from a flight attendant. He posted on his blog in 2007:

> If I rang the call button, I tell myself, I wouldn't ask for a Sprite. I'd just ask for water. Asking for a Sprite, it'd seem like I was interrupting them just so I could get my soda fix. Like I was some sort of petulant child who had to have his soda and was going to throw a temper tantrum if they didn't get it. Like a troublemaker, the kind of person they look down on. But water? Water they'd understand: it was a genuine medical request, a normal, physical human need. Something totally worth taking the extraordinary step of pressing the flight attendant call button.
>
> But I can't bring myself to do it. It seems like such an imposition.
>
> This, I suppose, is the actual problem: I feel my existence is an imposition on the planet. Not a huge one, perhaps, not a huge one at all, but an imposition nonetheless. When I go to a library and I see the librarian at her desk reading, I'm afraid to interrupt her, even though she sits there specifically so that she may be interrupted, even though being interrupted for reasons like this by people like me is her very job.

His insistence on a sort of social austerity had a tendency to actually deprive him, and make others at best feel awkward, and at worst take pity on him. His introversion, though, did not apply when it came to the Internet. Swartz wrote frequently and in great detail about his real-life conundrums: the needing water, the horrible stomach troubles, the cupboard. Posts like these, to his friends, read as cries for help. But then what did it mean when Swartz posted a media clip or shared an accomplishment? He clearly relished being written about in the press—and when the opportunities arose, he wouldn't shirk. He smiled for cameras, and was eloquent when interviewed. A 2005 *Wired* write-up of the Summer Founders Program hailed his not-yet-launched Infogami as a site that would let people "create rich, visually interesting websites" and quoted Swartz as saying, "Being around some of the bright lights of the technology world and having them expect great things helps you sit down and do it seriously."

When Reddit made it into the news later in 2006 he posted twenty-one links to press articles about it on his blog, apparently basking in the limelight. But the following day, he changed tack, writing a self-deprecating post that said he thought Reddit, at its start, was "childish," and even by 2006 was "just a list of links. And we didn't even write them ourselves."

In his frequent online writings, Swartz harnessed control of the story of his life. He was his own narrator and chorus, and it was in this style that "the cupboard," an annoying blip to Huffman, Ohanian, and Slowe, which lasted a matter of mere days, became a cog in the grander narrative of Reddit. "It became his thing, *the cupboard*," Slowe said later. "It went too far, and then he played it up—and he made it a story about how we put him in a cupboard."

(• •)

As 2005 turned into 2006, that winter was all time-sucks and misdirection for Reddit. There were more users, twelve thousand a day and counting, and after the code rewrite, Huffman was back to the habit of listening to users' desires. More than anything, users wanted tags. They wanted not an unending, perpetually flowing stream of random links, but rather, specified topics, and sorting of those topics. Delicious, the bookmarking site now also known as a popularity engine, was one of the first websites to popularize tagging and let users categorize content themselves.

Huffman was firmly opposed to tagging. Users' thoughts, even on fairly banal topics, were not subjective, he'd already learned. What might be considered "politics" by one person might be tagged as "left-wing liberal bullshit" by another. For about a week that winter, he was swayed by a combination of user pressure and Ohanian's willingness to experiment with it. Ohanian spent a week sifting through and adding categories to every single post that had ever been contributed to Reddit.

When Reddit launched its content-tagging system, Graham hated it. Perhaps more influential was the opinion of Zak Stone, Slowe's former cofounder, who was still close friends with Huffman. "He really brought me back to reality," said Huffman, who abruptly turned off the entire feature. Ohanian was pissed: He'd spent every waking hour for the past week fine-combing all of Reddit, a herculean effort, and just like that Huffman turned it off.

Huffman had a different idea of how to segregate out some of the content being submitted to Reddit. He envisioned separate pages, Reddits within Reddits, for topics. He made a page for content related to the 2006 Winter Olympics, Olympics.reddit.com. It felt newsy and current, and helped him and Ohanian hone the vision for what would eventually become subreddits. He then went on a tear of making international "Reddits" (a French subreddit, fr.reddit.com; a Bahasa Indonesia site, id.reddit.com; and an Esperanto page, eo.reddit.com). Users could submit their ideas for new sections on request.reddit.com. One user created ask.reddit.com, which would stick, and spez created NSFW, which very much stuck. It was originally intended to be content riddled with profanity, nudity, or simply not safe for viewing at work.

"Anything goes here, enjoy," Huffman wrote on the company's blog. Asked later about it, Ohanian said he expected a lot of curse words. "It wasn't supposed to just descend into porn." But the descent was deep, and almost instantaneous. Huffman later estimated that the first ever porn was uploaded to Reddit within five minutes of his having created the NSFW community. Within a month, NSFW was almost entirely porn, and the ecosystem of pornographic material on Reddit, which has since accounted for upwards of 10 percent of the site's traffic, began to develop.

Politics followed NSFW as the second significant and enduring subreddit ever created—simply because Huffman was sick of wading through political posts on the Reddit homepage. This segregating of content was a matter of personal taste: He'd always disliked reading political coverage, and the glut of it on Reddit was getting to him. To ensure users complied with posting all political links to the politics section, Huffman logged on as any username other than his main one, u/spez, and berated posters for not using r/politics for political content. It worked like a charm, effectively quarantining politics. At this point, and for roughly the next year, there were three subreddits linked to in a box on the right-hand rail of the site: popular, politics, and programming. NSFW would have to be discovered by users on its own; there was initially no linking to it from the homepage.

Before long, Huffman opened up a feature that let anyone create any subreddit—though that URL was hidden at first and therefore rarely used. It was another step toward giving the masses power over what they chose to see online—regular people rather than editors—and that decision steered the course for the company's future more than they ever could have foreseen at the time.

(• •)

In early December, TechCrunch's curmudgeonly founder and chief writer, Michael Arrington, began to hear whispers that Delicious, which had built up a loyal following of about three hundred thousand users, was talking with Yahoo. Apparently that sort of traffic registered as more than a "rounding error" to Yahoo's acquisitions team, because when Arrington phoned Delicious's founder, Joshua Schachter, to hound him for information, Schachter informed him that the deal was already done.

Arrington's post on TechCrunch pointed out that as of that day Yahoo owned the two most important players online in "tagging," Delicious and Flickr, which had been founded by Canadian entrepreneurs Caterina Fake and Stewart Butterfield, and which allowed users to store and categorize their photos. (Yahoo had purchased Flickr's parent company earlier in the year for upwards of $22 million.)

Huffman found Delicious to be far less interesting as a competitor after its acquisition. Was he still bitter about Yahoo? Sure, but he'd also begun to notice Delicious copying Reddit's features, and that had given him confidence. He started considering Reddit a serious threat to the userbases of both Delicious and Digg.

To outsiders, that seemed laughable. "When [Reddit] first came out, I remember looking at them and saying, 'They are a copycat, they're a clone,'" said Owen Byrne, a Canadian developer who built the first iteration of Digg. Although Slashdot was a nerd haven and Delicious appealed more to mainstream news junkies, Digg was widely seen as the strongest competitor in the nascent social news arena. It had launched more recently, in November 2004, as a collaborative project by four friends: Byrne; Kevin Rose, already a minor tech celebrity because of his appearances on the TechTV cable network; Ron Gorodetzky, a software engineer; and Jay Adelson, a former film editor and sound engineer. It functioned by letting users endorse ("digg") or dislike ("bury") links submitted by other users. It had a young, male, and geeky following, with front-page links often to gaming tips, tech product news, or sci-fi content. But in the ecosystem that was developing of similar news aggregation sites, it had a distinct advantage: In 2005 the Canadian web-design studio Silverorange had redesigned the site. Now it wasn't just a list of links. It had lovely fonts, visually appealing spacing, and little orange buttons showing the "digg" count of each link, which streamed down the site and could in short order be found around the web on news articles and blog posts. Digg, as a company, also had the benefit of acting like a tech company rather than a media startup: It raised a significant round of venture capital in October 2005. It could worry later about how it would make money.

Digg's userbase and traffic dwarfed Reddit's tiny following. Huffman, though, was steadfast in his conviction that Reddit would beat Digg. "I just had so little respect for what they were doing—I thought they were incompetent," he said, noting that he could see it plain as day on their site: Digg's engineers were struggling with issues he'd already solved, such as comment sorting and keeping spam at bay. "I knew how Digg worked. And I knew how Reddit worked. And I knew we were smarter."

He also thought Digg was messing up on another front: self-promotion. On Reddit, self-promotion—say, posting your own personal blog and voting it up from multiple user accounts you'd created—was considered spamming. The practice was also beginning to be culturally frowned upon by online communities. On Digg, however, there were loopholes often gamed by users, networks of friends, and newsrooms. Digg's front page was also somewhat chronological at the time, which made it feel like a blog rather than a popularity engine. "The Reddit way in my mind was so much better," Huffman recalls. "Good stories would be on the front page longer, and bad stories wouldn't be on the front page as long."

By early 2006, as the online social sharing space heated up, mentions of Reddit online weren't uncommon, and some sites were adding a Reddit social share button (a little alien) alongside the Twitter and Facebook icons. As the year rolled on, so did Reddit's momentum. Traffic grew, thanks in part to the new NSFW subreddit. By the middle of the year, media companies large and small started to notice traffic boosts when their links gained popularity on Reddit and landed on the site's homepage. Editors joked about Reddit's "hug of death," which lovingly bestowed upon a publisher so much traffic when their link hit Reddit's homepage that it sometimes crashed their entire website.

It was no longer so easy to dismiss Reddit as a Digg knockoff. "It became fairly obvious, fairly quickly, that they were more than just a clone," Byrne said. "They were a viable competitor."

As soon as the traffic was flowing, of course, there were those with blogs and websites trying to get a piece of it by posting and upvoting their own links. Reddit was, in part, self-policing: Other Redditors would readily downvote moneymaking schemes or spam, if it hadn't already been filtered by Huffman and Slowe's algorithms. Huffman himself banned users on the regular, most often "neutering" their content from being viewed by others, even though from their own device it would appear as if nothing about their account had changed. This concept now has a name, "shadow banning," and it would become infamous over time. Back in 2006, it was simply a superpower wielded by Reddit's founding team without much question or awareness by the community.

This cultural distaste for promotion was instigated by Huffman's philosophy that Reddit should be a place for genuine discussion, earnest free speech, and anonymity, but users solidified it even as there were those looking to exploit it. In July 2006, online media entrepreneur and investor Jason Calacanis posted on his blog that he was seeking to offer any of the top fifty users of a major social news or bookmarking site $1,000 a month to control their posts. He posited that sites such as Digg and Reddit were mostly driven by their power users, who spent hours each day on their social site of choice, making posts, upvoting posts by friends or acquaintances, and creating mini-communities within these sites. "I'm absolutely convinced that the top 20 people on Digg, Delicious, Flickr, MySpace, and Reddit are worth $1,000 a month and if we're the first folks to pay them that is fine with me—we will take the risk and the arrows from the folks who think we're corrupting the community process (is there anyone out there who thinks this any more?!)," Calacanis wrote. Before the era of corporate social media marketing, and "influencer" as a job title, it was a cringe-inducing but visionary perspective on how the social ecosystem would shape up over the following decade. Huffman couldn't help but repost Calacanis's crass proposal on Reddit, joking, "Cha-ching! We're outta here!"

Ohanian's job by this point had grown to include handling media attention. He did so deftly, emailing and Gchatting reporters and courting them in person. (Huffman had found his own media-friendly way of describing to the world *what does Alexis do?* He said, "I made Reddit. Alexis made Reddit *cool.*") One week, Ohanian took the $15 Fung Wah Bus from Chinatown to New York City to meet with reporters, and that included a coffee-and-cannoli date with Rachel Metz, a reporter for *Wired*. She didn't end up writing about Reddit. But she told some of her friends in the office about the fascinating little Boston-based company. One of them was Kristen Philipkoski, the wife of Kourosh Karimkhany, who'd recently been brought on at Condé Nast with a mandate to increase the old-media juggernaut's web presence. On February 22, 2006, a note from Karimkhany appeared in Alexis Ohanian's in-box.

> I'm a friend of Rachel Metz. I'm also the director of biz dev for CondéNet, the internet arm of Condé Nast, which, as I'm sure you know, publishes magazines like Wired, GQ, Vogue, New Yorker, Vanity Fair, etc. I'm intrigued with your technology and was hoping to set up a time to talk about possibly working together. I'm open the rest of the day today and Thursday, but will be traveling for a week starting Friday. Do you have time for a phone call? Also, are you based in Boston?

YOU ARE MAKING US SOUND STUPID

After repeatedly Googling "Condé Nast," Huffman, Ohanian, Slowe, and Swartz boarded a flight in early March 2006 to San Francisco to meet with Karimkhany. They rented a car and stayed with friends in the South Bay. None of them had spent much time in San Francisco, and they got turned around on one-way streets around *Wired*'s South of Market office. They found parking with just minutes to spare.

The *Wired* office was just as awesome as they'd anticipated. Karimkhany showed them the "beer robot" (basically a small kegerator) and "The Berlin Hall," which separated magazine staff from all the tech and online folks, and they were invited to try the arcade-style machines in the game room. They were fed lunch in the company cafeteria, run by Phil Ferrato, who treated the whole endeavor like his own farm-to-table restaurant. The tour ended in an oddly angled conference room in one corner of the former factory building. It had a remarkable view; its massive steel-frame windows gave an urban panorama topped with a distant view of the Bay Bridge.

The guys sat down, and in walked a distinguished, shiny-headed man whom Karimkhany rightly suspected would impress Ohanian and Huffman: *Wired*'s editor in chief, Chris Anderson. Swartz tried to play it cool; he adored *Wired* and had befriended a couple of the tech-and-gadget publication's writers already. He'd submitted articles, too, hoping to be published. It was plain to see he was self-conscious; Swartz did a lot of the talking, and bristled visibly every time Ohanian spoke. Huffman later recalled Swartz snapped at Ohanian, "You are making us sound stupid."

Keeping cool was, in this situation, imperative. They knew this little meeting had the potential to open up acquisition talks—and, like on a first date, they knew the subject of commitment should be avoided at all costs. They could not appear overeager.

Huffman and Swartz agreed together that they wouldn't be entertaining an acquisition offer. Not yet. But at that very meeting, Karimkhany brought up the concept of creating a partnership. Details were vague, but the four young men, who'd entered the meeting all stifled and sniping at each other, left giddy. To celebrate, the guys embarked on a couple days of earnest tourism in San Francisco, hiking up Coit Tower together and driving over the Golden Gate Bridge.

Within weeks, Karimkhany offered Reddit not an acquisition, but rather a way to test the waters on a partnership, to see if Reddit could really work with a major media company.

Despite the fact that the Condé Nast company is known for its glossy magazines, catering largely to a female audience, Karimkhany and his bosses, up to Steve Newhouse, liked the idea of bolstering the young, male, educated audience that its *Wired* title reached. But the opportunity that Karimkhany extended was one that seemed as if it could test Reddit's limits—and experiment in getting the site's infrastructure to reach an entirely different market: the women's-magazine demographic. To Newhouse, if they succeeded, it would be "proof of concept." The experiment would be a custom Reddit-like site, with all of Reddit's algorithmic power, but with the content (and color scheme) of a fashion and lifestyle blog. It would be called Lipstick.com. And for building and maintaining this pink Reddit clone, Condé Nast would pay Not A Bug, Inc. $10,000 a month.

(• •)

Karimkhany's proposal was incredibly fortuitous. Huffman forked Reddit and completed the build of Lipstick.com in a few hours. The new income meant Reddit would be able to pay Slowe, who'd been living on a meager grad student stipend. It would also easily cover their other expenses: rent, meals, and the few hundred dollars a month to keep the servers running. Not only did they have assurance that they wouldn't need to start scouring Graham's contacts for new investors within months, but they also had spending money. They went shopping for servers. Now they'd have not two but ten of them, which was too many to keep in their living room. They racked up their shiny new servers in a colocation center in nearby Somerville.

To Reddit, $10,000 a month for Lipstick.com was a boon. To Condé Nast, it was pennies tipped into a tidy experiment. To Karimkhany, it was a subterfuge. At the time he proposed Lipstick.com, he was already neck deep in a deal to help Condé Nast finally acquire Wired.com, which had eight years earlier been spun out from *Wired* magazine and existed as a separate web property operated by Lycos, which merged with a Spanish company, Terra, but later was sold to a South Korean one. At each juncture the parent company of Condé Nast, Advance Publications, had been party to attempts at reuniting the web property to the title. Newhouse later recalled it being a years-long, relentless pursuit. In 2006, once more, Karimkhany was hot on the case.

Karimkhany did like the idea of acquiring Reddit; he'd felt an affinity for the scrappy site from the moment he'd clicked through to a link of a blog post espousing an extremely well-thought-out theory to explain the victory of the rebels in *Star Wars*. "It was a community that was exactly who I was and what I was interested in at the time," he said.

Karimkhany had been hired in February 2006, hoping to bring into the Advance family something like MySpace—at the time the most popular social network, which Rupert Murdoch's News Corp acquired in July 2005 for $580 million—but for a women's-magazine audience. Websites such as Polyvore, a social commerce platform on which people expressed their fashion sense, were in his sights. But after visiting Reddit, Karimkhany started to see a different vision. He had in mind getting Wired.com and Reddit together under one roof, and harnessing a wide swath of young, Internet-savvy men, interested in tech and gadgets and video games. Steve Newhouse, the non-powerful scion of the Newhouse family that created Advance Publications, saw potential, too. Facing a changing media environment, in which web traffic was a potent tool for both sourcing of content and advertising, he recalled thinking, "If Reddit could build the right kind of community, it would be very compelling for that community to discover and share news."

To make it work, Karimkhany simply had to bide his time and keep Reddit occupied—which he did with the Lipstick.com contract. He figured he could simultaneously woo them. He heard that writer-actor-comedian Ricky Gervais would be attending *Wired* magazine's Rave Awards in San Francisco, and thought he shared some of Reddit's sensibilities and its wry humor. Karimkhany emailed Ohanian asking him to come out to meet the comedian at the party at San Francisco's St. Regis hotel by his side.

(• •)

Ohanian was feeling burnt out by the spring of 2006. His mother's health was deteriorating, and his workload only increased along with Reddit's popularity. He decided to take a short break, a weekend in the Outer Banks of North Carolina with his college buddies Thorman, Nguyen, and a few others. They'd done this same journey the year before, when they were all still in college, and it was epic. They'd taken flip cup to a new level by introducing an elimination component—when your team lost, you'd have to vote a member off, à la *Survivor*. Ohanian flew to Norfolk and drove to the Outer Banks. Then, before a single game of *Survivor* flip cup commenced, he opened his email.

Ohanian sighed but replied yes to Karimkhany. Yes, Condé Nast could book him a flight to San Francisco for the next day, a twenty-four-hour coast-to-coast trip. He explained to Karimkhany that Norfolk, Virginia, was the closest airport. He packed up his swim trunks, got back in the car he'd rented, and drove three hours to Norfolk for the flight.

The Rave Awards was the ritziest event Ohanian had ever attended, but he'd barely slept. The parade of minor Internet, film, and design celebrities was a blur. He never actually met Ricky Gervais. But it didn't matter to him in the slightest. What mattered to him was that he was putting in the effort with Karimkhany. Because whenever Karimkhany said, "Jump," Ohanian needed to be poised to say, "How high?"

(• •)

Back home, a host of factors had led Ohanian to make the potential acquisition his priority. Most of the factors stemmed from one human being: Aaron Swartz. Swartz and Huffman had grown very close over that winter while rewriting the site, building out its infrastructure, and managing its growth with new servers. They shared a bedroom, so the pair had been inseparable night and day.

Recently, though, the relationship had begun to fracture. Swartz had grown distant. He'd drifted away from his Reddit projects, including building feeds.reddit, and managing the Infogami integration. Huffman recognized that Swartz needed support and coaxing, and Ohanian sought advice from Graham and others about managing him. He tried complimenting Swartz's programming prowess, pleading, *Please build this, you will save us!* and incorporating Swartz in decision making, in hopes of giving him a stronger feeling of ownership of his work. Nothing helped. Swartz had taken to arguing that Infogami's old features should be integrated into Reddit. On other days, he'd campaign for rebuilding Infogami separately. Huffman and Ohanian didn't have time for Swartz's erratic ideas. They were plowing ahead with the site, bolstering subreddits and creating an on-site chat system. "We all started getting touchy from the stress and lack of productive work. We began screaming at each other," Swartz wrote later.

Swartz turned away from the group. Most days, he refused to work along with them. He took off abruptly and would vanish for hours. He was blogging on his personal site regularly, posting lengthy book reviews alongside his theories on dieting. He relaunched Infogami. Other projects were more quixotic. He wrote a program that would download material from the Internet Archive's Wayback Machine website, archive.org. He built and released a bare-bones Amazon search that loaded more quickly than the full Amazon.com site. He began researching early childhood development and education, with the aim to author his own text on the matter.

Swartz's physical and mental health began to concern the others. He'd bolt out of the apartment in the middle of the night; later he would explain that he'd run up and down the street as fast as he could for a few minutes. Sakillaris, Slowe's girlfriend, wanted him to eat more: Swartz had grown skinny, and possessed a staunch aversion to vegetables. A pathologically picky eater, he subsisted on mostly bland, white foods, claiming that too much flavor offended his sensitive "supertaster" palate. Even his mentors tried to intervene, albeit jovially. The writer Cory Doctorow, who cofounded the beloved nerd blog *Boing Boing*, joked, "You'd think, this is a kid who's really going to go somewhere—if he doesn't die of scurvy."

Sakillaris suspected Swartz might have a form of Crohn's disease—she spotted medicines taken by a friend of hers who'd been diagnosed with it—but she was never sure. Swartz had written on his blog about everything from ulcerative colitis to coughing up what he assumed were pieces of stomach lining. It was hyperbolic, a tone that illuminated not just physical but also mental anguish.

One particularly eyebrow-raising recent post was called "Eat and Code." Really it was about his Cheerios fixation.

In the post, Swartz claimed he'd found the perfect food for him: He could eat it anytime, it had little flavor, and it was readily available at the corner store. He ate it in his room, over his computer, handfuls at a time. Soon, yellow Cheerios boxes piled up in the corner. There was one problem: Cheerio dust. Pulverized oats had made their way under Swartz's fingernails, between pages of books, under keys on his computer, and in his phone. He became fixated on scraping the dust out of his electronics, where it had "apparently bonded with the metal." The dust was everywhere. "I began to discover that the Cheerio dust was also in my system, possibly even my lungs and giving me some Cheerio form of silicosis; they made it difficult to breathe deeply." He gave up the Cheerios. It didn't help.

Everyone working on Reddit agreed it might help to change their living situation. Swartz might be happier if they were closer to cafés and a vibrant neighborhood. Plus, maybe he needed some privacy? They found another three-bedroom apartment, this one on Elm Street near Davis Square. Slowe would move in with Sakillaris, allowing Swartz to have a bedroom to himself. The apartment at 279 Elm Street was a redbrick building on a commercial strip, above a one-hour photo developing shop, in between a tobacco store and an insurance agency. Across the street was a café, Diesel, which had the magical combination of Wi-Fi and air-conditioning, and became a de facto office once days got longer and hotter.

Now that he had his own private space, Swartz retreated into himself further. He stopped contributing code to Reddit altogether. Soon his daily routine involved little more than locking himself in his room, reading, blogging, and working on his book. "He wouldn't even come out," Huffman said of his friend. "I wouldn't see him for weeks. I would just hear him, and I would yell at him to, like, 'stop running around.' Yeah, he would basically jog in his room to get exercise."

Unlike Huffman, Ohanian had never clicked with Swartz. He

had mostly shrugged that off, having over the past year come to expect some lesser degree of respect from programmers because he was a "nontechnical" cofounder. "The challenge was he and I never had a relationship. I mean, he could always be a little rough and condescending," Ohanian said. "I never felt like he ever totally respected me." It had been a tough year, knowing that his mother's brain cancer was incurable; knowing that his friend was still suffering from the injuries of her fall. Huffman, who'd been by his side through it all, was a source of comfort. Swartz was the opposite. "I'd walk into the living room and there's someone who greets you with a smug grin as they get back to writing their book on childhood development, in the face of the fact they are ostensibly part of a team that you have given them equal equity for... That sucked."

Ohanian mostly kept his mouth shut. To vent, he'd call his parents.

By May, Swartz took his disenchantment public. He wrote on his blog, "I don't want to be a programmer. When I look at programming books, I am more tempted to mock them than to read them. When I go to programmer conferences, I'd rather skip out and talk politics than programming. And writing code... is hardly something I want to spend my life doing." He continued by announcing he was done programming.

A month later, Swartz had apparently gotten some blowback from that piece of writing. He posted what he called "a clarification," noting that he believed "many people misunderstood" his post, which had been titled "A Non-Programmer's Apology." He wrote, "I am 19 and live in Cambridge, Massachusetts, in an apartment with two others. The three of us together work full-time on the site reddit.com and I spend most of my days working on programming and various related tasks for it. In the nights and weekends I read and think and write. I'm working on a large book project, which I expect to take years, and which I don't discuss much on the Web."

Ohanian and Huffman gave up trying to manage Swartz. They had come to the realization that they had allowed a founders' share of their company to be owned by a very talented guy who was no longer interested in working with them, this nineteen-year-old genius with barely a lick of higher education who was writing a child development book. And they had allowed their tendency toward conflict avoidance to prevail in their relationship with Swartz. Reddit the website was thriving, doubling its audience every few months. Reddit the company was floundering. Ohanian repeatedly brought the situation to Graham, and they both came to the realization that "this is not a healthy company right now." Huffman knew it, too, and explained later, "The situation was so toxic we were, like, 'This is not gonna succeed; we should just sell while we can.'"

In hindsight, Graham knows they were all naïve. "Nowadays, if I saw a startup that was growing like Reddit was growing, I would really try hard to talk them out of being bought. But back in those days, especially since they were so young, it seemed like a lot of money for them, you know?"

(• •)

Karimkhany invited Ohanian to breakfast at the *Wired* office not long after the awards ceremony. Despite Ohanian's exhaustion, he again jumped. It was at this point that Ohanian recalls Karimkhany used the "a" word: acquisition.

This meeting single-handedly powered the next five months of Reddit's life. Now that an acquisition was on the table, Ohanian and Huffman finally cornered Swartz about being checked out of Reddit. The three made an informal agreement that as long as Swartz showed up to acquisition meetings and phone calls, "We would just let it go. We would make you really rich for really doing nothing and having almost destroyed this company—as long as you go along with this," as Ohanian described it later.

When matters needed to be discussed by all three, Swartz would come out of his room and hop on a phone call or listen to Huffman talk, as if nothing had changed, as if he'd been there the whole time.

Huffman remembers it coming to a head a couple of times. Once, he recalled, Swartz bristled at Huffman being "in charge." Huffman, who at the time was setting up conference calls with the lawyers and doing most of the talking while negotiations progressed, snapped back, incensed, "If I'm not in charge, who is? Somebody has to do this stuff."

Swartz replied, "If you don't want me here, I'll just give you back my stock and leave."

Huffman thought, *That sounds great. That's exactly what we want.* But he sighed and looked at his old friend and said, "Oh, Aaron, you don't have to go that far."

Years later, Huffman realized his mistake in not taking Swartz's bait. "We should have fired him and moved on," he said. But back then, the arguments were still few, the negligence easily dismissed as innocent. "We didn't hate each other yet. Things weren't really that bad. That was sort of the beginning of the bad times."

WE ARE THE NERDS

When Sakillaris pulled up to the house, the sun was just starting to bounce over the rooftops of the shops lining Elm Street. She was accustomed to waking up early and driving to work, so it wasn't too much of a stretch to leave home before dawn and pile four boys into her car to take them to the airport before heading to the office. After all, this was going to be a big day for her boyfriend—Slowe was going to New York City, just for a meeting! Now *this* was executive behavior, she thought. Could her boyfriend soon be an executive at Condé Nast? Could this dysfunctional crew somehow manage to impress some of the savviest media-company poobahs in the world? She sighed. Maybe it was all just wishful thinking.

"Good morning, loves! Your ride is here!" Sakillaris called as she swung open the door to the walk-up. The guys were still rushing around, lacing up their sneakers and taking swigs of coffee. Sakillaris, the fashion buyer, caught a glimpse of Ohanian, and was disturbed that he was wearing his typical T-shirt and jeans. This probably meant Huffman was wearing his usual khakis—and Swartz was in two-sizes-too-big jeans and a saggy hoodie. "Put on a suit, guys! At least a tie!" she yelled to all of them.

Ohanian shouted back, "No way!" He left his coffee mug in the kitchen sink and headed for the door. Crammed in the backseat of the car, the guys were laughing and trying not to elbow each other. Sakillaris answered a phone call and the guys whispered to one another, mimicking her bubbly phone voice. "Okay, byeee! Love you!" she said. ("Okay, byeeeee! Love you!" she heard four falsetto voices echo.)

Sakillaris gave a side-eye and warned the men they'd need to show some respect to Condé Nast, one of the biggest media companies in the entire world. They should take this seriously, she said.

Ohanian explained that this *was* serious. He'd given it thought, and his Reddit T-shirt was not accidental: The lack of pretense involved in *not* putting on a tie can go a long way for founders, he said. It would show the fancy-pants executives at the most esteemed magazine publisher in New York City that they mean business—in that they didn't give a shit about big-business convention. On this, he saw eye-to-eye with Swartz, who'd later write on his personal blog, "Suits . . . are the physical evidence of power distance, the entrenchment of a particular form of inequality." A banker wears a suit. Real hackers wear T-shirts and sandals, or a hoodie and shorts—or whatever the fuck they want, while they devote all their mental energy to building something awesome, Ohanian argued. As Sakillaris pulled into Logan International Airport, Ohanian ended the conversation, finally, by declaring, "We are the nerds!"

(• •)

The T-shirts worked. Or at least they hadn't derailed the acquisition courtship, which was still gaining momentum by midsummer. In July, Slowe and Sakillaris had been together just four months when they decided to travel to Paris. Slowe needed to attend a physics conference in Austria, so tacking a week onto the trip seemed logical.

They stopped over in London, where they did a whirlwind tour:

Buckingham Palace, London Bridge, Piccadilly Circus, the London Eye. Slowe stopped to take Sakillaris's photo in front of a Starbucks, where they'd spotted a Reddit Snoo sticker on a concrete pillar. Next stop, Paris. It was sweltering there in July, but as they trekked to the Eiffel Tower, Sakillaris looked *très Parisienne* in a black lace top and massive black shades.

They were taking a rest on a beige bench when Slowe's BlackBerry started buzzing. He knew the guys back home had a conversation slated for that day with Karimkhany from Condé Nast, so he took the call and got the updates. Sakillaris paced around him, occasionally wandering off to buy a bottle of water or look at street vendors' souvenirs, before heading back to the bench to wait. It was here, under the Tour Eiffel, that Ohanian told Slowe that Karimkhany had called, and said that Condé Nast was ready to begin officially discussing an acquisition. Not A Bug, Inc. would need lawyers to connect to Condé Nast's legal team. There was lots to hammer out, but at this moment, it looked like it might just happen.

Around dusk, Slowe and Sakillaris wandered over to the Left Bank and sat down to dinner in a café. Another buzzing in his pocket. This time, it was Huffman. Yes, everything was in order. Yes, Swartz seemed to be on board—at least enough to hope to make this work. Huffman and Ohanian had spoken with Karimkhany. They'd spoken with Graham. YC was in; Condé Nast was in. Condé Nast was going to, should their lawyers be able to hammer out a deal that would make everyone happy, acquire Not A Bug, Inc. It would be a multimillion-dollar deal. The Reddit guys were going to be rich. Or at least a little bit rich.

"Wooooohoo!" Slowe shouted as he hung up with Huffman. "Woohoo!" Sakillaris hollered. They hugged. The French couple at the next table over sent them a bottle of wine, assuming they'd just gotten engaged.

Two days later, on Bastille Day, Slowe and Sakillaris toured the Louvre. Slowe was still high on the Reddit news, and high on life, here in Paris with the woman he loved. He bought a crazy costume ring at the Louvre gift shop, and, once he and Sakillaris were outside near the glass pyramid, Slowe got down on one knee to propose. He didn't know much about how these things worked, but he rightly figured that with the single-digit fraction of Reddit that he had been promised, he'd soon have enough money to buy her a real ring.

(• •)

Back home, Slowe's life returned to its usual pace. He spent his daytimes at the lab and his evenings making dinner for himself and Sakillaris in their little $2,000-a-month flat in Somerville. He spent countless lab hours hunched over his computer, ostensibly reworking configurations for his experiments, but really, thanks to a pair of earbuds, listening in on hours upon hours of conference calls between the Reddit team and their lawyers, including Boston-based Mark Macenka, Condé Nast's lawyers, and Karimkhany's team. It was Slowe's first exposure to concepts like "due diligence," and it was a slog.

Days turned into weeks, and soon, three months. It was the most drawn-out, complicated deal Karimkhany worked on at Condé Nast—including the ostensibly more complicated *Wired* digital deal (which took roughly a month). In the scheme of corporate acquisitions, this was not a particularly complex deal at its outset. The assumed price tag was roughly $10 million, but the exact figure would fluctuate a bit based on how the founders' and investors' stock and stock options would be paid out.

Huffman had thrown a wrench into the conversation. He wasn't persnickety about the contractual language; he had one big, if simple, request—and it was one that required altering the acquisition price and the payout schedule, and the percentages allocated to all parties, including Y Combinator, Graham, and a stock option pool to be left open for future employees. At the close of the deal, Huffman wanted to be a millionaire.

It was a weirdly rigid demand that ruffled Condé Nast's lawyers:

They were not accustomed to this sort of Silicon Valley–style acquisition, where Huffman's behavior was not just the norm, but mild, even. Graham recalls Condé Nast's lawyers being draconian, "partly because they were just inexperienced" in the way Silicon Valley deals Graham had experienced worked, but also all Reddit parties involved recall there being a "New York" vibe to the negotiations, a particularly curt and abrasive nature that felt like a combination of bureaucracy and backlash.

Still, Huffman's monetary demand and the rash of paper cuts from the Condé Nast lawyers were nothing compared to how Swartz complicated matters. Swartz took umbrage with specific wordings and general concepts alike, particularly relating to intellectual property and the types of ownership Condé Nast would have over Reddit's future development. He had real and perhaps valid concerns about how a corporation as large and formal as Condé Nast would treat Reddit, which had already developed an ethos of free speech and openness, highly valuing user anonymity. Reddit was an unusual company, and Swartz insisted it should be treated as such going forward. He also wanted to protect his own intellectual property. His concerns repeatedly gummed up the works. Karimkhany would be on the phone with Condé Nast's legal team in New York, another business development chief, and from Boston, the four guys, plus Macenka. Swartz would throw out an objection, such as, "Well, if I write a book, do you guys own it?" The teams would assure him no, but he'd want to carve that out in the contractual language.

Huffman recalls that at times, Swartz would tweak wording in the contract without telling anyone—altering a line like "The company has the right to use your likeness" to "The company does not have the right to use your likeness." Sometimes, weeks later, a lawyer would notice the wording change and be irate. "It was like, 'Dude, we all signed this. This is not a joke,'" Huffman said. He fumed about it privately.

But, as usual, he and Ohanian avoided conflict, and chalked the behavior up to Swartz's immaturity. "It's hard to be mad to someone to their face—especially Aaron," Huffman said. "He was so hapless."

From the Elm Street apartment, perhaps the most difficult thing to uphold wasn't just decorum but their agreed-upon deception. "Aaron was doing zero work, but we made believe to Condé that we were still one big happy family," Huffman said. "He would come out of his room, and we'd basically talk about acquisition stuff. He would help with that. The plan was, we were going to sell, we would all get paid, and then he was going to quit on day one."

(• •)

By summer 2006, Ohanian had become a regular on the short flight between Boston and Baltimore. He took the first flight the morning his mom, Anke, was slated to have yet another brain surgery, this one at Johns Hopkins Hospital. Chris and Anke departed for the hospital at dawn so they could swing by Baltimore–Washington International Airport and pick up Alexis.

When Chris pulled up to arrivals, their son—usually easy to spot—was nowhere to be seen. Chris started calling Alexis's phone, which went straight to voicemail. He finally decided to leave Anke, who was dressed and ready for admission into pre-op, in the car to go search for Alexis. How could Alexis keep them waiting so long? They were lucky to have gotten Anke into Johns Hopkins for her treatment; now they'd be late for what could be a life-changing surgery. Chris kept dialing Alexis's cell phone, and his voicemail messages grew increasingly frantic. Finally, he left a message saying, "We're getting the hell outta here, buddy. I don't know where you are but we're gone!"

As Chris and Anke raced to the hospital in a panic, Alexis Ohanian woke up in a start, in a pleather airport seat. Shit. He'd fallen asleep. How come he hadn't heard his phone? He pinched it out of his pocket and saw it flashing. There were a dozen messages now, likely all from his dad. He grabbed his bag and ran outside, knowing he'd fucked up, eager to feel his mom's embrace, hoping they were still waiting. He paced down the line of unfamiliar cars and cursed himself: He'd stayed up all night working, so he could be sure to not oversleep for his super-early flight. He hadn't timed it well: He'd ended up in Baltimore earlier than his parents could get there. He'd found a seat—and apparently had dozed off.

Fuck. He was disappointing Steve by not being there this week to help. He had utterly let down his dad. He wanted to be there to hold his mom's hand. Now he was just standing on a curb in a city he knew mostly for its hospitals, feeling guilty and alone.

THE DEAL

The other year, when I was living in a cabinet, someone emailed me to ask if I had found a decent place to stay. 'Oh, don't worry,' I said. 'I'm sleeping outside the Coop,'" Swartz wrote on his blog the last week of October 2006.

His friend didn't believe Swartz for a minute—that he'd sleep outside of the Harvard University bookstore, which was known colloquially as "the Coop." In fact, he was lying to her. He hadn't slept there—yet. He'd scouted it out, noting that it was a popular spot for homeless people to camp out, in sleeping bags or on cardboard boxes. It had a nice, semi-sheltered alcove. And, hell, it was in one of his favorite places in the world, Harvard Square. Why shouldn't he sleep there? Why shouldn't Swartz, whose bank account would receive a seven-figure deposit within one week, not scuff up a sleeping bag and rest his head where the homeless do? And if he did, why shouldn't he blog about it?

It made perfect sense to him. So one day in late October, Swartz made meticulous preparations for becoming temporarily homeless. He buried a set of his house keys in a park. He dressed in sweatpants, multiple pairs of socks, and a bland T-shirt, so as not to stand out. In hopes of further blending in, he dirtied his sleeping bag by rolling it on the ground. He slid precisely enough change into a pocket for two subway fares, spending one on the way to Harvard Square, then burying the other along with his house key in a patch of dirt nearby.

Swartz unrolled his sleeping bag alongside a wall of the Coop, just down an alley off Brattle Street. From 10 p.m. until midnight, he watched a musician play, sell CDs, and encourage listeners to visit his website. Then Swartz tucked into his sleeping bag, positioned alongside the building, away from the five or so others who had done the same, "all tiled in nicely with each other, all in a different sort of gear." He slept until 5 a.m., when he woke briefly, and then dozed until 8 a.m. It had rained. Gear in tow, he tiptoed to avoid puddles as he went to unearth his subway fare.

"It was right where I left it and I got onto the train without incident," he wrote. He rode the train home.

(• •)

By October, sixteen months after its launch, Reddit had amassed one million monthly readers. And the deal with Condé Nast was nearly done.

The final price tag of just more than $10 million was not one that stood out in 2006, the largest ever year for corporate deals. Reddit's was not the sort of corporate M&A that made evening news headlines, as did Disney's nearly $8 billion acquisition of Pixar, or the $1.65 billion that Google had recently paid for YouTube. Instead, it was one of hundreds of small deals each year that don't bubble to front pages and rarely slipped through the lips of those at Silicon Valley cocktail parties. Media companies, such as Reddit—particularly fledgling ones, unproven by time or market forces, and unprofitable—were typically flying under the radar. (Wired.com's acquisition by Condé had been in the same ballpark, at $25 million.)

There were outliers, though, even in the media industry, and those had the result of making the Reddit deal feel awfully small. In August 2006, Digg cofounder Kevin Rose had appeared on the cover of *Business Week* wearing a backwards baseball cap and headphones and giving two thumbs up while the headline blared, "How This Kid Made $60 Million in 18 Months." The amount wasn't remotely accurate, but the cover stuck, making the Reddit cofounders' few million dollars feel small.

Perhaps the most similar deal with a major, head-turning price tag was the sale of MySpace's parent company to News Corp the prior year, for $580 million. At the time, MySpace had roughly sixteen times the number of monthly users as did Reddit—and, unlike Reddit, it was already profitable.

For Reddit, a media company just one year old, with two founders, one co-owner, and one employee, the acquisition price was reasonable—and perhaps also generous. Especially considering the then-unknown fact that the team behind the company was burnt out, fractured, and frustrated. Ohanian and Huffman had come to see the acquisition as an out, of sorts. It was a path "to part ways with someone who's been pretty toxic for the team, and also to give Reddit the support it needed," as Ohanian characterized it later. He couldn't wait for the feeling of relief when, hopefully, it would all be over. When he'd be a millionaire—imagine that, he thought—and he'd be able to tell his parents that all his complaints and all this suffering he'd gone through over the past year and a half were worthwhile.

Huffman, who had been working largely alone in the apartment that summer and fall, surrounded by the pain his two best friends were going through—Ohanian flying and driving so often to see his mom, and Swartz right there, feet away from him, rarely coming out of his room—knew the arrangement needed to end. He missed his girlfriend, Katie, who'd stayed in Charlottesville, and he wanted a new life—to move to San Francisco and get out of this damn apartment. He was frustrated after the months of negotiations, months he'd been treading water and upholding the deception that they were a functional team.

From where Steve Newhouse sat, the acquisition process seemed neither arduous nor unusually long. But Huffman, Ohanian, and Slowe were beaten down after nearly six months of phone calls hammering it out. Still, they chose to view their uncertain futures optimistically. They began to see the forthcoming acquisition not as an endpoint but rather as their smoothest path to keep building cool things. (Karimkhany's gentle coaxing may have had something to do with that.) Now they did not need to worry about the fact that they didn't have the funding to scale, to hire another programmer, or to do anything aside from keep Reddit.com online. An acquisition would make their bigger problems someone else's.

(• •)

As October wound down, a final sprint of phone calls led to a sense of calm. There were no more questions. The deal was closing. There were papers to sign on October 30, but they were the final papers, and they'd be finalized the following day, on Halloween. Ohanian, Huffman, Swartz, and Slowe hung up with Macenka, with Karimkhany, and with the legal team at Condé Nast. Good riddance, Huffman thought. Then he started shaking.

He walked to his bedroom, shut the door, and sat down on his bed. The months of stress, of keeping a poker face, of hiding his fear that this would all fall apart—all the emotion he'd built up seeped out and he was a puddle. Tears welled up and he laid his body down, just sobbing and sobbing into his pillow.

When day broke, Huffman stood upright.

"And then we signed the papers," he said. He was a twenty-two-year-old millionaire. Ohanian was, too, at twenty-three, and Swartz, at nineteen.

Huffman had known for months that this day would come. The day came. "I was just kind of like, yeah, whatever."

PART II

CHASING THAT MOMENT

On Halloween 2006, Kristen Sakillaris opened her email at work. She clicked on a note from Chris Slowe that read, "The deal is done!!"

She knew immediately what it meant: We're not poor anymore. She loved her job as a retail buyer at the parent company of T.J. Maxx, but it only brought in about $45,000 a year. Chris's grad student stipend was about $25,000; somehow, he still managed to pay a share of the rent. She bought groceries and, well, everything else, down to the shirts on his back. It also clicked for her: The potential for this outcome had been part of why he'd been doing Reddit, driving to his friends' house every evening after every long day at the Harvard physics lab. This was why he'd regularly come home at 2 a.m. and check Reddit one more time before collapsing into bed, only to rise at 6 a.m. and start over. It also meant that a cross-country move was almost certain—and she'd have to break it to her tight-knit and highly protective Greek Orthodox family that their only daughter would be leaving for San Francisco. Now, at least, she and her fiancé would have some footing on which to start their own little family, thanks to his single-digit-percent ownership stake in Reddit. The thought almost made her squeal. "Like, my fiancé is successful! Not that he wasn't successful before, getting a Ph.D. at Harvard," she joked. She hit reply to the email and wrote, "Are you taking me out to a steak dinner?"

At the Davis Square apartment, each of the three men woke up earlier than usual, anticipating the news. They were already armed with an announcement ready to post on their blog, but each had a nagging feeling that there would be still more to hammer out. There had been a phone call from the lawyers with additional tax-related questions, and one from Karimkhany that morning—but now that they'd had their coffee and their cereal bowls were stacked in the sink, it was eerily silent.

Huffman, Ohanian, and Swartz each stared at their computer screens, eyes darting through emails. Swartz whiled away a portion of the morning hunched over his laptop, obsessively refreshing TechCrunch, waiting for a story to appear. He grew so frustrated with his own impatience that he started writing a script that would automatically refresh the page and alert him when the story posted. An agreement between Condé Nast's publicity at *Wired* and TechCrunch meant Ohanian couldn't post an announcement that he'd written to Reddit until the news went live on TechCrunch.

In his head, Ohanian rehearsed what he'd say to the reporters who called—a slate of calls would take up most of that afternoon. Huffman figured he had an hour before the press calls started, so he walked downstairs to Elm Street, to do something each of the four young men would do that day: check his ATM balance. It wasn't until the machine spit out a receipt and he saw it printed out, right there between his fingers, seven figures, that he thought: *Holy shit, we really did this.*

Just after 11 a.m., the TechCrunch article, written up by the site's founder, Michael Arrington, went live. It described Reddit as a "social news site that has always played second fiddle to Digg," but noted, "Reddit does have an active and loyal userbase. Users praise Reddit for having a very quick load time and no advertising."

On the phone a little later with Arrington along with Marshall

Kirkpatrick, one of TechCrunch's writers, Arrington, a notorious curmudgeon, expressed pleasure that a link to his couple-paragraph news announcement was sitting at the very top of Reddit's own homepage. He seemed impressed when Huffman and Ohanian estimated that almost eighty thousand individuals landed on Reddit online every day, for a total of more than seven hundred thousand daily clicks. When Arrington quipped that he'd bet they'd see more traffic than usual today, Huffman agreed, and with characteristic humility joked, "From our smoking web servers, I hope that's the case. Otherwise we have other problems."

Arrington marveled at the leanness of their operation—just four employees—but Huffman and Ohanian wouldn't disclose financial details, and Arrington's ballpark guess of $20 million was in the end too high. At the end of the interview Arrington issued a prescient observation. Facebook had recently made dramatic changes, which caused a user revolt. If visitors to Reddit were indeed as loyal as they seemed, he said, Condé Nast had better tread lightly on tweaking the site, or risk alienating a fickle online audience, which was Reddit's most valuable asset. He said, "I suspect they will be pretty sensitive to any changes at all."

Most of the other press was glowing. A twenty-two-year-old and a twenty-three-year-old had spun $12,000 and someone else's idea into a web property deemed worthy of joining the mainstream media in one of its most revered towers. This little online bulletin board with just five categories of posts—deemed "bookmarklets" at the time by some—had broken one million monthly readers the previous month, giving hope that it might just be a window into the future of how magazines could breathe new life into their online presences and reconnect with readers.

In the midst of the excitement, Ohanian took a break from press calls to phone his mom. Teary-eyed, he told her the news. He didn't know it at the time, in the middle of this stressful shock to the system, but that phone call has over the years become a few minutes that he came to think of as the happiest of his life. Telling his mom that all his hard work, all the risk, had been worthwhile.

He recalled years later, "It was so happy. And now I'm just chasing it, chasing that moment."

They hung up, and Ohanian got an idea: He knew he'd given his mom, who knew she was dying, that sense of relief every parent wants, knowledge that her only son would be okay—not just this year, but for the rest of his life. Her voice that day had sounded peaceful. He knew he'd have the luxury of spending much of the next year by her side. He wanted to give his dad a little something, too. His father, Chris Ohanian, had taught him so much. He'd worked late nights at his little travel agency for him, and he'd made young Alexis's childhood mantra: "I can do everything." Ohanian called FedExField, connected to ticketholder operations, and upgraded his dad's Redskins season tickets from Section 437 to the club level.

MILLIONAIRES' BALL

The three new millionaires decided they should go out. It was Halloween, after all. By some sense of obligation to mark the occasion, they agreed on the very same place Huffman and Ohanian had gone on the night they were initially rejected from Y Combinator: the Border Cafe, a Tex-Mex restaurant strung with multicolored Christmas lights. Swartz posted on his blog, inviting local Redditors to join them for fajitas and margaritas.

Halloween was Ohanian's favorite holiday, and he was the first of the crew ready to go out on the town, having dug out his old Jack Sparrow costume, complete with white-pirate-guy dreadlocks attached to a floppy tricorn hat. Huffman donned bunny ears and an oversized bow tie. Slowe came over after wrapping up his lab work, but as for a costume, he drew a blank. Sakillaris had him covered after a stop at CVS for some hair gel and spray-on color. Once the makeshift mohawk was complete, Slowe threw on a leather jacket. He'd be a punk rocker, with electric-blue sideburns.

One person couldn't be convinced to run to the drugstore to assemble a festive outfit. Swartz wouldn't take off his typical uniform of Reddit T-shirt and jeans. Wandering down Church Street on the way back to Harvard Square, where they'd hit up a divey bar called Hong Kong, he got heckled about his lack of costume. "I looked them straight in the eye, scrunched up my face to look a little angry, and said 'I'm a dot-com millionaire' with utter seriousness. That was my costume." Slowe recalled that Swartz, who also wore a Stanford baseball cap and a corduroy blazer the color of peanut butter, told him he was dressed as "a conformist."

On his blog two days later, Swartz burned the whole scene, lambasting Ohanian for flirting with waitresses, trying to pick up young women on the street, and attempting to bribe people into voting for him in a costume contest. Never mind that Swartz was underage at a bar, he claimed that he was disgusted by his mild-mannered friends having "suddenly become showmen, a horde of girls at their feet" before even consuming a Scorpion Bowl of the Kong's notorious liquor punch. "By the time we finally reached the bar, my head was pounding and my stomach was nauseous, and I didn't want to go in, I didn't want to be here, I didn't want to know these people. I went home instead and watched a show about a serial killer and found myself identifying with the lead."

In reality, the party was pretty lame. A few friends dropped by with rounds of congratulations. Before long, each gave a hug or high five and went on their way. Soon, Huffman, Slowe, and Ohanian were left feeling obligated to keep sipping from the Scorpion Bowl, even after there was really nothing any of them wanted to say. "It was a really small party considering we had sold our company," Slowe said. Ohanian described it as "anticlimactic." Sakillaris apologized for having to work early the next morning, and ducked out. She later said, "I don't think they knew how to celebrate."

She was correct. These were men who'd never learned how to let loose. They'd spent the past year and a half since graduating college mostly in front of their computers, coding, designing logos, and emailing investors.

The three millionaires sat at the Kong, staring at an almost empty mixing bowl of Windex-colored punch. On its lip rested five extra-long straws and a soggy paper umbrella. The world still felt awfully small.

(• •)

On the following evening, November 1, Sakillaris and Slowe were in high spirits. Slowe's head was still ringing a bit from the hangover he'd nursed most of the day, so they'd decided to unwind at home. They shimmied around each other in their little kitchen, hand-tossing dough and mixing sauce for pizza. Sakillaris cranked up the oven as high as it would go and turned to Slowe. "We should invite Steve over!"

He dialed Huffman on his BlackBerry. But when Huffman answered, there was a bustling in the background. "Hey, man! I just landed!" Huffman said. Slowe was confused.

"Dude, I'm in San Francisco!" Huffman replied.

He explained to Slowe that the previous night, he'd opened his laptop, checked to make sure the Reddit servers were still functioning after a record-breaking traffic day, and then searched for plane tickets. He was done with this place. Done with being so cramped in living quarters, and yet so lonely. If he couldn't be with Katie while she was finishing school, he could at least be with his friends. He missed fellow entrepreneurs Justin Kan and Emmett Shear, who'd moved west in September, and wanted to start right away on his new job of shepherding Reddit into its new life. He had emptied a laundry bin of clothes into his suitcase, and cushioned his Xbox into the middle. He bought a ticket for the next morning to SFO.

Now he'd landed. Weighted down by his heavy duffel and a suitcase, he shuffled quickly out of the terminal. The air felt liberating as he rolled down the window and directed his cabdriver to take him to 2140 Taylor Street in Russian Hill. The driver laid on the gas to power up a steep hill lined with a pastel array of Victorians, and then pulled over. Huffman craned his neck to take in the "Crystal Towers," which he and his buddies had discovered by Googling "San Francisco apartment rental furnished" and clicking on the top result. What Huffman saw was a dingy twelve-story concrete-block building complete with balconies and a heated outdoor pool that had sounded nice on paper, but in person gave the air of an old roadside motel.

Apartments at the Crystal Towers were ideal for these young men whose most valuable possessions were laptops and servers, not armchairs or dining tables. It had another feature beneficial to the startup life, in which a company launched from a living room couch might still be growing strong two decades later, or dead within weeks: month-to-month leases. "We basically told everyone to move there," Kan explained. Matt Brezina and Adam Smith, who'd entered Y Combinator's new "startup school," Graham's West Coast autumn version of the summer incubator, with their startup dubbed Xobni (a "smarter address book"—its name is "in-box" spelled backwards), crashed on Kan's floor for a couple weeks before moving to their own apartment a couple floors down. Summer 2006 YC graduates Trip Adler and Jared Friedman, who were starting Scribd, also took an apartment. Smith's MIT fraternity brother Drew Houston, who'd become famous in this little universe for having scored 1600 on his SAT and having built online-poker-playing bots for fun, needed a place. He rented a one-bedroom and created a way to sync files online called Dropbox. Within months, Crystal Towers was so filled with YC entrepreneurs that the guys took to calling it "the Y Scraper."

To Huffman, the Y Scraper was a slice of heaven. There, he was finally surrounded by people as dedicated as himself to building world-shaking technologies. They were the real deal—the Silicon Valley he longed for back when his dad brought him out west for a business trip. Plus, they knew how to have fun. Especially Kan. On weekends, Kan would rally a pack of the guys into going bar-hopping, or, failing that, throw an impromptu house party.

But even if Huffman was surrounded by hackers, he was technically now a company man. He rose early each weekday, caught a Muni bus, and commuted to a 1920s factory building in the South of Market neighborhood. This was Condé Nast's home for *Wired* magazine, and despite smatterings of semi-stylish leather furniture, it was distinctly un-Condé. Drafty and bare, the open-plan office was all concrete-colored carpet squares and broad metal-casement windows. It was sweltering in late summer due to glitchy air-conditioning, and so cold in winter that employees surreptitiously kept space heaters under their desks.

Huffman camped at a desk near Chris Anderson, *Wired*'s editor, until a conference room—the only real sizable conference room—was prepared for the Reddit team. Plenty of days, five o'clock would roll around, and Huffman would reappear at the Y Scraper, thirty-pack of beer in hand. He'd stop by Kan's place, and his roommate, Michael Seibel, would turn down the episode of *Scrubs* he'd been watching.

Kan and Shear had sold Kiko on a whim in a truly bizarre fashion the prior year after Y Combinator: They'd listed it on eBay. The listing had boasted an AJAX infrastructure, forty thousand users, and the domain name. It also noted that for an extra $1,500 on top of the final auction price, the founders would fly to the winning bidder's location for a week and teach them how to use it all. The opening price on August 16, 2006, was $50,000. Kiko.com sold later that month to Tucows, a Canadian telecommunications company, with a final price tag of $258,100.

Now they'd teamed up with Seibel, their friend from Yale, to found something new. Kan had a wacky idea of wearing a video camera on his head and live-broadcasting every moment of his days and nights. He'd call it Justin.tv. Shear coded what would be Justin.tv all day—well, starting around noon—and most evenings. His main break was the near-daily arrival of Huffman. Seibel would cook elaborate themed dinners—sushi, or UK cuisine, replete with Yorkshire puddings—and then the guys would play video games and plow through the thirty-pack. Kan said, "It was almost like living in college again."

Like college—except with an air of *The Real World*, perhaps as envisioned through the sensibility of Philip K. Dick. They pondered the logistics of Kan live-broadcasting their every move to the world; they debated whether the bathroom, sleeping, or showering were off-limits. (No, no, and no: Kan could simply point the camera to the ceiling when he deemed necessary.) Building their camera rig system, which would transmit a continuous video signal to the

Internet, was an undergrad they'd found on an MIT listserv, Kyle Vogt. Vogt was a robotics-obsessed engineer who'd already experimented with self-driving cars and had competed on the TV show *BattleBots*. He flew to San Francisco after his fall semester ended, to crash on the couch and finish up the hardware during winter break.

With him, Vogt had brought a camera prototype. It was a black device a bit smaller than a soda can, with a headset that could perch above Kan's right ear. One Wednesday night in January, a couple days after Vogt arrived, the guys decided to take the camera out in the world for a test run. The four Justin.tv guys plus Huffman killed a fifth of rum between them before departing the Crystal Towers for a dive called Mojito.

It was their favorite bar in North Beach, just a block from historic Caffe Trieste. They'd sent out the beta-testing link to the Justin.tv website to about fifty friends, but weren't sure anyone was watching. Still, they wanted to test the practicality of the entire endeavor: the camera's battery, Kan's tolerance for wearing it, others' social reactions to it.

The camera met immediate resistance. A discussion with the bouncer over whether Kan could broadcast from his head camera while at the bar ended in a compromise: He could wear the headset so long as he kept the camera portion pointed toward the ceiling, instead of at fellow patrons. Not an hour later, Kan wanted to have some conversations off-camera, so he asked, "Anyone else want a go?"

Huffman volunteered. He nestled the camera behind his right ear, faced the camera to the front, and sauntered up to the bar to order another round.

"Hey, man, so that thing is a camera?" the bartender said. Huffman affirmed. "There are some San Francisco 49ers in here right now. So dude, sorry, you're going to have to turn that thing off."

"No problem," Huffman replied.

When he returned to the bar for another round a half hour later, Huffman hadn't moved or turned off the front-facing camera. The bartender was irate. He yelled at Huffman and waved a card in the air. "Listen, I've got your friend's credit card, and I'm not going to give it back until you turn that thing off," Huffman recalls he said.

"Make me," said Huffman, reaching over the bar and plucking Seibel's credit card out of the bartender's hand. He took a step back and bolted out the front door.

After a couple blocks, Huffman's conscience elbowed him. What if someone thought he stole the credit card—didn't understand it was his friend's? What if they hadn't been charged yet? He hadn't done anything wrong—so why was he running? He realized he'd been the asshole in the situation. He turned around and headed back to Mojito to apologize.

As he turned into the doorway, he found himself face-to-face with an SFPD officer who, according to multiple accounts, grabbed one of Huffman's arms, twisted it behind his back, and began questioning him. Kan and Seibel bolted out of the bar to find Huffman, and saw him right there, in the officer's grasp.

"You know, you can't hold me here," Huffman said.

"Sure I can," the officer said.

Kan recollects Huffman said, "I don't have to cooperate with you." And a moment later, the officer, fed up, announced he would be taking Huffman in.

Huffman was still wearing the camera—and Kan was feeling protective. "Well, if you arrest him, you gotta arrest me, too!" Vogt stared on, owl-eyed. Seibel, a large man with a calm demeanor, shook his head, marveling at the scene unfolding in front of him. A small crowd had gathered. "It seemed like literally out of Hollywood," Seibel recalled later. "It all happened just because he had strapped that camera on."

Seibel and Vogt stared at each other in amazement at the scene unfolding before them, their buddies being arrested, before realizing they'd left Shear inside the bar. He'd missed this entire scene— but he couldn't miss what would happen next. They plucked him away from a conversation with three girls and ran back outside. They saw the police van pulling away, with their friends in it. Seibel recalled, "Right then, a taxi pulls up to drop someone off, and we jump in the taxi, and say, 'Follow that police van!'" They urged the reluctant driver along, and sped in pursuit down Columbus Avenue.

As much adrenaline as was in the backseat of the cab, the cabbie was clearly uncomfortable. Shear's phone buzzed. He picked up. "Holy shit," said the voice on the other end. "Did Justin just get arrested?"

"How did you hear that?!" Shear said.

"I was watching!"

It was crazy. And validating. Maybe Justin.tv would work. Day one and they had an audience.

The cab slowed at Broadway and its driver turned around. "Where do you want me to go?" he asked. The SFPD van had turned—illegally—from Columbus. The driver refused to follow.

"We basically spent the rest of the night flying to different police stations, trying to figure out where our friends were," Seibel said later. (Tuning in to Justin.tv was no longer an option, as the headset had both run out of batteries and been confiscated.) At each station, in the wee hours of the morning, their inquiries were met with blank stares, and any searches police information officers made on their behalf turned up dry. They arrived home as the sky was starting to turn from black to midnight blue.

About an hour later, in shuffled Kan and Huffman. They'd spent a very unpleasant hour in a bare-bones police van, were transferred to a bus full of fellow drunk young men, which was followed by a few hours in SFPD's SoMa drunk tank. Their suspicious-looking camera sat in police custody for that time, but was handed back to them with their change and belts at dawn. "Every person we met that evening was a total asshole. That probably includes us," Huffman said later. He had breakfast at Denny's before hobbling home and calling Katie. She was not amused.

They were apologetic—especially to Kyle Vogt, twenty years old and impressionable, and whose invention they'd simultaneously pushed to its social, technological, and legal limits. Vogt, who had been in San Francisco three days, was in disbelief and awe. Years later he confided in Seibel that Huffman's and Kan's antics had made him think, "This is gonna be a great company to work at." He didn't fly back east after winter break and dropped out of MIT.

(• •)

No one was certain what Aaron Swartz would do after the acquisition; he'd long displayed skepticism of large, capitalist enterprises— though he liked *Wired*—and no enthusiasm for continuing with Reddit. But he and the cofounders had kept up appearances of being a functional company for so long that he just went with it. He moved to San Francisco almost as quickly as Huffman. It was his first time living in the Bay Area, and his first time working in a real office, with strangers for colleagues. To Huffman, Swartz seemed a little uncomfortable in his own skin. A week after the acquisition, he'd posted a long fictive account on his blog of a rich fraudster burning and flushing money for laughs and bribing police. Swartz seemed to be working through how he could maintain his intellectual hacker underdog identity while, well, rich. The piece he wrote, which he titled "The Millionaire's Ball," included the line, "In the old days the new money was made through theft and abuse of office. Now any random computer programmer—or even the people who hung around them—could find themselves saddled with a pile of cash."

There were a few work days that Huffman thought went well, and during which he'd deliberately spent time trying to introduce Swartz to some writers at *Wired* whom he'd met—people he thought Swartz might just admire or get along with. He was establishing new roots for himself, for Swartz, and for Reddit. This just might work.

Then, only a few days in, a new post appeared on Swartz's blog:

Wired has tried to make the offices look exciting by painting the walls bright pink but the gray office monotony sneaks through all the same. Gray walls, gray desks, gray noise. The first day I showed up here, I simply couldn't take it. By lunch time I had literally locked myself in a bathroom stall and started crying. I can't imagine staying sane with someone buzzing in my ear all day, let alone getting any actual work done.

Nobody else seems to get work done here either. Everybody's always coming into our room to hang out and chat or invite us to play the new video game system that *Wired* is testing. The upside is that while we haven't gotten much of our work done, we have managed to do many other people's. Various folks from around the office have shown up to have us help them with their technical problems, which we usually solve fairly quickly. We joked that we should get transferred to their IT department instead of Web development.

Huffman resented it immediately. He recalls he told Swartz, "No, what happened was I offered to help and you followed me over there while I fixed their thing for them. Then you wrote about how *they're* wasting *your* time." Huffman was fed up with Swartz for again "misrepresenting reality." This was his friend, someone he'd taken care of so many times. This was the final straw.

Huffman confessed to Karimkhany what had been going on: Swartz having been an active member of the Reddit team had been a façade. He explained the rift between them. The way Huffman saw it, his code, his sweat, his ingenuity had made Swartz a millionaire—and Swartz was not keeping up his end of the bargain. No longer was he even keeping up appearances. "Nothing ever fit, and Aaron had a terrible attitude," Huffman said. "He fucking hated it."

Slowe was concerned about his friends, now a continent away, but also about the optics for Reddit. "There was this acquisition and then one of the first things that happens is there's this exposé from one of the cofounders about how terrible it went?" Slowe said. "*Great.*"

Within weeks, Swartz stopped coming in to the office altogether. Karimkhany was concerned, but then an article appeared on

Wired.com placing Swartz in Berlin. Without telling anyone, Swartz had gone to the Chaos Communication Congress, a popular hacker convention. "It kind of tweaked our noses," Karimkhany said. As a former journalist, he suspects he would have approved Swartz's trip, if only to bring in an interesting perspective on digital rights. But Swartz hadn't asked. It looked like a giant fuck-you.

When Swartz eventually returned, Karimkhany, a diplomat of a manager and an easy talker, sat down with him. He asked Swartz how the company could make his transition easier. Did he need more days away from the office? Did he want to work remotely? Swartz insisted there was no problem, and that there was nothing Condé Nast could do to make him happier.

Karimkhany was baffled. But he took Swartz at his word.

YOU AREN'T A BANK TELLER

Ohanian always loved the idea of New York City. He'd been drawn to its energy, the constant clamor of taxis down Malcolm X Boulevard in Harlem, the performers in Union Square. Now was his chance to, once again, be a real New Yorker.

He'd been born and raised for the first few years of his life in Brooklyn. He romanticized downtown Brooklyn and Fort Greene, where his mom, Anke, and dad, Chris, brought him home from the hospital to the Kingsview co-op complex.

Not long after the Condé Nast acquisition, Ohanian arrived with his big duffel bags to stay with his girlfriend, Liz Nagle, in Park Slope, Brooklyn. He'd only been dating Nagle for a couple months, so "moving in" wasn't a term they'd used—heck, she only had a tiny studio apartment. He'd signed a lease in San Francisco with Huffman, and spent many weekends in Maryland by his mom's bedside. But that little Brooklyn studio had a certain allure, and Condé Nast had agreed to give Ohanian an office on the sixteenth floor of its second New York City headquarters at 1166 Sixth Avenue.

On his first day as a Condé Nast employee, Ohanian was all nerves. He woke up thankful his dad had taken him shopping—

they'd bought a bunch of stuff at Men's Wearhouse after his dad warned him, "You can't show up like a bum—these people just made you millionaires!" Nagle dug out her iron, and, for lack of an ironing board, they laid down towels on a table, and Ohanian clumsily pressed out the wrinkles of his new shirt. Nagle helped fasten his tie, and the two of them set out from her little studio apartment for the F train. She worked at Little, Brown, a book publisher, not far from Times Square, so she agreed to chaperone Ohanian's first commute and show him the proper speed with which to swipe his new MetroCard.

When Ohanian arrived, he instantly realized the tie was too much. He met with Steve Newhouse, one of his new bosses and the chairman of Advance.net, the digital arm of Condé's parent company, Advance Publications, which was owned by his father, Donald, and uncle Samuel Irving "Si" Newhouse. It was Ohanian's first time seeing a Newhouse since the acquisition, and his chest was thumping. But Newhouse was placid and calming. He coached Ohanian through some of the lighter demands that would be made on him as Reddit's project manager—including from magazine editors throughout Condé Nast, who Newhouse explained might occasionally ask him for tips on using emerging technologies or explainers on Internet zeitgeist. But Newhouse told him the relationship ended there; Reddit would be operating independently of the media properties.

"Don't feel like you are responsible to some editor or executive just because of what their title is here; do what you need to do and what's best for you," Ohanian remembers Newhouse saying.

Ohanian was relieved. The press announcements of the acquisition had included many mentions of integrating Reddit into Condé's digital properties, and creating licensable technology that Condé could sell. None of this was mentioned now. "Oh, yeah," Newhouse continued. "You don't need to wear a tie; you aren't a bank teller."

A MOMENT BEFORE DYING

C hris Slowe's BlackBerry buzzed and buzzed. Sometimes this
happened while he was at dinner at Kristen's family's house—
her phone's reception was shoddy in Newton, Massachusetts, and
so the pair was accustomed to Slowe getting all the calls. Slowe and
Sakillaris had spent much of the month packing up and getting
ready to move west.

But this evening in January, it wasn't one of Sakillaris's friends
calling. It was Ohanian.

"Dude, did you see what Aaron did?" Ohanian almost yelled
into the phone. "Oh man. It's bad." He gave Slowe the recap:
Earlier that day, Swartz had posted a blog called "A Moment Before Dying," a narrative of the quotidian morning of a guy named
Aaron, who suffered from embarrassment at having been a pudgy
kid, and now was crippled by "searing pains in his stomach, as if the
food winding its way through his gut had spikes and was tearing
apart the walls of his intestine." The post repeated the phrase "the
day Aaron killed himself" four times.

Slowe pulled up the post. This was classic Aaron. He was trying to be controversial. Or was he? There was the impossible-to-ignore possibility that it could be real. Swartz could already be dead.

Slowe ran in and told Sakillaris. "I have a key to the apartment still. I'm going," he said. He grabbed his jacket and looked straight at Sakillaris. "I don't think I can go alone."

"Oh my God. Oh. My. God," she said. "What are we walking into? Christopher, are we sure we want to walk into this?"

(✦ ✦)

Just an hour earlier, Karimkhany had been packing up his briefcase in the Times Square headquarters of Condé Nast, so he could head home to California, when Ohanian rushed in. "You have to read this," he said, handing Karimkhany a laptop displaying Swartz's blog.

The kid hadn't been at his desk for much of the past two months, and something would have to be done about it, Karimkhany thought. He'd stopped contributing code, and barely even communicated about work with Huffman. He'd posted a few pieces of writing demonizing San Francisco (a dark, cartoony, mask-filled world) and complaining about "the existential terror I feel every day walking the streets." Of the Berlin trip, Swartz had said in an interview elsewhere, "Heh. I bet the first time my boss finds out where I am is when he sees my photo on the front page of his own website." Karimkhany felt he'd been made a fool of.

Now, sitting with Ohanian's laptop in front of him, Karimkhany read the tiny serif words on the manila screen. He looked at Ohanian, and then dialed Swartz. No answer. They called Huffman, who did answer. Ohanian called Paul Graham, who was walking through the UC Berkeley campus. Graham paced the campus, calling various people in Swartz's life, for the next hour. With every call to Aaron Swartz that went to voicemail, the possibility grew: This was a suicide note.

They called the Cambridge police.

(• •)

In Boston, Swartz cowered against a concrete wall, trying to look invisible. His face tensed up and the hairs stood on the back of his neck at the slow groan of a police siren. It sounded distant, but he strained to discern whether it was growing closer. Or was that a fire truck? Were those blue and red lights? Shit. He fucking hated those guys sometimes. He knew it was them—and that the police were coming for him.

He'd been sitting chin-to-knees on the couch in the windowless living room of his empty apartment all evening, weary of the concerned messages from friends. He'd tried to ignore his phone; he couldn't deal with the incoming calls. But when he heard commotion on the street three floors below, and thought he saw a police car coming up Elm Street, his paranoia won. He checked his voicemail. He called his mom back.

After zipping up his gray hoodie and covering his head the best he could, Swartz set off. He looked back over his shoulder and saw cops in front of his door. He ducked behind a pillar. "I know exactly what to do in these kinds of situations; I've seen it in all the movies," he wrote later. "Turn off the wireless on the cell phone, pay for everything in cash, don't use RFID cards, stick to sidestreets. I stick to sidestreets, but I still hear the cop sirens buzzing down all the major roads. There are major roads on every side of me."

He checked his voicemail. There were messages from Ohanian, Huffman, and, oh God, Karimkhany. He didn't need this. He pocketed his phone and walked. When it vibrated again, he stopped and sidestepped into the space between two retail stores on Elm. "Yes," he said flatly.

"Aaron. Okay. What is going on?" Karimkhany asked. "What is going on in your head?"

Swartz was sheepish, and asked whether they'd called the police. "Why are there cops outside my door?"

"This is happening because we are worried about you," Karimkhany said.

Swartz laughed. "I just wrote a short story," he said. "I don't know why you have to make a big deal about it."

"Well, I can tell you I am sitting in a room of English majors and none of us read it as a short story," Karimkhany said. "We read it as a suicide note."

After hanging up with Karimkhany, Swartz, his hoodie still up and his head down, continued walking down Elm. Once he'd gone several blocks he settled down in front of the Rosebud Diner. He squatted near a row of bushes. His phone buzzed again. It was Slowe.

"Aaron, what are you doing?" Slowe demanded.

"Um. I'm hiding from the po-po," Swartz said.

Swartz refused to go home, but agreed to stay put. Slowe and Sakillaris met him in a tiny triangular park in the middle of the street in front of the diner.

"Hey," Swartz said, when Sakillaris approached.

"You don't say 'hey.' That's not what you do in this situation," Sakillaris said sternly. Then she gave him a hug.

"It was a joke," he said. "I didn't mean any harm."

The evening was turning to night, and none of them had eaten dinner. As per usual, Sakillaris's first impulse upon seeing Swartz was to feed him. Swartz, as usual, didn't want to eat. But once they sat down at the diner and they explained to Swartz the severity of what he'd done, he ordered plain pancakes.

That night in the diner, Swartz muttered an apology, then tried to change the topic. It clicked with Sakillaris: Swartz wasn't sorry at all. "That's when I was like, *He doesn't think the same as other people*," Sakillaris later recalled. "He doesn't really understand the consequences of his actions." She explained to him that he owed apologies to a lot of people: his mother, for one, because he'd written mean things about his family in that note. Graham, who'd been pacing the UC Berkeley campus for hours, clutching his cell awaiting updates. His concerned readers who'd posted comments urging him to seek professional help. All of Condé Nast, for putting up with his incivility, delinquency, and possible slander.

"But I'm not cashing my paycheck, so it doesn't matter if I'm working," Sakillaris remembers him saying. Swartz was steadfast in his beliefs as always, but his ability to construct and communicate his perspective was faltering. His alternate reality didn't fly with Sakillaris. She was fed up. "I was like, *That's not how the adult world works.* Meanwhile, I'm realizing that I'm a grown-up. We were grown-ups explaining the world to Aaron."

Swartz's life up to this point had not prepared him for this. He'd grown up affluent in Highland Park, Illinois, enabled in his various endeavors by his parents, who nurtured his intellect and allowed him to drop out of high school. "He was freed of all the disciplining experiences of life," said Lawrence Lessig, a Harvard law professor and political activist, who'd worked with Swartz. "His parents got him out of school early, which was great because it allowed him to become somebody who wasn't the product of puberty in a public school. But it was bad in the sense that it gave him a confidence about his own judgment, which is dangerous."

Over the past two years, Swartz had grown from boy genius—whose poor decisions and detrimental habits could be viewed as endearing or quirky—into a man. He was now confident but often stuck in his own head, where he was immune to the consequences of social interactions, of convention, of diet, and of law. On several occasions he'd been handed large sums of money to complete his Internet projects, where he answered only to his friends who continued to admire his genius and therefore hold his behavior to few, if any, standards.

From a shiny red vinyl booth in the boxcar-style diner, Slowe called Karimkhany and Ohanian. "He's with me right now," he told them. "He's fine. He's safe."

Karimkhany was relieved. Still, there was the matter of: *What now?* He was concerned about Reddit's future within Condé Nast. He was concerned that by morning all the tech blogs would be eating up this fictitious post about a founder's apparent suicide after seemingly being fired. He'd figure it out. But first he needed to stabilize Swartz. He dialed Swartz's parents on his way to the airport.

"I basically laid it out on the table: I think your son needs help. People are getting worried about him," Karimkhany recalls. "I tried to be as diplomatic as possible, but basically said, 'I really think you guys should be doing something about this.'"

(• •)

Within twenty-four hours, the fear Swartz's colleagues felt had been replaced by feelings of betrayal. Swartz was asked to resign.

Days later, Aaron's mother, Susan Harns Swartz, posted on her personal blog:

> I had to endure several phone conversations with Aaron's immediate boss...(your typical crawled-out-from-under-a-rock, lying-to-cover-his-ass middle manager), who expressed to me his great concern for Aaron's welfare and then turned around within minutes and fired him!...I say good riddance to bad corporate rubbish...Barely 20, he has other projects he wants to begin, books he wants to write, classes he wants to take. We wish him only the best and send him all our love.

On January 24, 2007, Swartz posted a photo of himself wearing a T-shirt printed with the *Wired* magazine logo font that had been doctored to read: FIRED.

In the *Wired* office, a woman from human resources had approached Swartz and asked him to collect his belongings. "She never says that she is escorting me, but she does stand behind me wherever I go," he wrote later. "I think I am supposed to leave. I leave. The sun is shining brightly. It's a beautiful day."

THE PHYSICIST, THE INFORMATION COWBOY, THE HACKER, AND THE TROLL

One Thursday night in January, Kristen Sakillaris opened a tube of lipstick and thought back to the glass pyramid at the entrance to the Louvre. When Slowe had gotten down on one knee that day last summer and proposed to her with the costume ring, she never doubted she'd get a real ring someday. She imagined a massive, joyous Greek wedding, with hundreds of family and friends dancing all night in a big ballroom.

Sakillaris was standing in her parents' bathroom, buttoning up a simple white shirt, exhausted from saying goodbye to all her long-time colleagues that afternoon during her final day at work. She smiled to herself. This wasn't what she'd had in mind. But the Greek Orthodox priest was downstairs, waiting in the living room. She and Slowe had gotten his blessing for a quick little ceremony: a simple recitation of vows and marriage certificate signing, at home, before she and Christopher—she and her family always called him Christopher—began their new life together in San Francisco.

Sakillaris sighed. It felt strangely illicit; this little living room ceremony would be her little secret between her immediate family and the Slowes. It was the glass ring of weddings. At least they'd be—

on paper, and in the eyes of the law—husband and wife when they flew out to San Francisco the next day to look at apartments. She could get on Slowe's health insurance. She blotted her rosy lipstick and walked downstairs, eager to hold her fiancé's hands and say her vows for the first time.

(• •)

"So this is what a commute is like," thought Slowe one morning a few weeks later in early February 2007, as he stared out the window of the 30 Stockton Muni bus. It was exciting, what with the occasional view of the San Francisco Bay and the bus's rapid climbs up harrowingly steep streets. As the bus lurched forward and stopped he suddenly saw a streak of bright blond...Steve! Their plan to meet on the bus before Slowe's first day working on Reddit in the San Francisco office had worked. They'd pulled it off, this little feat of urban-transit logistics, like they'd pulled off so much else over the past year. A feeling washed over him amid all his uncertainty about how this day would go: The band was back together again.

He and Kristen had flown out the morning after their little living room ceremony. They'd discovered that what they'd heard from friends had been correct: San Francisco was damn expensive. They had snatched up the first apartment that seemed acceptable, a little one-bedroom in the city's Marina neighborhood.

Once in the office at 520 3rd Street, Slowe found a new Mac-Book Pro waiting for him. He was issued a badge and invited to join in for lunch at the fancy *Wired* cafeteria anytime. But his greatest joy soon became working on a real daytime schedule, alongside Huffman. With the new routine and full-time hours, he could finally flex his programming muscles and learn more intense code-writing from Huffman. It felt legit.

Huffman was happy, too. It had been a long time coming. It had been lonely sitting at his desk after Swartz was gone. And awkward. He couldn't wait to show Slowe his place and, more than anything, his new Porsche. It was a killer car, an old black 911 convertible, a splurge courtesy of his cut of the acquisition payout. He'd sent away for a custom license plate, too: It would read SPEZ.

Together in the little conference room each day, Slowe and Huffman worked in tandem, splitting the jobs of systems administrator, chief technology officer, programmer, and product manager. What felt to them like a boatload of bureaucracy—endless legal documents, adding a site privacy policy and terms of use, were minor in the scheme of things.

Huffman was given great authority to run Reddit as he chose. With his Harvard experience, Slowe handled corporate life more gracefully than Huffman, the countless emails searching for signatures and approvals for the proper forms. Huffman continually bristled at such things. They'd first butted up against Condé Nast red tape just days after the acquisition. Their new corporate overlords, as they jokingly referred to them, emailed the Reddit team instructions on how to install a remote-desktop-control software called Timbuktu. It was a common software used by companies with IT departments, so a fix could be made to a user's system remotely. But to these hackers the software amounted to spyware. "It was the first time we were like, 'Hahahahaha...NO,'" Slowe said. Condé Nast followed up on their inaction by physically mailing them disks with which to install the program. Huffman and Slowe responded by physically placing the disks in a drawer and slamming it shut.

Aside from quarterly goal-setting meetings with Condé and Advance executives, Reddit was mostly left to its own devices. Maintaining its growth—rebooting servers, keeping Reddit online—took nearly all of Huffman and Slowe's energy. It meant there simply wasn't time for branching out into a hypothetical integration with Condé Nast sites or building side projects for their new parent empire. It didn't hurt that most of Condé Nast didn't comprehend this bizarre site with anonymous users posting increasingly on everything under the sun in informal, distinctly un-magazine-like language. Early Reddit staffers would later recall *Wired* editors walking past their corner, poking a head in, and then explaining to their guests or interview subjects, "This is Reddit. We don't really know what they do."

"It wasn't very professional. We were just doing what needed to be done to keep it going," Huffman said. "It was a lot of fun."

(• •)

The next step would be to bring in reinforcements. Jeremy Edberg had been nothing if not persistent. He'd met Huffman and Ohanian back in 2006, at a tech gathering hosted by Paul Graham in Boston. Over lunch that week with Ohanian, Edberg told the kid, seven years his junior, that when Reddit was ready to hire, call him. He handed Ohanian his résumé.

Ohanian laughed it off, having never considered that anyone, ever, would be asking to work for him.

When news of Reddit's acquisition was announced, Edberg emailed Ohanian. Huffman and Ohanian had gotten to know Edberg over time, in part due to his username, Jedberg, which was very active on Reddit. (In fact, it was his username online in many places; at work and among friends in person several people had taken to calling him "Jedberg," just as many people called Huffman "Spez.") By March 2007, it was official: Jedberg would be Reddit's first real hire. Reddit announced his hiring on its blog, noting that he is "quite handy with a puter" (he'd been a senior systems engineer at eBay). Edberg's title was chief architect of Reddit. Ohanian also wrote in the post, "Despite what his corporate title may be, he's reddit's 'Information Cowboy.' Yee-haw."

Edberg, baby-faced and pale, didn't cut an intimidating figure— but unlike the rest of the Reddit team, he had experience working inside large corporations, so he wasn't timid about telling Condé Nast how things should be done. His first task at Reddit was writing a new deployment system, so that when site updates needed to be made, deploying them didn't take a half hour. He got code deployment down to less than one minute. He helped Slowe rerack the servers, and soon all the site's traffic was flowing through a center just blocks from the South of Market office. He also tackled the perennial issue of email. He'd make Condé Nast happy by accepting email through the company's existing system, but also employed Reddit's own servers to reroute all messages to their @reddit.com addresses, for which he instituted strict spam controls.

Within months, Condé approved another position, and Huffman and Slowe announced on Reddit's blog that they were hiring. They received dozens of applications, but one stood out. He'd done a stint in the U.S. Army, and despite lacking a computer science degree was trying to make it in Silicon Valley. He'd started in an IT department and worked his way up to creating software. "I get all hot and bothered about writing distributed systems," Huffman recalled David King, writing in his cover letter. King, twenty-four, appeared straight out of central casting for "hacker," with his oversized black T-shirt, long brown hair, and neatly trimmed facial hair on a handsome, angular face. When Huffman emailed King a coding challenge, he responded in a day with a tight program in an esoteric coding language called Erlang. Huffman was sold.

Slowe and Huffman had begun a massive project, overhauling Reddit.com's codebase. It had been a longtime and significant priority of Huffman's to keep the site loading quickly and, for users, functioning well (programmers call this keeping a site "perky"). Thanks to numerous small changes and additions to its functionality over the past years, the codebase had become unwieldy. Plus, there were portions of code that were now unused, features built and never launched, or pulled back on, such as the complex recommendation engine Paul Graham had pushed so hard for at Reddit's inception.

With a team of four in place in the conference room overlooking SoMa's tech-company epicenter, it felt *good*. Reddit was ready to grow. Huffman and Slowe felt proud that they'd learned to navigate Condé Nast human resources well enough to hire, which allowed them finally to get ahead of the game on site maintenance. What they lacked was a plan for the future. "The plan was always like ... well ... ," Slowe said. "We never really had much of a product plan beyond whatever was in Steve's head."

(• •)

"There is one and only one social responsibility of business," the economist Milton Friedman wrote in 1962. And that is "to use its resources and engage in activities designed to increase its profits." Huffman knew what he was getting into when Reddit was acquired by a massive corporation: Reddit would have to make money.

On March 28, 2007, he posted something on Reddit that loyal users found both inevitable and despicable.

> Part of the reason reddit was acquired was so that eventually it could be used to sell advertising. We wanted to delay ads until we could debut all the new stuff we're working on, but it's taking longer than expected, and the powers-that-be are getting antsy. So, sometime later this week we'll be flipping the switch to turn a few ads on.

What read as a straightforward announcement was also a subtle attempt to manage the opinionated and vocal Reddit community's expectations. It made plain what was inevitable, and provided warning that might mitigate damage upon users beginning to see ads on the site. It also spoke to Reddit readers as intelligent beings who'd see the logic of such a moneymaking concept—but at the same time gave a whiff of antiestablishment sensibility in calling the "powers-that-be" "antsy." This was Huffman's style: It conducted the necessary business, but felt genuine, not whipped through a PR machine.

About eighteen months into its life, Reddit's breadth now extended well beyond Huffman's sensibility, but many of Huffman's own personal sensibilities had *become* Reddit. His good friend Kan said it's plain to see that Huffman contains all the "best and worst qualities of Reddit." He's intelligent, helpful, and generous—the friend you want to call when you're in a jam. He's rational. He's socially very liberal, veering libertarian—someone who believes in social justice. But his sense of humor is wry. He'd definitely make fun of an overly earnest post by a bleeding-heart liberal, or "social justice warrior," as they became known online.

He's also a total troll. Huffman's friends had learned never to leave their cell phones unlocked around him, because if the opportunity arose, he would text their ex-girlfriend something like, "I really love you. I made a huge mistake." Likewise, Reddit.com could be a total trollfest.

At times Reddit had the vibe of water-cooler gossip in a computer science TA break room. A typical post might feature file encryption technologies or concern security breaches at power plants. But simultaneously there existed posts on Reddit in which commenters were becoming action-oriented, posting about causes and sharing links to donation sites. There were rational (mostly) discussions about news, much of which circumvented the mainstream media or exposed flaws or hypocrisies in reporting. The upvoting of comments served to highlight the most cogent arguments, which made it feel like the smartest guy in the room got his voice heard.

As Reddit grew, it was becoming clear that control couldn't rest solely with Huffman. Users were handed more and more power to control corners of the Reddit universe. In late May 2008, Huffman more broadly opened up the ability for any user to create a section of Reddit—what would become known as "subreddits." By default, the user who created the section, say, r/atheism, would be its moderator. Users quickly created r/WTF, r/lolcats, and r/offbeat, sections with little purpose aside from wasting time but that would over the next decade amass millions of regular viewers and loyal subscribers. There was higher-brow Reddit, too: Subreddits for entertainment, photography, and art flourished. For example, photos of the eerie art installation of a tiny freestanding Prada store in Marfa, Texas, got upvoted.

Even though he'd been fired, Swartz's influence could also be felt. He'd in public been calling himself a cofounder of Reddit, which annoyed Huffman. But his free-speech absolutism, which infused posts on his blog, had already been embraced by much of Reddit's community. Swartz had written:

So I have my own justification for freedom of speech: because we can. Human freedom is important, so we should try to protect it from encroachment wherever possible. With most freedoms—freedom of motion, freedom of exchange, freedom of action—permitting them in full would cause some problems. People shouldn't be free to walk into other people's bedrooms, take all their stuff, and then punch the poor victims in the face. But hurling a bunch of epithets at the guy really isn't so bad.

Swartz extended the free-speech argument into a digital context, raising compelling points about the function of the Internet to transmit content at a time when few people were thinking about the effect of laws on our digital lives. "I fight laws that restrict what bits I can put on my website," he wrote, sweeping all online posting of content, infringing on patents, distributing copyrighted works, child pornography, and encryption of content into his free-speech bucket.

While Swartz's perspective was extreme, Reddit had, by design, always been infused with a free-speech ethos. As "the front page of the Internet," it believed in giving the power to users to elevate stories they believed in, to give them the placement they deserved at the top of the page. There was no editorial masthead doing the deciding; it was the people. With that came some content that was extremely different from what you'd usually see reading your hometown daily. There were curse words and many mentions of penises and boobs, and jokes. There were explicit photos of the aftermaths of traffic accidents and bear attacks.

And thousands of young hackers and scientists, cut from a similar cloth to Swartz's, posted often on related issues: copyright, government secrets, and individuals' privacy rights. Doing so was safe here, among like-minded peers, and behind a pseudonymous account name.

MISTER SPLASHY PANTS AND THE LARGE HADRON COLLIDER

Perhaps as compensation for the previous year's anticlimactic post-acquisition Halloween, over the messy first year of Reddit's life within Condé Nast, Ohanian and Huffman had learned how to celebrate. In August 2007, the crew flew back to Boston for Slowe and Sakillaris's actual big Greek wedding celebration, in which Huffman and Ohanian were groomsmen. It was everything Sakillaris—now Kristen Slowe—dreamed of: Greek Orthodox ceremony and a big party. For the nerds, they played the *Star Wars* theme before their first dance.

For the one-year anniversary of the acquisition, in late October, Reddit hosted not one but several open-bar boozefests around the country. New York City's was in a dive bar tucked beyond Avenue B in the East Village. Steve Newhouse attended, as did his younger cousin, S. I. Newhouse. Gawker wrote up the scene, noting the presence of the media-empire family, despite their general allergy to tabloid-style coverage. The media-gossip site dubbed the rest of the crowd "Silicon Alley's scruffiest."

Ohanian, despite traveling many weeks—jetting back to Virginia to see his mother as her cancer and treatments intensified, or out to

San Francisco for work—had grown comfortable with his new corporate life, commuting from Park Slope to Times Square, working some eight hours out of his beige office, and heading home or out to dinner with friends. He felt distant from Huffman, from Slowe and the team in San Francisco, but stayed connected online, on IM, and, hey, working alone wasn't so bad.

Mostly he watched his screen, alert to posts bubbling up on Reddit. A slice of his job was to be Condé Nast's digital sage, to inform in a presentation any department that asked for a primer on online publishing and managing the communities that develop there. He'd met with magazine editors in New York, and he sometimes stumbled in his mandate to apprise them about the future of digital. The learning curve at Condé Nast was steep.

Ohanian traveled to London to meet with representatives of various Condé Nast properties around Europe, to give what amounted to a pitch deck on the importance of publishing online. He remembers entering a mansion, all beautiful boardrooms of the sort he'd only seen in movies or on television, and kicking himself for not paying better attention in art history class. To Ohanian, it was surreal to be surrounded by a flurry of servants dashing around the stately table filled with European publishing's biggest names. He wore an ill-fitting suit and was not accustomed to spending time with people of power or wealth. "I felt like an outsider in that world, and 99 percent of the time I couldn't relate to these people," he said. But while he delivered his presentation, he noticed that some of the editors and publishers were nodding. Afterward, they asked engaged questions. He quickly got over his imposter complex.

(• •)

Much of what Ohanian did day-to-day, however, was observe and stoke the happenings on Reddit. Around lunchtime one day in November 2007 back in New York, he spotted something that made him laugh rocketing up Reddit's front page. The organization Greenpeace was attempting to raise awareness in a campaign against whale poaching by putting a tracking chip in a whale so that it could be watched by the masses online. In order to personify the creature they chose, Greenpeace created an online contest to name the whale. Suggestions included Kaimana, which in Hawaii means "power of the sea," Manami, Japanese for "love of the sea," and Libertad, Spanish for "freedom." Then there was this gem: Mister Splashy Pants.

Reddit user _black wrote a post: "Please vote Mister Splashy Pants."

Ohanian loved the goofy name for a noble beast, and users seemed to be rallying behind it. He quickly mocked up a whale, in the style of the Reddit alien, and swapped out the site's mascot for the day.

Reddit wasn't the only place online that rallied for Mister Splashy Pants. A 4chan poster had originally called out the contest, and environmental blog *TreeHugger* joked that "Splashy" was not an appropriately dignified name for such a majestic creature. But once it was on Reddit, the votes racked up—fast. Within a day, Mister Splashy Pants went from having 5 percent of the vote to 70 percent. Greenpeace was flabbergasted. It decided to pause, then reopen voting, perhaps in hopes of undoing the damage. Reddit only redoubled its efforts. Ohanian changed the site's mascot once more, to a fighting whale with flipper-fists raised.

When votes were tallied, Kaimana, Manami, and all the rest were in the dust. Humphrey took second place, with 4,329 votes, or 3 percent of the vote. Mister Splashy Pants had 119,367 votes, or 78 percent.

Greenpeace in the end reluctantly accepted Mister Splashy Pants as the tracked whale's name. It had a killer—if short-lived—little merchandise business on its hands, selling Mister Splashy Pants sweatshirts and the like. The wide exposure of the program, in part due to this absurd name, likely contributed to the Japanese government calling off its whaling expedition, one of Greenpeace's aims.

The Splashy Pants episode was a turning point for the community, at least in the eyes of Ohanian. "That was around the time it became clear that if something hit the top spot on a subreddit or hit the homepage, it was ready to take off to the rest of the Internet," he said. Within a year, sites such as Gawker would be regularly mining Reddit for content—and taking all the Internet glory for finding viral hits. Internet glory, of course, meant traffic. (Some media properties were better at monetizing that traffic than others; Reddit did not think like a traditional media company and was very slow to match its content with targeted advertising.)

The concept of virality on Reddit had taken hold. Its hotness algorithm, plus its karma tracking, were dual secret engines, chugging away out of the awareness of all but the most avid technologists and programmers but starting to influence more and more of the Internet and popular culture.

(• •)

Around the globe on September 10, 2008, on the front pages of newspapers were reports that the Large Hadron Collider, an ultra-powerful particle collider in the world's most complex laboratory, the European Organization for Nuclear Research, was complete, and had begun conducting initial tests. These news stories were geek catnip: This was the single largest machine on the planet, assembled over the course of a decade in a bunker underground. The mass fascination was in part due to the spine-chilling nature of the thing: The *New York Times* ran an article in advance of the collider's launch weighing the odds that its use could open up a black hole.

Photographs accompanying the articles showed a gigantic metal tube and a handful of scientists wearing hard hats and khaki blazers inspecting the magnificent creation. On Reddit, users marveled at the potential uses of—and destruction that could be caused by—the Large Hadron Collider. They weighed the value of its potential research versus its massive, $5 billion price tag. They also noted that one of the scientists in the photos, with tiny spectacles and goatee, looked a lot like Gordon Freeman, the protagonist of the video game *Half-Life*.

The cult classic character Freeman is a theoretical physicist employed by a vast underground research laboratory. *Half-Life*'s plot is dystopian, and hinges on Freeman's experiment inadvertently opening up a space-time rift that allows aliens to pour into his research facility. In the game, he fends off a series of bizarre creatures, including something called a "headcrab" (picture a breadbox-sized crab...that can latch onto one's head), with an assortment of weapons, the most basic of which is a distinctive red crowbar.

A Reddit user who went by Mad_Gouki posted in r/gaming, "Dear Reddit: We should buy a red crowbar and send it to Cern/LHC." The post garnered dozens of upvotes immediately, and rose to the top of the gaming subreddit. Ohanian spotted the goofy idea's quick ascent—he'd grown up playing *Half-Life*, and like hundreds of other Redditors found Mad_Gouki's idea ingenious. Like the stellar community manager he was becoming, he jumped on it.

Reddit was quickly becoming an insider-y cauldron of nerd ideas, news, and pop culture. The inside joke you'd once only get a chuckle for sharing with your gaming buddies now had potential to spawn a movement. Ohanian had witnessed this happen with Mister Splashy Pants, and wondered to himself whether he could help amplify this crowbar joke into another Internet-zeitgeist-steering moment on Reddit—one that would make the popular r/gaming community feel special, and perhaps get the company a few press hits.

Ohanian ordered a crowbar from Home Depot. When it arrived at the Reddit office in San Francisco, where he'd been working recently, he spray-painted it red to resemble the initial weapon in *Half-Life*.

Ohanian posted on his personal blog, "Upon learning that the Cern lab would be recreating the ill-fated Black Mesa project, Mad_Gouki thought it'd be prudent to send them a red crowbar for the pending alien invasion. Chris knows a few fellow physicists working at the lab, so we'll do our best to get this in the right hands." Along with the crowbar, a guide to *Half-Life*, and a headcrab headdress he somehow procured, he included a note: "Get this to Gordon Freeman. He'll know what to do."

Ohanian also documented his actions on Reddit's blog, and the press bit. *Engadget*, a tech blog, Destructoid, a gaming site, and plenty of others ran short items on the stunt. One day, Ohanian received an email that read, "Thanks so much for the crowbar. I took a bunch of photos for you." Attached was a series of photographs of the Gordon Freeman look-alike, whose name was Sandro Bonacini, reenacting scenes from *Half-Life*. A colleague at CERN, Stefano Michelis, posed wearing the headcrab hat. Ohanian was floored: This was sublime serendipity, this scientist willing to play along with a little Reddit in-joke. He uploaded the photos and submitted a post to r/gaming. Tech and gaming blogs loved the photos—and on Gizmodo, Kotaku, and similar sites, the story coming full circle got a lot of media play.

"Within six months or a year, a lot of these communities realized that they didn't need a moderator or an administrator to do this," Ohanian said later. Huffman may have built Reddit's structure and suffused it with his personality, but Ohanian nudged its tone and capabilities. He'd helped alert the hundreds of thousands of Redditors that they, too, could harness the enthusiasm—and sometimes the money—of the crowds of like-minded people dwelling alongside them online. In Ohanian's mind, there were endless ways to harness the power of the ever-expanding group of Redditors. There were charities to benefit, individuals to uplift. What he wasn't considering at the moment was that if this community of individuals could use their collective power for massive good, they could also commit terrible ills.

(• •)

One of the little pleasures in Ohanian's life was receiving random packages from a stranger named Erik Martin. They were bizarrely curated randomness: DVDs of Korean films he'd never heard of and likely would never watch, Colombian dance records, stickers, retro flyers, anime trading cards. The only discernible connection was that everything seemed to have been dunked in cool sauce.

Martin had come across Reddit years earlier, through reading Graham's website. When Ohanian finally met Martin over lunch, after Martin had relocated to New York City to work for a small film company, Ohanian found himself sitting across from a guy very similar to himself: easy to smile, earnest, with a wry sense of humor tucked beneath a scruffy face and warm brown eyes.

Ohanian thought Martin was both charming and resourceful. He learned that Martin had helped orchestrate a "scene" by the comedy collective Improv Everywhere inside a Manhattan Best Buy store. (During the "mission," in which about a hundred actors dressed as clueless retail employees, agent "EMartin" had kept his cool all while being escorted out of the store and interviewed by police.) The pair hit it off, and when Ohanian had a puckish idea, he often ran it by Martin.

Martin was a real-life MacGyver. He'd grown up the son of a Swiss immigrant inventor and entrepreneur who treated the family's Chapel Hill, North Carolina, living room like a laboratory-slash-communal-office. His dad did the tinkering and inventing; his mom handled the marketing. A rotating cast of employees would come in while young Erik got ready for school and still be there working—usually on something environmental-science- or laboratory-robotics-related—when Erik returned. "I had total mad scientist shit in my backyard," Martin said. His toys and sports equipment were often taken over by his father's projects; one day he returned home from school to find that his basketball hoop had wood furnaces and piping strung up it.

Ohanian asked Martin to take on some freelance work, engaging with Reddit users who had questions, answering email, and helping establish the brand. Or, rather, at this point, brands. While Huffman liked Reddit's fairly narrow focus on news and programming content, both Condé Nast and Ohanian were eager to branch out. The strategy at the time, spearheaded by Ohanian, was to snatch up hip-sounding URLs and launch additional Lipstick-like Reddit clones. The two most memorable ideas were We Heart Gossip, a site for celebrity news, and The Cute List, a site for posts about animals.

Ohanian purchased hundreds of URLs; dozens upon dozens were never used. It became clear within months that Ohanian's entire premise was flawed. He'd underestimated the extraordinary difficulty of building freestanding brands without organic traffic coming from a greater beast. He wasted a good part of a year attempting to build small communities such as The Cute List. Still, Martin proved himself a hard worker during this time.

It wasn't long before Ohanian was telling Martin that Reddit wanted to bring him on full-time. "It turned everything around for me," Martin said. In New York, Martin had lunch with Huffman, who'd flown in to meet him. Martin realized uncomfortably late that the barbecue lunch on Manhattan's west side, not far from the *Intrepid*, was an interview for his dream job. He got nervous sitting just feet from Huffman's soul-piercing light blue eyes. He sensed that Huffman was reserved but judgmental, saying later, "If you have any sort of weakness, he will sense it."

Martin needn't have worried. By Halloween 2008, it was official: Reddit's blog featured the headline "welcome, erik—manager of community, slayer of trolls." His username, hueypriest, was also included.

The San Francisco office made another hire that fall: Mike Schiraldi, a jovial guy with fast coding fingers who also happened to be deeply obsessed with Reddit. He'd read a *Wall Street Journal* article about Reddit power users and, jealous, set out to reach a karma level of 10,000. He cracked the top ten of all-time biggest Reddit posters.

During Schiraldi's recruitment, Huffman sensed he had doubts and asked him to meet with Karimkhany. One afternoon in early November 2008, Karimkhany took Schiraldi on a walk around South Park, an oval green space not far from the office. Schiraldi acknowledged that he'd become distracted by Reddit's biggest rival, Digg, having just raised nearly $30 million in fresh investment from venture capitalists. Its founder, Kevin Rose, had recently been on the cover of *Inc.* magazine. "How are we possibly going to compete? Reddit has six people. What's the plan for competing with this giant company?" Schiraldi asked.

"This funding for Digg is the best thing that's ever happened to Reddit," Karimkhany said.

Schiraldi raised a heavy eyebrow, but was calmed by Karimkhany's confidence. He took from their chat that massive investments, such as Digg's millions, meant adding board members and shareholders whose fiscal priorities could meddle with a company's values and its vision. He remembers Karimkhany saying, "They're not going to be happy running Digg the way it is, they're going to want to change everything to make it more like Twitter." Schiraldi accepted the job.

The following day, Condé Nast, whose magazines had brought in $3.2 billion in advertising revenue over the past year, but whose newspaper revenues were tanking, announced a company-wide hiring freeze and multiyear reorganization of its vast array of newspapers and websites. What it had in mind was streamlining its digital staff. Among those laid off was Karimkhany.

BENIGN NEGLECT

F or all the phenomena Ohanian spotted and nurtured, there
were others he simply missed.

For example: Ask Me Anything, one of the most popular and
prominent concepts for interacting on Reddit. To follow the concept back to its start, one must look to Ask Reddit, the original
subreddit where users would seek answers to questions such as, "Is
it a good idea to replace my desk chair with a stability ball?" or
"Tomorrow is my day off. Should I finish my Christmas shopping
or go play with manatees?"

Occasionally, an expert in a certain field would emerge and gain
a lot of upvotes for their answers of substance. Certain Q&A sessions started to resemble a phenomenon that had been going on
online for a while. In 1999, Slashdot had begun posting interviews
based on crowdsourced questions. They were funny, confessional,
and wide-ranging. Proof that this new breed of online earnestness
had traction could be found in the launches, that same year, of sites
UrbanBaby, full of confessional posts from New York moms, and
Something Awful, a humor site predominantly trafficked by young

men, which featured a Tell/Ask forum with contents such as "Ask me about working in a crematorium."

Despite that Q&As on other forum sites were fairly well established by 2008, Ohanian wasn't yet seeing the cues that this sort of group interview with an individual could work on Reddit. Instead, he took the Q&A concept in a glitzier direction.

Together with Martin, Ohanian decided to stage production-heavy video question-and-answer sessions with high-profile individuals, such as Adam Savage, the apricot-and-white-haired founding host of the Discovery Channel show *MythBusters*, and writer Christopher Hitchens. Through their Condé Nast connections, Martin and Ohanian got Hitchens, a *Vanity Fair* contributor, to agree to sit down with them. They flew to Washington, D.C., Martin lugging his camera and tripod into Hitchens's town house.

They were served lunch, and Hitchens poured each of them a whiskey. Then the writer escorted them to a separate apartment across the hall from his home. Another round of whiskey was poured. A bottle of wine was opened. Hitchens sat down behind Martin's laptop and read a question from the screen: "What historical figures, events, movements, or books do you feel have been ignored, or underemphasized, in the public education of young people?" Hitchens paused. He had read the username attached to the account that had submitted the question, PSteak. "Well, *Mr.* PSteak, which I think you must be, because I don't think there would be a *Mrs.* PSteak. Could I be wrong about that?"

After insulting the user, Hitchens noted that the founding of the United States as a secular democratic federal republic is understudied, and said, "We don't show the grip and the grain of how revolutionary our revolution was." He spoke about the Iraq War and the Socratic style of debate. But the magic that came from the interview wasn't strictly in the responses. It was in hearing him interact with users—regular Redditors. Hitchens simply reading out loud their usernames, some unpronounceable or slightly obscene, was validating to the Reddit community. It wasn't just Ohanian and

Martin and the bottle of Johnnie Walker Black that had been invited into Hitchens's private lair for an afternoon: It was everyone on Reddit.

Video, however, turned out to be cumbersome (it would take Martin weeks to edit a single question-and-answer session)—especially given what was already happening organically. By May 2009, a subreddit dedicated purely to the form r/IAmA, named after the first words a user volunteering to answer questions would write—as in, "I am a slumlord. Ask me anything!"—was created. Today, they're mostly known as "AMAs," as in "Ask Me Anything," and they are easily Reddit's most known feature. (Early and long-time Reddit employees still call them "IAmAs," pronounced *eye-am-uhs*.) Celebrities, Nobel laureates, and politicians—up to President Donald Trump—have participated in them. Some of the most popular of all time, though, are still those by intriguing everymen possessing useful information. One by a vacuum repair specialist was for years one of the most widely viewed Reddit threads.

By the end of the year, fifty thousand individual accounts followed r/IAmA. It contained incredible stories of cheating death, professional accomplishment, and bizarre wonders of modern medicine. "I was blind for two years. AMA." "I am a debunker of 9/11 conspiracy theories. AMA." There was simply a post titled: "My dad started reading Reddit, and I asked him if he's read IAMA. He said: 'Oh yeah, where you pretend to be someone and then everyone tries to prove you wrong!'"

(• •)

In 2008, America's housing bubble burst and the recession it precipitated was a dam to the river of funding that had begun to flow into Silicon Valley. Reddit, tucked inside of Advance Publications, under Condé Nast, was insulated from the market forces that would lead to the crib deaths of so many other small companies. But the company-wide hiring freeze instituted the day after Schiraldi was hired meant growth internally was no longer an option.

Karimkhany was no longer there to handhold them through Condé Nast and Advance Publications' bureaucracy.

During these lean years, Reddit was largely left to its own devices by Condé Nast, in a rare example of corporate benign neglect. "We did almost nothing to integrate Reddit into the rest of the company, and we probably should have done even less," Bob Sauerberg, Condé Nast's president, said. "We left Reddit in San Francisco and let it find its own way. Mostly we wanted to make sure we didn't screw it up."

Steve Newhouse, who served as chairman of the digital arm of Advance Publications, had been a Reddit ally from day one. He kept a close watch over Reddit, but he did not want his family's company to be the great corporate entity that devoured the promising startup. As time passed, the strategy solidified, as it became clear to Advance leadership that Reddit was so different from its other media properties, such as the *New Yorker* and *Teen Vogue*, that in order to see it thrive, they'd have to manage it differently than other holdings. Newhouse wanted to see Reddit scale— grow in traffic and user engagement—and held the staff to meeting growth goals they'd set together at quarterly meetings with him and the head of the digital division, Sarah Chubb.

Insulated in its own little Petri dish, Reddit deftly continued to grow, serving up 120,000 page views a day by mid-2008. Huffman had begun to feel more surefooted in his role as CEO and engineering lead. He and his team were tackling big problems, keeping the site secure and spam-free—well, at least trolling and self-promotion weren't completely rampant. Ohanian was throwing himself into his work more than ever, though he lacked direction. He knew idea generation was his wheelhouse, as was making the site profitable, and he took some stabs. He dreamed up business development deals. He embarked on a Reddit merchandise push, creating alien T-shirts, onesies, and mugs on CafePress.com and hawking them on an online storefront. He decided the video AMA format should be spun into a concept that would be called "Reddit TV."

A rift of priorities was developing. Some of these initiatives, particularly the merchandise, had the engineers in San Francisco scratching their heads. Shouldn't Ohanian be spending his time selling ads instead of hawking gear? Some of it simply had to do with Ohanian being in New York City, with Condé Nast corporate. To Huffman and his team, not much good seemed to come out of corporate. They poked fun outwardly, and stewed inwardly.

Huffman was particularly annoyed with HR. Just before the hiring freeze, while Reddit was actively interviewing engineers, he had extended a job offer to a developer he was courting, Vineet Kumar. Huffman thought he had done all the necessary work human resources required. He asked for paperwork to be signed to finalize the hire. In return he heard just crickets. "I did the interview, we negotiated a salary. Sign the fucking paper," Huffman said. "Then months went by and we ended up losing him." Kumar took a job at Google. Huffman wishes he'd handled it differently; he wishes he'd gone straight to supervisors, brought the issue all the way up to the Newhouses, but admits he was obstinate. He had chosen to believe that if he played by the rules as he knew them, things would work out. They did not. Huffman seethed.

Slowe, meanwhile, discovered that his buddies on either coast weren't communicating well. He'd occasionally work on a project for Ohanian and later realize Huffman didn't even know it was under way. He'd ask Huffman to do a code review on a project, and Huffman's response would be, "He asked you to do *what*?" Slowe explained, "Alexis felt Steve wasn't helping him with stuff, and I think Steve just didn't know what he was supposed to be doing."

(• •)

On March 15, 2008, Anke Ohanian died after nearly three years battling cancer. The family held a small funeral the following Tuesday in Ellicott City, Maryland.

After his mother's death, things shifted for Ohanian. His desire to stay in New York, where she'd brought him home from the hospital, where he was close enough to visit her any weekend he desired, waned; coincidentally, his girlfriend, Liz Nagle, had moved to California to get a master's in English at Stanford. Ohanian packed up out of the Condé Nast annex office, and moved in with Huffman to an apartment on 16th Street in the Mission District, which Ohanian lobbied should be their new home, as it had a more hip, more Brooklyn vibe than the North Beach neighborhood of Crystal Towers.

It started out well. Huffman loved hanging out with Nagle; they always liked each other. But for Ohanian and Huffman, being around each other twenty-four hours a day wasn't healthy. They got along personally, for the most part, but their passions at work weren't in sync, and when they disagreed over whether to use their meager staff resources to bolster the site's technological back end (Huffman) or build new, splashy media components (Ohanian), Huffman's core team in San Francisco would side with him. The resourceful and charismatic Ohanian didn't accept losing well. When Huffman and Ohanian would start sniping at each other in the office, there was never an opportunity for them to cool down, because at the end of the day they'd have to get into Huffman's Porsche together, to drive home together.

"We'd have some blow-up fights at the office," Huffman said. "I remember being pissed leaving work, I would drive us home and I remember not speaking to him in the car. That's when things were starting to deteriorate."

Reddit TV was one of the issues—on the surface at least. Huffman wasn't entirely on board with the idea. Feeling like he needed to take control, Ohanian enlisted the help of both employees and contractors to build it out—behind Huffman's back. Huffman felt undermined that he had been kept out of the loop, and also betrayed. He'd been actively working on his management skills, including delegation, and told Ohanian, "Look, I can't manage this team if I don't know what people are doing. If you want to do this thing, just tell me, we'll do it." He remembers Ohanian sniping back that if he did that, it would never get done: "I remember getting so pissed the hair stood up on my arm. I just left the room. I was very, very angry."

Huffman didn't deal well with his own anger. He returned thirty minutes later, put on his headphones, and kept his mouth closed. The pair did not speak for the rest of the day. By then Huffman knew this was untenable. This—working with Ohanian, working inside a little piece of a massive corporation—wasn't where he wanted to be.

TOOLS, YO

On August 20, 2009, a post rose to the front page of Reddit featuring a link to a Craftsman band saw from Sears's website. Near the top of the page was a breadcrumb trail of subcategories under which the product was listed. Only instead of the saw's category reading "Bench and stationary power tools," and subcategory reading "band saws," when users clicked the link, the category hierarchies were "Fucking Big Ass Saws" and "Fuck Yeah!" listed under the broader category of "Tools, yo." Other users quickly jumped on what appeared to be a structural issue in the Sears site's database, which allowed users to modify how these category names displayed just by tinkering with the URL.

How could Redditors resist? They could not and began experimenting with Sears's site. More than a dozen screenshots of and ideas for these ridiculous links crept up in popularity on Reddit. A slew of zany and profane categories began to be cached on Sears's servers, meaning they would stick around for about thirty minutes, displaying themselves for unsuspecting users. On Reddit, one post mimicked a conversation with Kmart customer service about the efficacy of "baby launchers," a subset of "infant swings." The Sears corporation was, unsurprisingly, livid.

This sort of thing had happened before: Something on Reddit would offend an individual or corporation, sometimes ones that did business with Advance Publications. Their complaints typically resulted in corporate calling Ohanian, a smooth talker who by 2009 was accustomed to dealing with this sort of thing. He'd get on the phone with the aggrieved party and explain a concept that had been dubbed "the Streisand effect." He'd refer the person on the line to the Wikipedia page explaining that doing what the company was typically requesting—removing the offending item— would most likely result in the unintended consequence of publicizing the information more widely due to backlash. In 2003, Barbra Streisand attempted to have photos of her Malibu beach house removed from the Internet, which led to the images being widely disseminated everywhere. Usually Ohanian could help the individual or company with a strategy to go forward without censoring the offending link—perhaps suggesting that they thank the Reddit community for pointing out the bug.

But on this day, Ohanian's phone was off. He was at a Y Combinator Demo Day, listening to pitches from the new summer 2009 class. Without him to defuse the situation, Sears's fuming only intensified.

The complaint got escalated to Sarah Chubb, the longtime president of Condé Nast Digital. She called Huffman, and they went back and forth on it over multiple phone calls. Huffman was livid at being micromanaged; to him this was censorship. He raised his voice, and his colleagues took off their headphones to listen. Relenting to Chubb, Huffman deleted the post, but warned her it was the wrong decision: "This is gonna blow up!" he said. "It will blow up."

Indignant and enraged, Huffman messaged the user who'd created the post, explaining how he was being forced to remove it. He recalls egging on the poster: "You should blow this up."

The user obliged, querying on r/AskReddit, "Where did my post about Sears.com's URL-hackable categories go? Am I actually being censored!?" Huffman, as u/spez, commented on the post. "As a matter of fact, yes. I was ordered to take it down. Pretty awesome of them." Redditors took that bait and went into full Internet troll mode to wreak havoc against both Sears and Condé Nast, on the site and off. More than a dozen submissions dedicated to the campaign, now known in Reddit lore as "Fuck Sears," were upvoted to the front page of Reddit. The Streisand effect was alive and well.

Offline, *Wired* magazine took the brunt of the bile. After finding phone numbers for *Wired* online, one Redditor set up an autodialer. When the staffer would answer, they'd hear a recorded message in a robot-tinged, singsongy voice that Mike Schiraldi recalls said, "In our world never censor the press." Phones were quickly taken off the network, but voicemail boxes jammed up with thousands of the eerie messages.

The original post's commenters begged for more details about the removal. Huffman responded by nodding to the fact that his three-year earn-out—the time he was required to stay at the company to satisfy terms of the Reddit acquisition—expired shortly. "Ask me again in a couple of months." It was a sure sign: This event had tipped the balance in his decision making about his future. Huffman knew for certain: He'd leave Reddit.

(• •)

Huffman was sick of the bureaucracy, sick of his hand being forced. He was sick of the stress and was frustrated he'd become so out of shape—he'd lost twenty pounds over the past couple years and couldn't even play a game of pickup basketball without becoming winded. He plotted his life after Reddit. He'd have a bachelor party in Vegas, marry Katie that fall, and they'd go to an island—any damn tropical island, a honeymoon in Bermuda would be nice—and then get out of San Francisco. He'd move to Virginia with her. He'd bring his Porsche, of course, and get away from this all.

The first step toward freedom would be his wedding. For it, the entire Reddit crew would fly to Virginia and drive out to the countryside, to a sprawling three-hundred-acre hillside resort called Airlie. It was a place the Huffmans knew well: Steve and his sister, Amanda, had been driven past it hundreds of times on their way to the Wakefield School.

The night before the wedding, everyone gathered at Airlie: the Huffmans' four half brothers, Graham, Katie's med school friends, and lots of San Francisco startup friends. Ohanian had a custom Reddit shirt made for the groomsmen to wear at the rehearsal dinner that evening: a tuxedo-printed white T-shirt with a Reddit Snoo logo. Afterward, they ran around the pastoral grounds aiming air guns at one another.

The evening of the wedding, the skies opened up. The entire event had to be moved indoors at the last minute. Ohanian delivered a warm, loving—but not especially intimate—toast. It was short. Funny—but only superficially. Ohanian listed the attributes of Katie Babiarz, now Katie Huffman: ridiculously smart, extremely affable, beautiful. He credited her for their success, for encouraging them to attend Graham's talk in Cambridge. He apologized in jest to Katie for all the times she likely had to explain to her colleagues at medical school that her fiancé "works for a website." He listed Huffman's attributes: "Steve is male. Which is exactly what Katie was looking for." He explained that Huffman subsisted on Cheez-Its and pizza.

Ohanian said that he, as an only child, was losing a brother. That part was already coming true: Their friendship had been tainted and wouldn't soon be repaired.

The new Mr. and Mrs. Huffman danced a graceful ballroom first dance; Katie had been required over the years to learn some of Steve's moves. Then the Huffman siblings performed a showcase dance that brought everyone in attendance to their feet.

On Reddit, a post titled "Congratulations Steve and Katie!" lived on the homepage. (The team had tinkered with the upvotes, adding thousands, to effectively pin it to the top.) But not all was festive. As the celebrations continued through the night, a pair of bugs was beginning to wreak havoc on hundreds of comment threads on Reddit. Originally it was contained to the particular page on which a comment was posted, but then it jumped from users' comments to their user pages and then multiplied into infinity, creating a torrent of comments orders of magnitude greater than what Reddit could support.

The servers were overwhelmed, and the site went completely dark the following morning. Everyone decamped to Five Guys in the airport. All the YC friends, who were split between two flights home to San Francisco, shared one Internet connection, thanks to a MiFi-style device carried by Emmett Shear. The group of hackers worked through their hangovers to diagnose precisely what had happened, and how to patch it to get the site running, but two facts became obvious. One: There was no easy fix. Two: They probably shouldn't have erected what amounted to a big, blinking marquee reading "Gone Fishing" atop the homepage.

As their flight boarding announcements cycled down to the boarding doors closing, it became clear they needed help, so the crew did something unorthodox: They asked for it. While most of the code that made Reddit function was open to the public, certain aspects were kept quiet—aspects that helped prevent gaming the site's algorithms, spamming, and precisely this type of hack attack. Still, they went into a moderator IRC (Internet Relay Chat) channel, and invited users began posting details they'd noticed about the worm's function and advice on remedies. An avid user named Max Goodman, who went by u/chromakode, volunteered to help. He wrote a patch and sent his code to Jeremy Edberg.

Edberg had a slow connection on the flight, too slow to communicate with other staffers. He received the patch from Goodman and reviewed it. He wondered what else could happen on the site with everyone who worked on Reddit physically up in the air all at once. He shrugged and deployed Goodman's fix.

Once the guys landed in Oakland and piled into a taxi with Shear and his personal Internet hotspot, they saw that the patch—for the most part—had worked. They had a lot of cleanup to do. Four of them huddled on laptops as the cab bumped over the Bay Bridge, their faces illuminated by the screens as the streetlights and glowing office towers of San Francisco grew closer.

(• •)

As Halloween 2009 approached in San Francisco, the holiday, this anniversary of the acquisition, felt bittersweet. Ohanian recalled how his life had changed on that Halloween three years earlier. This one would be his last hurrah.

Like Huffman, he'd made up his mind to leave after his three-year contract expired with Condé Nast. It was time; on some level he trusted Huffman's intuition and decided to follow suit. It had been far too long since he'd worked on anything that wasn't Reddit—like those nonprofits he'd started back at UVA. Could he again do some good for the world outside of the corporate sphere?

It had become clear during weeknight evenings, when he was alone with his laptop, that he was already moving on. In his spare time, he'd begun working on a new website. He took one of the old URLs he and Huffman had stashed away because they were too funny to let expire, Breadpig.com, and began building what would become a nonprofit to support independent creative projects.

He'd go out with a bang, at least. They'd throw a huge Halloween party for loyal Redditors that night at a sports bar in Potrero Hill called the Connecticut Yankee.

Before the party, they'd accomplish a bit of hardware handiwork they'd begun that past spring. Back in mid-May, the company had transitioned all its operations and the site's storage to Amazon Web Services. It had been a bit bumpy at first—the team pulled an all-nighter to figure out how to fix the site's performance when its servers weren't sitting inches from one another, until Huffman coded a fix. They'd kept the old servers around in case of trouble, but five months had passed without significant incident. So for Halloween, finally, they'd physically decommission them.

The five guys loaded into Schiraldi's gray Toyota Yaris and went the few blocks over from 3rd Street to Spear and Harrison, to the ColoServe facility where Reddit's servers were racked. It wasn't a particularly ceremonious goodbye, but the men laughed together about the times they'd previously set up the servers inside their little conference room inside *Wired*, then hauled them down the building's rickety freight elevator, which sounded like a jet engine when on the move, and loaded them into the trunk of the Yaris. "When we had five people and a trunk full of servers in the car," Schiraldi said, "I'd push the pedal down and we'd be moving at like nineteen miles an hour and there'd be sparks flying from underneath the car." Ohanian shared in the laugh, but truth was, he wasn't present for most of these memorable days. He'd been alone, traveling, or working out of the Manhattan Condé Nast office. No matter, he thought, this was a new chapter. His sentimental self felt he'd been forever changed by this experience building Reddit; his logical side knew the money he'd made would help him in his next endeavor.

To the others—to Schiraldi, Edberg, King, and Slowe—the future was similarly hazy. They'd each agreed to stay put. They figured that, together, they could keep the site running. They also figured Martin in New York could be an envoy to Condé Nast and Advance Publications. No one, Martin included, was sure he could fill Ohanian's shoes in terms of being the media-ready, polished face of Reddit. Slowe would be senior engineer, and the team's default leader. He'd built the basis of the site's algorithms, and knew them thoroughly, but he did not consider himself a superb programmer like Huffman. He wasn't sure he could have puzzled through an epic challenge, like the web server migration, alone. Plus, setting goals—and convincing the slate of corporate managers at quarterly meetings that Reddit was keeping up—would be new. Without a leader, could Reddit really function?

Each of the three men was also keenly aware that the moral authority of a founder was a formidable force—in negotiating with media, with sales, and with their bosses at corporate. They'd now be without this force. There was also the less tangible: Huffman had made Reddit, and infused its very tone with his own wry humor, skepticism, and wonder. Spez *was* Reddit. Without its very soul, could Reddit really function?

PART III

PART III

TAKE ME HOME

As a teen and young adult in the Bay Area, Dan McComas had been big into the punk music scene, and had helped open a club in Berkeley for young people to hang out and find community, called 924 Gilman Street. As an adult, he led engineering teams at a series of startups, including a news reporting nonprofit called The Bay Citizen. He loved Reddit, as was increasingly common among programmers like himself. But he gravitated toward something other than the coding advice: He loved the site's potential for community-building. In 2009 he'd encountered a thread that had morphed from a silly idea to a full-fledged crowdfunding effort—and a contest. It read, "Anyone else remember that JetBlue $600 for a month deal? What if we sponsor some unemployed redditor to travel around and do stuff for us, like courier packages, or do requests for us as compensation?" It was actually happening: One of the first campaigns on the crowdfunding website Kickstarter was already under way to accept donations to buy at least one "All You Can Jet Deal" ticket.

McComas felt a tiny pang of remorse for being too old, and, well, too employed to volunteer himself. He'd long grown out of his punk past and was settling into middle age. He'd married, had a couple little kids, and let some extra pounds accumulate on his already large frame. But he thought it was awesome that this "really big community was able to bring a subset of their users together and effect something in the real world." The least he could do was help.

He and his wife, Jessica Moreno, donated a few hundred dollars, enough to bump the adventure up from one to two travelers, and assisted in organizing a meetup in San Francisco near Reddit's office for the first day of the pair's journey. Two Redditors, u/Draynen and u/77or88, were flying sixteen stops around the United States, from San Francisco to New York City, from Portland to Long Beach. When they landed in San Francisco, they had some beers at the meetup and met some of the real Reddit team, including Ohanian and Huffman. McComas then kept up the generosity and took them out for Mexican food. This was a neat thing, he thought. He wondered what else he could come up with and set in motion online.

(• •)

On November 10, 2009, McComas posted on Reddit, "Would anybody be interested in a Reddit gift exchange (secret santa)." Upvotes poured in. McComas created a subreddit, r/secretsanta, and over Thanksgiving break built out a rudimentary sign-up system, which randomly matched any interested Redditor with another, whom they'd send a small gift. The gift-giver would then receive a gift of their own, via snail mail, from a third Redditor. Participants could plumb the person's Reddit account, and any other social media accounts the individual wanted to share, to casually stalk their online identities for clues as to what would make a good gift. It would operate strictly on an honor system, with two core rules: Spend at least $15 and don't be a dick. McComas hoped it would be a giant daisy chain of goodwill and creativity.

McComas was sitting on his parents' couch, along with Moreno, when the sign-up on RedditGifts.com launched. Within minutes, hundreds of emails asking basic questions about the sign-up process started flooding his personal account. When he checked the site, he saw that more than two thousand people had already signed up. Some started calling his personal cell phone. He wondered what he had unleashed. His parents were not amused by the 5 a.m. calls—but Moreno was getting a kick out of it. She took over responding to users—and on that day she went from full-time mom, which had been her job for much of the past decade, to co-founder of what came to be known as Reddit Gifts.

That first year, 2009, forty-three hundred people in sixty-two countries signed up. Gifts mailed from stranger to stranger that year included handmade paintings, a guitar, and $1,500 sent to a cash-strapped college student. There was a stuffed shark, with a note that "this gift will require surgery." The recipient clearly enjoyed it; he posted a series of photos of himself preparing the shark for "surgery," complete with gloves, a scalpel, and fake blood. The images document the careful extraction of the rest of the gift from the fluffy shark's belly.

TechCrunch wrote an article about the gift exchange, and McComas even spent some of his Christmas Eve doing television interviews. By the following year, 2010, Reddit Gifts had 17,079 participants from 102 countries—and 95 percent of the individuals who signed up sent a gift. Nearly half a million dollars had been spent sending presents from Internet stranger to Internet stranger. McComas got more ambitious. He added a new gift exchange for midsummer that Reddit dubbed "Arbitrary Day." A book exchange followed.

As his own family's holidays became entirely consumed with managing the Secret Santa, McComas, who was still working a full-time job, knew his little project had become too big for him and Moreno to handle. He sent a note to Erik Martin, who in the wake of Huffman and Ohanian's departure was in charge of business development, saying he and Moreno were going to have to shut down RedditGifts.com. Martin didn't want to see that happen, and before long McComas and Moreno were in the *Wired* office, sitting around a table with an Advance Publications VP of strategy and corporate development named Andrew Siegel, along with Erik Martin and Jeremy Edberg.

McComas later recalled that meeting, at which gradually more Reddit engineers poked their heads in and sat down, as being incredibly awkward. It was like a job interview of the worst kind—a barrage of questions he and Moreno answered ably, but not apparently to the liking of anyone in the room. McComas saw cold eyes and blank stares. Martin was a friendly addition; they'd met before. But no one else seemed very warm to the idea.

Still, within four months, Reddit, via Advance Publications, would acquire Reddit Gifts for a meager sum that was nonetheless enough to be life-changing for McComas and Moreno's family. One of the terms of the acquisition, changed in contract during the arduous, months-long conversations McComas and Moreno endured with the Advance Publications legal team, was that they would be required to work independently. They were not to physically join the Reddit team; they were expressly forbidden to work out of the *Wired* office.

(••)

As the plane carrying Steve and Katie Huffman broke through the clouds and descended into the Washington, D.C., area, Steve could see that the earth was coated with white. He hadn't considered the possibility of snow. But once the newlyweds had loaded their bags from their quick weekend trip into his Porsche, Huffman was elated. He hit the gas and peeled out of the parking garage. Other drivers were barely plodding along, and Interstate 66 was nearly empty, save for a silky coat of snow.

Huffman had shipped his car—not the black convertible, but rather a newer, red 1996 Porsche 911 with a lowered suspension that he had traded for on a whim—to Virginia. He worried he'd gotten swindled on the newer car, but shrugged it off, because it was "fucking cool." Also he figured the hard top was appropriate for the East Coast weather, and the suspension would be incredible for navigating empty country roads at high speeds.

He was right. And it was exhilarating, that snowstorm, and driving the lowered car through blowing snow and over ice. "I remember thinking, 'You people are all giant pansies, you can't drive in the snow,'" he said. "We had these eight-lane roads to ourselves so we were just flying around."

The couple, now married, had finally moved in together in Virginia, where Katie was in medical school. They'd been together since college, but had been living apart since graduation, seeing each other during Katie's summer breaks. She'd flown out and hung around San Francisco, and on weekends they piled backpacks into his black Porsche 911 convertible with the license plate SPEZ and road-tripped down Highway 1. Those had been good days—to Huffman, the best days. For 2010, he wanted all good days.

During the long days in Virginia, Huffman took flying lessons, obtaining his pilot's license. He worked out obsessively, using the commercial at-home regimen known as P90X (its tagline: "Extreme Home Fitness"). He made friends with his new wife's medical school colleagues. He drove too fast down empty country roads and he played countless hours of *Call of Duty*.

In part, he was deeply content: He and Katie were enjoying life as newlyweds, and were completely in love. But Huffman later admitted, "I was also kind of depressed. I remember being really sad at times because I missed my friends and I felt like I lacked purpose in my life." The twenty-six-year-old was quieter online, and he neglected his old friendships out west, even though he was lonely. He and Ohanian, in particular, weren't speaking.

(• •)

Alexis Ohanian's father, Chris, had heard all his family's stories of the Armenian genocide. His dad was the child of two survivors of the genocide who'd fled to the States and had raised him in upstate

New York. His mother's Armenian parents had also fled, settling in France. Chris Ohanian rarely repeated these stories to his wife and son—Armenia was part of their family history, but it wasn't a part he wanted to relive often.

Although Alexis may not have grown up steeped in the darker aspects of his family's past, he remembers always being interested in his ancestry. As the son of one recent immigrant, Anke, who was from Germany, he'd learned the German language in high school, and adored his German grandmother. He'd traveled to visit her several times, sometimes making the transatlantic flight alone as a teen. He was more in touch with the German part of his roots, but he also remembered moments from his childhood when Armenian relatives would pull him aside and whisper bits of the family history. They told him he was special, because his birthday, April 24, was on the day of remembrance of the country's atrocities. They told him the last survivors of the genocide were dying, and the wisdom they could yield was being lost. He should go, and learn.

As he left Reddit and 2009 turned into 2010, Ohanian decided to learn more about his father's side of the family. As it happened, an opportunity arrived close to home. Liz Nagle, his girlfriend, worked at Kiva, a not-for-profit that makes small loans to help entrepreneurs in developing countries. Through Nagle, Ohanian met with one of Kiva's founders and urged him to begin operations in Armenia. In 2010, the average annual income of an Armenian was less than $10,000 in U.S. dollars, and only 51 percent of the able-bodied population was employed.

Ohanian and Nagle signed up to spend three months in Armenia helping local banks connect with rural entrepreneurs. They rented an apartment in the capital, Yerevan, from an older woman with whom they could barely communicate, and adjusted to life in a developing country. Despite the lack of creature comforts, Ohanian felt good. "As soon as the plane landed," he said, "I felt grounded."

During daytimes, he and Nagle would travel with a local bank employee on field visits to prospective entrepreneurs. To Ohanian, this entrepreneurship looked wholly different from the Silicon Valley variety. These were sheep farmers spinning wool and weaving textiles for sale at a local market, or farmers who'd reclaimed vineyard land and were beginning to ferment grapes into spirits. To help these entrepreneurs, many mornings Nagle and Ohanian would take a bus and then hike, or hop in a dilapidated car, out to the snowy mountains of extinct volcanoes in the countryside, or to a dingy suburb. There, they'd visit a market stand or tromp through the fields, to see the sheep or sample the wine. Other days, their tasks were more sedentary: They were also charged with set-ting up an office, complete with computing system, in a small space Kiva rented in Yerevan.

During the roughly three months he was away, even as Ohanian explored his roots and dove into new experiences, Reddit weighed heavily on his mind. He spent many evenings on the site, both as a user and an admin (his privileges weren't revoked upon leaving). He spent time emailing with Slowe, offering advice, and promot-ing the fund-raising Reddit had begun in the wake of the massive earthquake in Haiti. He also spent some time emailing the New-houses, Condé Nast's power nexus. By this point, Ohanian counted Steve and S. I. Newhouse as friends. He was half a world away from it all now, but a thought had begun to creep in: He still wanted to be part of the future of Reddit. Maybe there was a way.

(• •)

Adam Goldstein was like a younger, shorter, less technical version of Steve Huffman. Both were blond, bespectacled programmers who'd ingratiated themselves with older mentors who could help them achieve their ambitions. For Goldstein, a fortuitous rela-tionship with the technology writer David Pogue led to the then sixteen-year-old meeting Huffman, who was just a few years his senior. Goldstein approached Silicon Valley from an analytical per-spective, and Huffman appreciated that he made for a stimulating conversation partner. The two became good friends over the years, thanks to online chats and in-person visits: Goldstein stayed with

Huffman many times during trips to San Francisco, and even worked out of the *Wired* office with him for a time, while creating a publishing startup with *Wired*'s editor, Chris Anderson.

By 2010, Goldstein was twenty-two and in his senior year at MIT, where he majored in EECS—electrical engineering and computer science—as well as mechanical engineering, with a minor in economics. On weekends, he participated in parliamentary-style debate tournaments, for which he arranged travel and accommodations— which meant long nights searching for hotels, ground transportation, and flights, both domestic and, when the championship was in Botswana, international. It was a massive time-suck. He knew he should be studying, sleeping, or hanging out with his girlfriend rather than obsessively checking airline websites, but he'd also get little pangs of pleasure when he'd discover a particularly underpriced flight or interesting route, or could exploit some loophole to collect rewards points or frequent flier miles. "There were some little hacks in there that were fun, but mostly it was agony," he said. With the agony came a revelation: He wanted to be spending his time on a project that made people's lives better, or at least easier. He wanted to—as had Ohanian and Huffman—make a dent in the universe. He thought: What if he made a better travel site? He wanted to make a search that was more useful than Kayak. And he knew he didn't want to do it alone.

He took a shot and called Huffman. After the initial phone call explaining his startup idea, Goldstein flew to Virginia to meet with Huffman. Huffman wasn't at all convinced that travel was an area they should try to tackle. But with the caveat that if travel search failed, he would get to choose their next startup idea, Huffman said yes, he'd help. Goldstein couldn't believe his luck. Huffman had become a minor legend for having created Reddit, and he could easily have raised funding from a venture capital firm for any idea he'd wanted. Instead, he partnered with a virtually unknown twenty-two-year-old, on an idea whose premise he'd deemed unsound.

Over the following weeks they made plans. They'd move together to wherever Katie Huffman's medical residency required that Huffman relocate after her graduation. They'd live together, and they'd code the site together. Nervously, Goldstein decided he'd need to approach Huffman again. Before they started work in earnest, they should divide responsibilities. He knew he wanted to handle business growth, and that Huffman was the superior hacker. He wanted to be CEO. It was his idea, after all. Gingerly, he approached the topic of roles. Huffman said, "Why? Do you want to be CEO?"

Goldstein hesitated. "Uh, yeah."

"It's yours," Huffman said. He'd been there, done that. He didn't need to do it again.

After a flight out to the Bay Area to meet with Paul Graham, they decided to join the next Y Combinator class that summer, out in California. Goldstein flew to San Francisco the day after he graduated MIT. Fortuitously, Katie Huffman got accepted to a medical residency there, so Steve Huffman came out, too. His Virginia respite was over.

Over the course of eighty-five days that summer, they created their travel startup, which they dubbed Hipmunk, like chipmunk without the C.

THE ONES THAT GOT AWAY

A pple Inc.'s App Store had debuted to much fanfare in July 2008. As the iPhone became ubiquitous, so did apps tailor-made for its iOS operating system. The notetaking app Evernote was an early hit. There was a MySpace app, an AIM app, and even old media was on board: The *New York Times* had an app. Reddit, perpetually strangled of resources, and with what Ohanian referred to later as a "mountain of other, more pressing development," did not.

Before Ohanian left Reddit, he had decided that it needed its own app. But who would build it? From the burgeoning network of Y Combinator alums, he contracted a web development firm called 280 North to create iReddit. The app launched on Valentine's Day 2009, and though he was off the payroll, Ohanian wrote a post for the company blog, explaining, "We decided $1.99 was a reasonable price for this app; it will reward 280 North for their great work and help us cover a few more servers." The app allowed users to view stories, vote, comment, and share links. It also contained a funny feature inspired by the UrbanSpoon app: One could shake their iPhone and be served up a new random thread. It was all pretty bare-bones, though: It lacked a search function and any ability to view one's own account activity.

Because Reddit's code was open-source, meaning it was available online for developers to scope out and build upon, there was opportunity for others to create their own view into Reddit and co-opt its potential in the emerging mobile world. Most notably, a blue-eyed Australian named Jase Morrissey had built a mobile Reddit viewer that was intuitive to use on a phone and beautiful in full-screen mode on the iPad. Morrissey was an avid Redditor, and he liked to browse it late in the evening, but the site's tiny fonts strained his computer-weary eyes. His app, called Alien Blue, featured larger fonts and what he called "late-night colors." It became a user favorite, and quickly surpassed iReddit as the most popular mobile way to view Reddit.

(• •)

Apps weren't the only opportunity that Reddit lacked bandwidth to exploit. Alan Schaaf, twenty-one, spent most of his 2009 winter break from Ohio University alone in his apartment, playing *World of Warcraft*. Break was almost over, and students were returning to campus, so Schaaf invited a couple friends over to his house at 20 South Shafer Street in Athens, Ohio. He brought up a crazy idea he'd been thinking of channeling his energy toward. "You guys know what sucks on the Internet? Broken images," he told his friends.

One of the many slow-loading and now-foreign-seeming aspects of the pre-2010 Internet was the fact that uploading and sharing photographs and screen grabs was a hit-or-miss endeavor. Certain image hosting services would yank images that took up significant bandwidth and replace them with marketing materials. Remember all those broken images and "upgrade to pro" links? They didn't make any sense to Schaaf. His friends, mostly fellow computer science majors, agreed.

Reddit, as a repository of links, suffered mightily from this unfortunate reality, and Schaaf himself was an avid Redditor whose username was u/MrGrim. He spent the next month working many evenings, sometimes overnight. He powered through with a supply of Mountain Dew and the occasional midnight pizza, keeping the lights low and trance music streaming.

On February 23, Schaaf posted to Reddit, "My Gift to Reddit: I created an image hosting service that doesn't suck. What do you think?" The line linked to his new website, with its hand-designed logo that read "Imgur," as in *image-er*. Boy, did Reddit's community of users like it. Four hours after its release, Schaaf realized that the space he'd allocated in a shared server—using his dad's $5-a-month HostGator account—wasn't going to cut it. He upgraded to a service offering one terabyte of bandwidth per month. Imgur blew through that in twenty-six days. Schaaf found a host in the UK offering three terabytes a month. After three months, he was being charged overage fees. Traffic continued to surge, tied largely to the continual growth of Reddit, which at the time was tripling in size annually.

Imgur was almost entirely dependent on Reddit for traffic, and grew steadily as Reddit did. Its content mirrored Reddit's, and fed into it—it was almost a way to view Reddit in visual form. In some ways, though, Imgur was everything Reddit was not. Unlike Reddit, Imgur functioned as one gigantic community, unfractured by subchannels or niche interests. This meant the site had a shallow learning curve. To join the fun on Imgur, one only had to upload a single photo. Schaaf explained later that his own mother, who barely understood the site, one day posted a photo of their family cats, who were named for *Dragon Ball Z* characters. It became one of the top posts that day. Users differentiated themselves on Imgur only by their unique pseudonymous usernames, such as cuntsparkle. ("He's like an Imgur celebrity," explained Schaaf.)

Improbably, out of that little house in Athens, Ohio, grew a site that would come to for years host nearly every image posted to Reddit. Any Redditor who'd ever seen or shared an image with a white text block-letter caption likely had Imgur to thank: Imgur was Reddit's meme engine. The only problem was: Reddit didn't own Imgur. Nor did it foster a great relationship with its colleague in Internet meme-spreading. Early on, Slowe invited Schaaf to join a private Reddit chat channel, in IRC, so that he could communicate with the Reddit team. Schaaf says he lurked often, and learned much of Reddit's inner workings. He had dinner with the team—but nothing came of it, aside from some casual Internet friendships with certain Reddit staffers. Mostly, Reddit kept Schaaf at an awkward arm's length

Without Reddit's support, Schaaf equipped Imgur pages with tiny advertising links, and made enough money that by his senior year he ditched his summer desk job working for an aerospace contractor. Within three years, Imgur was serving more than 1.5 million images a day, and its website received more than 400 million monthly visits. It was a virality factory well on its way to becoming a functional social network.

As the years passed, the relationship between Imgur and Reddit would become less sanguine. Rumors circulated that Yahoo might acquire Imgur for up to $500 million. By 2017, Imgur was the eleventh most popular website in the United States. As the sites grew in tandem, every shift in strategy or traffic surge on Reddit over the years hit Imgur like a post-quake tsunami. The tension between them was evident when Schaaf was asked what over the years Reddit had done that greatly affected Imgur. He said, "I'm drawing a blank." Imgur has never been officially affiliated with Reddit. It was an obvious acquisition target on whom Reddit or Condé Nast never officially trained an arrow. The sites were symbiotic for years, without having any trace of official affiliation. Schaaf wasn't necessarily bitter, though. "There's no official Reddit *anything*," he said with a shrug.

(• •)

At Reddit, it was a sometimes daily struggle to keep the site online. Denial-of-service attacks were frequent; sometimes simply too much traffic to a new subreddit would crash the site. It wasn't uncommon for *Wired* staffers to hear shouting coming from the drafty brick-colored conference room. If the site stayed down too long, the team would shrug and do shots of "downtime vodka."

It was just four of them in San Francisco now—Jeremy Edberg, the systems architect; Mike Schiraldi, the engineer; David King, the hacker; and, running the show by default, Chris Slowe. In New York there was Erik Martin, who'd crafted himself a role that's now known in Silicon Valley parlance as "community manager," and that at Reddit entailed responding to every problem an individual user reported having on the site, including but not limited to harassment, copyright infringement, and doxing (having their personal information published). In addition, Martin handled business development, sold ads, did publicity, and forged partnerships. Adding employees, beyond the occasional intern or contractor, was still out of the question. With capital investments seemingly beyond their reach, Reddit's tiny team looked for opportunities to keep them going wherever they could.

After a catastrophic earthquake devastated parts of Haiti in January 2010, killing more than one hundred thousand people and demolishing nearly three hundred thousand buildings, Redditors donated, through a Direct Relief link on the site, more than $188,000, a number that staggered the Reddit crew. They were inspired to see their own site move that kind of cash and do some good in the world.

The fact that Reddit could deliver this sort of impact and get so little additional resources from Condé struck some nerves, too— particularly Schiraldi's. He'd been pretty insulated from Slowe's dealings with Condé Nast corporate, but when a team of executives from New York made a trip to San Francisco and one of the higher-ups popped in to greet the Reddit team and take questions, things blew up.

Schiraldi seized the opportunity to ask a so-obvious-it-was-bold question that had been boiling for the past two years: "When do we get to hire some more people?"

The response was to the point: "You guys really need to step up your revenue if you want to be able to hire anybody." They were flabbergasted. And pissed. The loose network of superiors they dealt with at Condé Nast and Condé's digital arm had consistently advised them to focus on growth, on traffic. By any reasonable metric, the site was doubling in traffic every eight months—an astronomical success. They'd done back-of-the-napkin calculations, and suspected Reddit would soon have more traffic than all of the other Condé Nast media properties' websites *put together.*

Slowe, the perpetually coolheaded manager, lost it. The moment the executive left was one of the only times his colleagues could recall seeing Slowe, face and ears red, completely fly free from his relaxed demeanor. He'd been leading the team in the direction he'd been given—grow now, make money later—and what did that mean now? Had they been misled? Had he fucked it all up? Did they even have a chance to succeed if this was the way in which corporate was going to communicate with them?

Reddit had in the past made meager attempts at selling advertising. Slowe had designed, built, and promoted an entire "sponsored links" system, wherein users could boost sponsored content and target particular communities on Reddit for a payment. The team was at work bolstering a self-serve ad platform, which was popular among blog sites at the time. It made sense for Reddit, Slowe thought, to make sure there was no middleman between the site and its users. Heck, Condé Nast wasn't selling many ads for them, so they'd have to do it themselves. Out in New York, Martin took it upon himself to cold-call potential advertisers who'd previously gotten positive comments on Reddit about their companies or products.

But these efforts were fledgling, and the four developers had a long list of site maintenance issues that consumed them. Five staffers supported nearly three hundred million monthly page views. Who among them was supposed to be marketing ad products? It felt unsolvable.

An incident in mid-2010 further exacerbated the revenue issue.

Plenty of San Franciscans were energized around this time by an upcoming ballot initiative known as Proposition 19, or the "Regulate, Control and Tax Cannabis Act." It was to be on the statewide ballots that November and had the potential to legalize marijuana sales across California. The Reddit community, which veered socially liberal, libertarian, and contrarian, loved the concept.

One advocacy group, Yes on 19, decided to advertise on Reddit, and, using its self-serve advertising platform, signed up for $10,000 worth of promotion. The Reddit team was over the moon: finally, a significant ad buy that was a snug fit with the Reddit community.

Condé Nast, though, was not pleased. The company's lawyers decided Reddit could not run the Yes on 19 ads. (A subsequent statement explained, "As a corporation, Condé Nast does not want to benefit financially from this particular issue.") On Reddit, the ad-pull bubbled into a controversy, especially on the site's forum for cannabis enthusiasts, r/trees. Under a post titled "WTF REDDIT I thought you were cool...," users asked, "What is wrong in the head with Condé Nast?," and many wrote that they were installing ad-blocking software in protest.

Slowe posted in the internal IRC that everyone should gather. Erik Martin called in from New York. The team was irate: If Condé Nast wanted them to increase revenue, why were they turning down this money? Slowe said, "There's this thing that I want to do but I'm not going to do it unless every single person here signs off on it. If the company's line is they don't want to accept money, I think we should just let them have the ads for free." Everyone agreed. Martin said the consensus was it was a cool idea, and they all thought, "What's the worst they can do? They can't give us less money or fewer resources." Together, the team drafted a post, which made the following points:

1. This was a decision made at the highest levels of Condé Nast.
2. reddit itself strongly disagrees with it, and frankly thinks it's ridiculous that we're turning away advertising money.

3. We're trying to convince Corporate that they're making the wrong decision here, and we encourage the community to create a petition, so that your anger is organized in a way that will produce results.

"It was signed by every single member, not just the employees but the contractors and our interns. Everybody who we've considered a Reddit employee undersigns the post, because we needed to make sure they couldn't fire all of us," Schiraldi said. The post also announced that Reddit would indeed be running the ads Yes on 19 submitted. Only it would be running them for free.

The tone of the comments on r/trees shifted immediately. "It's over, so quickly too. Reddit rocks," the top commenter wrote, amending an originally enraged post. "The users thought this was the greatest thing we ever did," Schiraldi said. "Obviously they're going to worship us for making that decision."

(• •)

The cannabis ad situation cleverly flipped the usual dynamic between Redditors and any commercial initiative the company pursued. But money was on the minds of staffers still. They desperately wanted to hire a new developer, and the tone of conversations with their bosses had indicated that they would not be permitted to do so unless they were on solid track to bring in roughly $1 million in revenue the following year.

Whenever Reddit announced anything revenue-related in its blog, comments would boil with anticapitalist vitriol. Schiraldi described the response as "Reddit is so corporate. Reddit is selling out. You guys shouldn't be making decisions based on what's best for the bottom line. Reddit should be more like a public good." He would usually reply with something like, "That's great. Call your congressman, have him give me a call, and we'll let them know when to start sending the checks."

Some users, more rationally, suggested that the site should

accept donations. It happened so frequently that Schiraldi began to wonder, *Could that work?* What if Reddit acted like NPR and did a pledge drive? Or what if it created some sort of subscription service to unlock premium features?

Schiraldi approached Reddit's major ally at corporate, S. I. Newhouse, with the idea, couched in another plea for additional resources. Newhouse's response was vague; he indicated repeatedly that he was on their side about hiring—he wanted to get Reddit additional resources. But he also expressed the new reality: Reddit was expected this year to contribute at least a token sum to the corporate bottom line. He told Schiraldi, in essence, that he'd need time to get his head around that idea. Then: silence.

Days went by. Sick of waiting, Schiraldi decided to play another hand. He pitched Slowe on a plan to launch a donation campaign that would give Redditors extra features, which he'd tongue-in-cheek dubbed "Reddit Gold"—without approval from corporate.

For Slowe, it wasn't a difficult decision, but he knew it was a monumental one. If he did it, it would piss off corporate—and that could have major repercussions. "Here we are, this absurdly successful—in the scheme of things—site, that is owned by a major media company with deep pockets. And they are starving us of resources to the point where we have to beg our community for donations. How does that look?" Slowe said later. But he'd long felt that he lacked leverage against Condé Nast Digital. The company had turned down his request to hire Max Goodman, the talented programmer who'd saved all their butts when the comment bomb hit the site and nearly all of Reddit's staff was on an airplane. More recently, the revenue incident left him reeling and feeling helpless. The revenue demand had been clarified to the team: They needed to contribute roughly $1 million for the following year if they were to hire additional engineers.

If Gold worked, Slowe thought, at least it would move his team toward their revenue goal. The timing was right; Slowe at this moment wasn't afraid to taunt Condé Nast: "Go ahead, fire me." He'd over recent months spent several evenings over beers chatting with

Huffman about Hipmunk, and his interest had been piqued. Huff-man had infected him with the idea that it would be awesome to work at a fast-growing startup—one able to attract outside investment and spend big on engineering talent. Slowe hadn't told Schiraldi, but he already had a backup plan: He'd leave Reddit.

Once Schiraldi secured Slowe's approval, he built the entirety of Reddit Gold in eleven days. The team waited to launch it until the following Friday morning, when they knew that most of the executives at Advance Publications in New York City's Condé Nast Building would be leaving the office early. Schiraldi imagined them shutting down their computers, grabbing their weekender bags, and piling into black cars out to the Hamptons. Finally, the New York publishing world's "summer hours" perk had something to offer Silicon Valley.

On July 9, 2010, Schiraldi posted a plea on Reddit's blog, along with the launch of Reddit Gold. He wrote, "Reddit needs help . . . It seems like every week something comes up that slows performance to a crawl or even leads to a total site outage. And we almost never get a chance to release new features anymore." He explained that even with four engineers working full-time, plus the middle of the night and on weekends, just to keep things going, new features or site repairs were impossible.

"The bottom line is, we need more resources." The plea continued with a frank admission that Condé Nast allocated "resources proportionate to revenue. And Reddit's revenue isn't great." It promised donors, who could give any amount they chose, that they would someday receive additional Reddit features. Immediately, all they'd get would be a gold trophy to display on their user page. "It's kind of a lame offer, we know, but if the program is a success, we'll be able to give subscribers better incentives in the coming months," Schiraldi wrote. "In the meantime, I suppose it's more or less a pledge drive."

With the post unleashed, the four developers packed up and walked in an anxious pack down 3rd Street to an Indian restaurant. They would, for a moment at least, avoid the vitriol that was sure to rain down from New York. Schiraldi put his cell phone on the table, facedown.

With menus in front of them, they didn't feel guilty about the act of defiance—because they didn't see it as such. Instead, they saw it as an act of desperation akin to stealing bread to feed your hungry child. "If we don't do this, the site is definitely going to die, so there's no point in not pissing them off," Schiraldi said. "It's better to piss them off and have the site live."

Not an hour later, Schiraldi picked up his phone to check Reddit's PayPal account. He was floored. Seeing his face, Edberg, King, and Slowe checked their screens, too. On that first day, they pulled in enough donations to easily hire an additional programmer. Within six months, they'd have raised $250,000. It was enough that their defiance blew over quickly with corporate—and enough to give Reddit the resources that would help the developers stop treading water and start building again.

It was a victory in all minds but one: that of Steve Huffman. When he, from his workstation at Hipmunk, read the blog post, he thought it sounded hapless. "You sound really pathetic," he thought. "It's like, come on, guys, have some self-respect." When confronted later with the fact that Reddit Gold *worked*, Huffman didn't backpedal.

"I don't know," he replied. "It didn't *not* work."

GEEK WOODSTOCK

In late summer of 2010, a Redditor using the moniker mrsam-mercer posted a hazy, middle-of-the-night idea: Redditors should gather, in character, as avid Tea Partiers. Together, five hundred thousand strong, they would mock ultraconservative talk show host Glenn Beck's Restoring Honor rally, which had occurred the prior weekend in Washington. The rally had ostensibly been a fund-raiser for the nonprofit Special Operations Warrior Foundation, but it was also a parade for ultraconservative values, featuring Sarah Palin and Beck, who took to a stage to argue that all Americans, re-gardless of religion, should trust in God and embark on "turning our face back to the values and principles that made us great." To some liberal Redditors, it almost begged to be parodied. To do so, they'd recruit as their leader in this massive stunt the man who made a living portraying a caricature of conservative pundits: Stephen Colbert, the host of Comedy Central's *Colbert Report*.

The post had been written by twenty-eight-year-old Pittsburgh resident Joseph Laughlin at 5 a.m. Later that morning, it was quickly climbing Reddit's front page, with 7,000 upvotes. Then it spread elsewhere online. Individuals created Facebook pages for the "event." Fans of the idea sent emails to staffers at *The Colbert Report*. Others hacked together a quick website promoting the hypothetical rally.

On Reddit, users strategized in comment threads, plotting the best way to get Colbert's attention and spur him into action to organize this rally. Instead of pestering Colbert and his team with emails and letters, they decided to aim at his heartstrings, by targeting DonorsChoose, the crowdfunding platform for classrooms, of which Colbert was a board member. Money poured in from the Reddit effort so quickly that the organization's servers were crippled due to the traffic surge. Within weeks, more than $100,000 had been earmarked for educational charities in the name of Stephen Colbert, much of it via Redditors. The DonorsChoose campaign wound up with close to a quarter million dollars.

Colbert and *Daily Show* host Jon Stewart, who had been simultaneously pondering a rally of the like, kept mostly mum on the outpouring of support. Colbert noted he wanted doves sent from God to signal he should rally; Redditors released white pigeons outside his office and mailed stuffed waterfowl.

Laughlin was blown away. He commented on his original post that "the thought of Colbert himself actually maybe seeing this is probably the coolest thing that's ever happened to me so far in my life."

Turns out, Colbert had seen it. He announced that an event—which he dubbed the "March to Keep Fear Alive," and which would mirror a same-day rally by Stewart called the "Rally to Restore Sanity"—would be held in October in Washington, D.C. Before the rally, he sent Ohanian a note thanking Reddit for the contributions to DonorsChoose. "The track record of your hivemind speaks for itself," he wrote. He noted that "with the momentum you've created, we could stage a hundred rallies."

As October 30, the date of the rally, approached, Redditors, comedy fans, and fed-up citizens converged on Washington, D.C. The team at Reddit—and their enthused spouses, interns, friends, and even a Newhouse—boarded a flight. Reddit lacked the budget to do much itself, but thanks to the site's massive donations, the team of employees had been invited to join the DonorsChoose tent. They'd also booked a few bars for afterparties, in hopes that many loyal Redditors would show up.

(• •)

Alex Angel slammed the door of her parents' silver Lexus, which they'd pulled over a few blocks away from the National Mall; it was impossible to drive any farther. The Wesleyan astrophysics major panned her head toward the crowd and brushed a strand of hair out of her eye. What the hell was she walking into? There were humans absolutely everywhere, carrying signs, wearing absurd costumes, milling about, shouting, sitting, running. Having grown up outside of Washington, D.C., she'd been to plenty of activist events at the National Mall, but this was next level.

She made her way into the crowds and passed mock protesters wielding signs such as "Give me apathy or give me whatever," "Poster board is a terrible medium for expressing complex arguments," "That's what she said," and "CAPSLOCK IS NOT PERSUASIVE." There were thousands upon thousands, and many seemed to share the native sensibilities of the Reddit community, a sort of wry sarcasm that Angel had come not only to adore but also to intuit. She grinned when she spotted a couple of signs and T-shirts featuring the little Reddit alien.

As Angel ambled on, her goal was to find her new colleagues at Reddit. For the past year she'd been obsessed with the programming subreddit, and loved reading posts on astronomy and astrophysics. (She'd recently changed her college major to astrophysics, and had formerly worked building lasers for the U.S. Army in its Night Vision and Electronic Sensors Directorate.) Not long before, she had seen a Reddit post looking for an unpaid intern, and, logged on as u/cupcake1713, had sent Erik Martin an email. Never mind that it was likely extraordinarily below her pay grade and entirely irrelevant to her prior experience. Martin wrote her back, taking her up on her offer to work unpaid while she finished school. Since then, she had been taking a train to New York City roughly once a week to work alongside Martin, sometimes out of the younger S. I. Newhouse's cubicle in the Condé Nast office. When she wasn't studying, she worked on Reddit from her dorm, analyzing advertising traffic, putting together case studies, and building PowerPoint presentations about the efficacy of advertising on Reddit. From early on, Angel was a pro at understanding the community. Once, when users were joking about Reddit Gold and said, "Why isn't there Reddit Silver?" she opened up MS Paint on her computer, scrawled the word "silver" over an envelope icon, and sent it to a user to display on his profile page trophy case.

This weekend in D.C., at the Rally to Restore Sanity and/or Fear, Angel was still brand-new at Reddit. Aside from Martin, she only knew her colleagues by their screen names. Her task was to meet people, and to interview Redditors for potential blog posts. At this moment, elbowing through the rowdy hordes, she knew it would be a challenge to even find them.

The core Reddit crew had all woken up far earlier than was comfortable to meet at the very un-Reddit hour of 7 a.m. in the lobby of their hotel, the Savoy Suites in Georgetown. The ramshackle band toted seven tiny folding stools and huge boxes of T-shirts onto a shuttle bus.

When they arrived on the National Mall, it was already bustling. By midday, the center of the mall was becoming so packed that movement became difficult. Comedy Central's permit for the event estimated sixty thousand attendees; more than two hundred thousand showed up. Getting to the Reddit–DonorsChoose tent was nearly impossible.

None of the Reddit crew saw Colbert or Stewart or any of the other boldfaced names perform. They'd been confined to the little tent, which was positioned far from the stage and facing away from it. By the time of the performances, the crowds were leaning in on all sides, threatening to topple the little shelter. It didn't matter; it was the high of a lifetime. They had helped make this. Actually seeing Reddit T-shirts and signs around and knowing that their site had helped draw thousands of real people into the sunshine of the National Mall was affirming in a way no comment thread could be. The rally was ridiculous, hilarious, and whip-smart in its criticism of politics and mainstream media. It was, as Ohanian would later declare, "Geek Woodstock."

Stewart took the stage unironically arguing for reasonableness in public discourse and lacerating "the country's twenty-four-hour politico pundit perpetual panic conflictinator," a.k.a. cable news. Colbert satirized right-wing fearmongering, and musicians Yusuf (formerly known as Cat Stevens) and Ozzy Osbourne performed a mash-up of "Peace Train" and "Crazy Train," until out came the O'Jays, playing "Love Train." After the show ended late in the day, the Reddit team, dehydrated and claustrophobic, began the long hike out. Now the fun—Reddit's slate of six after-rally parties—would begin.

When the crew ambled into the one they assumed would be the largest, at One Lounge near Dupont Circle, it was already over capacity. Slowe remembered having to walk up past a massive line snaking out from the door. He approached the bouncer, saying, "Hey, this is my party." With their Reddit T-shirts, with aliens and mail icons in the bright Reddit orange-red color, avid Redditors had stood out to one another in the National Mall. But here there were alien icons everywhere. Slowe later recalled, "Whenever we would say we're from Reddit it was like freaking rock stars walking around the place."

The venue was cavernous: a series of dimly lit rooms connected by narrow hallways. In each room, a group of Redditors perched on banquettes and around tables, exchanging contact information, scanning each other's QR codes for a Reddit-powered game, and completing scavenger hunts designed to foster in-person conversations among usually pseudonymous Redditors.

At 1:30 a.m., Angel finally pulled herself away from a conversation and ducked out of the bar, her head buzzing. To her surprise, the streets were still dense with people—was it really as late as she thought? She checked her watch. She'd heard from many people inside that the Metro was jam-packed, impossible to ride on this day. Later she heard it was the biggest one-day ridership the Washington, D.C., Metro had ever experienced. She breathed in the cooling air and set out for a long walk through Georgetown, across the Francis Scott Key Bridge toward Rosslyn, Virginia.

Angel didn't consider herself a "people person," but she admitted to herself that she'd had some good conversations that night. All these people she had known by their screen names—those her family considered her strange "Internet friends"—had been transformed into real humans. She'd met not just the Reddit crew, including cofounder Steve Huffman, but also two fascinating engineers she'd soon work with, David King and Neil Williams. She liked them. "It really opened my eyes, like, 'Oh my God, there are all these people who are my age, older, younger, who have totally different backgrounds, and here we all are united over this one thing, and we are physically present and having real-life conversations.'" Once in Virginia, Angel hailed a taxi and rode back to her parents' home, still in awe of the crowds and the mass enthusiasm that Reddit had helped create.

EXODUS AND ILL WILL

One day not long after the Colbert rally, an email arrived in the Reddit in-box from their biggest competitor, Digg. A group of Digg engineers wanted to invite the Reddit crew to lunch. Slowe and the others puzzled over it: curious, indeed. Was this an olive branch?

It had been a particularly tense past few months in Digg-Reddit relations. On May 28, Digg's Silicon Valley celebrity founder, Kevin Rose, posted a video to YouTube announcing Digg version 4, as a "publisher preview." The company, which had accepted three rounds of venture capital funding to the tune of $40 million, was taking an overt step to become more friendly to large publishing companies. Users were highly skeptical and bemoaned not only the new look of the site, but also its prioritization of sponsored content.

Ohanian posted on his personal blog "an open letter to Kevin Rose." In it, he wrote that "this new version of digg reeks of VC meddling. It's cobbling together features from more popular sites and departing from the core of digg, which was to 'give the power back to the people,'" quoting Rose himself from 2004. "Now what matters is how many followers & influence a user has and how many followers & influence they've got. Where have we heard this before: Twitter? Facebook? GoogleBuzz?" Ohanian credited Rose for helping start a movement online of community-shared content, but then unleashed this kicker: "It's a damned shame to see digg just re-implementing features from other websites."

"Guy Who Copied Digg Slams Digg for Copying Twitter," blared the resulting TechCrunch headline. In response to the article, Paul Graham posted the article link to Hacker News and retold the story of Reddit's founding, specifically noting that Huffman and Ohanian hadn't known of Digg's existence until weeks into building their own site. Ohanian then posted a follow-up on his blog with details to support Graham's account, noting that he'd sent Huffman an email on July 11, 2005, at 11:48 p.m., alerting him that a competitor site named Digg had launched. (Digg actually had launched in October 2004, perhaps unbeknownst to both Reddit and Graham; Huffman had put Reddit live in late June 2005.)

Despite these squabbles, Slowe, Schiraldi, King, and Edberg couldn't say no to the Digg invitation. They figured, at worst, there was wisdom in keeping their enemies close. Upon entering the office in an industrial building in San Francisco's Potrero Hill, Schiraldi remembers being wowed by Digg's two whole floors of space—one of which seemed to consist of a lot of break rooms, vintage arcade games, and foosball tables. The other floor was offices and cubicles for Digg's sixty-plus employees.

They sat down in a conference room, where the seven Digg staffers whom they were meeting—more folks than all of Reddit—already had their cafeteria-style lunches on plates. It was slightly disturbing to the Reddit guys that separate pizzas had been ordered to feed them. Schiraldi later recalled rolling over a joke in his mind: "They wouldn't intentionally poison us—there's no way."

The entire crew of seven Digg-ers and four Redditors posed for a photo after their meeting. Inexplicably, one of the Digg staffers wore a Reddit T-shirt. Edberg had made sure to document the full, bizarre meeting, writing a blog entry afterward that he titled "Into the Lion's Den."

The hilarious post was catnip for serious Reddit fans, especially the newest ones, who had begun to make an exodus from Digg for Reddit. Edberg noted that the Reddit team hadn't felt the need to be cagey about their struggles. "Since we're open-source, we were able to freely discuss our technology and the issues we run into," he wrote. The two teams discussed their database management system, Cassandra, and exchanged business cards so they could stay in touch.

Something else happened in that meeting that they did not publicly note: Everyone called a secret truce and agreed to share their internal traffic numbers. Reddit knew it was climbing like mad— Slowe was particularly proud recently of being able to scale up, about 50 percent, to deal with the additional traffic due to a user exodus after Digg's version 4 was introduced. Reddit knew its internal metrics, and the analysis it paid for from Google Analytics, showed wildly higher numbers than did public sources such as Compete, Comcast, or Nielsen. What they didn't know was that by certain metrics, Reddit was already bigger than Digg.

"They told us their traffic numbers first because they were super proud," Edberg said. "And we went, 'Oh wow! That's really great. Here's ours.'"

The Reddit crew left the meeting with heads appropriately inflated. They were keenly aware that they were four young men running a site that had served more than four hundred million page views to more than eight million individuals a month—at a company without a CEO. They were once again flabbergasted by their situation, which seemed both unprecedented and increasingly untenable.

By the end of 2010, Digg had already reached its peak of popularity. Users had begun to flee. Shortly after the launch of Digg v4, users staged a revolt they dubbed "Quit Digg Day," in which they voted up on Digg all links submitted through Reddit. A quarter million Digg visitors went to Reddit that day.

As the group rode back up the elevator to the *Wired* office,

Slowe took a deep stream of air in through his nose. "Funny thing," he said. "I'm leaving Reddit."

(• •)

Inside Reddit, Slowe's departure left a power vacuum. He'd been a good leader, the obvious choice to have succeeded Huffman. Martin, in New York, was managing the business side of operations. Who would fill the void in San Francisco? There was Schiraldi, a quick, driven worker eager to both start and ship new projects. At another desk along the drafty window there was David King, a slower, more fastidious programmer. Then there was Jeremy Edberg, the experienced systems architect. "Once Chris left, I think we all sort of felt that we were the new leader," Schiraldi said. "And that was not a good type of thing."

Slowe's open HR slot had been filled with a programmer named Neil Williams—albeit at a lower salary and title. So Edberg presented himself as the de facto head of the ragtag Reddit band, and maintained, "The way it worked was the senior engineer was in charge—and that was me for about a month." Occasionally there were power struggles. Schiraldi felt slighted, and bristled at anything he considered to be a power move by Edberg.

By March 2011, King had been poached by Huffman and joined him and Slowe to code Hipmunk's flight finder. Schiraldi left shortly thereafter for Google, which ended up tripling his pay. Suddenly, only Edberg was left, managing one brand-new engineer, Williams. He imagined his bosses in New York, having fancy lunches, traveling on jets, hiring droves of developers fresh from college—Condé Nast must have two hundred of them, he imagined—though he never was quite sure technically who was his boss. At one time, he knew, the Reddit team seemed to report to Condé Nast's CTO, Rajiv Pant. But now he communicated more with Bob Sauerberg, the president and CEO of Condé Nast, directly. Which meant when there was something he needed—new servers, for instance—he felt that he couldn't bug the head of

Condé Nast with that. Instead, he'd just file an invoice. Sometimes it would get approved. Other times, he recalls hearing, *It will just take some time*. And that "some time" ticked on and on.

On its blog in April 2011, Reddit announced that Martin was Reddit's general manager and would be moving to San Francisco. They'd hired—finally!—a developer named Max Goodman, a.k.a. u/chromakode. But the biggest news was that Ohanian, by this time back from Armenia, would also be rejoining the team, as an adviser to Reddit and Condé Nast.

Edberg had fancied himself a pro at handling the bureaucracy—but fact was, he hadn't made many inroads. Now Martin was his boss? Did he answer to Ohanian? It wasn't clear, but it didn't feel good. Management didn't like the arrangement, either. At 10 a.m. on June 17, 2011, Edberg posted to the Reddit blog a long and bittersweet look back at his tenure and noted that as for his future, "Well, I don't actually have anything lined up just yet." A team from HR flew out to San Francisco and sat down with him. They informed him there would be a lot of paperwork to sign, seeing as this was an executive departure. They informed him his lawyer could be present. He did without.

(• •)

Ohanian's services were also enlisted that year by Goldstein and Huffman, who had decided they needed help in August when they were heads-down coding Hipmunk, prepping for its official launch at Y Combinator's Demo Day. They wanted to refine their branding, make sure the little jet-setting chipmunk that was part of their logo was perfect. And they'd need to drum up some press.

Hipmunk hired Ohanian full-time, despite that Huffman and Ohanian had barely spoken over recent months. They hadn't settled all the complicated feelings between them; both chose to keep their emotions bottled up and their friendship separate from their work relationship. "We never talked about the Reddit stuff. So we were friendly," Huffman said. "Friendly-ish."

Ohanian would manage marketing, and report to Goldstein. Goldstein was highly disciplined, but several years younger, and he was new to managing employees. Ohanian, for his part, hadn't reported to someone since high school. He was accustomed to a great degree of automony, following his own pace and pursuing his own goals.

When they started working together on Hipmunk, Ohanian had flown out to San Francisco and for weeks crashed on the couch at the combination home/office Goldstein and Huffman shared, which was owned by Goldstein's aunt. Ohanian whipped up a logo, in a font inspired by that of his favorite team, the Washington Redskins, and finalized the puffy-cheeked little "hipmunk," a grinning flying chipmunk mascot.

By Hipmunk's launch, in 2010, Y Combinator was in its eleventh class. Out of Mountain View, it had established itself as an enviable boot camp for building a tech company, and Paul Graham had been dubbed "The Start-up Guru" by *Inc.* magazine. Demo Day for the first time was a big press event, with A-list investors such as Ashton Kutcher present. Goldstein nudged Huffman after their presentation to go talk to Demi Moore, who'd come along with Kutcher; he demurred. Goldstein approached Kutcher, and ended up securing investment from him. The press, after Demo Day, adored Hipmunk. "It was insane," Goldstein said. "Huge, like nothing we expected, and nothing YC had ever seen before." More than ten thousand people tried out Hipmunk on its first day—and the site didn't crash. It was in prime position for the limelight, and boasted having sold $350,000 in plane tickets in its first week. Meetings from Demo Day set in motion a $1 million seed investment round from venture capitalists, and a subsequent $4.2 million series A.

The press hits drove most of Hipmunk's initial usage, and its traction, and it had Ohanian to thank for that. He arranged the company's presence the following year at South by Southwest Interactive in Austin, including dozens of press meetings where he handed out luggage tags featuring the chipmunk-wearing-vintage-aviator-goggles mascot. Meanwhile, Hipmunk hired up in San Francisco, expanding to eight coders and salespeople in San Francisco's SoMa neighborhood. After SXSW, Ohanian went home to New York City.

Although Hipmunk benefited from Ohanian's media blitz, the arrangement didn't last long. Ohanian was prone to distraction, taking on ten projects when one required his focus. He worked in spurts, and then seemed to disappear at times. Huffman saw the rift between his old friend and the disciplined Goldstein and told Ohanian, "You and Adam don't work very well together." He recalls that separately, he told Goldstein, "Alexis is not built to be an employee." After some months it was clear that Hipmunk didn't want or need a remote marketing employee.

Goldstein flew to New York City and met Ohanian at a bar near Union Square. Six months into Hipmunk, Goldstein was no longer writing code; he was jetting around the country, meeting with airline executives, making deals to aggregate their flight-search results. He told Ohanian that working remotely wasn't working. Hipmunk wanted to build a marketing team in San Francisco. It was uncomfortable, but in the end they both agreed they'd move Ohanian to an advisory role.

Goldstein, once alone, broke down. "I just remember being so, so shaken up by the conversation," he recalled.

Inside, Ohanian was stewing. He hadn't had a performance review; he had no inkling there'd been a problem. He simply hadn't considered this. It stung. He dialed Huffman. "What did I do?!" he demanded. There was a pause on the line. "I don't know," Huffman finally said. Ohanian later realized he'd been acting too much on his own—and perhaps with too much ego about his talents. In hindsight, he said he didn't have a good blueprint for how to interact with Goldstein. He had just made decisions and acted as he would have as a founder—full steam ahead.

Ohanian knew he had also snarled his relationship with Huffman. "I think about a year in I had invested very little in my working relationship with Steve. He was doing his CTO thing and

I was doing my, like, marketing PR guy thing," he said. "That was a mistake."

When Ohanian left Hipmunk, he wondered if he was also walking away from his relationship with Huffman. They'd never resolved things from Reddit; now another professional cavern was between them.

FREE-SPEECH SANDBOX

On December 17, 2010, a Reddit user named BadgerMatt posted an AMA he headlined, "My story as an anonymous kidney donor and my plea for your help." His plea wasn't personal; he posted a link to donate to the American Cancer Society through the website JustGive. "I wrote out my experience (it was filled with medical complications) and made my request for charity. Everything was going perfectly," he said. He typed away late into the evening, answering questions and posting photos of his kidney in the operating room and of the resulting scars. He went to bed.

As BadgerMatt slept, other Redditors got suspicious. His account was only two weeks old: red flag. He hadn't posted or commented much, but just two days prior, BadgerMatt had posted another improbable and fantastic story: another red flag. (His previous post, from December 15, was titled "How I got an uncooperative eBay buyer to pay for her purchase. Was it unethical?" It detailed how a woman bid $600 for his tickets to a game, then pulled out of the transaction. He created a fake account and offered her $1,000 for the tickets, which she then purchased—then, you guessed it, pulled out. The story yielded more than 3,000 karma points and more than four thousand comments in four days.)

When BadgerMatt woke up and checked the site, his kidney post had tanked in karma, with −350 points, and commenters were calling him a crook and a scammer. The top comment on his post was now "DO NOT DONATE TO THE KIDNEY PERSON. IT IS FAKE."

His phone rang. Again and again. He'd been doxed. His identity—his real name and phone number—had been exposed. "People got ahold of my contact information and were making me and my family's life hell," he said. His Reddit mail icon glowed orange-red, and when he clicked it, he saw dozens of private messages telling him that he was a horrible person, a scum, and deserved to die. He tried to correct the record but found he was banned from commenting on his original Reddit post.

"My father-in-law has cancer so I thought it'd be neat to use the publicity from the story to drum up donations in his name," Matt explained. He'd earned a couple hundred dollars in donations, but had also been harassed, doxed, bullied, and barred from defending himself.

BadgerMatt did the only thing he could think of: He created a new Reddit thread. He titled it "Redeeming Myself" and posted more photos from the surgery. He also included lab reports and letters confirming the date of his operation. "People began apologizing at that point," he said later. But not everyone: The user who had started the witch hunt sent Matt a message reading, "Sorry, but it's not that big of a deal, it's just the internet."

It's just the internet. It's also a concept that might be called Reddit's dissociative identity disorder. By 2012, Reddit had one hundred thousand communities of avid readers, who had donated tens of thousands of dollars to classrooms, to natural-disaster victims, and more than $80,000 to build a massive wall protecting the Faraja Children's Home in Kenya from attackers after a user posted a photo of a man who'd been slashed in the face by a machete while attempting to defend the complex. It was home to whimsical helpfulness—who hasn't heard of the once-popular subreddit "Random Acts of Pizza"?—and, of course, the world's largest Secret Santa program.

Two significant conceptual and organizational forces on Reddit.com had helped fuel Reddit's massive growth over the past couple of years, even though its team remained small. One was the introduction of nonlink posts. Anyone could by this time create a freeform post about anything—a unique experience they wanted to share, the fact that they were looking for work, or a plea seeking advice. These were called "self" posts, and this was the kind of post that u/BadgerMatt had made.

The second transformative development had been the proliferation of subreddits, which any user could create and manage themselves. Reddit's little sections were curated by an army of thousands of volunteer moderators from around the world, who watched over their troves of fascinating content. Moderators, in exchange for upholding Reddit's content policy (no spamming, no doxing, and the like), were allowed to run their own little corners of Reddit, with extra rules of their choosing.

Subreddits were wide-ranging: r/LifeProTips, where users would post often-funny life hacks, and r/todayilearned, which was filled with fascinating "aha" moments or strange historical coincidences. On r/personalfinance, individuals asked for help getting out of debt, and strangers chimed in with worthwhile tips. R/DIY, r/Frugal, and r/HomeImprovement captured a feel-good, self-starter vibe, spreading advice and praise for completed projects. There was an emerging porn ecosystem, but there was also r/spaceporn, with beautiful images of outer space, and its sister sites, r/EarthPorn and r/FoodPorn. (Of course some clever pornographer had to take that to its logical backlash-to-the-backlash place, and also create r/EarthPornPorn, in which users could view images of humans au naturel amid nature.)

There were also super-specific topics that were catnip to niche enthusiasts: sharing close readings of *Calvin and Hobbes* comic strips (r/calvinandhobbes); crafters who wanted to swap work with another crafter (r/craftexchange); and an array of sports team and video-game subreddits limited only by the number of sports teams and video games on the planet. There were also offshoots and specific subsets of these hobbies: For gay video-game enthusiasts, there was r/gaymers. For practicing Buddhists trying to get their kids to eat healthier or clean up their toys, there was r/BuddhistParents.

By this time, users had launched a couple of ridiculously popular sections that have become Reddit hallmarks, such as r/nosleep, dedicated to true-sounding long fictional tales specifically crafted to keep their readers up all night, and r/trees for marijuana enthusiasts. (Upset that their logical subreddit name had been snapped up, a cohort of arborists later snagged r/marijuanaenthusiasts to post their gorgeous images of actual trees.) Other subreddits, such as r/woahdude and r/StonerPhilosophy catered to a subset of r/trees subscribers, and were best viewed after having consumed "trees."

For all the whimsical and the delightfully wry content these volunteer moderators ushered into the world with the help of their subreddits' followers, these so-benevolent Redditors had also gotten people fired, harassed a sexual assault victim, and launched dozens of witch hunts against demonstrably innocent people. It was a community left to, essentially, police itself. Even the moderators, in charge of making rules for their subreddits, and detecting or banning rule-breakers, were sometimes themselves culprits. In one particularly bizarre case, a moderator of r/trees had attempted to solicit donations for a pro-pot nonprofit—without actually setting up a nonprofit. Users were livid; the moderator was banned.

(• •)

As Reddit grew, its underbelly also gained girth. Buried deep beyond the front page, forums glorified gore, white supremacy, anarchy, fat shaming, porn, and, most disturbingly—at least in the eyes of the law—content that looked a lot like, and sometimes was, child pornography, including illustrations of sexualized children and photos of barely clothed teenagers.

Some of this content was sucked from or mimicked the sort of stuff shared on 4chan, the popular anonymous message-board site. 4chan's primary differentiation from Reddit was that it stripped away even any modicum of identity; there were no usernames at all and each commenter appeared as "anonymous." It had been launched in 2003 by a smart, scrawny New York teenager named Chris Poole in his parents' basement as a way to share Japanese animation images, but by the early 2010s was known as a haven for trolls and niche, sometimes noxious content of all sorts.

To many, Reddit's dank subreddits, with moderators volunteering their own hours to run apparently horrific communities of Internet sludge, were just as despicable.

One of Reddit's early operating assumptions was that users wanted "freedom *from* the press," as an early team T-shirt read. The gatekeepers who determined what was on the front page of the *Wall Street Journal* and *New York Times* weren't welcome here: This was a place where the crowd decided what was deeply interesting. To avoid that "gatekeeper" effect, the people operating the site should be hands-off and let the community be self-organizing. This perspective was a simple, rules-minimizing precursor to the "we are a platform, not a publisher" argument so many Silicon Valley media companies would later adopt. But the ideology didn't foresee some of the ways in which it could be abused.

The philosophy within Reddit assumed that humans were fundamentally good—and thus staff admins and moderators should allow users to treat the site as a free-speech sandbox. Now users were building the most bizarre and disturbing creations. There were narcissists trying to attract attention. There were classic trolls looking to antagonize other users into fights. There were contrarians looking to get a rise out of moderators, alarm Reddit staffers, and perhaps get a peek behind the company's green curtain. Others endeavored to test the limits of their abilities (and the law) in this new frontier of the wide-open Internet, trying to see what they could get away with while hiding behind usernames.

R/jailbait was a forum dedicated to being a safe space for people sexually attracted to underage girls. Participants dubbed themselves "ephebophiles," though the world outside this twenty-thousand-strong community would call them pedophiles. The subreddit, moderated by a user named Violentacrez (pronounced "Violent Acres"), featured mostly photos of teenage girls, most in bikinis or revealing clothing. The initial aim of forums like this, some community moderators claimed, was to poke fun at, satirize, or warn against the sort of unintentionally sexualized images of kids that pageant parents or brands would freely post online. They were photos that would seem banal amid a stream of vacation snaps from a friend on Facebook. Assembled in this context, though, they took on an entirely different and deeply disturbing meaning.

When Erik Martin was asked in an AMA what he thought about subreddits such as r/jailbait and r/PicsOfDeadKids (which was accurately titled), he responded that the latter was obviously a "troll subreddit created to get a reaction," and admitting that most people found it offensive. He raised a question of context: "What if the name of the subreddit was /r/autopsyphotos or /r/doyoureallywanttogointocriminalforensics and they were sincere in their discussion of these images?" What if they were only historical photos? Only adults? Where was the line? "The point is I don't want to be the one making those decisions for anyone but myself, and it's not the business Reddit is in. We're a free speech site with very few exceptions (mostly personal info)." He added that the morally questionable forums were something that must be stomached and "are part of the price" of a free-speech site like this.

Among Reddit staffers, the debate was a significant one, but one with near-universal agreement that keeping rules simple and minimal was necessary. Making detailed policy as to where lines would be drawn on specific use cases wasn't just undesirable from a legal standpoint, it was impossible from a bandwidth one. While the community team could watch new subreddits as they were created, and cut off obvious problems as they germinated, they didn't have the resources to police every image of the thousands upon thousands uploaded daily. As the site was designed, this was the moderators' job. But should a subreddit be held responsible for illegal content? Should a problem user? When should Reddit itself be held responsible? The answers were murky.

Jailbait was a traffic hit. It generated millions of page views each month, and for a time "jailbait" was the search term bringing the most Google traffic to Reddit, just behind typing "Reddit" into the search bar. (For a significant period, the second most used search was "Reddit NSFW," or "not safe for work.")

On August 16, 2011, however, Reddit's administrators wiped the entire jailbait forum from the site. Responding to a user request for more information, Martin wrote cryptically, "The Reddit gods banned it. It was going to get out of control fast with the mod drama so we banned it." After a multitude of additional queries, Martin clarified, taking direct responsibility for the ban and revealing that he'd gotten into a fight over Instant Messenger with the head moderator, Violentacrez. His reasoning for the ban wasn't the noxious content but rather "specific issues and a bunch of new mods with bad rap sheets." The subreddit was reopened two weeks later; apparently Violentacrez had reshuffled his moderator slates to Martin's liking.

On September 29, the CNN news talk show *Anderson Cooper 360°* featured a segment about the jailbait section of Reddit. Legal commentators accused the company of hiding behind the First Amendment and refusing to take responsibility for its content. Jeffrey Toobin, a writer and legal pundit, said that while a telephone is considered a common carrier, meaning a phone company cannot be sued for inflammatory things one might shout through its lines, a website is very different, in that it "exercises some control" over its posters. Websites have rules—they have terms of use, after all.

A week later, r/jailbait was gone, again—this time for good. The logic? It threatened the "structural integrity of the greater Reddit community," according to the banner that had been erected to greet would-be visitors to r/jailbait. The limits of free speech had indeed been tested, the gray area plumbed, and, finally, Martin made the call that repeat violations of the site's rules were wreaking too much havoc. The backlash accelerated quickly, with Redditors jumping to declare a "new age" of Reddit "policing" users. In fact, it wasn't an isolated shutdown; plenty of subreddits had been quieted in the past, temporarily or permanently, for bad behavior by users or moderators. One prone to skating on particularly thin ice with Reddit admins, as staff were known, was r/Anarchism. There, getting banned by advocating rape, acts of terrorism, and the like had become a badge of honor for users. Moderator drama was a perennial issue for the Reddit team.

Still, to the outside world, the perceived isolated ban on r/jailbait was jarring, considering there were myriad dark corners of the site, still open, still flowing day after day with photographs of women cowering after being beaten; long, blatantly racist threads; and revenge porn. Violentacrez himself moderated a universe of more than 250 of these outré subreddits. "There were rules we would've made as human beings, or wanted to make," Martin said later. "But we didn't think we should be in that position."

Within months of shutting down r/jailbait, Reddit solidified the move as policy, banning all sexual content featuring minors. Still, it was careful to anticipate complaints that Reddit was censoring free speech. On the blog, Reddit staff posted:

> We understand that this might make some of you worried about the slippery slope from banning one specific type of content to banning other types of content. We're concerned about that too, and do not make this policy change lightly or without careful deliberation.

In hindsight, the statement reads as an overly defensive reaction to taking a logical action: shutting down the obvious places within Reddit where child pornography was being found.

BLACKOUT

After he was dismissed from Reddit, Aaron Swartz had moved back to Boston and begun dabbling in politics. He'd helped launch the Progressive Change Campaign Committee, a political action group. He'd launched a website to fund-raise for and promote Al Franken's 2008 Senate campaign.

But nothing had galvanized him like a 2010 phone call from a friend alerting him to the existence of a Senate bill called the Combating Online Infringement and Counterfeits Act. The bill would have authorized the U.S. attorney general to seize and halt use of any Internet domain found to be dedicated to copyright infringement. When Swartz delved into the specific language of the proposed legislation, he realized it could have significant ramifications for free speech. Swartz had studied the U.S. judicial system's reactions to First Amendment cases. Even though expression had strong judicial support even in extreme cases, such as pornography, he saw issues of copyright as a "blind spot" for justice. He said, "This bill would allow the government to devise a list of websites that Americans were not allowed to visit."

To Swartz, it was a war—"a battle to define everything that

happens on the internet in terms of traditional things that law understands. Is sharing a video on BitTorrent like shoplifting from a movie store, or loaning to a friend? Is reloading a webpage over and over again like a peaceful virtual sit-in, or a violent smashing of shop windows? Is publishing government documents like brave whistleblowing or international espionage? . . . The way we answer these questions will shape the next era of our society."

Swartz knew copyright was a slippery thing—easy to violate, so much so that he pointed out that the website of the bill's sponsor had been written in part with copyrighted code. So he asked himself: What do you do when you're a little guy facing a terrible future with long odds and little hope of success? He started an online petition. He called a few friends, and they stayed up all night hacking together a website they called Demand Progress. The friends emailed it to friends, and before long the online petition went viral, quickly amassing two hundred thousand digital signatures opposing the bill.

Ron Wyden, a Democratic senator from Oregon, put a hold on the bill, calling it a "bunker-buster bomb" aimed at the Internet. But a year later it was alive and well again, sailing through committee under a new name: PIPA.

PIPA, the obvious title for the mouthful the House titled its bill—Preventing Real Online Threats to Economic Creativity and Theft of Intellectual Property Act, or the PROTECT IP Act—had a sister bill in the Senate called SOPA, the Stop Online Piracy Act. Led by Swartz, Demand Progress railed against them, and spread the word far and wide through the Internet and Silicon Valley and the tech press.

Hollywood, via its powerful lobby, the Motion Picture Association of America, was seeking stricter protections for copyrighted materials online. The deep-pocketed trade group had a formidable leader in Chris Dodd, a former Democratic senator from Connecticut. Dodd had made smooth work of pushing for the initial bills in Washington and helping them amass additional support from corporations. Some, including Sony and Nintendo, hired their own lobbyists to push for SOPA and PIPA, according to data compiled by OpenSecrets.

The intensifying SOPA/PIPA debate had caught the attention of Alexis Ohanian. He was mostly living in Brooklyn, and had begun making small seed investments of about $5,000 in about two dozen startups. He put some time into Breadpig, his nonprofit arts endeavor, and continued casually advising Reddit. He hired an employee to help juggle it all.

From the million-dollar apartment he owned in Brooklyn, which featured giant factory windows offering remarkable views of the East River and lower Manhattan, Ohanian watched online conversations about the legislation bubbling up. He also got an email about SOPA from the founders of Fight for the Future, a nonprofit that campaigns for open Internet access. The organization was scraping together an anti-SOPA campaign and wanted Ohanian's help. He had friends at Google who were organizing a trip to Washington to meet with representatives, and he happily joined.

The way Ohanian and plenty of other advocates of what has come to be known as "Internet freedom" saw it, the bills were written in a way that ignored the needs of technology companies large and small—especially those, like Reddit, that were powered by user submissions. The Digital Millennium Copyright Act, a 1998 law that upholds copyright law, dismissed Internet service providers and other companies from being held liable for being used to transmit copyrighted works. SOPA and PIPA, however, proposed putting websites that "facilitated" copyright infringement on the hook for all content uploaded by users. (Others that did business with sites violating copyright—payment services, ad networks— were also thought to be subject to potential punishment.) That wasn't realistic in the eyes of Ohanian and his fellow tech emissaries.

By the end of their visit, Senator Jerry Moran, a Republican from Kansas, signed on to a statement against PIPA. Utah Republican Jason Chaffetz later brought up Ohanian's own wording during a House Judiciary Committee discussion of the bill, saying, "We're basically gonna reconfigure the Internet...without bringing in the nerds."

For months, Swartz and Ohanian effectively worked in tandem on Internet freedom, without ever teaming up or speaking. Since Swartz had been forced out of Reddit, he'd communicated occasionally with Huffman, but very rarely with Ohanian. Now the two were on the same path, marching toward the same goal, with a wall of mutual mistrust between them. Behind the scenes, and behind a screen, Swartz and his colleagues drummed up signatures, circulated blog posts and petitions, and raised money. In front of TV-station cameras and at the center of rallies, Ohanian leveraged his handsome face and natural charisma.

Ohanian wanted to get Reddit involved. He flew to San Francisco and took a couple Reddit staffers, Marta Gossage and Ricky Ramirez, out to dinner on December 19, 2011. At a Japanese-fusion steakhouse in San Francisco's Mission Bay, over a clawless lobster special and custom cocktails, he picked the brains of the engineer and community manager, who were in the trenches of Reddit every day. What action could Reddit take? What if they enlisted celebrities to tout the cause? The idea of blacking out the whole of Reddit—or even portions of it—to protest the bills was floated, but it seemed both far-fetched and heavy-handed to the staffers. "We only saw that as a nuclear option," Ramirez said. They wanted the Reddit community to steer any action it took—rather than foist something on them.

At this time, in late 2011, SOPA and PIPA weren't yet mainstream news. Ohanian reached out to the team working with Margaret Brennan, a fellow UVA grad, at Bloomberg Television, asking if there was any way he could come on the air to discuss SOPA. She bit. Things still didn't seem to be gaining media traction in any significant way, though.

Impatient, he flew to the Turks and Caicos for the twenty-ninth birthday of his girlfriend, Sabriya Stukes. While Ohanian was on the beach, he got an email: The House Committee on Oversight and Government Reform had requested that he testify before them on January 18. This was it, he thought: the big time. He threw himself into prep mode, seeking advice. He turned to Michael Seibel, his fellow Y Combinator alum and Justin.tv executive (whose stream-ing media service struggled with preventing illegal broadcasts of sporting events, and could almost certainly be forced out of exis-tence under the proposed laws). Seibel, who had started his career in politics, taught Ohanian how to write a testimony and anticipate lawmakers' questions.

Seibel also shared with him a story from college, when he'd at-tended a talk by Henry Kissinger, the former secretary of state under Richard Nixon and Gerald Ford. In a room with plenty of detractors, Kissinger had opened the floor to questions by noting that he had only six answers prepared, so whatever the gathered students asked, he said, he'd be likely to give one of his six answers. "I always thought that that was so on point, because people tend to get in trouble when they start ad-libbing," Seibel later explained.

With his six major talking points prepped, Ohanian readied for January 18, 2012. He would attend a big anti-SOPA rally. He would do TV appearances for twenty-four hours straight, arranged by his new employee, Kat Manalac. He would testify before Con-gress alongside First Amendment lawyers, chief executives, and prominent venture capitalists. "I now had this quiver of things to say that were quick and pithy and perfect for the sound-bite medium. Plus I had the red tie, white shirt, blue suit," he said, wait-ing a beat for the joke to sink in, the very idea of this hip Brooklyn jeans-and-sneakers guy bedecked in the default cable news guest uniform. "I stole the tie from my dad."

(• •)

On Reddit, particularly in r/politics, commenters had begun pick-ing apart the language of the bills: They pointed out that SOPA/PIPA would dramatically expand the government's ability to shut-ter or block websites that even linked to content that potentially infringed copyright. The bills were clearly written by nontechnolo-gists; they were overly broad, such that their passage could hamper e-commerce, dampen free and open communications online, and strip the country of startups, jobs, and innovation. In addition to engaging in heated discussions, the Reddit community also presented achievable, accessible calls to action. One Redditor condemned GoDaddy for lobbying to support the acts, saying he would be transferring his fifty-one domain names and suggesting that other Redditors use December 29 as Move Your Domain Day. GoDaddy withdrew its support for the bills that day. By the turn of the new year, moderators were pondering more significant protests, such as putting up banners over their subreddits or blacking them out.

Meanwhile, Jimmy Wales of Wikipedia had proposed an official online blackout date. On r/AskReddit, moderator andrewsmith1986 wrote, "Let's discuss SOPA, Askreddit." He explained that he'd been discussing with other moderators whether they should shut down for twenty-four hours. "We aren't admins so we cannot close all of Reddit but we can shut down our respective playgrounds." In response to his question, whether users would be okay with the subreddit being shut down for twenty-four hours, he got resounding yeses.

Reddit's community team had been observing as moderators organized, with more of them volunteering to black out their sections for a full day of protest. They took a vote, and came to a conclusion: They'd do it. They'd do just what Ohanian had floated weeks ago: Black out the whole site.

On January 10, 2012, a Reddit blog post declared, "The freedom, innovation, and economic opportunity that the Internet enables is in jeopardy. Congress is considering legislation that will dramatically change your Internet experience and put an end to Reddit and many other sites you use everyday." Reddit went on to announce that eight days later, it would make its entire website, all ten-thousand-plus subreddits, unreadable for twelve hours, in protest of the two pieces of copyright legislation.

Reddit went dark at 8 a.m. on January 18. Its site, which displayed at the top an outline of a gray, frowning alien over a black background, read, "SOPA and PIPA damage the internet. Today we fight back." Reddit.com had been transformed into a lengthy list of links and notes urging users to contact their government representatives and an explainer of the bills, written by Reddit systems administrator Jason Harvey. It was perhaps the most visible face of that day's Internet blackout, which spread to more than 115,000 websites and blogs, some of which went completely dark; others, such as *Wired* magazine, displayed creatively crafted messages about Internet censorship on their homepages. Wikipedia turned to shades of gray and displayed the words "Imagine a world without free knowledge," and included a tool for contacting members of Congress. More than eight million people used it, according to Wikipedia. More than 350,000 emails were sent to representatives via SopaStrike.com, and individuals posted more than 2.4 million tweets about SOPA on the eighteenth.

Reddit and its kin killing SOPA and PIPA was an alluring narrative. Even before January 18 arrived, though, Republican senators had begun to pull their support. The White House had issued a statement opposing the bill, saying it would "not support legislation that reduces freedom of expression, increases cybersecurity risk, or undermines the dynamic, innovative global Internet." Shortly thereafter, the Democrats pulled the bill before the vote. A Senate vote on PIPA scheduled for January 24 was delayed indefinitely. The House Judiciary Committee also put the brakes on its legislation. Ohanian didn't go to Washington that day; there was no longer need for testimony.

A massive online protest was no longer necessary, either, but it happened anyway. The tech companies' victory lap took much of the credit for what Swartz and his grassroots movements had set in motion. "It was stopped by the people. The people themselves. We killed the bill dead. So dead," Swartz later said. Ten million people had signed the petitions stemming from his original effort more than a year earlier.

Instead of going to Washington, Ohanian stayed in New York, doing televised hits on MSNBC and CNN. Then, still in his TV getup, red tie from his father included, he hustled to the intersection of

Third Avenue and 49th Street, where a group called New York Tech Meetup had organized an "emergency meeting" in protest of the bills. The location, kitty-corner from legendary steakhouse Smith & Wollensky, was chosen because it was parked squarely in front of the offices of New York senators Charles Schumer and Kirsten Gillibrand. "We're here because we are fighting against wholesale destruction of one of the healthiest parts of the American economy," Ohanian's voice boomed out from the speakers. He was confident; he spoke in sound bites. The fight to stop SOPA, in Ohanian's words, was not just a fight to save Silicon Valley; it was a fight to save our very democracy.

Ohanian would, for this and all the press that followed, be called "The Voice of His Generation." Ben Huh, founder and CEO of the website network Cheezburger, and an unabashed policy wonk, said, "He represents the idea we have about young, smart people doing good things on the Internet." Senator Ron Wyden credited Ohanian "and the movement he leads" as being "hugely helpful in winning the battle against SOPA and PIPA." *Forbes* published an article calling Ohanian the "Mayor of the Internet." BuzzFeed one-upped *Forbes*, noting, "Alexis Ohanian wants to be *president* of the Internet."

Ohanian was barraged by press questions for an hour after the protest. When asked where the idea for blacking out Reddit that day came from, he took a lot of the credit for bringing the blackout to the World Wide Web, but also extended praise to users of Reddit. "The spirit of Reddit has always been: Let the community do the hard stuff," he said. "We can create a great system, and get out of their way."

After stepping away from the microphones, Ohanian passed by a man with wire-rimmed glasses, slouched shoulders, and a mop of wavy dark hair: Aaron Swartz. He wore a black wool bomber jacket. They nodded to each other but didn't catch up or reminisce. This was the last time Alexis Ohanian saw Aaron Swartz.

MEET YOUR NEW CEO

To Condé Nast Digital, Reddit was a wondrous traffic beast: It had been more than doubling in page views every year, and was up to a billion a month now. But nearly five years after the acquisition, it was still a financial disappointment. Potential advertisers were still wary. There were the site's darker corners to worry about, along with the bizarre actions of the community, which was increasingly difficult to rein in.

Steve Newhouse, who ran digital operations for Advance Publications, didn't see Reddit as a liability—just as an entity that was best kept at arm's length from the glossy magazines. He had supported the Reddit team's strategy of focusing on traffic growth, and felt proud of the initiatives the scrappy group had undertaken. They'd taught him about open-sourcing a site's code, and he'd taught them about maintaining quarterly goals. But in 2011, Newhouse decided it was time to try something new for Reddit.

Bob Sauerberg, Condé's president, was on board. He and Newhouse figured that if Reddit was allowed to raise venture capital funding and behave more like other Silicon Valley startups, the company would have a chance at competing with the likes of

Facebook and Twitter. Reddit would also have more flexibility to hire new employees, to pay them competitively, and to offer stock options. Plus, given investors' enthusiasm for heavily trafficked money-losing websites, an independent Reddit would almost certainly be worth a lot more to the market than it was to Condé Nast. (Which meant, if Advance Publications retained ownership, it would, eventually, be worth a lot more to it, too.) In September 2011, Reddit was spun out as an independent business. Advance Publications would retain ownership, but now through holding shares of the company.

The Newhouses had been in touch regularly with Ohanian at this point, and involved him in certain conversations about spinning out Reddit. Ohanian was particularly close with Steve Newhouse and his younger cousin, S. I. Newhouse, who'd gotten more involved with Reddit's operations, and with whom he'd stayed in touch over the past two years. The Newhouse family had seen Ohanian's star rising as he began to deliver public speeches about the history of Reddit. They had other dealings with him, too: The Newhouses were among his biggest backers when Ohanian launched an investment fund, Das Kapital Capital, in 2010.

As the spin-off plan took shape, Ohanian was offered the chance to return to what he'd created and take the reins as chief executive. Or alternatively, he could take a spot on the board of directors for Reddit—become an adviser who could dip in and out as he pleased. "Reddit didn't feel like what I needed to be doing," he later recalled. He didn't pursue the CEO position. Instead he joined the board, and accepted stock options in the new iteration of Reddit.

Steve Huffman was kept out of the loop. He had for the past two years been focused intensely on building Hipmunk, which had just been named one of the best websites of the year by *Time*. He'd come to envision himself as a hardworking professional, doing the unglamorous work of trying to grow a small company. He was slinging plane tickets while simultaneously trying to bolster Hipmunk into a viable competitor to Kayak and the other big online travel agents.

Over the years, his connections to Reddit had dwindled—in part because he'd hired his former colleagues over to Hipmunk. He and Ohanian were not on speaking terms. Reddit was dear to his heart—he considered it the best thing he'd ever built—and he'd dipped in occasionally for the most ceremonial of events, such as the rally in Washington, but now he felt increasingly alienated from the tiny team at Reddit.

As Condé Nast made its plans, Huffman wasn't asked for advice. His role in Reddit was merely obsessive lurker.

On September 6, 2011, Reddit's general manager, Erik Martin, posted on Reddit's blog that Reddit was no longer "a division of Condé Nast," and instead would stand on its own as "Reddit, Inc." under the greater umbrella of Advance Publications. The post explained that the new arrangement would set up "reddit so that it can better handle future growth and opportunities." He cited a statistic that when Reddit had been acquired in 2006, it received about seven hundred thousand page views per day. As of the post, Reddit regularly got that much traffic every fifteen minutes.

Steve Huffman read Martin's post and seethed. He realized almost immediately that Ohanian had likely been involved in the spin-out. He knew his former cofounder, his former best friend, had been there, having somehow inserted himself in the company's bureaucracy they'd once together bemoaned. He felt waves of anger and embarrassment hit him: He'd been intentionally kept in the dark for, what, months? Years? There were pangs of jealousy at the fact that Ohanian would be returning to serve on Reddit's new board. Over days and weeks, Huffman dwelled on the situation, and came to the realization that Ohanian must have received shares of Reddit in a deal to lock in his board position. That fact didn't just sting; it burned.

(• •)

Yishan Wong hadn't been seriously looking for a job when he read the news about Reddit's spin-out and clicked through to Martin's post. The blog explained that a CEO search was under way, to help

Reddit reach its full "unbridled potential." Reddit "wouldn't seriously consider any individuals for the CEO position unless they understood the community and were passionate about serving its needs," Martin had written.

Wong, a former Facebook engineering manager, had already had a successful career, even by high-flying Silicon Valley standards. With a carefree look of floppy black hair and chin stubble, he was now running an incubator, mentoring young startup founders. He had a good life—a wife and little kid. He drove a blue Tesla.

The fact that he didn't *need* a job didn't stop Wong from immediately imagining what his life would be like as Reddit CEO. Nor did his recognition that he wouldn't be an ideal candidate. Sure, he'd managed people at Facebook, as he had also done as senior engineer of applications at PayPal. Lately, though, he'd just been advising startups. He figured that while his work experiences might qualify him to start his own company, they wouldn't enable him to jump in as a growth-oriented executive of an existing one. *But, Reddit!* He unabashedly loved the site. He'd had an account since 2005 and wasn't just a passive lurker; he posted often.

By the time an executive recruiter working with Advance reached out to Wong, the idea had already taken hold. Steve Newhouse and Andrew Siegel, who'd taken over as vice president of corporate development, stressed to Wong that the Reddit team was small. "That was actually good, because I don't think I'm qualified to run a large company," Wong recalled. "So it was like, 'All right, technically I could lead a company about this size.'"

His attitude read as humility, due perhaps to Wong's credentials: He was basically Silicon Valley royalty. Facebook engineers were becoming well respected, and on top of that, Wong was a member of the so-called PayPal Mafia, the exclusive club of PayPal employees who became legends not just for constructing that payments infrastructure, but also for what they'd gone on to accomplish; Wong's former coworkers had founded Palantir, LinkedIn, Yelp, Yammer, YouTube, Tesla Motors, and SpaceX. Others had become venture capitalists who invested in their former colleagues' companies, along with Facebook and Zynga. It was a web of friendship and money. And Wong was, at least on paper, a Mafioso.

After the Advance executives conducted interviews, a handful of candidates were sent to meet Ohanian. Sitting down with Wong, Ohanian learned quickly that while the skilled hacker didn't share his own jump-out-of-your-seat enthusiasm or easy charisma, he did have a certain gravitas, and a wry sense of humor. He possessed a set of skills extremely important to Ohanian—technical chops. "The product was still just frozen in time and Reddit was missing opportunities because it wasn't improving," Ohanian said later. "What intrigued me about Yishan is that he was deeply technical, a well-known engineering leader within a well-known company. Reddit needed that kind of leadership."

Perhaps even more important, Wong had been a longtime avid Redditor. As such, he held dear a certain slate of beliefs that had become gospel among many dedicated moderators, and central to Reddit staffers' ethos. His beliefs skewed libertarian, and he was firmly in favor of defending freedom of speech, however extreme. He was comfortable justifying Reddit as an online home for anything not illegal beyond a reasonable doubt. Wong was the type of hacker with a gleam in his eye, a natural troublemaker and underdog—albeit one who'd been made financially comfy due to his past at PayPal and Facebook. "He had characteristics that Alexis and Steve had at the start," Martin recalled. "He had a little touch of anarchist."

Newhouse and Sauerberg decided Wong was their man.

(• •)

During the fall of 2011, while Yishan Wong was in talks with the board, the still tiny Reddit staff felt like they were living inside a snow globe perched on an executive's desk at Condé Nast. Occasionally they'd feel a tapping or shaking, but mostly they were isolated, with only a hazy and distorted view of the machinations beyond their near-distance sight.

Erik Martin had relocated to San Francisco, and as Reddit's general manager was tasked with leading the team. Martin quickly become an empowering boss. In the eyes of employees, he was honest, compassionate, and creative. He encouraged employees to explore new concepts by giving them tools to learn, and then challenging them to produce something that would benefit the site or its community. He'd rather an employee spend an hour working on a crisis plan based on hypothetical problematic situations than putting out a handful of minor garbage-can fires. Martin was the company's first nontechnical leader, and he'd managed to create a cohesive group and grow it into a strong if scrappy creative force.

Martin broke the crippling hiring freeze by learning to work the very system of paying contractors he'd despised when he had been a contractor himself. He'd discovered that if he brought on potential employees as freelance contributors, he could gradually work to make them full-time staffers, once he had enough evidence to display to the Newhouses and other Condé Nast executives that they were providing great value.

Martin had recruited Marta Gossage, a former community manager at LiveJournal, whose job there included monitoring the site for posts by suicidal teenagers. By the end of 2011, Gossage was handling a wide range of legal issues for Reddit, alongside Martin and Alex Angel, who also now occasionally worked from the San Francisco office. Now there were not one but two women at Reddit. Everyone worked days amicably but quietly—engineers in full headphones-on concentration mode. Some days, Gossage would see the clock on her computer tick past six, and if there were no major problems to address, she'd suggest over chat that they play a board game. Everyone wheeled over to a table, or went to the café across the office, and settled into Cards Against Humanity, or Telestrations, a parlor game that combines elements of Pictionary and Telephone.

Martin had also finally managed to hire u/chromakode, a.k.a. Max Goodman, the engineer who'd solved the *Jurassic Park*–style comment bug infestation during Steve Huffman's wedding. He had also brought on the new systems administrator, Ricky Ramirez, back in September 2011. A month later, a free spirit named Josh Wardle, fresh off completing his master's of fine arts at the University of Oregon, joined as "resident artist" (though in this scrappy system in which titles meant little and everyone lent their talents where useful, Goodman continued illustrating the custom "Snoovatars," such as Gossage's red-shirted one in homage to her long-standing amusement with the TV series trope of "red shirts" being stock characters who'd be the first to die in an episode).

The Reddit Gifts team—Dan McComas and Jessica Moreno—was still quarantined from entering the office, but occasionally Gossage was sent as an envoy across the bay to visit them in their Alameda digs. Gossage, reservedly friendly and midwestern, possessed a sincere adoration of Reddit and Internet culture, and blended into the team of hackers with her understanding of legal issues and site moderation. That fall of 2011, they all became exceptionally close, confidants in building their crazy machine that allowed anyone to say anything.

What the little team heard from Advance Publications generally had trickled down through Martin, or sometimes Ohanian or S. I. Newhouse. Martin had been told that he and the staff would be looped into the post-spin-off CEO search; they'd all be able to sit down with candidates, ask their questions, and generally assist in the interview process. A check-in with management after the January 2012 blackout to protest SOPA and PIPA indicated no sign that progress had been made toward finding Reddit's new leader. They were told there were no candidates.

Within weeks, another message came through the pipeline, introducing them to Wong, their new chief executive.

The shocking news was met with ire. The Reddit team already nursed some mistrust of their corporate overlords in New York, who, as they saw it, had at times starved the site of desperately needed resources. If the staff had been involved in the process, this moment could have been a turning point. Instead, the Reddit staff interpreted it as a shackling. Immediately, the little fishbowl office convened a meeting. Its subject: whether to simultaneously submit letters of resignation to the board from every last one of them.

The engineers and community managers decided against resigning en masse. In March, Yishan Wong was officially issued a badge and given a desk in the *Wired* office, becoming CEO of Reddit. Max Goodman created a custom Snoo, like all employees received, of the alien holding five parrots—because one of the goofier images returned by a Google image search for "Yishan Wong" was him wearing a lei and holding a bevy of birds.

In a discussion of the new executive on Reddit, most top comments either implicitly or explicitly said, "Don't fuck it up." Ohanian, as u/kn0thing, replied to one, saying he'd verified that u/yishan had one of the oldest Reddit accounts, dating back to the days when he, Huffman, and Slowe were first creating the site in Somerville, Massachusetts. He also wrote, "I'll do everything in my capacity...to make sure he doesn't fuck it up."

NOT BAD!

Heading into 2012, there were a couple of competing narratives about Reddit. On one end of the spectrum, there was creepshot Reddit. On the other was bright and shiny Ask Me Anything Reddit. R/IAmA was by 2012 easily the best-known section of Reddit due to celebrities posting and answering questions from regular folks. R/IAmA had long since ditched its video roots, morphing into a lower-maintenance, simpler version of the thing that basically just required an interesting person to get on their laptop (or, well, have their staff transcribe their thoughts—though just as on Twitter, even high-profile individuals often simply typed themselves, as it was easier). Celebrities such as Dave Grohl, Madonna, Larry King, and Bill Nye had done AMAs. Astronaut Chris Hadfield had answered questions from the International Space Station.

Despite that politics was a popular topic on Reddit, politicians were tough gets for AMAs. "We'd call up press secretaries on the Hill," Martin said, "and most of them would say, 'I have no idea what you're talking about, fuck off.'" The politicians who had bitten on Martin's asks in the past didn't really want to do a genuine AMA: They'd ask to collect questions in advance rather than participate in real time. So even if one surmised that Alexis Ohanian's tweet at 10:45 a.m. on August 29, 2012—"there's a really special AMA coming later today"—was promoting a political AMA, no one suspected the president of the United States would be logging on to answer questions.

Reddit's team had long dreamed of an AMA by the president, and Ohanian had nurtured friendships with Barack Obama's digital campaign staffers over the years—visiting campaign headquarters in Chicago, and frequently mentioning the idea of doing an AMA, or even a series of video fireside chats (as he'd envisioned them, in the spirit of FDR).

His hustle had perhaps planted a seed. By mid-2012, as Obama prepared for a "youth tour" of swing-state campuses as part of his re-election campaign, Stephanie Cutter, the deputy campaign manager, approached Teddy Goff, the Yale graduate who'd worked his way up in Obama's campaign staff to digital director. "We've got two chunks of his time" to spend on digital efforts, Cutter told Goff. They'd already done a Twitter live Q&A. Goff suggested an AMA. Cutter approved.

Within an hour, the team had reached out to Reddit. "POTUS is doing an AMA."

Goff, along with the Reddit team, opted not to promote the president's scheduled thirty-minute appearance on r/IAmA, to limit potential technical issues due to flooding their servers and to limit spam and hack attacks. Martin knew there'd be a huge risk of individual users attempting to game the Reddit algorithm to have their questions appear at the top of the page; he also feared DDoS attacks. Martin was petrified that news would leak, even from Reddit's tiny twenty-person staff. So he conferred with Wong—he had let the systems administrator know in advance, so he could ready the servers. The rest of the staff would have to wait until the day of the event. Just ten minutes before the first Obama post, Martin told moderators of the r/IAmA section, in a glowing note that credited them with making this happen. (It also urged them to refrain from gaming their own system.)

On the afternoon of August 29, in Charlottesville, Virginia, the same place Ohanian and Huffman had first created Redbrick Solutions, Barack Obama spoke to students at the University of Virginia at an open-air arena several blocks off campus. After the speech, he shook hands, greeted a few students, but then hurried to a beige holding room with linoleum tiles and a flimsy standing lamp, desk, chair, and MacBook Pro. A campaign staffer took a photo of the president, and Goff posted it on Reddit along with the headline "I am Barack Obama, President of the United States—AMA."

"So what is this?" Obama asked, staring at the screen. Goff briefed him for less than a minute: Reddit was an insanely popular social news site, meaning it was crowdsourced rather than being run by an editorial team. Earnest, pithy, voice-of-the-people.

"Yeah, yeah, yeah." Obama nodded. Slightly reassured, Goff replied, "All right, you know how this works?"

"No. I have no idea," the president replied.

No matter: Obama dug in. He typed straight into Reddit, "Hey everybody—this is barack. Just finished a great rally in Charlottesville, and am looking forward to your questions."

Submit. The president was live on Reddit.

The plan was for Obama to dictate answers to Cody Keenan, a speechwriter. But Obama didn't hand over the laptop. "I'll just keep going," he said. He began to type out answers to questions on economic issues affecting young people, funding the space program, and the White House's beer recipe. Advisers James Kvaal, David Plouffe, and Jen Psaki and photographer Pete Souza milled about, ducking into the room occasionally.

At first, Reddit users were skeptical, just as Goff feared. Despite the photo Goff had uploaded, and the link to a tweet by the president to serve as verification of identity for the AMA, Martin had to step in and post as an administrator to reiterate to the masses that, yes, this indeed was the chief of state posting. The questions for Obama, simultaneously, were building up at an accelerating rate. Within ten minutes, there were 278 comments. By 4:15, before Obama had even answered just one question from users, Reddit's servers were sputtering.

Jason Harvey, the systems administrator in San Francisco, had set up a dedicated connection for Team Obama, so that if Reddit crashed, it wouldn't waste the president's precious thirty minutes of time; he could at least go on answering whatever questions were already live. Harvey had prepared by adding 30 dedicated servers for the thread to the existing 150 already handling the site's usual traffic.

They weren't enough. The systems admin team struggled to manage the servers, at one point believing that the president had lost his connection through an endpoint they'd provided. The AMA quickly became the first thread in Reddit's history to become more popular than the site's front page. At one point Reddit was receiving over one hundred thousand page views per minute. It overwhelmed the site's load balancers. As soon as Harvey spotted a bottleneck, he'd discover that the bottleneck had moved to a different, often more difficult position. Many individuals were only seeing a cached version of Reddit, which meant they could view but not participate in the AMA. "Basically everything that had a breaking point reached that breaking point and broke," engineer Ricky Ramirez later recalled.

Meanwhile, Martin and Angel in San Francisco hustled to communicate the technical setbacks to the team in Virginia while simultaneously monitoring for profanities, rants, or racist remarks from pseudonymous Redditors. When a reporter reached out to Erik Martin over Google chat, he replied, "Chaos over here."

The Reddit team was so focused on managing the mayhem within Reddit that it hadn't considered at length whether the Obama AMA would put them in the spotlight to the world beyond. Then President Obama decided to answer the query "What are you going to do to end the corrupting influence of money in politics during your second term?" In his reply, he brought up the 2010 Supreme Court decision that paved the way for super PACs that raise and spend unlimited funds during election cycles, writing, "Over the longer term, I think we need to seriously consider mobilizing a constitutional amendment process to overturn Citizens United (assuming the Supreme Court doesn't revisit it). Even if the amendment process falls short, it can shine a spotlight of the super-PAC phenomenon and help apply pressure for change."

Obama's campaign manager, Jim Messina, had previously signaled that the president didn't support the *Citizens United* decision, but this declaration that the president would want a constitutional amendment to block its effects—this was news. The *Wall Street Journal* published a story almost immediately.

All in, the Obama AMA mostly read like a press conference, albeit one with a reference to beer. After thirty minutes and eight questions, Obama was due to sign off. Goff, over the president's shoulder, clued him in to one of Reddit's most wholesome in-jokes. "There's this thing about Reddit where people say, 'Not bad,'" he told Obama. "Just trust me, that's a thing."

Obama typed:

> Speaking of balance, though, I need to get going so I'm back in DC in time for dinner. But I want to thank everybody at reddit for participating—this is an example of how technology and the internet can empower the sorts of conversations that strengthen our democracy over the long run. AND REMEMBER TO VOTE IN NOVEMBER—if you need to know how to register, go to Gottaregister.com. By the way, if you want to know what I think about this whole reddit experience—NOT BAD!

The response amounted to a digital standing ovation—more than two hundred thousand people were at one point on Reddit watching this unfold simultaneously. Ripples spread far; the AMA immediately snatched the evening news cycle away from the Republicans and cracked the top ten trending topics on Twitter. Reddit scored heaps of press exposure, including a profile by revered media columnist David Carr in the *New York Times*, who called the site "a staple of digital life for the young and connected." Martin's team stayed humble, writing on Reddit's blog, "Did it go perfectly smooth? Nope. Is this the absolute perfect format for politicians to answer questions? Nope. But it worked."

Still, there had been one significant, if at the time entirely super-ficial, disappointment. It was a cleft bemoaned by Reddit readers and staffers alike: an awesome question that went unanswered. Even federal employees in the White House speculated in days after the AMA about its unknown answer and needled Goff for not alerting the president to the query. The absence of a POTUS response to this particular question launched a hundred tweets, several news articles, and a twenty-five-hundred-word think piece in the *Atlantic*.

"Would you rather fight one horse-sized duck or 100 duck-sized horses?"

THE ID

Eight hundred years ago, a couple miles outside the small central Italian town of Cupramontana, a group of hermits carved a communal lair into a cliff. In these caves enveloped by hills rich with towering oaks and maples, the clan formed its own religion and, as years passed, an isolated worldview. The hermitage was dubbed Eremo dei Frati Bianchi, or the Hermitage of the White Friars. Its residents were men who'd forsaken the structures of the outside world in order to live silent lives of self-abnegation and study, in hopes of somehow improving what they saw as a depraved, mismanaged society.

By 2008, when Aaron Swartz found himself here, the hermitage had long been abandoned. But its caves and surrounding brick structures had been restored. The monastery known now as Eremo by this time functioned as a venue for scientific conferences and miscellaneous events. It was something of a monument to independent-minded outsiders everywhere, a reminder that the radical idealism of opting out of the conventional world was conceivable.

Swartz walked the lawn in the mid-July heat and gazed into the

friars' caves while visiting Eremo for two days of a "visioning retreat" convened by an international consortium known as EIFL,
whose stated mission was to expand access to scholarly works in developing countries. "Open access" was a key issue here, as in parts
of Africa and Asia, access to academic journals was out of reach. It
was simply too costly. The days at the retreat were jammed with
policy discussions, the nights with lengthy dinners at nearby restaurants, where over wine and large, long meals, conversations with
librarians from all over the globe—particularly developing cities,
with which Swartz was unfamiliar—stretched beyond midnight.

Swartz came to Eremo passionate about open access to information, but his argument had been more philosophical than
practical. Here it was set upon a sturdier foundation. These librarians from developing countries presented him with actual examples
of cases where individuals and, as he learned, wide swaths of the
planet's population were genuinely deprived of information. Their
libraries, where they existed at all, were outdated, their online services severely restricted. It clicked: Rich people in Western culture's
most elite institutions could easily pay to access information. What
about a researcher or student in Cambodia or Accra? "It genuinely
opened his eyes," said Monika Elbert, an EIFL official who organized the retreat, of Swartz's experience there.

Swartz did not hesitate to act on his new insights. One evening
in Eremo, he signed his name to what others would not, or could
not, as employees of governments or universities. While librarians
may not have been willing to publicly voice these thoughts, for fear
of becoming unemployable, Swartz let surface no such trepidation.
He wrote:

> Large corporations, of course, are blinded by greed. The
> laws under which they operate require it—their shareholders
> would revolt at anything less. And the politicians they have
> bought off back them, passing laws giving them the exclusive
> power to decide who can make copies.
>
> There is no justice in following unjust laws. It's time to

come into the light and, in the grand tradition of civil disobe-
dience, declare our opposition to this private theft of public
culture.

We need to take information, wherever it is stored, make
our copies and share them with the world. We need to take
stuff that's out of copyright and add it to the archive. We need
to buy secret databases and put them on the Web. We need to
download scientific journals and upload them to file sharing
networks. We need to fight for Guerilla Open Access.

With enough of us, around the world, we'll not just send
a strong message opposing the privatization of knowledge—
we'll make it a thing of the past. Will you join us?

It was titled the Guerilla Open Access Manifesto, and signed,
"Aaron Swartz. July 2008, Eremo, Italy." Swartz posted it online.

(• •)

Aaron Swartz had already begun a transformation by the time he
left Reddit in the early winter of 2007. He'd publicly disavowed
the programmer's life, and had on his blog been ripping into the
startup culture and what he'd dubbed the "existential terror" of
San Francisco.

He publicly decried overhearing chatter at cafés about funding
rounds and programming languages. Separately, in a piece of seri-
alized fiction he portrayed Google as a ruthless, omnipotent tech
overlord. He chided his peers for wasting their talents building
websites that were "the mental equivalent of snack food." He also
wrote that skilled individuals who enter a profession are doing it
wrong; they'd only "get bossed around and told exactly what to
do" by more powerful individuals.

When Swartz had escaped San Francisco that year in favor of
Cambridge, "the only place that's ever felt like home," he'd turned
away not just from the startup life, but also, seemingly, from the
entire capitalist structure that allows corporations to grow and

flourish. He realized he couldn't effect change by simply not show-ing up to his cubicle, or by cowering from the towering menaces posed by organizational bureaucracy, government inefficiency, and "power" in the hands of organizations and individuals. He'd de-cided to stand up to the systems he despised.

In Cambridge, he found projects to protect his days from what he perceived as a great enemy: stagnancy. "What was so striking about Aaron is that he always wanted to solve the harder problem, not just to find some issue-specific workaround, but to understand how whatever system he was thinking about worked, and then to understand how to make it work better, however unusual such changes might be," said writer Clay Shirky. Swartz read widely and strove to spend his time on things that mattered. There was, for one, bringing public access to information—some of which was in the public domain, which meant it was ostensibly owned by the cit-izens. These were government files and court documents that were now available online but were stored behind paywalls and within systems architected in the 1990s. They were workable for journal-ists and interested companies, but the interfaces were clunky, which meant accessing many of their records was cumbersome for average citizens—who should be able both to act as journalists and to lo-cate their own information—to reach.

Some of Swartz's idols were already on the case. Brewster Kahle of the Internet Archive was interested in "freeing" information, particularly government court cases. Carl Malamud, a freedom-of-information advocate Swartz had admired since his teenage years, had founded a nonprofit group called Public.Resource.Org. In 2008 Malamud put out a call for hackers and librarians to help him liberate an out-of-date and cumbersome public records system called Public Access to Court Electronic Records (PACER). Swartz, then twenty-two, raised his hand.

PACER typically charged citizens 8 cents per page of records they wanted to access, in order to refund courts the cost of upload-ing and storing the documents. But PACER had run a surplus of $150 million and had recently begun a trial program to offer its records up for free at seventeen major libraries around the country, which was where Malamud imagined the downloads by an army of freelance information warriors could take place.

Swartz emailed Malamud that he estimated he'd be able to capture four terabytes' worth of PACER records. Malamud emailed him back, "We're going to have fun with this," and noted that Swartz's contribution would "definitely make the point." Swartz replied, "awesome. :-)."

In a Chicago library, Swartz mass-downloaded more than twenty million pages from PACER, using a script that taxed and then crashed PACER. The entire PACER library program was put on emergency suspension. The act was brazen, even for Malamud, who told Swartz, "You definitely went over the line." A government official told librarians that federal agents were conducting an investigation into the download.

To Swartz, this was all in the name of good—albeit super-niche—activism. Malamud, who had plentiful ties to courts, was protective of Swartz and urged the young man to stay anonymous. But Swartz, rarely publicity-shy, posed for a photo for the *New York Times* in a story about the massive PACER download.

(• •)

By 2009, the Federal Bureau of Investigation had opened a file on Aaron Hillel Swartz. It noted that two Amazon IP addresses used in the mass download of PACER documents had belonged to Swartz. The bureau had searched for wage reports for him for the year and found none. Vehicular reports: none. Criminal record: none. It had located his Social Security number, and his parents' address in Highland Park. In February, the FBI directed the North Chicago Resident Agency to surveil Swartz's parents' home, but when it did, it found their house on a heavily wooded dead-end street without other cars parked—and decided staking it out would be impossible; they'd be too easily detected.

The FBI, before long, also took note of Swartz's own blog, on which he'd written about the bureau. He had flippantly admitted knowledge of the investigation. A post by Swartz seemed to mock online dating conventions, asking potential candidates for a mate, "Want to meet the man behind the headlines? Want to have the F.B.I. open up a file on you as well?" (Swartz and his parents by this time had received phone calls from the bureau, and had referred them to an attorney.)

Swartz did not meet with federal agents, who seemed to have determined little about his and Malamud's motives. The file was closed on April 20, 2009.

Perhaps a bit rattled by his brush with law enforcement, Swartz turned to more mainstream activism. He embarked upon online campaigns to oppose proposed legislation that could limit the distribution of copyrighted works online. He mobilized opposition to CISPA (the Cyber Intelligence Sharing and Protection Act), SOPA, and PIPA, the same bills that Reddit would rally against and over which it would go dark in protest. In addition to his political action group, the Progressive Change Campaign Committee, he worked on a Democratic congressional campaign in Rhode Island. He was something of an activist and something of a freelance idealist, juggling multiple projects in nonprofits and politics.

Still appealing to Swartz, though, were projects related to what he saw as "freeing" valuable information. What he'd discovered in Eremo hadn't drifted far from his mind—nor from his long mental list of ills in the world that required fixing. He had set up a website, GuerillaOpenAccess.com, which hosted his writing from Eremo, and which linked to another site, the Content Liberation Front. There, individuals were encouraged to upload copies of any academic journal articles from sites such as JSTOR, which stands for "journal storage," to the Internet Archive, or to work toward "liberating entire journal archives from these sites and uploading them," or to send databases to an address in Cambridge, Massachusetts, Schwarz's home.

In September 2010, Swartz flew to Budapest to speak at the Google-sponsored Internet at Liberty conference. He lectured on

Born in November 1983 in Lansing, Michigan, Steve Huffman grew up in Warrenton, Virginia, outside of Washington, D.C., where he and his sister were raised mostly by his mom and stepdad. He was a serious, studious kid, who by high school seemed to excel at everything he attempted. He was student body president, editor of the school's literary magazine, and Athlete of the Year. *Courtesy of Jeanette Irby.*

Alexis Ohanian was born in April 1983, in New York City. After a few years in Brooklyn and Queens, the Ohanian family moved to Columbia, Maryland. Ohanian was an athletic, social kid with a big heart and a mischievous streak. He's pictured with his mother, Anke, a German immigrant. *Courtesy of Chris Ohanian.*

Ohanian and Huffman met their freshman year at the University of Virginia, bonding over video games such as *Gran Turismo.* Four years later, they had an idea for a startup. They were accepted into a summer program that soon would become known as Y Combinator. Over three months, they set out to build "the front page of the Internet." *Courtesy of Jessica Livingston.*

Y Combinator began in June 2005. Eight groups of young men received a $6,000-per-person stipend for the summer. The group, overseen by Paul Graham (far right) and Jessica Livingston (far left), brought together several soon-to-be well-known tech figures, including Huffman and Ohanian (third and fourth from left), Chris Slowe (fifth from left), Justin Kan (front seated), Aaron Swartz (immediately behind him), and Sam Altman (arms crossed). *Courtesy of Kate Courteau.*

After Y Combinator ended, Aaron Swartz's company, Infogami, merged with Reddit. Swartz moved into the apartment Huffman, Ohanian, and Slowe, the Harvard graduate student who'd become Reddit's first employee, shared on Washington Street in Somerville, Massachusetts, carving himself a temporary sleeping nook inside a kitchen cupboard. *Courtesy of Alexis Ohanian.*

By early 2006, Reddit was being courted by Condé Nast, and the small team (from left, Ohanian, Slowe, Huffman, and Swartz) visited the office of *Wired* magazine in San Francisco. After meeting with executives there, they climbed Coit Tower and drove across the Golden Gate Bridge. *Courtesy of Chris Slowe.*

The acquisition was finalized on October 31, 2006. Reddit became part of Condé Nast, and Huffman, Ohanian, and Swartz became millionaires. The three young men, plus Slowe, invited friends to a celebratory Halloween dinner, followed by drinks at a Cambridge dive called Hong Kong. Huffman and Slowe threw together costumes at the last minute; Ohanian wore his trusty Jack Sparrow costume. *Courtesy of Kristen Slowe.*

Swartz refused to dress up for the evening, telling anyone who asked that he was dressed as "a conformist" or "a dot-com millionaire." *Courtesy of Chris Slowe.*

When Ohanian, Huffman, and Slowe attended the rehearsal dinner for Paul Graham and Jessica Livingston's wedding in 2008, they wore polo shirts and khaki shorts—the same outfit Graham wore daily. *Courtesy of Kristen Slowe.*

Hundreds of thousands of people gathered on the National Mall in Washington, D.C., on October 30, 2010, for Jon Stewart and Stephen Colbert's Rally to Restore Sanity and/or Fear. The event, in part conceived of and promoted on Reddit, was billed as an antidote to the ugly political mood dividing the United States in the run-up to the 2010 mid-term elections. *Kimihiro Hoshino/ AFP/Getty Images.*

Reddit's mascot, Snoo the alien, made abundant appearances at the rally. Reddit staffers were floored by encountering so many Reddit users in person. "To see Reddit manifested like that was really impressive," Ohanian said. *Courtesy of Antonio Zugaldia, via Creative Commons.*

After the rally, attendees dispersed to several Reddit-organized afterparties. At One Lounge in Dupont Circle, the Reddit crew—including community manager Erik Martin, community intern Alex Angel, programmer Neil Williams, systems administrator Jeremy Edberg, and cofounder Huffman—mingled with Redditors. *Courtesy of AlfredoFloresPhotography.com.*

Ohanian left Reddit in 2009 and devoted himself to investing, speaking, and political activism. In 2011, he became a prominent spokesperson against proposed anti-piracy legislation known as SOPA and PIPA. In this never-before-published image from January 17, 2012, Ohanian speaks at a rally in New York City, wearing his father's red tie. Aaron Swartz, who was pursuing his own activism, watches from a few feet away. This was the last time the two men saw each other. *Photograph by Phillip Stearns.*

Erik Martin, Reddit's New York City–based community manager, was promoted to general manager of the site in 2011. He and some of his teammates moved to San Francisco to work out of the *Wired* office. He's pictured, at right, with Ben Huh, founder of the Cheezburger Network. *Courtesy of Victoria Taylor.*

In 2011, executives at Advance Publications decided to spin Reddit off as its own entity, allowing it to take outside investment and act more like a fast-growing startup. Alexis Ohanian would join a new board of directors, and Facebook veteran Yishan Wong would be hired as chief executive. *Courtesy of Yishan Wong.*

Wong raised funding for Reddit and grew its teams both in San Francisco and New York, where it hired Victoria Taylor (center) to manage the site's most public-facing aspect: question-and-answer sessions with notable individuals. Here, Taylor poses with r/IAmA subjects *The X-Files* stars Gillian Anderson and David Duchovny. *Courtesy of Victoria Taylor.*

eddit's traffic continued to grow rapidly fter it was spun out from Condé Nast— it claimed 731 million unique visitors in 2013. At a staff gathering on January 29, 2014, Victoria Taylor (center) posed with Josh Wardle (second from right), ho designed many of the site's notorious April Fools' Day projects. The site's ormer chief architect, Jeremy Edberg, is at back. *Courtesy of Victoria Taylor.*

After Wong's dramatic exit from Reddit, Ellen Pao was named interim chief executive. During her tenure, she made moves to cut down on-site harassment, and endured a trial resulting from her lawsuit alleging gender discrimination and sexual harassment at venture capital firm Kleiner Perkins Caufield & Byers. *Photograph by Jason Henry.*

Shortly after leaving Reddit in 2009, Huffman began work on a new startup, a travel-search site called Hipmunk, with cofounder Adam Goldstein (left). The pair found some success, raising more than $40 million in venture capital. Still, Reddit was never far from Huffman's mind. *Courtesy of Hipmunk, Inc.*

To celebrate Reddit's tenth anniversary, staff gathered at a gallery and event space in San Francisco's SoMa neighborhood. Former employees, such as Chris Slowe, David King, Jeremy Edberg, and Mike Schiraldi (front row, left to right), showed up, to the surprise of several current staffers. So did Ohanian, who was now chairman of the board. When Steve Huffman walked in, heads turned. *Courtesy of Kristen Slowe.*

Ellen Pao resigned from Reddit after eight months, after a revolt led by moderators. Alexis Ohanian (left) might have seemed an obvious choice to step in. Steve Huffman was still building Hipmunk, but a subtle campaign to persuade him to return had been underway for years. *Courtesy of Garry Tan.*

Huffman was in Sonoma celebrating a friend's birthday during the revolt. He didn't want to leave Hipmunk, but once he got on the phone with an executive from Condé Nast, he said: "I'll get it done." Huffman returned to Reddit as chief executive on July 10, 2015. *Courtesy of Reddit. Photograph by Lei Gong.*

Just weeks after Huffman returned as CEO of Reddit, the company invited select reporters and photographers to its office, to tell the executive comeback story. Huffman appeared on the covers of magazines, including *New York* magazine, which asked "Can Steve Huffman Save Reddit From Itself?" *Photograph by Jake Stangel.*

Under Huffman's leadership, Reddit continued its climb from geeky obscurity to the fourth most popular website in the United States, a distinction it attained in 2017. Huffman and Ohanian were finally back together, sometimes working side by side. *Photograph by Jason Henry.*

After Huffman returned to Reddit, he convinced Slowe (pictured with wife Kristen), Reddit's first employee, to rejoin the company, too. In 2016, Huffman gave him a broad mandate: "Go do stuff, Chris." As Reddit's staff doubled in size that year, Slowe was promoted to chief technology officer. *Courtesy of Kevin Warnock.*

Ohanian met tennis great Serena Williams in May 2015 while in Rome at a media conference. Williams announced their engagement (on Reddit, naturally)—and gave birth to their daughter, Alexis Olympia Ohanian, in September 2017. They married two months later in New Orleans. *Courtesy of Alexis Ohanian. Photograph by Mel Barlow and Allan Zepeda.*

Before the ceremony, Ohanian and his groomsmen gathered in the second-floor living room of an old Victorian home in New Orleans. When Ohanian fumbled to secure his bow tie, Huffman stepped up to help. After his wedding, this was the first photograph Ohanian posted on social media. *Courtesy of Alexis Ohanian. Photograph by Mel Barlow and Allan Zepeda.*

enforcing ethics and accountability of those in power, corporations and the government, and about the importance of online free expression. At the end of the day, he dined with some activists who'd obtained funding from progressive-minded billionaire philanthropist George Soros to open up JSTOR documents to the public.

JSTOR had become a flashpoint in the copyright-activism zeitgeist. Just three months earlier, an article in openDemocracy dubbed it "problematic" that JSTOR was off-limits to people who could benefit from its rich trove of humanities research. At dinner, the activists bemoaned that the money it would take to make meaningful change in access was far more than they could obtain, even from Soros. The conference ended on September 22.

Swartz moved swiftly once back in Cambridge. Within three days, he had purchased a new Acer computer and hardwired it to a Massachusetts Institute of Technology network. Using a guest-access account "GHost," to which he attached the name Gary Host, he employed a computer program to initiate download sessions of the JSTOR database at a rapid clip. This was called "scraping." It violated JSTOR's terms of service and threatened to topple the stability of the whole system's servers, which were located seven hundred miles away in Ann Arbor, Michigan.

As Swartz saw it, he had begun the liberation of JSTOR. As the library database saw it, a guest user within MIT was methodically stealing its protected works. Within months, police were video monitoring MIT's Building 16 computer science area. The feed revealed a slight young man with a long mop of shiny brown hair repeatedly entering a telephone-and-computer-network closet called 16-004t. Investigators discovered that the man had set up a laptop under a cardboard box. Over several weeks, it downloaded some two million JSTOR articles—one hundred times more than all other JSTOR users during that time. The value of the downloaded content was intangible, and difficult to prescribe a dollar amount to, but in the midst of the ordeal, MIT estimated to police that a chunk of it was worth $50,000.

At about 3:30 p.m. on January 4, 2011, police spotted the man tinkering in room 16-004t for several minutes. He removed a hard drive from his bag and appeared to bend down to the laptop, which officers from the Cambridge police, Boston police, and Secret Service had responded to that very morning and had left in place. It had been processed for "latent prints." The man was gone moments later.

Just after noon two days later, the man appeared again. By that time, Swartz had logged in at MIT through many IP addresses, in a months-long dance with JSTOR, which repeatedly banned MIT addresses from its services. Now, though, Swartz had multiple devices doing the scraping; Grace Host, a Mac, had joined Gary Host, the Acer. Both ran a script he'd written in Python, called keepgrabbing.py.

When Swartz entered 16-004t on January 6, at 12:32 p.m., MIT police captain Jay Perault was watching the live feed from the camera set up inside the closet. Perault saw the young hacker cover his face with his bike helmet—perhaps to shield himself from the camera or nearby MIT employees—and pack his bag before turning off the light and ducking out. He seemed to have packed up items—Perault noted that he seemed to have taken the laptop. MIT officers had been dispatched to the area, but when they arrived, Swartz had vanished.

Minutes later, MIT police captain Albert Pierce was driving down Vassar Street when he spotted a young man on a bike who resembled the suspect. Pierce did a U-turn and rolled his unmarked car up to Swartz, who stopped. Swartz was abrasive, even upon being shown Pierce's badge. He muttered that he didn't talk to strangers and remarked that Pierce's colleagues weren't "real cops."

Swartz pivoted away, swinging his leg over his bicycle. He paused, hoping the interaction was over. It was not. Swartz zagged his bike off the street and threw it down. Then he ran.

Pierce chased Swartz on foot toward Central Square. By this time, Michael Pickett, the Secret Service agent already on the MIT JSTOR hacking case, had spotted Swartz fleeing. He and another local officer joined the pursuit.

Swartz, running up Massachusetts Avenue, was now being tailed by Pierce, who'd returned to his car. Years ago, Swartz had practiced running these streets on nighttime sprints when he couldn't sleep. He'd run through Cambridge back in 2007, when police went searching for him after he'd posted what was widely read as a suicide note. Now he was trying to change the world—and here he was, again, fleeing a siren. This time he ran toward home, where he knew the police could probably just break down his door anyway. But maybe his sprint would buy enough time on foot to pick up his other devices.

Swartz did not make it home. He was arrested on Lee Street, a residential lane about a mile from MIT and a few blocks from his apartment. It was clear to the officers that they'd located the man on the video; this man had with him a thumb drive that contained the script keepgrabbing.py. Swartz was charged with two state counts of breaking and entering during the daytime with intent to commit a felony.

(• •)

Breaking and entering would be the cleanest of the charges piled on Swartz over the following year, all stemming from the late 2010 and early 2011 download of more than four million academic journal documents from JSTOR. In July 2011, a federal grand jury indicted Swartz for wire fraud, computer fraud, and for recklessly damaging a protected computer. By September 2012, another nine felony counts were added. Local charges were piled on, too, but were dismissed. Ultimately he was charged with two counts of wire fraud and eleven violations of the Computer Fraud and Abuse Act.

When the federal charges were unsealed in July 2011, the *New York Times* dubbed Swartz—who'd taken a job with one of his mentors, Lawrence Lessig, as a fellow in the Edmond J. Safra Center for Ethics at Harvard University—a "folk hero" and a "respected Harvard researcher." The press was largely loving toward Swartz, the former teenage prodigy, a member of the Internet elite, the crusader for open access online. His friends and allies made glowing statements to journalists, and reiterated, as did his friend David Segal, the director of Demand Progress, that arresting Swartz after the indictment "makes no sense."

MIT Media Lab's director, Joi Ito, petitioned the university to have Swartz's case considered a "family matter," and to remember that MIT's policy was that anyone on campus could log into JSTOR or other library databases freely and easily. But the measure of indifference with which MIT had treated the entire endeavor of Swartz to this point, and its general culture of permissiveness toward technical pranks and pursuits, mattered little to U.S. attorney Carmen Ortiz. She persisted doggedly in making the case against Swartz and held it up as an example to hackers everywhere: "Stealing is stealing, whether you are using a computer command or a crowbar."

To the U.S. Attorney's office, this was big-time—taking down a major hacker. The Secret Service searched Swartz's Cambridge apartment on February 11, 2011. After agents observed Swartz—who'd seemed calm—walk out of the apartment building, and then break into a sprint on the street, they followed him to his office at Harvard and searched that as well. They seized as evidence all his devices, including an iMac, three iPods, and three cell phones, including one that agents found buried in Swartz's living room closet: his old Sidekick, with which he had spent so many afternoons curled up on the Washington Street apartment couch and which had accompanied him when he slept in the cupboard. They kept it as evidence, moving it between the Boston Field Office vault and a lab, and eventually assessed it as having zero monetary value. Courts subpoenaed his friends. Investigators searched for a motive, and fixated on Swartz's writing from years prior, particularly his Guerilla Open Access Manifesto, with its aggressive title and frank advocacy for the sort of illegal activity in which he'd subsequently partaken.

It was right there, clear as sunlight online, along with all of Swartz's rambling blog posts, allegories, and news updates. It was a direct call to action, a manifesto in which he declared himself opposed to following "unjust laws," and in which he issued the plea to liberate information from its legal home and redistribute it.

The charges against Swartz carried a maximum fifty-year imprisonment and $1 million fine.

(• •)

Swartz regarded himself as extraordinarily different from other humans. It's a not uncommon worldview, especially for a man in his early twenties, for whom life had been so fortunate that he was accustomed to being revered. He'd long had trouble interacting with people from other walks of life, especially those in service professions. In part it was a disdain for imposing upon others with quotidian requests—such as the glass of water when extremely thirsty while on an airplane. But privilege, too, was part of the unnavigable rift between Swartz and others. "Most people, it seems, stretch the truth to make themselves seem more impressive. I, it seems, stretch the truth to make myself look worse," he'd written back in 2005.

He'd been long isolated from others due to his temperament's strange cauldron of humility and high self-regard; isolating, too, were his illnesses, and his sheer intellect. During the course of the investigation into his downloading actions, on his blog, the world's long-standing window into the mind of Aaron Swartz, he went silent. Harvard suspended his fellowship and banned him from campus. He stepped down from his position at Demand Progress, and ended a romantic relationship with journalist Quinn Norton. He grew further isolated, and lived in fear of another sudden arrest.

The adult world had come upon Swartz. He knew he would not be forgiven after performing with a smile that exposed his fleshy, cherubic cheeks, as he had so many times before. His malfunctioning digestive system was not easily blamed.

As months passed and the threat of trial continued to loom, the press remained sympathetic. In the intellectualized worldview shared by Swartz and some of his free-information activist cohorts, the question was not "Did Swartz commit a crime?" but rather "Why was it necessary for Aaron Swartz to be labeled a felon?" Swartz read and posted a review of Kafka's *The Trial*. The whole thing, for a time, seemed like a bad dream—both to those close to Swartz and to those reading the news. Like it might just vanish at any moment or be closed, as had been his last FBI file. As had most consequences he potentially faced earlier in his life. He told almost no one about his arrest. To his new girlfriend, Taren Stinebrickner-Kauffman, he simply called the whole matter of the federal charges "the bad thing."

After some months, he was able to throw himself into new political work. He worked on writing software that incorporated computer learning to aid in political organizing. He worked on drug policy and addiction research. He prepared to revive a government watchdog website he'd once set up. His personal life, too, shifted and gradually seemed to improve; he'd moved to New York, and in with Stinebrickner-Kauffman, to a nice, new-construction apartment in Brooklyn's rapidly gentrifying Crown Heights neighborhood.

Swartz switched lawyers, and defense strategies, but the expenses of preparing for trial had bled his personal wealth, plenty from the sale of Reddit, almost dry. Money was a stress, and the strategy for the trial another huge strain. He spent a lot of time debating with himself over taking a plea deal. Prosecutors had offered him a possibility of doing half a year in a low-security prison if he pleaded guilty to thirteen of the federal crimes. It would avoid the trial. Swartz, via his attorney, declined. For New Year's, to ring out 2012 and in 2013, he went to Vermont with Stinebrickner-Kauffman, in an attempt to forget his misery. Instead, he got the flu. He asked his girlfriend, "Am I always going to feel like this?"

(• •)

Back in Brooklyn on January 11, 2013, Swartz was still sapped of energy, and stayed home while Stinebrickner-Kauffman went to work. She'd hoped that day they'd grab dinner with friends in the evening, but wasn't able to reach Swartz for hours. She headed home after work to their small but pristine shared apartment. She'd hoped Swartz would be feeling better.

Walking in, Stinebrickner-Kauffman saw Swartz hanging from a window, a belt cinched around his neck. His body was cold.

(• •)

The suicide of Aaron Swartz became a global news story within a day. Websites popped up to eulogize the brilliant young programmer who'd always been willing to stand up for his beliefs. He was a hacker with a heart—a man who'd sought to change the world, and who'd actually made a dent in the free flow of information online, starting at age fourteen, when he'd helped create the framework for RSS. He'd been the impetus behind rewriting Reddit into the programming language Python. Now he was dead, at age twenty-six.

On Reddit on January 12, the top post was a photo posted by Erik Martin, titled simply "AaronSW," Swartz's Reddit username. It was a sharp portrait, taken by Jacob Appelbaum, a hacker, security researcher, and friend of Swartz. In the image, Swartz's face is scruffy, but his brown eyes clear. He's closed-lipped, smiling warmly, in a dark hoodie. Appelbaum later posted on Twitter, "I'm pretty upset but so is the entire internet—@aaronsw touched a lot of people. It isn't wrong to say how we will all personally miss him."

Around the world, on newsstands and screens, press articles detailed (through accounts from Swartz's friends, lawyers, and mentors) the debilitating stress he had suffered while under federal investigation, and the terrible threats of outsized punishments wielded by prosecutors against this young, good-hearted man who'd caused little harm. With the federal trial having loomed over him, writers didn't have to grapple to draw out a motive for Swartz's action. Few mentioned his ongoing struggles with depression and illness. Instead they pondered: Was the government overzealous in pursuing him?

At his funeral the following Tuesday, Aaron Swartz's father was unambiguous. In a steely voice, Robert Swartz told the mourners at the packed sanctuary of Highland Park's Central Avenue Synagogue, "Aaron did not commit suicide, but was killed by the government." Said Stinebrickner-Kauffman a week later, "Aaron's death should radicalize us." She chided the government for denying Swartz his constitutional right to a speedy trial. He died because a prosecutor and a U.S. attorney, who had immense individual power over his life, "were more interested in making a high-profile example out of Aaron than in justice or in mercy."

Eulogies by academics and friends at Swartz's funeral and at a massive memorial service hosted by the Internet Archive in San Francisco on January 24 channeled some of Swartz's own energies. They portrayed him as a provocative, brilliant young man who sought nothing more than to make this world a better place. They called for action at turns, and wallowed in sadness at others. Tim Berners-Lee, the computer scientist best known for creating the World Wide Web, posted on Twitter, "World wanderers, we have lost a wise elder. Hackers for right, we are one down. Parents all, we have lost a child. Let us weep."

Neither Huffman nor Ohanian attended either the funeral or the memorial. They mourned privately: Ohanian at the loss of another human passionate about ideas dear to his heart, Huffman at a man who'd been his best friend and closest confidant for the greater part of a very formative year. Swartz's early involvement in Reddit was one of the many gold-plated items he'd left on his résumé, and in legend, too. Swartz had often called himself a cofounder of Reddit—and there were the ephemeral strands of influence he'd weaved into the early code, and his posts in the days of enthusiasm after Swartz's Infogami joined Reddit to form Not A Bug, Inc. Beyond his tangible contributions to the site's code and content, there was something intangible—something perhaps greater—to the spirit of the untamed hacker, the young man alone, bubbling with provocative thoughts and code, that rang true at least as an aspiration to so many Redditors. The ethos of open information, of hacking for good, of kicking dirt at the establishment, was undeniably contained within Reddit. Swartz was Reddit's id.

In the wake of his death, Swartz was transformed from a niche activist into a modern-day martyr to coders and tech employees chafing within their cubicle farms, a fallen hero to all those who felt disconnected from the seemingly arbitrary moves of government restricting their freedoms—or snooping in their business—online. To those who wish they could do more to foster equality of education, of access to information, he became a hero. Mention of the name Aaron Swartz became a rallying cry against government overreach in prosecution, against Internet regulations, against the surveillance state, and in favor of reforming computer-crime laws.

Many posthumous awards and a few poignant acts of cultural dissent followed. When Anonymous hacked the State Department website on February 17, 2013, they declared, "Aaron Swartz this is for you." Anonymous also hacked MIT's website, and part of the U.S. judicial system's web presences, all in Swartz's honor.

Within days of his death, a memorial appeared in the industrial-hip neighborhood of Greenpoint, Brooklyn. On the side of a building above a bodega emerged a black-and-white graffiti portrait of Swartz, smiling slyly, gazing into the distance. Beside the image were words, painted in black, in a typeface that reads as early MS-DOS, but was really an iconic font created in 1970 and popularized by mostly science-fiction book titles. It was a poor approximation, but to casual viewers it gave a distinctly digital vibe, and perhaps was a sneaky reference to the never-realized better world we'd all, decades ago, imagined computers might bring. The words read "RIP AARON SWARTZ."

PART IV

PART IV

OMNISCIENT GUARDIANS OF THE DEPTHS

Every weekday morning, Michael Brutsch said goodbye to his wife at their home in suburban Dallas and made his way to the offices of First Cash Financial Services, a large, publicly held company that operates payday lenders and hundreds of pawnshops.

Brutsch was a programmer and application developer; he managed the systems that moved money around for the company, and the digital infrastructure for keeping hundreds of pawnshops compliant with federal regulations when they dealt with firearms.

Brutsch's family depended on his work, particularly his wife, whose diabetes and fibromyalgia made his work-provided medical insurance highly valuable for them. It was a good job, which Brutsch had held since 2004 after a string of positions that barely lasted a year each. It could be difficult to find another; he wasn't traditionally educated. What he hadn't taught himself about systems administration and programming he picked up in the Air Force in the early 1980s, back when the military machines interfaced with ARPANET.

To his neighbors, Brutsch likely appeared to be an upstanding member of the community. Online, he was something else entirely: one of the most notorious trolls the Internet had ever known.

In the evening, Brutsch would drive home and relax, watch some TV, and sit with his computer, often on his bed, with his wife sprawled out next to him with her own laptop. She would scroll through Reddit, posting or commenting on adorable photos of cats—they both loved cats—or sometimes images of fairies or dolphins, or checking in on the fibromyalgia subreddit, which she'd created (its tagline: "A pain in the everywhere"). He would log in, too. Behind his username, Violentacrez, Brutsch would check in on the array of subreddits he moderated.

There were occasionally new posts on r/incest and r/rapebait that needed to be deleted for potentially qualifying as child pornography. He'd hop on IRC and alert any Reddit employees who were still online. On r/jailbait, there was the opposite problem: People sometimes posted images of girls who were definitely older than seventeen. Delete. If he had extra time after doing what amounted to janitorial work in the Internet's sewer system, Brutsch would check in on the mainstream Reddit universe, where he frequented r/movies, r/funny, and moderated r/creepy. Or he would scheme up new subreddits, such as r/ChokeABitch, r/hitler, r/JewMerica, and r/n---erjailbait.

On October 3, 2012, Brutsch was at his desk doing another part of his job as a Reddit moderator: answering questions from a reporter. He did this sort of thing occasionally, and only through his pseudonym, Violentacrez. The interview was conducted over Gmail chat, ostensibly for a profile of him on Gawker. But as the interview with the reporter, Adrian Chen, progressed, Brutsch became suspicious of Chen's motives.

It had come to Chen's attention that Brutsch had been known to attend in-person Reddit meetups where he would introduce himself to others. He wrote to Violentacrez, "It seems like you're not super careful about keeping your identity under wraps, if you meet people in real life. A lot of trolls I've talked to would never do that or give out as many details about themselves as they do."

Violentacrez typed into Gchat: "have you been given my real name?"

In fact, Chen had been chatting with Violentacrez over Gchat in preparation for calling Brutsch. The reporter wanted to match the man's voice to that of Violentacrez, who had been recorded on radio shows, which Chen had listened to in hopes of positively identifying Brutsch. He just had to work up the nerve to pick up the phone and confront the man he'd come to suspect was the mastermind of the darkest, deepest, most disgusting caverns of filth on Reddit.

Chen responded to Brutsch, simply, "yeah."

"That's not good," Brutsch responded.

Chen wasn't fully prepared, but knew what he had to do. He immediately picked up the phone and dialed the work number he'd tracked down for Brutsch. A familiar voice answered—the voice he'd heard identified as Violentacrez on podcasts previously.

It said, "So, are you going to out me?"

(• •)

As Yishan Wong settled in to his new dream job as Reddit CEO, he scheduled an AMA for himself for April 20, 2012. Wong was nervous, but not ill-prepared. He'd been studying how the Reddit community responded to various tones and which subjects had the propensity to turn into minefields. Plus, he was adept at navigating other social sites.

Wong had become a power contributor on the Q&A site Quora, developing a reputation as a Silicon Valley insider who frequently and unceremoniously pulled back the curtain. In response to queries from strangers, he discussed Facebook and other tech companies with a remarkable earnestness. He was blunt, and that read as honest. For instance, when a Quora user asked who ran Mark Zuckerberg's personal Facebook page, Wong, who'd been Facebook's engineering director, wrote simply, "He does."

On the day of his AMA, Wong logged in as u/yishan and saw the questions rolling in. How would he fix Reddit's remarkably slow and ineffective search function? (He wrote he'd work to make it faster and more accurate.) He was asked about improving the site's self-serve ad platform and about making money in general. (Yes, Wong wanted to fix it; no, advertising wasn't the entire solution.)

When asked about revenue, Wong posited that Reddit should be viewed not just as a corporation, and not just as a community. Instead, it was a hybrid of these things: a city-state, an entity with its own legal system and employees and that provided services as would those of a small government. Reddit employees would serve the community of people who dwell there and "form communities and institutions and culture and provide the real character." He continued, "Ultimately, you are beholden to the people who give you money. Thus, I want an arrangement where most of our money comes from redditors." He proposed a hypothetical advertising model wherein ads originate from members of the community.

To a user who asked him about the Reddit "hivemind," Yishan responded that "'managing' the community is kind of like beekeeping." Redditors were like bees—difficult to manage—and the best he could do was create conditions to keep them happy. "Flowers and stuff," he wrote. "But occasionally something will piss off the bees," he continued, and "they will swarm around and sting you. You really can't do anything about it, but also the swarm eventually goes away. And like beekeepers, you just need to be wearing decent protection, or have a thick skin."

All in, Wong was pleased with the AMA. He did not get downvoted into obscurity, nor get eaten alive by snarky commenters, so the community, the city-state, the beehive—whatever it was—seemed to *like* him well enough.

He was already proud of the bigger picture he'd helped set in motion for Reddit's future. At the tail end of Reddit's departure from Condé Nast, Wong helped negotiate a recapitalization for Reddit, which would give it, by some estimates, an ample $20 million to operate going forward. In the office, he hypothesized to employees about taking on additional strategic investment from advisers who'd help steer the company. He also imagined using a tool employed by the heavy hitters of San Francisco to help attract and retain talent: equity. He wanted employees both to feel appreciated and have skin in the game.

But managing details of the recapitalization and new corporate structure was both time-consuming and mind-boggling. Wong saw the corporate structure in terms of Reddit's connection to Condé and Advance Publications as incredibly complex and weird. Setting up the new structure created for him an "enormous amount of stress," and before long he came to know the same tiresome bureaucratic battles that those running Reddit before him had seen.

The hivemind online seemed open to Wong's stewardship, but inside the office he still had a remarkable struggle that hadn't yet turned around from the moment he was hired. The staff was no longer mutinous, but they still harbored skepticism of their new boss.

When it came to uniting and managing an unsympathetic staff, Wong was a novice. He recalled later that he was "not aware of the degree of dysfunction on the team," noting that over time this became a "huge problem." The team was young, most in their twenties, and in love with the idea of what they'd already been working on. They were not just reluctant to change; they were putting up walls.

(• •)

To Reddit's staff, change was not just scary; it was almost inconceivable. The five full-time employees and several contractors had been largely in control of their own, and Reddit's, destiny. Under Condé's light-touch management, they'd managed to serve up more than a billion page views a month. They had their own metaphor for Reddit's community—an ocean, a vast and untamable realm composed of hundreds of massive and unique ecosystems, of which they were omniscient guardians. It possessed wide swaths of beautiful coral, incredible Technicolor creatures. But it also had dark depths, and deep trenches within those depths, in which terrifying predators lurked, and underneath which plates could shift, and a destructive volcano could spring up.

Each employee had developed in-depth subject-matter knowledge of Reddit's darkest and most problematic trenches, particularly those in the scrappy community team. Marta Gossage specialized in legal matters and became adept at reporting crime and potential suicides to authorities. She'd also been a clever spam fighter, taking down botnet rings that would post and upvote content aimed at directing traffic or making money. She called out publications at which she'd found too many upvotes from one IP address; individuals located in or near the offices of *Forbes* and the *Huffington Post*, she said, were the worst offenders at trying to game Reddit's popularity algorithm to promote their own posts—something Reddit did not allow.

Gossage developed a daily triage routine. After waking up early in her apartment on Manhattan's Upper West Side, she'd spend an hour or more checking in on recently problematic subreddits, such as whatever was bubbling up at the time in the Violentacrez universe, say, r/picsofdeadjailbait, his attempt to outfilth r/jailbait, which was now banned. Next, she'd check the subreddits where moderators lobbed their complaints and questions, such as r/modnews, r/modhelp, and r/modclub. With the worst out of the way, she'd make breakfast and brew a pot of coffee. Then she'd dig into reported messages—private comments users had received and flagged as abusive, offensive, or pornographic. She took to calling this portion of her morning "Dick and Coffee."

The single biggest category of messages Gossage had to review was pictures of penises. There were so many dicks! They were, by and large, sent by men to unsuspecting and unwilling women, some of whom had either previously posted photos of themselves on Reddit or had asked for relationship advice. Gossage would view each reported message and attached image—shooing away her boyfriend if she was working at home—and diplomatically explain to the users who'd sent unsolicited pictures of their genitalia that this was unacceptable. She'd coach them in the basics of online etiquette. Most men were defensive, and she often found herself arguing with repeat offenders, some of whom might send dozens of unique pictures in a single day.

Banning users was a judgment call for the community team. Sometimes it was clear-cut, but when a member of the community team had to make a difficult decision on content or take action based on a user's bizarre behavior, they'd simply call or chat one another for a "sanity check." "We had so few rules for so long," said Alex Angel, who'd stuck with her Reddit internship through graduation and was now living in New York City and working as a community manager at Reddit. "It was manageable and it worked. Only when catastrophic events happen do you reevaluate everything that you stand for."

The most time-consuming subreddits were not necessarily the most noxious ones. What most bedeviled Reddit's small community team was the endless infighting between various subreddits with opposing viewpoints. Another problem: hostility between white and male-centric subreddits (known for veering into misogyny and white supremacy) and the minority groups and women who had to worry about harassment across Reddit. Sexism, both casual and overt, was so rampant across Reddit that a Reddit business manager once told a reporter that she'd recommend women altogether avoid r/gaming, which at the time had 1.5 million subscribers, because it was simply too hostile to women.

In September 2011, a victim of sexual assault posted her story to the women's forum r/TwoXChromosomes, including photos, and Redditors accused her of lying and faking her wounds with makeup. In December, a fifteen-year-old posted a photograph to the atheism subreddit and was met with hundreds of comments about what they wanted to do to various parts of her body, whole comment threads filled with quips about rape and blood and memes pondering child abduction.

By this time, a group of Redditors had launched a section of the site dedicated to chronicling and fighting the types of racist, misogynistic, homophobic, transphobic, and other objectionable content that bubbled up all over: r/ShitRedditSays, or SRS. It was moderated by a uniformly feminist league who dubbed themselves "Archangels." SRS was to be a water cooler for activists, and a place to make fun of straight, able-bodied, white, gender-inflexible men. It also became known as Reddit's "thought police." SRS occupied a strange cranny within Reddit. In many ways, it is hostile to Reddit's prevailing culture. Typically, even the top posts on SRS have a net negative karma; voting is actually discouraged. "Pretend the rest of Reddit is a museum of poop. Don't touch the poop," its rules read.

Naturally, a counterforce arose to attack what they saw as whiny social justice warrior behavior. The most prominent anti-SRS subreddits were named r/antisrs and r/SRSsucks. These forums—loosely antifeminist and strictly pro–free speech—birthed a rapidly expanding universe of affiliated subreddits, including r/SubredditDrama, r/menkampf, and r/subredditcancer, which sought to expose corruption among "social justice warrioposters."

There being no straightforward way to explain the variety of arguments arising from these warring subreddit clusters, using the gender binaries made sense to some. Some dubbed the anti-SRS sites the Himisphere. The original SRS sites it took on were known to some as the Shevil Fempire. The dueling factions may have been confusing in the early 2010s, but after the 2016 election cycle and its aftermath, they're much more recognizable as the seeds of identity-conscious leftists and factions of the alt-right.

In this little battleground, threads devolved so quickly into finger-pointing, hate speech, and doxing, it was hard for the handful of Reddit community managers to keep up. These metastasizing rival forces were noxious and pervasive in their tactics: They engaged in mass attempts to silence or sink rivals by downvoting their points of view (or, conversely, upvoting en masse content they wanted to see rise on their opponents' subreddit). At times they seemed almost entirely dedicated to being Trojan horses within Reddit, invading subreddits they didn't like (which is known on Reddit as "brigading").

Another all too effective tool in each side's arsenal was co-opting tactics, and even vernacular, from 4chan and video-game chat. The resulting vibe was trollish and alienating to outsiders. "Crush the Redditors with your Dildz," one graphic on SRS read. ("Dildz" would be dildos, just the sort of weapon individuals who are fighting men who disparage women imagine their sexist targets would imagine their league of gnarly feminists wielding. Go ahead and read that sentence again.)

Vote brigading was strictly against Reddit's etiquette, but subtle and complex instances snuck by. Battling spam was hard, but fighting users who'd engage in spamlike or harassing behavior on their own was harder—particularly when individuals teamed up. Reddit's handful of community managers had to solve these conundrums while being harassed themselves. For Alex Angel, many days were entirely taken up policing the SRS universe and its opposition. She mostly kept to protocol when issues arose here and elsewhere, trying to message moderators through modmail, the internal Reddit mail system, where she was sometimes known as Alex. Her somewhat feminine Reddit handle, though, may have hurt. She'd frequently step in on problem Reddit threads, asking people to knock off their behavior, and commenters would sometimes note that an admin, u/cupcake1713, was a girl. They doxed her and posted her photos in threads.

Erik Martin, their boss, took on some of the toughest tasks of community management himself. He dealt with grisly content, pictures of violence, corpses, hate-speech-like threats, and sexualized images of minors. When r/MensRights would be labeled a hate group by the Southern Poverty Law Center, or when Reddit would be accused of harboring a child-pornography ring, he'd be the one journalists called, whose name would appear in the press, associated with this stuff. He directly interacted with the most problematic users who created the worst content. He sometimes met them in person and often would bring along Mog, his chocolate brindled pit bull mix, whose name rhymes with "dog."

This small and highly collaborative team formed a united front that, over time, had developed its own coping mechanisms and internal sense of humor in response to dealing with such an array of complaints, bizarre questions, and sporadic threats. This stuff— government subpoenas for private user data, floods of dick pics, instances of child porn—could not be understood by their partners at home. They were isolated together, and began to see themselves as special; each had contributed insurmountably to this delicate, beautiful, and wild ecosystem. It wasn't all dank troughs: These employees had fostered positive communities, witnessed charities bolstered by Redditors' support, seen cancer victims embraced and lifted up by the community. Each employee deeply adored Reddit. At one point, Martin posted, "I love not knowing what Reddit-tomorrow will bring. It's like being in love with someone who has a constantly expanding and mostly beautiful multiple personality disorder."

With all that in mind, Reddit's staff couldn't fathom how someone with Wong's background—the way he was prone to ranting online; the way he'd been entrenched in Facebook's bureaucracy—could ever be the Triton of their raging ocean.

For Wong, this collective everyone-is-hunkered-down-in-battle mode appeared to be an unseemly defensive posture with the broader Reddit community. He diagnosed his new staff as "all smart, good-hearted people, who had been basically subjected to this horrible environment, for years, and therefore traumatized." When chaos erupted on the site, priority number one was not pissing off the far-flung network of volunteer moderators, not causing additional infighting among warring subreddits, not inciting additional harassment of other moderators or of themselves, and, most paramount, not inspiring a mass exodus from the site.

"The day that Digg died" remained a fresh memory; they were uniquely sensitive to the fickle nature of online communities. "They were unwilling to make any changes with the site for fear of the community uprising," Dan McComas said, "and that led to deep stagnation in the company and resistance to any sort of change at all."

Given this raging sea of dysfunction, did Wong have any doubts going into his first chief executive stint? "Yeah, and I probably should have listened to them," he said. "I think one of my biggest mistakes was not exerting my authority more strongly when I had joined. Now I understand why when a new CEO comes in, they often wipe out the entire executive staff and replace it with their own people."

(• •)

As Wong finally settled into the job, an introductory dinner was planned for the entire staff. Even McComas of Reddit Gifts—technically part of Reddit, though he and Jessica Moreno had never quite been treated as part of the team—was invited.

Wong also invited McComas in for a one-on-one meeting. Over the course of it, McComas came to realize that Wong had "no idea we were part of Reddit." Nor did he know that McComas and Moreno were still owed a significant amount of money, which was part of their Reddit Gifts acquisition, being paid out over time. Still, the men kept it copacetic, and McComas explained to Wong that he and Moreno were in the middle of planning their family's move to Utah. To Moreno and McComas, the move was a bittersweet prospect. They loved the Bay Area, and McComas had spent his whole life in or near San Francisco. But Reddit had for the most part treated them like outcasts; what they'd earned from the acquisition was nice, but it wasn't enough to buy a home in or around San Francisco. They'd prepared their young children for the move, to a new home they could actually afford, near their relatives. They'd already packed up their stuff and hired movers.

On the night before they were set to drive the last of their belongings to Salt Lake City, McComas got an email from Wong. It was jarringly formal. Wong explained that Reddit had reviewed their plan, and the company could not afford to pay out the rest of the Reddit Gifts contract. Were they being fired? "All of a sudden, everything was thrown into craziness for me," McComas said. He enlisted help from the best lawyer he knew—his own father—and set off a long chain of debate, with many phases of negotiation, over his contract and the fate of Reddit Gifts. During it, Wong officially proposed that Reddit Gifts relocate to San Francisco.

McComas and Moreno felt more comfortable potentially walking away from more than half a million dollars than moving their family right back to the bay. Wong held the purse strings, but Moreno and McComas still had significant power in the negotiation: Should they walk away, Reddit Gifts could vanish into thin air. So a new, bizarre deal was reached: Reddit Gifts could potentially earn the rest of its acquisition deal, but only if it became profitable. In the meantime, McComas and Moreno would take meager salaries.

In Wong's mind, the money was everything. "Basically I had to take away the earn-out in order to keep us from becoming too unprofitable." He instituted a goals program to incentivize McComas and Moreno to make money, and then receive their rightful earn-out. It was a strange situation, the first of several unorthodox deals he would seek to broker.

McComas and Moreno were permitted to stay in Salt Lake City, and to make a single hire. They moved into the cheapest office McComas could find: a $300-a-month bare-bones space behind a Dunkin' Donuts in Salt Lake City. He and Moreno, an intern, and their new programmer hire, Lesley Brownlee, worked hard. They badly wanted to succeed. Days, evenings, anytime they were in the office they heard staticky voices through the drive-through speaker tallying change for orders of Boston Kremes, Munchkins, and iced coffees.

(• •)

On October 12, 2012, at 4 p.m., Adrian Chen's powerful exposé of u/Violentacrez, the man who had created or moderated more than five hundred of the vilest forums on Reddit, went live. Gawker's "Unmasking Reddit's Violentacrez, the Biggest Troll on the Web" revealed a forty-nine-year-old Texas man named Michael Brutsch as a prolific Redditor who specialized in keeping racism, violence, gore, porn, and an entire universe of sexual abominations turning on Reddit.

At the time of the article's publication, Brutsch's latest significant project had been r/CreepShots, where individuals contributed and upvoted surreptitiously snapped photos of women, primarily close-ups of asses in tight pants. Brutsch had been enlisted to help run the community after it erupted in controversy when a teacher in Georgia was fired for allegedly posting photos of his students.

Despite all the horrific content on his subreddit, Brutsch had a reputation as an effective moderator. For all the controversy and headaches he caused Reddit, he'd been in touch with Reddit staffers for years, sometimes alerting them to illegal content concerns, clueing them in to budding controversies, and generally keeping them abreast of the latest from his sprawling evil kingdom. Better the devil you know, thought Reddit employees. Multiple employees have referred to him casually as a "nice guy." Chris Slowe, who'd already left Reddit, but who dealt with Violentacrez during his tenure, had said, "We just stayed out of there and let him do his thing and we knew at least he was getting rid of a lot of stuff that wasn't particularly legal. I know I didn't want it to be my job."

Back in August, Violentacrez had attempted to explain his trolling philosophy to the Daily Dot, a web publication that covers Internet culture. "I think it's interesting how many people defend my right to act the way I do," he said, still hiding behind his screen name, "while decrying my posts themselves." He was a ringmaster, pitting Reddit's do-gooding outrage machine and its unbending free-speech value system against each other. Sitting alone at his computer, it allowed him to marvel, "People take things way too seriously around here." For this sort of spouting, u/Violentacrez had become a legend and a leader to other moderators of a certain stripe. He was a cult hero pushing the limits of what's legal to publish, and simultaneously the most public, notorious troll the Internet had ever known.

Now his actual human identity, Michael Brutsch, was out there in the world, tied forever to his despicable behavior as Violentacrez. Behind that screen name was a suburban cubicle-dweller, a husband of a woman whose health was dependent on his insurance, a dad. His boss called him the Saturday morning after the article posted to fire him. Brutsch posted via his "clean" Reddit handle, u/mbrutsch, "Well, I had already told my boss about the impending article last week. He thought I was exaggerating the potential fallout. So when he called Saturday morning, I just said, 'Told you so.'"

Chen's article was an immediate hit online, garnering twenty thousand page views in minutes. The hivemind of Reddit was absolutely outraged. The one thing it held dear was, "Don't post personal information," ever. "No doxing" was one of just five rules Reddit staffers vehemently upheld and communities were expected to follow (the others were: no attempting to game the algorithm, no spam, no breaking or interfering with the function of the site, and no child porn). The Gawker article was doxing in the extreme—never mind that the rest of the world, which included investigative journalism, didn't adhere to the same rules as did Redditors. Within thirty minutes, the link to the Gawker story was banned from being disseminated on Reddit.

Not that the article's publication was a surprise, at least on Reddit. It had been a full nine days since Chen, the reporter, had called Michael Brutsch at his desk. The pair had continued communicating, and Brutsch had grown increasingly petrified of the potential fallout. He told Chen he wasn't concerned about his family finding out—heck, they knew. His wife went by the moniker not_so_violentacrez, and his son even completed an AMA under the handle Spawn_of_VA. But he had a mortgage, his wife had a disability, and he believed the doxing would cause him to be fired. It also could cause the trolls to come after his real name.

In desperation, Brutsch offered to shutter his account, to shut down the offensive forums. He offered to be Chen's "sockpuppet" on Reddit—whatever that means. "I'm like the spy who's found out," he told Chen. "I'll do anything. If you want me to stop posting, delete whatever I posted, whatever. I am at your mercy because I really can't think of anything worse that could possibly happen."

Brutsch deleted his Violentacrez account that week, leading to widespread speculation about what was going on. The following day, chat logs leaked, and soon word circulated within Reddit about Chen's forthcoming story. A moderator, u/POTATO_IN_MY_ANUS, who claimed to communicate with Violentacrez, posted in r/Subreddit-Drama that Chen was attempting to dox Violentacrez, with evidence as to his reaching out to other mods. He took the opportunity to call Chen a "scummy journalist who really, really hates Reddit," and to speculate that it was a senior Reddit employee who gave Brutsch's contact information or identity to Chen.

Among Reddit moderators, a "Ban Gawker" campaign began to bubble up, complete with a dedicated forum, r/BanGawker. By the time Chen's exposé of Brutsch was posted on Gawker, all Gawker links were being banned throughout portions of Reddit, including the popular r/politics. A moderator of the forum wrote, "As moderators, we feel that this type of behavior is completely intolerable. We volunteer our time on Reddit to make it a better place for the users, and should not be harassed and threatened for that." Amid the debate, which drew in every Reddit employee, a prominent moderator got to the core problem for Reddit: "Without assurances of anonymity, I have very little motivation to put in the many hours I spend moderating." Martin responded to him, saying, "This is a unique case we have not encountered before." Another user replied, "It's not an unpredictable case."

Reddit's staffers had also, briefly, enforced a site-wide ban of Chen's story, which they justified by reasoning that its content violated the site's strict "no doxing" rule. What Reddit saw as doxing, the rest of the world saw as investigative journalism. And what Reddit saw as enforcing law, the rest of the world saw as blatant censorship.

Within a day, the site-wide ban was called off. Martin began apologizing in the press. Wong posted a long-winded explainer of the situation in a private subreddit for moderators, writing that Reddit came down against the ban for three reasons. One, it wouldn't stop off-site doxing. Two, it wouldn't hurt Gawker anyway. Three: the Streisand effect. "It would definitely raise the profile of the issue with the general public, and result in headlines like 'gawker exposes creepster; reddit engages in personal vendetta to defend pedophile,'" he wrote.

This did not end the controversy, as Gawker continued to follow the story and tech blogs and major newspapers followed suit, many after having interviewed Erik Martin, who stuck steadfastly to his this-is-a-tricky-free-speech-issue sentiment. Martin also defended the moderators who banned the articles. "They're constantly under attack from people who don't agree with them," he said. "And people say some really aggressive and scary things to them, and I think they are frustrated and worried that this sets a precedent."

Journalists were understandably unkind to what in their eyes amounted to blatant censorship. "In fact, for a website that made its name crusading against the stifling anti-piracy SOPA bill, Reddit users' [*sic*] and administrators have proved surprisingly adept at censorship when it comes to this article," Chen later wrote. Other press sentiments echoed Chen's online.

Wong countered with a post on the private forum r/modtalk. "We stand for free speech. This means we are not going to ban distasteful subreddits. We will not ban legal content even if we find it odious or if we personally condemn it," he went on. But he maintained the ban on posting of "personal information...because it incites violence and harassment against specific individuals," stating that it was necessary because of past instances of overzealous and wrongheaded "witchhunts."

Not all Reddit users found this argument compelling. As u/mtrice put it, "There is no actual philosophy behind the free speech rhetoric except to cash in on content other social networks won't allow."

THE INTERNET BUS

The very same week Reddit had been lit on fire with its most toxic controversy to date, Alexis Ohanian and much of Reddit's staff embarked on perhaps one of the more wholesome press events Silicon Valley had ever concocted.

The idea had arisen months earlier, in the wake of Reddit's SOPA blackout, as community manager Alex Angel, Martin, and Ohanian had pondered ways to continue the momentum against the threat of government censorship of the Internet. Politics was in the zeitgeist in the run-up to the 2012 elections. Someone suggested getting a bus—just like a presidential campaign! Ohanian, who was eager to continue championing online freedoms, and simultaneously to boost his own profile, was sold. The Mayor of the Internet would not fade quietly into a board seat.

Ohanian and Martin launched an Indiegogo campaign for the "Internet 2012 Bus Tour," and raised almost $20,000, supplementing it with contributions from donors such as Craigslist founder Craig Newmark. Reddit and Y Combinator funded the bus, which, once Martin located one, ended up being the very same bus that had once served as John McCain and Sarah Palin's "Straight Talk Express."

For the actual journey, which began in October 2012, Ohanian enlisted Martin, who had just been named one of *Time* magazine's 100 people of the year, and Angel, who also came for part of the tour, despite that she and Martin were in the thick of managing moderators' outrage at Gawker. Ricky Ramirez, the systems administrator who helped keep Reddit operating during the Obama AMA, also joined. They would help spread the word of why concepts like "net neutrality" were important, to farmers, to gas-station attendants—heck, to everyone. They'd solicit stories from midwestern moms who made a living selling handmade wares on Etsy, from teachers who earned spending money posting courses on Skillshare. However blithe their effort, Martin and Ohanian approached it in all earnestness; they'd solicited tech reporters to ride along, as well as a documentary film crew.

While on the bus, Martin and Angel attempted to keep up with their regular workloads—answering user complaints about harassment, deleting problematic new subreddits, and answering moderator and press questions about Gawker fallout. But it wasn't possible to do it all—especially because they'd forgotten to wire the "Internet" bus with Internet, and were dependent on Ohanian's personal Wi-Fi device. It was long hours traveling, then late-night stops at a hotel, and sometimes they'd pile back onto the bus at 6 a.m. to make it to the next day's event.

The tour wrapped in Lexington, Kentucky, where team Reddit hosted a big event along with their buddy Drew Curtis, the founder of the weird-news aggregation website Fark. Thanks to this massive road trip, Ohanian had collected inspiring stories of the Internet, and entrepreneurship, having changed the lives of individuals who never graduated from an Ivy League school nor pitched an investor on Sand Hill Road. Now he had another idea: a book. He'd taken it to literary agents, and a year after the tour, he would publish a hardcover book about the democratizing force of the World Wide Web, and how to start a startup, all inspired by his own story of founding Reddit.

(• •)

A couple years earlier, a junior partner at Kleiner Perkins Caufield & Byers, one of the world's largest and most established venture capital firms, which had backed 850 startups with hundreds of millions in funding, had reached out to Wong. Her name was Ellen Pao, and she told Wong she was interested in potentially investing in his latest project. Wong had no new project. He agreed to have coffee with Pao anyway, and they struck up a friendship.

During that time, Pao's life changed dramatically. She'd been involved in a brief affair with another partner at Kleiner Perkins, and she claimed another had made what she saw as inappropriate romantic advances. In the months that followed, Pao believed she was being excluded from meetings and was not promoted. In May 2012 she filed a bombshell twelve-page lawsuit accusing Kleiner of gender and pay discrimination and retaliation for previously reporting harassment. The firm terminated Pao in October. The media's reaction was mixed. Some heralded her as a rare advocate for equality in Silicon Valley's white-programmer-bro-laden culture. Other pieces dragged her husband's personal life into the mix, and detailed the "lurid" and "steamy" sex scenes from her lawsuit.

Throughout her legal tribulations, Wong was a friend to Pao. After she'd left Kleiner, she began formally advising him on transforming Reddit into a profitable company. She was one of several experienced executives whom Wong brought on initially as contractors. Members of the Reddit team were still irked that Wong had been hired without their consent; they saw Pao, with her Harvard degrees and her Sand Hill Road pedigree, as extremely buttoned-up and overly professional. To them she wasn't a real Redditor, she was a poseur.

Pao read the employees as passionate—they were youthfully enthusiastic, but wildly stubborn. They seemed simply unwilling to change the way they'd been doing things. This was a team that had exerted so much of their energy putting out fires that it seemed they'd lost the bigger picture: They were unable to focus their attention on something new, such as building new products.

Still, she thought the work was important; she found the content on Reddit itself inspiring and recognized its potential to reach a broader audience. There was lots of obvious work to do in terms of marketing and advertising. The state of ads on Reddit, she thought, was "the worst of both worlds"; they were at once ineffective *and* spammy-looking. She implored Wong to bring on a full-time business development executive.

"How about you?" Wong asked. Pao agreed.

THE 117TH BOSTON MARATHON

At 2:50 p.m. on April 15, 2013, a massive blast shook the street and sent shrapnel through the crowds at the finish line of the 117th Boston Marathon. Twelve seconds later, another explosion shook Boylston Street, in front of the Boston Public Library. Two pressure cookers that had been rigged into IEDs had exploded, injuring more than 250 and killing three people, including an eight-year-old boy. Boylston Street was still covered with blood and debris when President Obama vowed to find who'd done it, remarking that any responsible individual or group would "feel the full weight of justice." He also cautioned against the temptation to "jump to conclusions" before a full investigation was complete.

Less than ten hours after the blasts, on Reddit, dozens of discussions about the bombing had broken out on the site's main news forum. R/boston, too, was filled with threads. Just after midnight, a twenty-three-year-old professional poker player from England, who went by the username oops777, created the subreddit r/findbostonbombers to be "one single place for people to compile, analyze, and discuss images, links, and thoughts about the Boston Bombing."

The Boston Marathon bombing case encapsulated the inherent promise and peril of all of Reddit. The Reddit community had accomplished amazing feats of investigation previously—in 2012, one gearhead identified the make and model of the car involved in a hit-and-run from just an image of a single headlight—and would continue such massive multiperspective sleuthing in the future. This, however, was a different order of magnitude.

In its first day on the case, the subreddit was featured in *Slate*, where writer Will Oremus pondered with wide-eyed wonder that "Reddit Thinks It Can Solve the Boston Bombings."

Others were skeptical. Just five hours after it was engendered, r/findbostonbombers carried a post by u/rroach that read, "Does anyone remember Richard Jewell?," referring to the Atlanta security guard erroneously identified as a suspect in the 1996 Summer Olympics bombing. "Why am I bringing this up? Because this sub is dedicated to pointing to random people in a crowd photograph and declaring your suspicions. You're starting the trial by public aspect."

This warning did little to deter individuals from posting theories. Their hunches were based on tiny details in photographs sourced from individuals' Facebook pages, Flickr accounts, and surveillance footage, identifying potential movement of the bombs by searching Where's Waldo–style for backpacks, which could have been used to transport the two bombs, and even pinpointing the brand of pressure cooker purportedly used in the attack. They theorized about individuals at the scene, such as one who became known as "Blue Robe Guy," and "basically every brown person wearing a backpack," as Gawker summarized the efforts. One of these was "White Hat Guy," a man seen in a crowd shot next to a possible co-conspirator with a backpack. Redditors, though, quickly discerned that this image showed a high school runner, Salaheddin Barhoum, seventeen, and White Hat Guy his coach, Yassine Zaimi. Barhoum's Facebook, they noted, was full of tourist-style photos of Boston, and snapshots of him alongside the top-finishing marathon runners. An acquaintance noted that the pair had left the scene an hour before the bombing.

The next morning, a *New York Post* front-page photo of the student and coach ran with an article, "Bag men: Feds seek these two pictured at Boston Marathon." It did not name them, but essentially pinned the crime on the innocent student and coach. Posts online claimed Barhoum was terrified; he had already allegedly gone to the police, other Reddit commenters noted, upon realizing he needed to demonstrate his innocence, but was deeply fearful of appearing in public. Reddit users criticized the coverage—but then again, Reddit itself had initially proposed these two as suspects.

The moderators of the subreddit r/findbostonbombers, by this point, seemed to have a sturdy grasp of what could go wrong. The forum's rules were extensive:

1. We do not condone vigilante justice.
2. DO NOT POST ANY PERSONAL INFORMATION.
3. Any racism will not be tolerated.
4. Theories are welcome, but make sure you fact-check your sources.
5. Remember, we are only a subreddit. We must remember where helping ends and the job of professionals begins.
6. Do not make any images viral. Limit reposting images outside of this sub.
7. Finally keep in mind that most or all of the "suspects" being discussed are, in all likelihood, innocent people and that they should be treated as innocent until they are proven guilty.

The moderators also wrote, "r/findbostonbombers is a *discussion forum*, not a journalistic media outlet. We do not strive, nor pretend, to release journalist-quality content for the sake of informing the public." It included an email link to the Boston FBI and implored readers to send any major information about the identities of the bombers to the FBI or Boston Police Department. Within a day, r/findbostonbombers was an accessible source for tips, analysis, and speculation, and reporters, eager for any leads, any coverage related to Boston, flocked there.

Moderating the section, despite all the rules, was a Sisyphean task. Names were being posted, photos disseminated and dissected. "At one point I was banning dozens of people a minute for even the smallest infraction," a volunteer moderator who went by u/Rather_Confused wrote later in the r/offmychest forum. "It got to the point, on[e] infraction and you were banned, no waiting, no warning." He wrote that he knew the forum "could have potentially devastating effects" and that despite that "we did our best," it ended up giving "people an outlet and the media a target."

The press had indeed turned on Reddit. Alexis Madrigal of the *Atlantic* wrote a post entitled "Hey Reddit, Enough Boston Bombing Vigilantism." A *Wired* UK story was headlined "Reddit users are hosting a witch-hunt for the Boston Marathon bomber." And with each press report, however skeptical, the forum's subscriber ranks grew.

On April 18, the Federal Bureau of Investigation released grainy photographs of two suspects. The special agent in charge of the FBI's Boston division warned the public to stay away from other photos. "For clarity," said the agent, Richard DesLauriers, "these images should be the only ones—the *only ones*—that the public should view to assist us." He also stated that other photos could unnecessarily divert attention and create undue work for vital law enforcement. The *Washington Post* later clarified that DesLauriers was indeed speaking about Reddit.

Moderators of r/findbostonbombers immediately banned photos that did not include the suspects. Within three hours, though, two remarkable things happened on Reddit, one incredible, one despicable. The good: Reddit turned up a real, high-quality photo of one of the suspects. It had been snapped by Boston Marathon runner David Green and had been posted on his Facebook page. In the photo, a young man appears in the background behind three individuals apparently fleeing the blast. He is wearing a baseball cap, his unruly hair poking out in curls. His layers of clothing are visible, and even his scruffy facial hair can be made out.

And then, the ugly: In the subreddit r/worldnews, a comment

on a thread of the FBI's photos speculated that a Brown University student, who had been reported missing the prior month, was one of the suspects. His name was Sunil Tripathi. An hour later, the same tidbit was submitted to the r/boston forum by a Reddit user who went by u/pizzatime. The post included a link to a *Huffington Post* story about Tripathi's disappearance. The now thousands of armchair investigators and dilettante journalists dove into a new comment thread, speculating about Tripathi—pondering his disappearance, hypothesizing about whether he was Muslim, and questioning the FBI's involvement in his search. (Tripathi was not Muslim, he suffered from depression, and his family called him "Sunny"—all of these facts were overlooked.)

Around 3 a.m. on April 19, a Reddit user, honestbleeps, commented on u/pizzatime's post that Tripathi might be one of the suspected bombers, based upon an alleged report he saw in a tweet that claimed a Boston police scanner as its source. The report that Tripathi's name was mentioned on the Boston police scanner in conjunction with the bombings led other Redditors to congratulate u/pizzatime on the seemingly correct speculation. "Pizzatime always solves the crime," wrote Peel_Here at 3:07 a.m.

Through the night, enraged messages stacked up on Sunil Tripathi's Facebook page, one his heartsick parents had set up as part of their search for him after his sudden disappearance—they'd been told that missing people sometimes Google themselves, and hoped to show him an outpouring of love. The page included many beautiful recent photos of Sunil and his relatives; its comments, before that night, had been words of love and grief. After the Reddit theorizing, the page was covered with words of hate, and threats.

Around 11 p.m., twenty hours after the police scanner claim, Sunil's distraught parents, who had previously been assured by a contact at the local FBI that their son was not a suspect, took down the Facebook page. Within an hour, Sunny's mother's cell phone had fifty messages from demanding journalists and threatening strangers.

The worst hadn't even begun for the Tripathi family—Judy and

Akhil and their children, longtime Boston residents who'd spent much of the past two months in Rhode Island organizing a search for their son. Around 3 a.m., one day after the u/honestbleeps "confirmation" of u/pizzatime's speculation, a local journalist from Hartford, Connecticut, relayed the misinformation over Twitter, and journalists with a national audience chimed in. Luke Russert, a reporter for NBC News and son of the late Tim Russert, tweeted out a photo of Dzhokhar Tsarnaev—one of the actual suspects, who had not yet been named, and who, like Tripathi, was a college student with dark hair and a prominent nose—with the commentary, "This pic kinda feeds Sunil Tripathi theory."

BuzzFeed's Andrew Kaczynski credited Reddit with uncovering the information. "Wow Reddit was right about the missing Brown student per the police scanner. Suspect identified as Sunil Tripathi." Another BuzzFeed writer, Erik Malinowski, took suspicious note that the Tripathi family's Facebook page had been removed. Malinowski's tweet received some three hundred retweets, including from popular celebrity gossipmonger Perez Hilton. Just six minutes after his first Tripathi tweet, Luke Russert tweeted again, saying, "It's still early w unconfirmed reports, but if Redit [*sic*] was right with the Sunil Tripathi theory, it's changed the game 4ever."

Reddit wasn't right. Three years before social networks would fuel a vicious cycle of fake news—often aided by Russian disinformation outlets, domestic right-wing meme warriors, and politically minded propagandists—Reddit had seeded an entirely incorrect and highly damaging news cycle.

Two hours later, around 5 a.m. the entire theory fell apart. NBC reported that Tripathi was not a suspect. All of the online speculation, of which Reddit was a primary hub, had indeed turned into what the moderators and the press had feared: a witch hunt.

(• •)

On April 22, Erik Martin posted a long, thoughtful reflection on the witch hunt that had unfolded on Reddit. He apologized for the Reddit staff and millions of people on Reddit that it had happened—and noted that Reddit had apologized privately to the Tripathi family. Moderators had reached out to them, too. He wrote:

> This crisis has reminded all of us of the fragility of people's lives and the importance of our communities, online as well as offline. These communities and lives are now interconnected in an unprecedented way. Especially when the stakes are high we must strive to show good judgement and solidarity.

Martin also noted that the site's traffic had peaked on April 19, when reports came in that a second, real, suspect was captured. A quarter million individuals had been viewing Reddit simultaneously when Dzhokhar Tsarnaev was apprehended by law enforcement.

Sunny was found dead a few days later, his body floating in the Seekonk River in Providence. The fact he'd likely been dead for weeks did not lessen the pain that had been inflicted on his family.

MONEY ON THE MIND

Advance Publications, the private company that owns Condé Nast, was still Reddit's majority owner, but one never would have known it from reading most news coverage. "Their strategy," said Robert Quigley, a lecturer on new media at the University of Texas at Austin, "appears to be to pretend they don't own it." Reddit was a confounding property, to be sure: porn, programming, and men's rights advocacy were squarely out of line with the mix of luxury, fashion, and celebrity that filled the advertising-packed magazines for which the company was best known. Now that Reddit had been spun out as its own property, it was gaining even more distance from Condé and Advance.

In a blog post on August 6, 2013, Reddit's new CEO, Yishan Wong, explained the ownership structure, and noted that the second-biggest shareholder group after Advance Publications was a group that included the company's twenty-eight employees. The third-largest set of stakeholders, he announced, was a brand-new list of individuals who owned tiny shares amounting in total to less than 1 percent of the company. This cadre included a few well-known venture capitalists, such as Dave McClure, who ran an incubator called 500 Startups; Keith Rabois, a fellow PayPal Mafioso of Wong's and a partner at Khosla Ventures; Paul Buchheit, the creator of Gmail who now worked at Y Combinator; Thrive Capital founder Joshua Kushner, the brother of Donald Trump's son-in-law, Jared; and Marc Andreessen, the Netscape cofounder who'd cofounded the powerful venture capital firm Andreessen Horowitz. Also mentioned were some people familiar to the employees, including Ohanian, Pao, and Jeremy Edberg, Reddit's original systems administrator.

Wong's sudden announcement flummoxed some employees. He had assured them there'd be transparency internally when it came to bringing on outside "strategic investors." But they'd been kept in the dark. This clearly wasn't a major investment round if the names listed altogether owned less than 1 percent of the company. But what was Edberg's name doing there, next to Ohanian's? They'd heard the two did not get along. They'd speculated among one another that Ohanian may have pushed Edberg out of his job.

The move wasn't financial, according to Wong: "This was actually just to get us on the radar of several significant angels." That's not to say money wasn't on Wong's mind. It was: top of it. Wong obsessed over the concept known as "runway," a term popular among startups, which use it to describe the amount of time a company has before it runs out of money. As general manager, Martin had made a meaningful attempt to get Reddit to break even. Wong, though, had changed the curve by adding funding—but with it he had also grown head count, which meant his math was more complex. With every hire, every well-compensated consultant—and there were several—the roughly $20 million financial runway the company had to taxi down would grow shorter and shorter. Wong figured, at best, the company had a year and a half of funding.

Reddit by this time was making money in three ways: advertising, Reddit Gold, and Reddit Gifts. Lesley Brownlee, along with Dan McComas, had created a new feature for this year's massive Secret Santa exchange: a marketplace. It allowed vendors to list their products, sell them, and link them to the gift exchange so they could directly ship gifts to their match. Secret Santa had grown to nearly sixty thousand individuals from 125 countries by the end of 2012—enough of them used the marketplace that Reddit Gifts brought in a tidy profit, which was a revolutionary thing in the history of Reddit. It did not fail to impress Wong and Pao.

Pao and Reddit Gifts cofounder McComas had already hit it off as colleagues; she was congenial, he gung-ho about making a new ally in Reddit management. She made trips to Utah to visit them. In January 2013, she invited them to San Francisco, where she set up a meeting for them in a conference room at the St. Regis hotel, a place where she often conducted business (she lived there in a $3.85 million twenty-third-floor apartment). There, Pao helped McComas craft a budget and a proposal for growth going forward.

Before long, resources began flowing to the Salt Lake City office. It was given customer support, and the ability to hire at a rapid clip after that first holiday of profitability. The Gifts team grew to twenty people, expanding from its miniscule shop in earshot of a Dunkin' Donuts drive-through window to an eight-thousand-square-foot facility downtown. McComas was still embittered that he and Moreno had been deprived of some of the acquisition payout he felt they deserved, but he was at least relieved that his little creation was finally being allocated real resources.

Meanwhile, Reddit users were beginning to see changes to the site that made them wonder about the company's profit-seeking motives. In July 2013, users abruptly noticed that r/atheism and r/politics had been removed from the "default" subreddits that populated Reddit's front page. The homepage represented the splashiest, often most popular portions of Reddit: r/aww cute-animal photos; r/science, with links to advances published in medical journals; and general-interest topics such as r/pics, r/movies, and r/gaming. For the consistently popular but not controversy-shy politics and atheism sections, with more than three million and two million subscribers, respectively, to be moved off the front page was considered by many users to be editorializing, or pandering to potential advertisers.

Reddit maintained that the decision was not financially moti-vated. "We could give you a canned corporate answer or a diplo-matic answer that is carefully crafted for the situation," Alex Angel wrote in a blog post. "But since this is Reddit, we're going to try things a bit differently and give you the real answer: they just weren't up to snuff." Both pages had become known for their in-arguments and, sometimes, bad behavior. Her words appeared alongside an animated GIF of Ron Paul, a U.S. representative from Texas and frequent presidential candidate, dancing about in front of Technicolor lasers. Paul's libertarian views had made him a pop-ular figure on Reddit, and discussions about him often dominated the r/politics forum. "Overall, they just haven't continued to grow and evolve like the other subreddits we've decided to add."

In August 2013, Wong posted on the company blog a long, de-fensive explainer of "the business" of Reddit. "We want to address some more common recurring myths we see out there and be as transparent as possible about the size of the company, our business structure, profitability, and other questions we've encountered," he wrote.

> myth: reddit is making tons of money, so you are just lining someone's pockets by buying reddit gold.
> reality: reddit is not yet profitable.

Below that, he posted a numberless graph, showing a red line for expenses and a green one for revenues. Revenues trailed expenses by roughly a quarter throughout, with a noticeable fourth-quarter jump in revenue that past year, likely due to Reddit Gifts' new marketplace.

(• •)

Wong believed he could both turn a profit and manage to maintain Reddit's pseudo-anarchist soul. He knew he'd need to do a better job selling that vision to Reddit's growing userbase. To that end, he continued embarking upon a bizarre and unprecedented corporate strategy.

In February 2014 he announced that Reddit would be giving 10 percent of its advertising revenue receipts to nonprofits "chosen by the Reddit community...We want to show that advertising doesn't just support the Reddit platform, it also directly supports the causes and goals of Reddit as a whole."

Redditors, again, were mystified. So were staffers. Some stewed, while others voiced their concerns. The top-voted comment in response read simply, "Isn't Reddit operating in the red?"

Wong responded, "We're getting closer to closing the gap. Yes, doing this will widen the gap again but people are right: we think this is good for non-profits AND we are working to increase ad revenue by more than 11.1% anyhow. So it's less about a numbers game as it is trying to align things even more between ads and the will of the community."

Wong assumed the post would be read as benevolence, and a step toward fiscal transparency—heck, if they were going to tell the figure represented by 10 percent of revenue, they'd essentially be disclosing what all the $5-a-pop sponsored links in subreddits, plus the major corporate deals in the works, amounted to for the year. Reddit's internal ad operations team, run by Pao and Jena Donlin, was confident they'd be ramping up enough to have significant revenue by the end of the year. The advertising team included a handful of staffers, and Donlin estimated in early 2014 that ten Reddit employees, out of forty total, touched advertising in some way.

Another component of Reddit's revenue was Reddit Gold. Over the past year, it had evolved as planned, into something of a "pro" account for subscribers—though Reddit didn't quite bill it as such. "If any feature is so good that everyone needs it," explained Josh Wardle, Reddit's project manager for its community engineering team, "we don't want to make you have to pay for it." (One year of Reddit Gold cost $29.99 in 2017; benefits over the years have included extra on-site tools for subscribers that cost Reddit slightly more to run, such as being able to view hundreds of additional comments in a thread, create a custom alien avatar, and turn off advertising.)

Gold's membership base had become valuable to Reddit's developers, too: It allowed Reddit to test out potential features on a subset of loyal users before opening them up to the masses. Wardle, who had been hired in October 2011 as "resident artist," and whose first major project was digitizing fan postcards from Reddit users, had infused Reddit Gold's experiments with an art-school whimsy. One experiment was an on-site bot of sorts, which would alert a user when her username was mentioned anywhere on the site. Its charm was in its tone: an overly formal, Jeeves-like cadence—and Wardle dubbed it The Butler. After testing among the small Gold community, it was a hit, and was released to every Redditor. (The Butler's current iteration on the site lacks the mock formality; it is simply known as "username mentions" and sends Redditors a message to their Reddit in-box whenever their username is mentioned. Other bots would become common appearances within Reddit discussions in subsequent years.)

Reddit wanted to gamify Gold, adding a layer of interaction for users in order to gently encourage more sign-ups, as well as to transparently reflect their actual value to the company. For Redditors who'd purchased Gold, a little sidebar displayed the amount of server time their purchase had funded (say, about fifty-five hours for a single year's subscription).

Redditors didn't totally buy it, questioning the math Reddit employed. By October 2014, Wong posted another lengthy, somewhat prickly comment about Gold on r/howredditworks. It explained, in mostly nontechnical detail, how the "server time" calculation was made. "Roughly speaking at the moment, a month of reddit gold pays for about 276 minutes (about 4.6 hours) of server time. By buying a month of gold, you're helping to pay for one of our many hundreds of servers to run for 4.6 hours. Each server generates thousands of pageviews per hour (massive oversimplification), so by buying reddit gold you are helping to fund not just your own reddit experience, but reddit for many others." It only got sixty upvotes and two dozen comments.

That same week, though, u/RyuKenya had posted in r/today-ilearned "that despite having 70+ million monthly viewers, Reddit is actually not profitable," with a link to a July 2013 *Business Insider* story. In the piece, Wong was quoted about Reddit: "Yep, the site is still in the red. We are trying to finish the year at break-even (or slightly above, to have a margin of error) though." Unlike Wong's post, this one soared—it garnered more than three thousand upvotes, and caused Gold purchases to skyrocket for the next week. Wardle remembers this single user post as having created the biggest influx of new Gold subscribers ever.

Wardle and his team added a bare-bones bar graph to Reddit's homepage, consisting of a single bar that would show the percentage of the "daily reddit gold goal" based on new purchases. It would start empty and would reset daily. When the goal was met, that day's purchasers were invited to a forum, r/nameaserver, to suggest or vote on a new name for a Reddit server. On August 11 and 12, 2014, users voted to name servers Robin Williams and Doubtfire in memoriam. July 17 of that year, it was RIPMalaysiaAir17. Over the years, the servers have commemorated disasters, deaths, and the general zeitgeist. On June 25, 2017, the name chosen was a play on President Trump's bizarre, just-after-midnight tweet earlier that month, "Despite the constant negative press covfefe." The server's name: Servfefe. Other recent names include ServyMcServface, fidgetspinner, IllBe-YourServerTonight, Hillary-email-server, and SeanSpicer-porn-folder.

"The way our servers work, they get spun up and killed quite a lot," Wardle said. "So probably for a brief period, yes, we had one called Snowden. There was definitely one called Harambe."

Reddit's operations were managed across Amazon Web Services and employed between six hundred and one thousand servers at a time, scaling to more during busy times of day. There was no physical AWS server bestowed with a silver nameplate thanks to a vote of random humans scattered across the planet, so none of this makes a tremendous amount of sense. But damn if it isn't funny.

(• •)

When Wong pulled his ocean-blue Tesla onto Pioneer Way, a cul-de-sac in downtown Mountain View, in the spring of 2014, he saw several open parking spots in the lot to the side of Y Combinator's headquarters. But he drove past them. He wasn't trying to look ostentatious, and he knew his car was a little flashy. He wanted to make a good first impression with the guy he'd heard so much about: Sam Altman.

As Wong parked a good distance from the door, he noticed in his rearview mirror another Tesla—this one an even flashier lighter shade of blue. He trained his eyes on the mirror and saw it slowly pull into a spot. A couple seconds later, out stepped Altman.

If Wong's vision of growing and evolving Reddit as a "city-state" and trying to appease the community was rough going, his other objective, to move the company toward profitability, was tougher. By this point in 2014 it seemed too far-fetched to even put a timeline on. Instead, Wong decided to consider switching mind-sets—and possibly change the goal altogether. He could envision treating Reddit as a typical Silicon Valley startup. To that end, he had gone back to the place Reddit started, back to Y Combinator.

Wong and Altman stepped away from their nearly matching cars and walked together into Y Combinator. Wong took in the space, all clean lines and stark design. This office, like Paul Graham's original Cambridge one, had been built out by Graham's architect friend Kate Courteau. The scale, though, was entirely different here: There were rows of dozens of tables in the airplane-hangar-sized communal hall. The chaos-inducing tippy wooden benches that epitomized YC's earliest incarnation had been replaced by scores of white folding chairs. Overhead hung some twenty Herman Miller pendant lanterns. Persimmon was no longer a scattered-about accent color; there were entire bright orange walls. There was even an actual sign outside.

Altman, who'd once been known as the founder of Loopt, from the original class of Y Combinator back in 2005, retained a boyish air and tended to wear flashy sneakers despite having amassed extraordinary influence in Silicon Valley. He'd long been Graham's protégé, and as such had been an official investment partner at Y Combinator since 2011. By this point Altman knew that he was Graham's heir apparent: Graham had approached him in 2012 about the possibility of becoming president of the fund, the school, everything, someday. Recently, Altman had also been investing on his own, stretching his investment funds thin by putting funding into thirty to forty companies a year. His role at YC allowed him to easily diversify investments—so he was hoping to make a solitary, and significant, personal one soon.

Altman took in Wong quickly: He was smart. He seemed to deeply understand Reddit. Good. As the men chatted, Wong asked Altman about the investment outlook, which was reportedly becoming tougher for startups due to what the tech press had dubbed the "series A crunch."

"Oh yeah, it's really bad," Altman said, bemoaning the recent trend in ample early seed funding for upstarts, along with investors' hesitation to put significant skin in the game. "But you could raise money. Because you're *Reddit*."

By the time Wong slid back into his Tesla, he felt encouraged.

Altman was excited, too, and spent the evening rolling the idea around in his head. He loved Reddit; he felt like he understood Reddit and its growth. After all, it had been created by two of his friends back in 2005. Two days later, he reached back out to Wong and told him he'd like to take charge of putting together a major round of funding for the site.

Wong had a slate of requirements, and a longer wish list. He wanted certain investors to participate, including Peter Thiel, his former PayPal colleague who'd become legendary for his early investment in Facebook and interest in far-out ideas such as building government-free techno-utopian floating islands. Also on Wong's list of preferred backers were Hollywood types, including rapper Snoop Dogg and the actor Jared Leto. Wong also, as Altman recalls, wanted to prevent Reddit from getting screwed by investors.

He wanted investors who wouldn't try to steer Reddit into trying to grow too fast, or do anything to alienate users in the aim of making money. A sizable round of funding had the potential to put pressure on all his ideals, so he wanted to retain as much board control as possible.

Altman had ideas for handling each of Wong's demands. The plan he assembled included leading the round himself and putting in the majority of the funding. He'd take a seat on Reddit's board, but give voting proxy on his shares to Wong. However, that voting proxy would only apply to him; if Wong were to leave Reddit, the provision would expire, and Altman's voting power would be reinstated.

In subsequent weeks, far from the Reddit office, well out of earshot of Reddit employees, who were once again kept in the dark, Altman got to work. He piqued the interest of some of Silicon Valley's heaviest-hitting VC firms in joining the round. He even made quick work of the celebrity wish list, including Snoop Dogg. "That was a 'one phone call' kind of a deal," Altman later recalled.

(• •)

By the summer of 2014, Reddit was maturing as a company, and Wong had hired up; the company comprised twenty-eight employees, across many cities. In San Francisco, space was getting tight in the *Wired* conference room. Martin and the small team of community staffers gradually moved back to New York, where a couple of ad-sales reps now worked. Reddit's Manhattan presence expanded from one glass-walled cubicle in a SoHo WeWork space to two.

One of the new hires in New York City would be a community manager to specialize in moderating and nurturing the AMAs. An extensive search process yielded two candidates, both avid Redditors, one of whom worked in Hollywood public relations, and had experience wrangling celebrities through various Internet endeavors. She'd set up Twitter accounts and social media presences for the likes of Robin Williams and Eric Idle, a member of Monty Python.

Wong and Pao might have worried that the former publicist would be too slick for Reddit's geeky culture, but when they flew to New York to interview the candidate they knew from Reddit as u/chooter, they discovered she was an unpretentious midwesterner who wore thick glasses. She'd grown up in Wisconsin watching Monty Python and had triple-majored at Marquette University. This was Victoria Taylor.

Taylor had already coordinated and completed AMAs for some of her celebrity clients. She'd learned that authenticity was core to the Reddit process—and insisted her clients either type their answers themselves or answer the questions verbally, sitting next to her, and she'd transcribe them, using the subject's words and tone.

Through a gauntlet of interviews with many Reddit staffers, plus journalist George Anders, who was brought in to conduct a mock press interrogation, Taylor proved she was patient, capable, and cared deeply about her subjects. She was passionate about Reddit as a platform for honest discussion and had already demonstrated that she could curate the sort of content the community loved. She had a Rolodex of celebrity contacts and had already displayed that she could deftly walk them through very authentic-feeling AMAs. She could bridge the gap between Reddit and Hollywood. Martin told Taylor the job was hers.

Wong sought to professionalize Reddit in other ways. In July 2014, he hired a well-known startup consultant, who'd previously helped other YC alums during their growth toward "deca-corn" status, that is, a valuation of more than $10 billion. She was a marketing specialist, who'd made her name consulting on corporate culture and assisting startups in shedding their youthful skin. Her task was to help Reddit realize its potential as a massive media company, its potential to lure advertisers. She began by conducting one-on-one interviews with nearly every single employee, in every office. She started in San Francisco, then moved on to Salt Lake, Reddit's largest office, where a staff of twenty was working on the most promising aspect of Reddit's business, the Secret Santa program and its gift marketplace.

When she arrived, McComas welcomed her into his office and let her meet with his staffers both solo and in groups. But it seemed to him that her one-on-one meetings were becoming dish-fests, full of office gossip, which some younger employees recalled as fun and casual, but others remembered as awful. "She would go meet with the next employee, and tell them what the previous one had said," McComas remembered. He was not pleased, but he figured, as he did with so many other directives coming from Wong or his consultants (there had been others; Pao at first was just a consultant as well), that this was the cost of doing business. A few weeks prior he had gotten a call from Wong explaining that he wanted to give McComas a founder's share of Reddit as a perk; McComas and Moreno felt they were about to be further redeemed, despite that they were still earning a small fraction of what they felt due.

The consultant did not have an easy task. In New York, Martin met with her and talked strategy for growth, because to him it was clear that Reddit was at a crossroads. The strength of the team was its feeling of being a scrappy upstart, "like, there's ten of us versus the world!" Martin said. But as the company expanded, that vibe was being sucked away by increasing bureaucracy. Martin knew he loved working when he was making the decision himself to work twelve-hour days—not when he was being told to do so.

EVERY MAN IS RESPONSIBLE
FOR HIS OWN SOUL

On the last day of August 2014, a Sunday, hundreds of steamy photographs started appearing online. They were selfies in bathroom mirrors, in thongs and push-up bras. Or completely naked. Ranging from innocent—*hey I'm in a bubble bath*, which left things to the imagination—to downright pornographic, these images were explicit and frank, suggesting and, in certain cases, actually depicting sex acts. They were perhaps the most valuable porn of all time, due to the precise women who appeared in the photographs.

All of the images were private property, stolen by an amateur hacker from the personal iPhones of more than a hundred women so famous that their images are known worldwide. Among the boldface names were Kate Upton, Kim Kardashian, Eva Longoria, and Cara Delevingne. There were pop stars, models, Academy Award–winning actresses, athletes, reality stars, and, shockingly, two minors: gold-medal-winning American gymnast McKayla Maroney and MTV reality star Liz Lee.

The dissemination of private nude photos—perhaps by a jilted ex-boyfriend with a phone full of sexts—had already become sufficiently common in the age of the social web that it had been made a crime in several states and had earned a cringeworthy name: "revenge porn." In a cover story in *Vanity Fair*, the actress Jennifer Lawrence, one of the victims of the hack, said, "It's not a scandal; it's a sex crime." Although there was plenty of condemnation like this from victims and the press, it didn't stop hundreds of millions of individuals around the globe from sneaking a look. And many—the general public at least—didn't go to 4chan, the first place outside of the dark Internet where most of the photos were originally posted. The common gateway wasn't Imgur or Photobucket, where these photos were hosted. Instead, most people went to Reddit, where they saw a cascade of links to the images, in an easily accessible, aggregated, popularity-ranked list.

By Sunday afternoon, the phenomenon of sharing and viewing the lewd naked celebrity photos had already earned an ick-inducing name: the Fappening. (The etymology of the word stems from *fap*, for a sound effect indicating male masturbation, inspired by anime comics; the suffix *-penning* is a play on a popular hacker meme, "It's happening.") The photos almost immediately flooded Reddit's servers with traffic.

The images had hit 4chan that prior night, and by Sunday morning of Labor Day weekend, Reddit's employees, one by one, saw alerts piling up on their computers and cell phones. Slack, the in-office messaging system Reddit used, was where most of the official discussion was taking place. One by one, employees opened up the Slack app, and could immediately see the severity of the situation: Jason Harvey, the systems administrator, was online. Clearly the servers were getting hit hard. Reddit employees hunkered down with their laptops on Sunday afternoon, convening an impromptu emergency online meeting. A systems administrator rushed to keep the rest of Reddit from faltering, and temporarily took down the primary place where photos were being shared, r/TheFappening, a few times. Staffers were freaking out, watching site traffic spike, and trying to manage the server load. Others were fielding phone calls and photo takedown requests—agents and representatives of the actresses and models were calling. So were journalists.

Alex Angel, the community team's leader, had for the weekend driven with her boyfriend up to a friend's cabin in the woods for a massive Labor Day weekend pig roast. She had spotty service, but saw her phone going crazy, the emails and alerts piling up. On her computer, she checked the modmail and internal Reddit IRC. She thought, "Oh fuck. This is going to be awful."

Within ten hours, r/TheFappening, the main Fappening subreddit, had more than 50,000 subscribers; within twenty-four hours, 100,000, making it the fastest-growing subreddit of all time. In a single day 141 million people visited the site. The press and public, not surprisingly, blamed Reddit's employees and investors for allowing the stolen nudes to be disseminated. The FBI initiated an investigation.

As with most situations within Reddit that rose to mainstream media coverage, the issues requiring constant site effort and upkeep by staff were far more numerous and complex than explained by any outraged post in the tech press. The first, and simplest, issue was copyright. Reddit's community team had begun receiving and parsing through content-takedown requests. At this time, Reddit was a list of links to elsewhere and didn't host images itself, aside from tiny thumbnail images. They hustled to take down the thumbnails.

The letter of the law made its enforcement difficult—specifically due to what it failed to address. The Digital Millennium Copyright Act, which had been signed into law by President Bill Clinton in 1998, was straightforward about the digital rights of images taken by an individual: You owned your own photos. So takedown requests for Jennifer Lawrence's selfies were honored, at least in theory. But what about the photos stolen from her phone clearly photographed by another individual? As Wong put it later, "Someone can take any terrible picture of you and you don't have any rights."

All this meant, to Wong, the Fappening in general was "very controversial, but never at any point significantly lawbreaking. Or even close to lawbreaking." It was the same logic Reddit had applied to creepshots.

The images of minors, Reddit decided unequivocally to remove. They *were* breaking child-pornography laws. But once staff identified and banned an image, another user would recrop, reupload it elsewhere, and recirculate it on Reddit. Both volunteer moderators and staff administrators were overwhelmed.

(• •)

On September 3, the Tuesday after Labor Day weekend, the Fappening was in full swing on Reddit, and as the media returned to work, many writers hit Reddit with venom for despoiling America's sweetheart Jennifer Lawrence and all the rest. Despite the mob of public opinion entreating Reddit to act, largely it did not. Two days later, these stolen pornographic images were still being rampantly shared on the site. That meant Erik Martin's phone was ringing incessantly. Modmail was overflowing. Martin's staffers' in-boxes were jammed, too.

Martin ignored his ringing phone and sat down to write Wong an email. "I've always said to myself that if the day came where I no longer felt an intense passion for my job, I would step aside," he told him. "There are times when I sincerely and perhaps naively believed that day might never come. If I am honest with myself and if I am honest with my teammates, that day has come." In the midst of one of Reddit's biggest scandals, its longest-remaining staffer had just quit.

Wong called Martin to convince him to stay. But Martin's email, and words, were definitive. Wong let Martin in on some of his thought process of late, his significant personal stress, and his uncertainty about the future of Reddit. Some significant changes for the company would be announced soon; the men decided to keep Martin's forthcoming departure a secret. They did so for nearly a month.

In the San Francisco and New York offices that week, day after day, debates ensued, in person and over Slack, between community staffers, contractors, and those in other departments. Some old-timers didn't question it: Under the letter of the law as Reddit was being advised currently and had observed in the past, most of the links to pictures seemed legal. Other individuals, including some newer employees and contractors, were appalled. At least one appealed to the board. A rift arose in the offices, as the strain on the servers continued. Jason Harvey and Ricky Ramirez, the two systems admins, were sleep-deprived and weary by Friday. Women on staff had each individually been forced to reckon with the morality around defending the rights of the sweaty male hordes posting, reposting, and promoting these stolen photos. Wong worried that the Fappening would interfere with his fund-raising efforts. Still, lucrative traffic continued to flow in all week. The moderator who created r/TheFappening claimed that his page—with a quarter billion page views—had made enough money for Reddit to pay for its wildly expensive servers for twenty-seven days. And Reddit continued to defend its actions.

On Friday, Wong wanted to write a definitive post to communicate to the world Reddit's logic—and to urge the community to police itself. He sent around a draft to a few staffers he respected. This missive stated that Reddit the company deplored the "theft of these images" and did "not condone their widespread distribution," but also explained why Reddit was continuing to allow the dissemination of the images on its site.

At least one staffer advised Wong not to post it. They knew it would not land well. Experienced community staffers, in particular, had developed a sixth sense about what would rile up the most vocal Reddit constituencies—and, separately, the things that would goad the press. Wong published the post anyway, on Friday. It was titled "Every Man is Responsible for His Own Soul."

"We understand the harm that misusing our site does to the victims of this theft, and we deeply sympathize," Wong wrote. "Having said that, we are unlikely to make changes to our existing site content policies in response to this specific event." He added, "The philosophy behind this stems from the idea that each individual is responsible for his or her moral actions."

It read as smug—and definitive. It lacked transparency about what was really going on behind the scenes in the Reddit offices. There, staffers were beat down due to the raging debate over involuntary pornography, and over the sputtering servers, and something else, too: the fact that the site was being overrun by spam and viruses. Where there are eyeballs online—particularly in the pornier realms of the Internet—there are spammers wanting to capitalize on the avid clicking. "We had people spamming things like crazy, so every time we would block out some type of route to people spamming links, they would find another route around," Harvey said later. "So it was just an all-out slam of traffic from every end." Complying with the takedown notices and routine removal of the images of minors, too, were taxing the staff. It wasn't sustainable. Harvey knew it and the community team knew it.

Within hours of Wong's post, it was all over. The community team, led by Alex Angel, made the call to turn off the Fappening subreddit to the public.

Wong was understanding of the decision. He didn't fire, nor even reprimand, Angel. But he was frustrated. "And so just as I put up that thing saying we're not gonna take it down, we have to take it down for completely different reasons," Wong said. "So we look totally schizophrenic and crazy." While the media pummeled Wong for his bizarre post and flip-flopping, he asked Jason Harvey to write a report about the situation, explaining how it was handled and why the subreddit was taken down. Harvey, an engineer, not an English major and certainly no publicist, gave a thoughtful if sprawling account of events, explaining that administrators had gotten fed up with keeping up with the legal requests, taking down the photos of the few minors whose photos were part of the leak, and blocking all the spam. It was superior to Wong's response on that front, and Harvey got off his chest the fact that he'd "be ashamed to share publicly" the new traffic milestones Reddit hit that week.

> This nightmare of the weekend made myself and many of my coworkers feel pretty awful. I had an obvious responsibility to keep the site up and running, but seeing that all of my efforts

were due to a huge number of people scrambling to look at stolen private photos didn't sit well with me personally, to say the least.

Harvey did not explicitly note that for more than a dozen Reddit employees, the task of picking through the exploding garbage heap, keeping the Fappening from dominating Reddit's front page, and sorting through DMCA requests meant that for twelve hours a day their jobs were viewing stolen pornographic images that invaded other humans' privacy.

Wong later said the call to take down the Fappening was based on malware that started being circulated on the subreddit and was infecting users. It had come down to a filthy Internet cesspool of child porn, malware, and spam that Reddit was, in the end, incapable of dredging.

(• •)

Within weeks, the growth consultant Wong had hired delivered her report to him. She presented the CEO with a picture of Reddit the company as a disjointed enterprise, with disgruntled employees who loved the site's community but harbored varying degrees of uncertainty about the company that employed them. Problematically, they were spread across three separate offices, each with its own unique culture and perceptions. Plus, a handful of employees were dispersed around the world; one community manager was in Ireland, another employee in Indiana, yet another in Canada. Wong recalls she advised him that the employees either needed to be united in one office or spend a significantly greater amount of time together at company-wide gatherings. Wong emerged from the meeting convinced that to move forward as a company, Reddit needed its own culture, its own unity.

Wong was the type of person who, after taking in a situation and thinking about it for a few hours, tended to write out his thoughts. Sometimes those thoughts would take the form of an explanatory post on Quora, Reddit, or Medium. Other times, they would become long, late-night emails. He liked to type and to see his words lay out his argument in text—clean, plain, and definitive.

When he boarded his flight back to San Francisco, he put down his tray table and got back to work on one of these long, late emails.

(• •)

Wong's late-night-on-the-airplane email landed on screens in front of the faces of Martin, McComas, and Pao. The bombshell explained that every Reddit employee around the globe, from Ireland to Indiana, would need to relocate to San Francisco within one month.

Martin and McComas thought about how both their lives and those of all their employees would be directly and dramatically affected, and they became livid. Reading between the lines of Wong's note, they sensed panic.

McComas called his wife and Reddit Gifts cofounder, Jessica Moreno. "I told her and then I was just losing my shit. She was bawling," McComas said. After all, they were in Salt Lake City precisely because they didn't want to be in the Bay Area; they'd uprooted their family once to get away from Reddit, and they were happy now in Utah. Their team had grown to more than twenty people. The staff even celebrated holidays together—they had a big Thanksgiving usually a week early, in anticipation of the holiday work crunch. Now after all Wong had already put them through, they were being forced to move back, and forced to tell their new employees, many of whom had families there, to uproot, too? It felt like a bizarre torture. "We both left the office and I went home and just started drinking. I drank for, like, two hours straight and then passed out."

McComas told Wong he simply wouldn't do it to his employees: Wong would need to be the one to deliver his news to the Salt Lake City Reddit employees. So Wong boarded another flight and scheduled a company-wide staff meeting. Ellen Pao in San Francisco and Erik Martin in New York would each gather all their respective staffers together and they would all relay the massive news simultaneously.

(• •)

All of the San Francisco employees pulled up chairs and gathered around Ellen Pao. Her remarks were brief and matter-of-fact. Their lives were the least disrupted. In Salt Lake City, Dan McComas ushered Yishan Wong into a room. He put his head down for a moment, and began addressing the Reddit Gifts team, who were blindsided, some in tears.

In New York City, employees got up from their desks and walked down a narrow hallway into a little glass-walled conference room at WeWork. Martin looked around the room at Victoria Taylor, two advertising employees, and Alex Angel. He started his address with a heavy heart. "First, I'm going to be leaving Reddit," he said. There were audible gasps.

But then Martin stiffened up to deliver the real news, the reason everyone was gathered: Second, he said, the company was shifting strategy and was asking everyone to move to San Francisco. Employees outside the Bay Area had one week to decide whether they'd make the move. If they did, it'd be paid for. There'd likely be a significant bonus involved for those who stayed on. Those who wouldn't migrate would receive severance.

A New York City employee put forth a theory: "This is totally just a way for Yishan to fire us all." Martin assured them that was not the case.

Angel was floored: She'd just been packing up her apartment for a long-anticipated move to Portland in two days. Both Martin and Wong had previously signed off on the cross-country relocation, approving that she could work remotely. Angel had been promoted to head of community management back in January, reporting to Martin, the general manager with whom she'd worked closely since she started at Reddit four years earlier as an intern. She was accustomed to working from home and managing her team remotely. Now she was hit with a complete reversal. Without Martin in between her and Wong—and Wong's consultant army—she couldn't do it. She told Martin she was resigning.

Martin reported back to Wong that his team was upset, dismayed, and that the head of community had already jumped ship. Wong flew to New York City to meet with employees. He convinced Angel to stay and told her she was the exception to the rule—she could still move to Portland; she'd just have to come to San Francisco frequently.

Another New York City employee negotiated long and hard to not comply with the directive, despite that Martin, her most significant ally and friend, was heading out the door. She loved Reddit; she was vital to the community, and she persuasively presented her case to Wong. Victoria Taylor had helped nurture AMAs into a site-wide phenomenon, wherein moderators from across Reddit proposed subjects, and hosted their own. Taylor was not just queen of courting celebrities and deeply fascinating everyday Janes, but was also the Reddit employee lifeline to many important volunteer moderators of the site.

Wong decided that Taylor, too, could be an exception to his rule. She could keep her job, her perks, her office, everything, and she wouldn't have to move to San Francisco. Victoria Taylor could stay.

TINY BOXES

The timing was not optimal. No one knew that more acutely than Yishan Wong.

On September 30, 2014, precisely one month after the massive trove of stolen pornographic photographs of famous women nearly took down Reddit, the press reported that a slate of Silicon Valley investors had infused the company with $50 million in funding. It gave Reddit an estimated valuation of $500 million.

Employees were baffled yet again. From where they saw it, over the past year, all of Reddit had been flipped upside down in pursuit of increasing revenue. It had since been reiterated to them over and over that their job, their collective push, was toward building a sustainable and profitable Reddit; the only investors would be small, strategic ones, like the last round. Few of them had been looped into Wong's new strategy, which he, Pao, and Altman together had executed. Significant venture capital rounds were in their minds associated with fast-growing startups unconcerned by trivial matters such as *making money*.

Sam Altman, who'd led the round, assumed a new seat on Reddit's board, which was now comprised of Ohanian, Sauerberg, Wong, and

Keith Rabois, the former PayPal executive who'd joined Silicon Valley investment firm Khosla Ventures, but who had made only a small investment in Reddit. He was dubbed an "independent board member." Altman had taken the helm at Y Combinator earlier in the year from Paul Graham. Graham, Livingston, and their two sons would decamp from Silicon Valley before long for the English countryside.

If the press wasn't yet over the celebrity photo leak scandal, investors seemed to be. "The press never affected us," Wong recalled. "Investors never cared about whatever, they just wanted traffic."

Although the funding round looked like a move from a more traditional startup playbook, it included one rather bizarre element in its structure. The concept: 10 percent of the new shares of the company that had been created under the funding structure would accrue to Redditors themselves to thank them for the "central role the community plays in Reddit's ongoing success."

It was nutty, and it was dubious from its inception. Nevertheless, the press played along, with headlines such as "Reddit Raises $50 Million, Promises to Share Stock with Community." Wong knew it would be tough to pull off; he posted an explainer of how he hypothesized his latest strange financial decision might work. "We are thinking about creating a cryptocurrency and making it exchangeable (backed) by those shares of reddit, and then distributing the currency to the community. The investors have explicitly agreed to this in their investment terms," he wrote. "Nothing like this has ever been done before."

The post had a disclaimer at its top: "CAVEAT: KEEP IN MIND THAT THIS PLAN COULD TOTALLY FAIL."

(• •)

The year 2014 was a turnaround year for cryptocurrency; major retailers such as Overstock, Microsoft, and Dell began accepting Bitcoin, and to payments-startup insiders, some of the hottest scrappy San Francisco upstarts—Coinbase, Ripple—were in digital currency. Wong thought, if anything could manage his vision for distributing tiny fractions of dollars to Redditors, the blockchain might work. He hired a cryptocurrency engineer, Ryan X. Charles, to execute this vision for giving 10 percent of ad revenue back to millions of anonymous users, a project users joked should be called "creddits," but would become known as Reddit Notes. These hypothetical "notes"—for which a labyrinthine new blockchain system was to be developed by Charles and project manager Daniel Lim—were perhaps doomed from their inception.

For Wong's part, he admits that at the time he was not entirely in control. Running any company can spike one's adrenaline on the regular, kill the ability to lie down restfully at night, and take over any mental space one might otherwise devote to life's pleasures. Executives' friends suffer; their partners suffer. Their small children suffer their absence. Any chief executive must devote hours upon hours to the other groups of people who depend on them, who answer to them and to whom they answer: their employees, their board, their investors, and the press.

Running a company as anarchic as Reddit was worse. Over the course of less than two months, Wong had shepherded the company through not only the Fappening and the subsequent FBI investigation into the stolen photos, but also through other entirely unprecedented controversies, including what came to be known as Gamergate. Reddit had been part of countless legal matters. It had lost multiple longtime and beloved employees, and simultaneously, Wong had closed the deal for $50 million in funding. He said that around this time, he considered himself adept at handling precisely one crisis at a time. Four? Utterly impossible. He was beat up, from inside the company, from the press, from Reddit users. He was overtired. Everything started aching. "I was under enormous amounts of stress, and I was not really able to recognize and appreciate that," he recalled later.

The public criticism only mounted when news of the office consolidation leaked. David Heinemeier Hansson, a creator of the Ruby on Rails programming framework and a partner at the project management software firm Basecamp, got wind of Wong's decision to move employees to San Francisco and called it a "shit sandwich" on his blog. In reporting on the limited notice employees were given to decide, he wrote, "Can you imagine a more serious fuck you from your supposedly hip employer? You have one week (or hey, maybe even two weeks!) to decide whether you want to yank your kids out of school, whether you want to jeopardize your work visa, whether there's any way for your spouse to get a job 3,000 miles away." Wong was livid, and fixated on the leak of information.

On October 5, David Ehrmann, a former Reddit engineer who worked on the advertising framework, posted an AMA criticizing Reddit. As u/dehrmann, he wrote that he'd been frustrated at Reddit over how long it took to get things done, and felt employees were "disrespected" at multiple junctures. He wrote that Reddit was "two-faced about openness" and that there were "occasional edicts that seemingly materialized out of nowhere; It felt like there were a lot of politics in the background." He also commented directly on being laid off, saying he was given "no reason."

Wong did not handle this criticism quietly. Instead, he wrote and posted a lengthy response, noting that Ehrmann was *fired*, which he marked in boldface and bullet-pointed with four specific reasons, including "incompetence and not getting much work done." Wong dedicated most of the post to discussing the nondisclosure agreement Ehrmann had declined to sign. "When an employee is dismissed from employment at a company, the policy of almost every company (including Reddit) is not to comment, either publicly or internally. This is because companies have no desire to ruin someone's future employment prospects by broadcasting to the world that they were fired. In return, the polite expectation is that the employee will not go shooting their mouth off," he wrote. "Unfortunately, you have just forfeited this arrangement."

"Oh shit," one Redditor commented. "Mind == blown," another wrote. "This is so wildly inappropriate it makes me feel like someone must have control of Yishan's account. Their HR department must be in fits right now," wrote another. (Little did Redditors know that Reddit's HR department consisted of one recent college graduate, who also did bookkeeping.)

Throughout the fall, Wong tried to eliminate some stressors in his life. He appealed to the board about them. One was the crazy-long commute, from Burlingame to South of Market in San Francisco, and parking there every day. Altman suggested that instead of spending hours a day in his Tesla, perhaps Wong should expense an Uber every time and be able to open up his laptop, get through emails, start chipping away at his day instead of having idle time. Wong couldn't. His carsickness was too severe.

Wong fixated on the logistics of his commute as the root of all of his problems. Reddit needed a new office; why not make the office come to him? Commercial real estate in San Francisco was pushing $100 per square foot, which seemed unsustainable. South of the city, Reddit could afford to have a real campus, like all the tech giants. But a significant factor in the decision was Wong's own convenience. He told some employees that his wife would divorce him if he didn't move the office closer to home. (He later explained that doing so was merely an appeal to their empathy and, in hindsight, a mistake.)

The place he settled on was Daly City, a municipality just beyond the San Francisco city limits, near Burlingame. It's a suburb so idle it inspired the song "Little Boxes."

Daly City's dominant characteristics are that it is home to several big-box retailers, and it is surrounded by so many cemeteries that the neighboring community of Colma jokes that its estimated 1.5 million dead outnumber its living by a thousand to one. (Its unofficial motto: "It's great to be alive in Colma.") There is also a casino. San Francisco, with its third-wave coffee counters, scrappy art galleries, and rooftop event spaces, this was not. Mountain View, Palo Alto, or Sunnyvale, with their sprawling, sunny lawns and sushi restaurants with grapevine-covered patios, this was not. An article in *Slate* published in response to the proposed move pondered, "What's Daly City?," answering, "Daly City amounts to the Bay Area's equivalent of purgatory."

When Wong presented the plan, his staff reacted in horror. This was why they'd been asked to uproot their families—for *Daly City*?

The space Wong had found, the only Class A corporate real estate in Daly City, which was tucked next to an old movie theater, would require renovation—and he wanted to move quick. The board stalled. Wong insisted this was the right call. The board members had indicated that they would support him, Wong said, but they asked him to do his research first: Take a poll of the employees, so he would know whom he'd need to replace. Meanwhile, behind his back, a roster of top employees had sent a petition to the board, stating that they would quit should Wong move the office to Daly City.

That week, Alex Angel flew down from Portland to meet with Wong, to finalize the hires she was in the process of making to the community team. There were some fantastic candidates, including two who were longtime Redditors, who moderated many subreddits, and who knew the topography of Reddit well. They'd be natural fits. Their names were straight out of a 1960s children's book: Bill and Susie.

Angel went into the office and, before going to sit down with Wong, she caught up with her old colleagues, whom she didn't get to see in person often. She saw several new faces. Wong never showed. Angel recalls other employees coming up to her, concerned, and asking, "Alex, what's happening? You're the only person on the books who is supposed to be meeting with him. What's going on?" No one had any idea where their chief executive was. Wong had vanished. Days passed. He did not return.

UNBELIEVABLE BECAUSE IT'S SO WEIRD

Years later, Wong explained how his sudden departure transpired from his side. The chain of crises in late summer and fall of 2014 had left him exhausted and crumpled. He was sick of commuting in his car each day to get to and from a job he was fairly certain was in the process of inflicting him with chronic stress. The Fappening: stress. The funding: stress. The move: stress. With each employee who protested the move, more stress. "You have to do everything just right for everyone," he said.

Wong later divulged that at the board's behest, he'd taken the poll of employees. A couple hadn't answered, but just one said they would resign. It seemed clear to him that the move to Daly City would not incite a mass staff exodus.

He wrote out his thoughts and sent the board one of his long, late-in-the-day emails, explaining that if they didn't approve the move, that was it. He'd leave Reddit. "Yeah, I think I have a problem with authority," he later admitted. He sent it after 10 p.m., and asked the board to respond within two hours, a board member later recalled.

He later explained that he then walked out of the office, got into his Tesla, and embarked upon the long drive home. "And then I realized, once I was at home, I was like, 'Man, if they *do* agree with me, that's bad.'" It would mean the board had consented to all his demands, and he'd have to keep on doing the job. To keep on living this life. "I was hoping they would not agree."

Board members were blindsided by Wong's email. They knew agreeing to his demand could mean employees would mutiny. They did not agree. But none put a foot down.

Altman diplomatically responded that email was not the proper forum for the conversation. Twenty-four hours later, nothing had been determined. The board hadn't given Wong the definitive yes or no he sought.

"I was just like, *fuck this*," Wong later recalled.

He emailed back the following day, saying he was out. He didn't get back in his Tesla the next morning. He didn't go to the Reddit office.

He later acknowledged that quitting under these circumstances—over an unanswered ultimatum about office space—is "unbelievable because it's so weird." Still, he felt it was justified. "If the job had been an energizing one rather than one that had been so draining, this probably wouldn't have been an issue I resigned over," he said. "But it was."

(• •)

One circumstance Wong spoke candidly about, and several former Reddit employees have also acknowledged has afflicted them, is post-traumatic stress disorder, or PTSD. It's not a term thrown around lightly; the condition is commonly associated with combat veterans, bombing survivors, and rape victims. But it is one that's very familiar to most former community staffers and former executives at Reddit. Because many suspect they have it. A couple have been diagnosed; some have gone through extensive therapy. Wong said he believed his "particular strain of PTSD" had largely to do with his in-box. Years after resigning as chief executive of Reddit, he still cringed when opening his email, in part because it has at times been filled with horribly abusive messages. That would be fine, he said, if it was predictable. But the emails weren't. "I won't know which angle it's coming from," he said. "They're either accusing me of being a sexist white supremacist or some Nazi feminist destroying Western civilization."

Exposure to graphic messages, abrupt and out-of-context threats, and extremist viewpoints has plagued generations of Reddit employees. To the designated community team, it was staring at violent images, racist words, and sussing out what precisely constituted child pornography. It was the work of reporting bomb threats, possible suicide attempts, and illegal images of underage girls and boys to investigators. It was hearing the voices through the phone of young women whose jilted ex-lovers had posted pornographic images of them online, women violated and terrified about their futures.

Angel had developed an extremely thick skin after three years as a community staffer and one year managing the team. She was responsible for turning over child molesters and pornographers to the FBI, not to mention just routinely conversing with moderators such as u/Violentacrez, who ran Reddit's dank web of extreme pornography and hate-filled subreddits. Her job grew significantly more difficult when moderators figured out that she was a woman. Daily hate mail—she estimated about five messages each day—started to appear in her in-box. "It was usually just along the lines of 'fuck you stupid cunt,' or stuff like that," Angel said nonchalantly.

Other harassment that came with the job, and that she learned to brush off, was being doxed, threatened, and stalked. "I did have a stalker, which was fun," she mentioned, and then amended, "Actually, two, but one didn't live in the United States, so I wasn't worried about it."

One user who'd been banned repeatedly from posting on Reddit private-messaged Angel the Reddit office address and her phone number. Her name and photos of her were online; mods had previously connected her username with her real name and her photo.

She knew the reality: He had enough information to find her leaving the office and follow her home. "There were so many other horrible, shitty parts of my job," she said, "that it was just not even something to give a second thought to."

Dell Frost was hired as a community manager later, in April 2015, and during his brief tenure he witnessed the most tumultuous six months in Reddit's life span. He liked his colleagues, and the easygoing vibe of the office day-to-day. Still, he recalled his time at Reddit as the "most unhappy I've ever been professionally," and in one big breath could rattle off a list explaining why. Here goes: "Child molesters, child porn, vicious stalking, rape threats, serious harassment, people taking the harassment offline, and people filing police reports on each other. I had to report one person to the feds. So much shit. I dealt with that on a daily basis."

CLOSER TO YES

Alexis Ohanian squinted in the dark, staring out beyond the wraparound terrace to the hotel's lights shimmering in the ocean surf. The $600-a-night seaside bungalow in Bali at the St. Regis was one of the nicer places he'd ever stayed, but it wasn't huge, and he was feeling guilty. He could hear his longtime girl-friend, Sabriya Stukes, tossing in bed in the next room. Not that he could stop working on this balmy night in October 2014: He was trying to save Reddit, to his mind the most important thing he'd ever done. He looked down at his thumb, almost unconsciously scrolling his iPhone's contact list. It was almost 2 a.m.—but 10 a.m. in San Francisco. He had more calls to make.

Ohanian had just hung up with Sam Altman. He knew he'd still need to talk to Steve Newhouse—and Bob Sauerberg, another Condé executive. He sighed. Altman had filled him in on the situation; he knew what Newhouse was going to say: Reddit's current chief executive, Yishan Wong, had submitted his resignation, and the rest of the board wanted Ohanian to step up his commitment to Reddit, move from his birthplace and home of Brooklyn back—yet again—to San Francisco. Those three letters—C-E-O—were mentioned. "I wanted to be back so bad," Ohanian said later. "I'd never really let go of Reddit over the seven years I'd been gone."

If he really wanted to say yes, he'd first need to figure out whether things inside Reddit were as bad as he feared. Morale was supposedly terrible, and the company was bleeding employees. If he took the job, Ohanian would have to fix all that, somehow—alone. Unless he could do something no one else had managed: convince Steve Huffman to also return to Reddit.

What would he even say to Steve? Huffman, the prolific programmer, the esteemed Silicon Valley serial entrepreneur, the man who created the structure, voice, and very soul of Reddit, his late-night video-game-playing buddy, the best friend whose shoulder he'd actually cried on. They weren't even speaking now. Steve was no longer a friend—their business dealings had fouled it too many times. But Ohanian knew that to return to Reddit, he'd need Steve. But first, he'd need to call Steve. And he'd need to have something convincing to say when he opened his mouth to deliver the pitch, which amounted to that Huffman should return to Reddit as chief technology officer. Well, that was, if Huffman would even take his call. Ohanian looked down at his thumb and hit the name "Steve."

(••)

Huffman was in denial. Like Ohanian, he'd gotten calls from Altman and Steve Newhouse. He was more estranged from Reddit than his cofounder, but he'd been following the news. He had specific insight into how bad morale was at Reddit; he'd recruited some of Reddit's best engineers to come work for him at Hipmunk, so they'd gotten word back to him. Despite that, he still dearly loved the site he'd created. He knew he had a chip on his shoulder—along with a heap of something close to regret. He wouldn't take the acquisition back, exactly; he'd been so extraordinarily happy when he and Alexis sold Reddit that Halloween in 2006. What Huffman was nursing was a lingering feeling that he'd lost something special when he left Condé Nast. "How many people get an opportunity to work on something at Reddit's scale? Very few," he said later. "I felt like I had missed that. I was frustrated about my own decisions. I felt like it was healthier to not brood on it."

Over the years, with the help of a therapist and executive coach, Huffman had meticulously conditioned himself to keep his distance from Reddit, as if it were an abusive but ridiculously attractive ex-girlfriend. He still visited the site almost daily, mostly lurking, and only very rarely posting under his longtime username, spez. He had opinions, certainly, but he had been careful not to be critical of Reddit as a company or platform, even when decisions were made with which he disagreed. He knew it was healthier for him not to second-guess his past decisions, or think too hard about Reddit.

These factors, in addition to his dedication to building Hipmunk, meant that over the years, whenever Huffman had gotten a call to return to the company, his response had always been a steadfast "No." So when Altman called, nearly begging him, "Bro, it's time. It's your time. Come back!" Huffman recited his answer: "No."

Ellen Pao, now a senior manager at Reddit's San Francisco office, called him, too, after Wong's sudden disappearance, asking for advice. She later recalled that Huffman advised her not to attempt to bring Ohanian in: He wasn't a strong manager and didn't have good execution or follow-through. The day became a web of calls between Altman, Huffman, Ohanian, and Pao. Altman agreed with Huffman that it wouldn't be a good idea for Ohanian to step in as chief executive. Altman told Huffman he would happily explain that to Ohanian.

Not an hour later, Huffman heard his phone vibrating next to his keyboard. He glanced down to see Ohanian's name bright on the screen. He and Ohanian hadn't been talking much over the past couple years, so there was a friction to even engaging. When they finally talked, Ohanian asked Huffman if he would consider coming back to Reddit as chief technology officer—presumably with Ohanian as chief executive. Huffman scoffed, "Definitely not."

Only Huffman's closest friends knew the truth: He was absolutely dying to be back at Reddit. Even though he tried to suppress it, an inclination to dissent was bubbling up inside him. Huffman had noticed the change in himself. Over the last year, he'd become more mentally invested, and he didn't like the direction the company was going. "I had noticed myself unintentionally becoming more critical publicly of Reddit," he said, "which was frustrating." Now, with every phone call, he was getting closer. With every scandal, his head ached with frustration, and he grew closer to brushing away the rote answer. Closer to yes.

(• •)

Wong assumed he'd rattled the board with his sudden departure. He'd dropped off email—and so had they. For days he stayed near home, south of San Francisco, doing little of importance except picking his kid up from school. The silence over email was unnerving, though. Wong reached back out, making clear he needed to get out of the job, but wanted to be helpful in easing the transition. Once the channel of communications had been reopened, members of the board asked his opinion on who should replace him.

He said it would have to be Ellen Pao. He didn't advocate for Ohanian. And he figured that while McComas would likely be able to be swayed to report to Pao, the inverse would not be true. He knew it would be tricky and later recalled having advised them so. "Because Ellen represents, in the eyes of young white males, the SJW [social justice warrior] bogeyman."

Ohanian had flown back from Asia to San Francisco uncertain of Reddit's future—and his own. He'd still require a lot of coaxing and assurance if he was to step in as chief executive, especially without Huffman at his side. He was slated to meet with the two highest-ranking Reddit managers remaining, Pao and Dan McComas. When he sat down in a meeting room at the St. Regis hotel, he quickly got the vibe that McComas and Pao had already synced up on a plan, he later recalled. They presented him with a proposal, laying out what he later called a "compelling case" for Pao to become Reddit's CEO and McComas its senior vice president of product. Ohanian hadn't expected such a plan to unfold before him, but was a little relieved. He conferred with other board members and concluded, "It seemed like the path that would get us to some stability fastest."

McComas, for his part, had been in the midst of the ramp-up to Reddit Gifts' holiday season—his absolutely slammed-with-work time of year. Half of his team was currently moving their families from Salt Lake City to San Francisco, so all of life simply felt up in the air. The title SVP of product, and a raise, appealed to him. He didn't argue. So when it was his turn to talk in the St. Regis meeting, "I decided it was going to be her," he said. "Which was probably a huge mistake."

In her 2017 book *Reset*, Pao phrases this entirely passively—that Ohanian and McComas "both told me they thought I should run the company." This may have been strictly true, but she had already stepped up, done the work, made the phone calls, and set forth a compelling proposal to stop the bleeding.

Ohanian reported back to the rest of the board, and the board—now also comprised of Sauerberg, Rabois, and Altman—consented. Pao would be given the job, and the noncommittal title of "interim CEO."

THE POLTERGEIST

The press met Ellen Pao's ascension to the role of chief executive with excitement: She had already become a feminist hero of Silicon Valley for putting the spotlight on rampant gender discrimination in tech due to her 2012 lawsuit against white-shoe venture capital firm Kleiner Perkins Caufield & Byers. Journalists called her appointment "remarkable," and lauded the "striking statement" made by Reddit in turning over the reins of one of the most popular sites on the Internet, one laden with lascivious content, to a woman. Her gold-plated résumé (Princeton engineering, Harvard law, Harvard business degrees) as well as her recent accomplishments at Reddit (such as acquiring the popular mobile Reddit reader Alien Blue, and debuting an Ask Me Anything app) were widely praised.

Pao was polished, experienced, armed with $50 million in funding, and seemed poised to lead Reddit through an inflection point in its growth. Still, some of the press articles focused on a separate leadership change. Swooping in alongside Pao would be one of the company's original founders, a man who'd advocated for Internet freedoms, who'd led the fight against legislation that could have stifled online creativity, and who along the way had become an in-demand public speaker, a sought-after investor, and an idol to young would-be app makers and entrepreneurs. Ohanian had been made executive chairman of Reddit. Ohanian's new role would be in part to sit on the governing body by which Pao and Reddit would be held accountable. It was also, in part, operational. Ohanian recalls being told by his fellow board members that they wanted his eyes inside the company. He recalls being asked to physically be in the office, speaking with employees as much as possible, though he says it was made clear to him his authority as executive chairman would not be greater than that of the CEO.

"Alexis probably knows the Reddit community better than anyone else on the planet," Altman wrote on his blog. "He had the original product vision for the company and I'm excited he'll get to finish the job." (Bizarrely, Altman also noted that he himself had for the past eight days held the title of chief executive of Reddit.)

Despite the rush of press, Reddit the company was left battered. Employees felt exhausted from the months-long chain of continual change; many were in the midst of transitioning their lives to San Francisco, and the collective mood was glum. A few were relieved that Pao would be chief executive. "It was comforting to me that she was not an outsider," said longtime Reddit engineer Ricky Ramirez. But that December, there was no Christmas party. There was no celebration as McComas and some of his team from Salt Lake City settled in to their new lives and new desks in San Francisco.

Pao and Ohanian jettisoned Wong's Daly City idea, but they continued his move to consolidate all of Reddit in San Francisco. "We had major culture issues," Pao wrote, "and we needed to come together; I created a mantra: 'One Company, One Team.'" Someone shortened it to OCelOT, which inspired Pao to use many images of big cats in her presentations.

Still, those presentations at company-wide meetings didn't resonate widely. Employees chafed against the new projects Pao recruited teams of engineers and project managers to build, such as search engine optimization and advertising tools. They questioned the motives and form of these overt and typical growth strategies, employed by so many growing companies, and which often could boost page views and, ostensibly, revenue. Many employees viewed these methods as unsustainable and not jibing with Reddit's spirit of freewheeling growth driven by users.

Some were frankly intimidated by Pao's demeanor and her ability to get what she wanted out of any conversation—even if it meant the interaction ended with tears. Also noisome to some of them was the fact that she continued Wong's strategy of employing often-expensive consultants. Former staffers recall that she would occasionally bring in a legal adviser or professional, someone she introduced as "a friend," and then later they'd see that individual on LinkedIn promoting themselves as having been a formal adviser to Reddit for months. Many of the young hackers and scrappy community managers bristled against new systems being set in place, new structures, and new hierarchy.

(• •)

Pao approached rebuilding Reddit methodically. She wrote in her book that a board member, whom she did not name, advised her to clean house: Fire as much of the team as possible. Altman, the board member most often in contact with Pao, denies making such a statement, but recalls letting Pao know that if she met resistance from the team to go ahead and make staff changes. Pao knew sudden layoffs now would put Reddit at a dual risk of mutiny. The rest of the loyal staff could quit in protest, essentially crippling the site. So, too, could volunteer moderators and their users revolt. Plus, she'd determined that some of the site's code had been "kludged together" and was "impossible to make sense of or untangle if you weren't there when the emergency hack was created." She decided that for the time being at least, she needed to keep the old guard around to keep the site running.

As Ohanian shuffled his personal life and prepared for a half-move to San Francisco (he'd agreed to spend one week there for every one he spent in New York, as part of his new operational role; he was among other things trying to figure out how to manage the life of his Brooklyn-dwelling cat, Karma), Pao undoubtedly had cleaning house on her mind from early in her tenure as chief executive. One of her high-powered consultants had used the word "poltergeist" to describe Reddit's internal company culture—"a magnetic core of old-timers with a strong obstructionist culture that was like a black hole for new initiatives and that spun out people they didn't like." Pao wrote, "Whenever I had trouble understanding how and why something otherwise inexplicable happened, she would look know-ingly at me and say, 'It's just the poltergeist!'"

The "poltergeist," in other words, consisted of the staffers who wanted Reddit to stay made by Redditors, for Redditors. They were the ones who insisted that users—desktop users, who tended, they knew, to keep a Reddit tab open all workday—were only glancingly interested in mobile. They insisted that users paid no attention to the site's design, and staff therefore dragged their feet on changes. They were used to working together, all-hands-on-deck style, when a cri-sis arose; they were not used to staying in their professional lanes or abiding by their job descriptions. Keeping up with site requests, with helping the most avid moderators and users, were their priorities. Ship-ping product always fell second, third, or, well, whatever place was last in a list that regularly would be topped by a new perceived crisis.

At times, Pao attempted a soft touch to effect change. She held lots of one-on-one meetings to rally support for new projects; she bantered with staffers over binge-watching Netflix, and many en-joyed her quick wit. She had a sense of humor, those she chose to befriend found. But unlike anything they'd encountered at Reddit previously, she was a swift and decisive manager. Some of the old ways were not going to fly.

At a recent company-wide meeting about diversity and inclusive company cultures and how they could be emulated at Reddit, an employee sighed loudly and wrote on a paper tablecloth, "BALLS, BALLS, BALLS." Pao had witnessed other inappropriate behavior, such as conversation in the middle of the office about the aesthetic of penises. She emailed the full staff, writing, "You do realize you were talking about penises for ninety minutes, right?" and noted that both a student group and female job candidates would be coming through shortly. She received a response that defended the conversation and clarified that it was a substantive debate about penis aesthetics but also debated whether breasts were objectively aesthetically superior. Pao was fed up. She later wrote, "Women had been groped. Embarrassing things had been said. This was supposed to be a business."

Pao began to think of herself as the new sheriff in town. She banned hard alcohol in the office and forbade work-related events at which the central or sole activity would be consuming alcohol. She hadn't minded the mild drinking culture within Reddit's San Francisco office, where there'd been a bar stocked with hard alcohol. It wasn't often abused. But there was an oft-repeated rumor that Salt Lake City employees had gotten an underage intern so intoxicated he ended up wandering out of the office and stumbling down the street. "This wasn't fun and games," Pao wrote later. She knew this was a matter, too, of liability.

Pao made staffing decisions that she recognized as unpopular. First, she promoted Jessica Moreno to head of community. Pao saw Moreno as "the most thoughtful person on the team"; some staffers questioned Moreno's management style, which favored face-to-face communication and meetings over herself delving in to manage modmail requests, as past community managers had done, operating more like peers than supervisors. Employees also questioned Pao's promotion of Moreno's husband. McComas and Pao still got along very well; she perhaps overestimated how well he got along with other team members.

Former employees from this time bemoan many events, but most notorious was a string of terminations in early 2015. Alex Angel in Portland was told that Wong's offer to work remotely was no longer valid; she would need to move to San Francisco. Angel, the former rocket scientist who'd transformed her life and career to work for Reddit ever since that day at the Colbert rally when she was just a college kid in her alien T-shirt, said no. She had a life in Portland. She resigned and took the severance.

Also dismissed: cryptocurrency engineer Ryan X. Charles, who later said he was given no reasonable opportunity to pitch to the new administration his digital creation harnessing blockchain technology, which Wong had hired him to develop. There were others. Every few weeks, someone would not show up to the Wednesday all-hands meeting, and stop appearing on online chat—and everyone else would be left to speculate what happened. (Speculation was usually all they got, as most employees were careful not to violate the paperwork they'd signed in exchange for significant severance pay.) Some staffers privately began to call the Wednesday staff meetings "Wednesday Bloody Wednesday," because they dreaded learning what colleague of theirs wouldn't show.

This string of "involuntary departures," which typically ended in an employee being able to choose to resign and sign their exit paperwork, including nondisclosure and nondisparagement agreements, had begun the prior year, in 2014, while Wong was still CEO, but while Pao was consulting. The first to go, remarkably enough, was Marta Gossage, whose Reddit avatar was a red shirt.

One departure weighs particularly heavily on some former Reddit employees—that of David A. Croach, who was recovering from leukemia. Invariably, any list of grudges against Pao and her time at Reddit includes the claim that "she fired the cancer patient."

Community manager Croach was known to his friends as Dac, and to Reddit as u/Dacvak. He'd had a terrible past three years, during which he'd gone through chemotherapy for leukemia, undergone a bone marrow transplant, and endured months of hospitalization. Reddit had in many ways been there for him. During Croach's first round of treatments, when Martin was in charge, Reddit had even made a community blog posting about Croach's diagnosis and appealed to Reddit to help him find a bone marrow donor. Croach was able to work remotely for Reddit's community team for about a year, before the cancer came back. Martin and

Wong kept him employed at Reddit, and his job open, during his long second recovery.

Croach explained it all later in a Reddit post: He thought he was healthy enough to return to work again in late 2014. He flew out to San Francisco to meet with Pao around the turn of the new year and was planning his move out to the Bay Area as mandated. He claimed: "Less than a month later, in February of 2015, I received a call from Ellen stating that I was to be terminated in less than a week When I asked what the specific reason was, she had roughly stated that 'because of our discussion, you are too sick to properly fulfill your duties as Community Manager.'" Croach wrote that he pleaded with her; he'd been so eager to return to work. He pledged to get the okay from his doctor to move, to work forty-plus-hour weeks. He did note he was thankful that Reddit paid for one year of medical coverage as severance for him. For its part, when asked for comment at the time, Reddit denied that Croach's account was accurate but declined to comment further on employee matters. Pao later said she can't comment on employment matters, but made clear she'd "never terminated someone for being ill."

Some of the spirits of Reddit past, the individuals who had shaped its growth and steered its direction, just like this, were gradually and unceremoniously removed. What Pao lacked the power to do, even in her new position, was exorcize the poltergeist from the sprawling online lairs that comprised Reddit.com.

(• •)

"We're excited to announce eight new members to team Reddit. We've also just moved into our new SF office, fabulously decorated..." Thus began a post on Reddit's blog on January 22, 2015. There was the new head of commerce, Cameron Brain, who'd cofounded a handful of startups in rapid succession, selling bicycle parts, social media tools, and motorcycles. A new mobile engineer, a web security engineer, and two new community staffers were also on the list. Finally, there was a bespectacled, suit-wearing, briefcase-toting personalized Snoo for Zubair Jandali, Reddit's new vice president of sales.

Two hires came straight from Ohanian's roster of personal employees, who worked out of New York on Ohanian's public image and managing his investments. Michael Pope became creative projects manager, and Ashley Dawkins became Reddit's new director of outreach. The fact that all of a sudden there were new employees allowed to work far from San Francisco confused and riled some staffers who'd uprooted and those who'd been longtime pals of Angel and others who'd decided not to comply with the mandate to move to San Francisco and had lost their jobs.

To Pao, these hires amounted to a substantial victory; during Wong's reign, she'd witnessed him struggle to bring in new people, and noted that despite their joint efforts at improving diversity among the staff, including hiring four experienced women, "They all wound up leaving. It was the same old story: They weren't a 'culture fit,' and so year after year the almost-all-white, almost-all-male demographics stayed the same."

There were only two women on Pao's hiring announcement, but soon she also brought on bethanye McKinney Blount, an impressive engineer who'd founded and run Cathy Labs, an upstart that makes compensation analytics software for startups (Blount uses all lowercase for her first name as a remnant of her childhood writing style). Wong had previously attempted to hire Blount away from Facebook; Pao actually succeeded and called Blount one of her "proudest hires." Pao also brought on Melissa Tidwell, a former Google senior counsel who would now be Reddit's full-time general counsel—and its first African American executive. Around this time, Pao instituted a ban on salary negotiations during the hiring process, in an effort to help equalize pay. (Studies have shown that women are less likely than men to successfully negotiate for higher salaries and career advancement.)

Pao's efforts to make the company more inclusive were meaningful to many employees. Jandali, the new sales VP, who is Muslim, had recently lost his brother-in-law, his brother-in-law's wife and a friend in a hate crime. Pao gave him time off to grieve and supported him emotionally. He was thankful for this time and later cited it as one of many benefits to working at Reddit that helped him and his family. (Other benefits included a four-month parental leave policy and, at one time, a $1,500-a-month "health and wellness" stipend.) Jandali would thrive at Reddit, going on to manage deals with major corporate clients and managing a team of more than fifty people.

There were two floors of nearly nine thousand square feet of office space each available at 101 New Montgomery, a six-story blond-brick commercial building. For now, this reinvigorated team would only mostly need one floor, but Reddit finally had room for all of its workers under one roof. Reddit's "resident artist," Dante Orpilla, along with a few of his friends, spray-painted murals on what had been stark white walls. It resulted in a youthful-if-disjointed aesthetic: here, a three-foot-wide *Calvin and Hobbes* cartoon; there, a floor-to-ceiling duck being ridden by a small red-eyed Reddit alien wielding an upvote spear (officially titled "Horse Sized Duck," a work in acrylic and spray paint). They'd have to live with the dark gray endurance carpeting, but the rest of the space was nice; finally they had their own little kitchen, a café area with communal seating, and a television with multiple video-game systems. And it was not in nowheresville Daly City but rather in the heart of San Francisco's startup-saturated South of Market neighborhood. Y Combinator's own San Francisco office was within walking distance. Pao had also negated the possibility that she'd ever get burnt out by commuting, as Wong had. Ellen Pao's own home, in the St. Regis, was a single city block away.

10

On June 23, 2015, Reddit celebrated its ten-year anniversary. There were accomplishments to toast, and a post on the company's blog exhaustively listed them. In its history, there had been more than sixteen billion upvotes (and, well, two billion downvotes). Users had spent a whopping $29 million on each other in Reddit Gifts exchanges. More than thirty-six million user accounts had been created.

Some of the most popular posts of all time at this moment, precisely ten years in, included an r/Showerthoughts: "Waterboarding at Guantanamo Bay sounds super rad if you don't know what either of those things are," and an inquiry on r/AskReddit: "Which tasty food would be disgusting if eaten over rice?" (The latter gained traction because the original poster responded to nearly every idea by individually taste-testing it and rating the results. "Yoplait yogurt with rice: 9/10 . . . tastes like a foreign dessert." "Orange juice with rice: 3/10. I don't think most drinks are good with rice.")

To commemorate the event, and to show employees and their families some appreciation, Reddit booked a popular bar-slash-coffee-shop-slash-gallery-space down the street for a party. Employees were allowed to bring their partners; even Pao brought her husband. A monstrous ice sculpture of a "10" with an image of Snoo the mascot carved into its top had been commissioned, and orange-red gift bags for attendees included commemorative hoodies.

The night of the party, the thing to do was take a photo with the ice sculpture. There was also a photo booth, set up with props like silly hats and mustaches, for even more photos. There was an open bar, and the photos and mingling went on for hours. Some of the company's clients, and even former employees, popped in. There was Chris Slowe, David King, and Jeremy Edberg. Ohanian and Pao both delivered remarks, thanking everyone for coming, thanking family members for their support over the rough past couple of years. As the crowd swelled, Ohanian—eyes above most heads, with a clear view of a room at most times—caught a shock of blond hair coming in the door from the street. Other heads turned: Steve Huffman had arrived.

PART V

PARTY

REVENGE AND REVENGE PORN

S teve Huffman had been seeing a therapist for a few years, and perhaps thanks to the rising tide of Silicon Valley, that individual, Cameron Yarbrough, had transitioned from mere "therapist" to "executive coach." During sessions with Yarbrough, Huffman lamented his ailing relationship with Ohanian, and admitted that he had a litany of long-standing issues they'd been avoiding hashing out for years, Huffman later recalled. Huffman knew they'd both grown up, and grown even more different, but that didn't change the fact that he missed his old friend. At Yarbrough's encouragement, he reached out to Ohanian.

Huffman tried to plan a dinner for them, but even tracking down Ohanian, getting him to cement a plan, was "a pain in the ass," he said. Ohanian had mostly moved to San Francisco, but spent roughly half his time jetting around the world for speaking engagements and at his old home in Brooklyn.

So Huffman saw it as a minor victory when Ohanian appeared at 5A5, a steakhouse near the Embarcadero that Huffman loved, at close to the appointed time one evening in early 2015. Once

Ohanian was seated across from him, Huffman couldn't hide his frustrations. "Dude, I'm trying to make an effort and I can't get you to respond to my texts."

Ohanian, almost always considerate and charismatic in person, apologized. As steaks arrived at the table, and the men each nursed a cocktail, they began to hash out what happened back at Reddit so many years ago when Ohanian hired contract programmers behind Huffman's back, and, subsequently, when he took a board seat at Reddit without telling him. "You didn't even tell me you were going back," Huffman said. "Meanwhile, I wanted to be back, and then I almost felt like you were keeping me out."

Ohanian had his own beef: the time Hipmunk fired him without warning. He felt Huffman had a hand in that. He used the word "betrayed." Huffman knew Ohanian thought it hadn't been handled well; he didn't know exactly how bitter Ohanian had become about what he perceived as his having abandoned him by not stepping in between Adam Goldstein and Ohanian at the time. As the men talked, a central, unspoken question hovered above all else: Could they even trust each other? That's how distant Ohanian and Huffman had grown. They agreed to meet again for dinner.

During that second dinner, at a place Ohanian chose that specialized in seafood, which Huffman hated, as the pair swapped stories and spoke about specific points of tension, Huffman began to remember why they'd become friends in the first place. They shared a worldview, and, beyond the alienating scaffolding each had erected around the other in supposition and years of relative silence—*liked* each other. Even ten years later. Huffman and Ohanian gingerly began circling around another massive question: Could they ever work together again?

The next morning, during an intense weight-lifting workout with a personal trainer, Huffman excused himself abruptly. He vomited up the remains of a lobster roll.

(• •)

Months after the Fappening, Pao had come to look back on it with disgust. She and several staffers began to not only question their ability to respond to the worst-case scenario, but also to wonder: What if this sort of thing becomes the norm? Would we consistently make the same call? Who are we? What exactly *is* Reddit? Pao convened a meeting and asked the staff that question, albeit in its most extreme version: "Are we comfortable becoming 4chan?"

There were outliers, employees who believed that an anything-goes attitude was vital to Reddit's ethos. But by this time, more had begun adopting a nuanced view, advocating the necessity of protecting users from abuse.

It was starting to become clear that two of Reddit's tenets—user anonymity and an almost-anything-goes content policy—had together become toxic. The very concepts that made it possible for Reddit to become home to thousands of open, brutally honest, ingenuity-dappled forums that felt so much more genuine than the rest of the airbrushed-and-Photoshopped Internet had allowed users to hide behind u/names and cartoon alien avatars to say and do terrible things to one another. The real humans interacting there still had bodies, and those bodies—their colors, their shapes, their quirks—were fodder for abuse, hatred, and harassment.

Pao and her colleagues decided to move to stop one form of blatant harassment, the nonconsensual posting of pornographic images or videos, otherwise known as revenge porn. On February 24, 2015, Reddit banned it site-wide. The ban required only a simple update to the site's privacy policy, which dubbed the prohibited content "involuntary pornography."

The community team buried the news of the change on Reddit's blog. It was stated as an afterthought within a lengthy post announcing new moderator tools and staff changes. The day the ban took effect, March 10, Reddit's community team hunkered down in a conference room. They tag-teamed responses to questions with prepared answers. It was clean and systematic. Pao later wrote, "By the end of the day, there was no more revenge porn.

We'd won." This is an oversimplification. There was no way to "win" against this type of content; battling it was a continuing slog.

Still, the policy was something entirely new: a concrete wall. Erecting it became one of Pao's most significant accomplishments as Reddit's interim CEO. The decision was squarely in the zeitgeist (multiple nations and U.S. states were considering laws banning revenge porn; California had recently voted to pass one), and Reddit's move influenced other communities and social platforms to follow suit. Within weeks, Facebook put out a release reiterating that revenge porn, like all nudity on the site, was not allowed. Twitter updated its terms of service to forbid "intimate photos or videos that were taken or distributed without the subject's consent."

The same day the ban took effect, proceedings began in Ellen Pao's sexual harassment trial. She had prepared for the trial during every waking hour not spent at Reddit or with her husband and daughter. Still, she knew that her days on the witness stand would be arduous and emotionally gutting. She later wrote that she believed that Kleiner Perkins had organized a smear campaign against her, including hiring one of the world's best crisis PR firms. She suspected it had enlisted a troll farm to defame her online. (Brunswick, a firm Kleiner Perkins worked with at the time, said in a statement, "We never have and never would encourage or enlist anyone to 'troll' an individual or organization.") Pao also had heard they had hired workers in India to comb through the more than seven hundred thousand emails she'd turned over in discovery. She thought she knew what her adversaries were capable of, but her lawyers advised her to keep calm and on how to answer certain upsetting questions while on the stand.

Testifying was worse than she'd anticipated. Kleiner's attorney presented a chart of "resentment" that Pao had emailed to herself, which listed former colleagues and grievances she held against them. An attorney accused her of "never" having "done anything for women" herself.

The central argument in Pao's case was that after she ended a brief affair with firm partner Ajit Nazre, her standing and career deteriorated after Nazre and Kleiner retaliated against her. Her lawyers attempted to create a picture of Kleiner as being unfriendly toward women. The firm disputed these charges and presented evidence that it prioritized hiring women.

The trial went on for two weeks, with daily dispatches from the press analyzing not just the lascivious content, but also Pao's blunt and icy-seeming reactions. One called her "shrewd, and cagey." On the stand, she at times stared blankly at the attorneys in lieu of speaking. "I ended up coming across as distant, even a bit robotic, as I bit my tongue to keep my answers short and noncombative," she wrote later. Her relationships with male colleagues and her performance reviews were pored over, as Kleiner's attorneys attempted to make the case that the reason she was not promoted was due to her performance. Even the *New York Times* described the trial sensationally, comparing its content to *King Lear* and *Keeping Up with the Kardashians.*

Jurors began their deliberations on March 25, 2015. At stake was $16 million for sex discrimination and retaliation, and as much as $144 million in punitive damages.

Two days later, the decision came. Jurors rejected three claims by Pao. On the fourth claim, that Kleiner had retaliated against her after she filed suit, there was not a consensus. After an hour of further deliberations among the six-man, six-woman jury, it returned to the judge with the necessary nine votes in favor of Kleiner Perkins. Pao had lost on all counts.

Pao's case, though, had already mesmerized Silicon Valley, finance, and the media, and amplified entirely valid concerns about lack of diversity in technology and venture capital. It was now widely known that women comprised just 6 percent of venture capitalists; women and minorities were sorely underrepresented throughout all levels of the broader tech industry.

Leaving the courtroom, Pao waved to the jury. She was smiling and composed. Outside the courthouse, she made a very brief statement to the gathered press. "If I've helped to level the playing field for women and minorities in venture capital, then the battle was worth it."

(• •)

By May, the conversation about further reining in harassing content on Reddit was taking shape inside the San Francisco office. New committees met to discuss company culture, vision, and priorities. The revenge-porn ban empowered the discussion and gave it momentum. Meanwhile, Pao produced Reddit's new core values, a seven-item plan that would serve as a compass to employees. It included maxims such as "embrace experimentation," "default to transparency," and "remember the human." The latter had been a struggle for Reddit its entire life. The document looked like something a well-functioning company, with executives armed with MBAs who told them mission statements and core values were important, would do. It looked—and perhaps even felt—like Reddit was growing up.

Inside the office, action became swifter. Pao asked Moreno to find the worst subreddits and make a shortlist of candidates to ban. Doing so would be a major signal to users that Reddit was no longer afraid of them. That isn't to say things hadn't already gotten ugly in the wake of Reddit's revenge-porn ban. Enraged Redditors had Photoshopped an image of Pao to resemble Chairman Mao. A cadre of Redditors seemed to enjoy rendering Pao as Hitler, an obese person, or encircling her face with penises. Pao was aware that more abuse would come from a ban of toxic subreddits but still felt "we had an obligation and ability to take a stand."

Moreno homed in on subreddits that deployed hate speech and imagery against people of color, overweight people, and transgender people. The board approved removing r/fatpeoplehate, r/HamPlanetHatred, r/transfags, r/NeoFAG, and r/ShitN---ersSay. Notably not on this list was the overtly and enthusiastically racist r/CoonTown, which had about ten thousand subscribers. Pao later wrote, "We weren't touching any of the many, many subreddits giving people a forum to espouse hate of other groups and theories of genetic superiority. That, to my mind, was protected, because we wanted to encourage conversations and ideas."

Reddit hired a full-time security guard for the office and developed a crisis communications plan. On June 10, 2015, the community team hit publish on a blog post titled "Removing harassing subreddits," announcing, "We will ban subreddits that allow their communities to use the subreddit as a platform to harass individuals when moderators don't take action. We're banning behavior, not ideas." (R/fatpeoplehate was by far the most popular; by Reddit's own accounting, it had more than 150,000 subscribers at its peak.) A community manager removed the sites, and Pao and the staff waited. Within minutes, the banned communities popped back up, having been reregistered by moderators using different names. The sequel subreddits weren't particularly creative: r/fatpeoplehate2, r/fatpeopleantipathy, r/wedislikefatpeople. When those were repeatedly cut off before they had opportunities to flourish, individuals began retaliating against Pao, sending her increasingly angry and threatening private images and posting violent or obscene computer-edited images of her. She tried not to look at the messages, but community staffers did. Two remember being very rattled by them: They directly threatened Pao's safety and that of her family. They threatened to harm her young daughter.

It wasn't just Pao; other members of her team were getting doxed and threatened. "Threats carry a bit more weight when the people threatening you also publish your address," Pao wrote later. Aside from addressing the community team's safety concerns, she was stoic in her response. She didn't ask the community team to remove the many images of her; the only post they removed offered a $1,000 bounty for a real image of her being punched in the face.

Two of the moderators of r/punchablefaces, where this occurred, were banned. The third moderator locked down the subreddit, posting, "This isn't your new 'safehaven' for posting about your disliking of fat people. Neither is it your place to hate on the Reddit CEO." Moderators, albeit slowly, seemed to be getting the message, that they'd need to hold their communities to a new standard.

Within days, the attempts at creating clone subreddits of those banned slowed dramatically. The backlash harassment died down, too. It had worked.

There'd been a disappointing and little-appreciated side effect of the bans. The day they took effect, r/CoonTown, which had been widely cited in the press as having been left untouched by Reddit, experienced a rush of new subscribers and traffic. It gained four thousand subscribers in two days, doubling in size from the prior month. On June 11, 2015, it garnered 870,000 page views. "The reason for the influx appeared to be a rush for users to show support as the threat of losing 'Coontown' grew," wrote the Southern Poverty Law Center.

Journalists pondered the boundaries of speaking one's mind anonymously online. As Gawker noted, "Starting to crack down on harassment has positioned Reddit in an awkward middle ground—too CoonTown for the mainstream, too moderated-even-the-tiniest-little bit for those who cry censorship because a company (remember, Reddit is a business) won't give their No Fatties club a place to meet."

Still, Pao chalked the subreddit ban up as a win. It would be her last at the helm of Reddit.

FAME AND ITS INVERSE

The life of Alexis Ohanian had morphed dramatically by mid-2015. The intense drama unfolding within the Reddit office and on Reddit itself had nothing to do with it.

Since the publication of his book, *Without Their Permission*, more than a year earlier, Ohanian had completed a 107-stop bus tour—speaking mostly on college campuses to young, tech-savvy audiences about founding Reddit. He had appeared on TV talk shows, including *The Colbert Report*, and had become a sought-after public speaker, taking gigs on stages in Beijing, Dublin, Paris, Singapore, and Rome. He told and retold Reddit's story and evangelized for the free and open Internet. In his travels he was accompanied often by Elisabeth Garvin, a smiley blonde-haired woman in her early twenties, who acted as scheduler, friend, adviser, Lyft-booker, personal historian, photographer, and, sometimes, the world's most petite and inoffensive bodyguard.

Recently, Ohanian had begun trying to balance his globetrotting with focusing on his health: He'd been drinking more water, streamlining his diet, starting his days with a vegetable smoothie or the occasional Soylent (a meal replacement beloved in Silicon

Valley). He'd purchased a house in San Francisco's chic NoPa neighborhood (North of the Panhandle of Golden Gate Park). He'd also fallen in love with one of the most famous athletes on the planet.

Ohanian's romance with Serena Williams, which has played out in glossy publications and behind paparazzi lenses, improbably began in May 2015 while Ohanian was preparing to deliver a speech at an advertising conference in Rome. His laptop battery died while he was working on his presentation at a café one evening in advance of the Festival of Media Global. Eschewing work, he decided to have a drink. In the bar he spotted a woman who looked a lot like Kristen Wiig, the comedic actress, writer, and producer who was also the cousin of one of Ohanian's friends. Ohanian sent his buddy a Facebook message asking if his cousin was in Rome. Affirmative: She was there filming *Zoolander 2*. Ohanian introduced himself, and they stayed up drinking and chatting until 2 a.m.

Ohanian slept in, missing the breakfast buffet at his hotel, the Rome Cavalieri Waldorf Astoria, the site of the conference. The Waldorf Astoria offers panoramic views from a tree-covered hill above the city, a private art collection, and "aristocratic" rooms. It also boasts red-clay tennis courts. Searching for coffee and a snack, Ohanian was directed out back to one of the hotel's two pools where he could order food. Headphones on, he sat down at an empty table near a large group. He figured they'd keep to themselves, and he'd get a little work done. Not the case.

"Aye, mate! There's a rat. There's a rat by your table," a voice with an unmistakably Australian twang called to Ohanian. "You don't want to sit there."

Ohanian looked around. No rat. He shrugged. "I'm from Brooklyn, I see rats all the time," he replied. It wasn't immediately clear to him, but the group simply wanted to spread out—and Ohanian's mobile workstation was in their way. A tall and striking woman in the group laughed and fessed up. "No, we just don't want you sitting there. We're going to use that table."

Ohanian did a double take. He was "98 percent sure" the

woman who just spoke to him was Serena Williams. He didn't watch tennis—ever—but he'd of course heard of her, seen photos, and knew that she was widely considered the greatest living athlete. All of a sudden, the world's best tennis player was inviting Ohanian to join their group. They got to talking, about the conference that had brought Ohanian there, about Reddit. Ohanian didn't let on that he knew next to nothing about tennis.

Williams admitted she'd never heard of Reddit—but was intrigued by Ohanian's investment company. She later recalled that she'd long been interested in getting involved in investing—but knew little about the industry. Williams says she asked Ohanian for his number, to continue the conversation, and he obliged. Among her crew there at the pool was her longtime agent, Jill Smoller, at William Morris Endeavor Entertainment. When Williams departed for a dance class, Ohanian talked more with Smoller, who worked with his own literary agent. They sent him a selfie together. Smoller invited Ohanian to join their box that evening at Williams's match.

That night, Ohanian posted a photo from the match on Instagram, writing, "I guess I'm a tennis fan now." The photo itself belied how little he knew about the sport: In it, Williams was foot-faulting. "I didn't realize it," he admitted later. "That was really bad."

The faux pas didn't prevent the pair from continuing their discussion. Williams called Ohanian to ask about investments, and may have joked that she hoped he could see her play better. Ohanian wondered whether it was a genuine invite or idle conversation—but put his money on the former. He let her know he was coming to see her in Paris. "Worst-case scenario," he thought, "I go to Paris that weekend and I get blown off by Serena. Then I'll get to laugh about the story when I'm an old man."

Williams raised an eyebrow that Ohanian actually made the trip to France. Later, she didn't recall explicitly inviting him. "I said to myself, 'Huh. This is definitely taking an unexpected turn.'" Her agent arranged that the pair go out to dinner, only it wasn't precisely a date: They were chaperoned by both Williams's assistant and agent. The next day, though, before her match, the pair snuck a little time by themselves. Ohanian picked her up and they set out on a midday date on their own. "We grabbed an Uber and just started driving. We saw a zoo, and I was like, we should get out here," Ohanian said. They watched a leopard eat its lunch. They bought some candy. Williams recalled later that it wasn't long before she "started to look at him in a different way—not just a guy who was super tall. He had this incredible personality and infectious smile and laugh. He just also had a great set of values that couldn't be compromised."

Around this time, much of Ohanian's life took place in the air. He was still flying back and forth from New York to San Francisco, one week here, one week there. He broke off a five-year relationship with his Ph.D.-candidate girlfriend, Sabriya Stukes, which he'd found difficult to maintain since spending so much time in San Francisco. Before long, he was also flying to tennis matches nearly every other weekend, and routinely visiting West Palm Beach, Florida, where Williams lived and trained. Their relationship had leaked into the press a bit at this point, but Ohanian wasn't stressed about being spotted with her. He joked that he felt like he was an "antidote" to her celebrity. They'd notice photos being snapped of them by citizens and paparazzi, but rarely—at this point in their relationship—would such photos appear on celebrity-news sites. After they attended the Academy Awards together, Ohanian, who was accustomed to some measure of notoriety in San Francisco, where he was occasionally stopped on the street, was cropped out of some of the photos of Williams. In others published online, he wasn't named. He explained later, "It's like, here's Serena Williams and Roger Federer and, uh, *some guy.*"

(• •)

Huffman, by the summer of 2015, had also become accustomed to being spotted and called out in public. As with Ohanian, his height made him stand out at parties, bars, or just walking down the street, and his striking light blue eyes and thick shock of golden hair made him recognizable. Once, a fellow passenger in an Uber car pool ID'd him solely by his voice; he'd listened to hours upon hours of an online course Huffman taught called "CS253: Web Application Engineering."

When Huffman has to prepare for an event, speak onstage, or lead a meeting, he likes being "Steve Huffman, founder of Reddit." When he's out with friends, he does not. If asked at bars if he's Steve Huffman, he often replies, "No," and turns away.

Now that he was over thirty, he was confident in his desires. He knew he liked to build things, and on the weekends he liked to hang out with his friends from back in the Y Combinator days, spending afternoons in large groups lounging at biergartens or in backyards, or nights at dive bars or karaoke. All alcohol-fueled, all a blast.

Anonymity wasn't always easy: His friends, such as Justin Kan, Snapchatted and Instagrammed frequently, and given their success, they lived lives at times filled with conspicuous consumption. Kan, along with Emmett Shear and Michael Seibel, sold Twitch, which started way back when as Justin.tv in the Crystal Towers apartments, to Amazon in 2014 for almost $1 billion. That same summer, Huffman and his friends all flew to Ibiza for Seibel's bachelor party. Huffman dominated the club dance floors all over the Mediterranean island.

Also in the summer of 2014, Kan spent evenings and weekends enlisting a group of about twenty friends to prepare for Burning Man, the sixty-thousand-person, clothing-optional experiment in radical self-reliance that takes place at the end of August. As every Burning Man participant is encouraged to gift services or goods to others, Kan's camp would be called Bao Chicka Wow Wow and would provide warm pork buns to hungry residents of the temporary city.

Kan also wanted to create a mobile piece of public art, in the form of a massive "art car," as many roving vehicles of the playa are known. Huffman became very involved that summer in building it. On weekends and evenings, he'd head out to an East Oakland do-it-yourself industrial art and hacker party space called Nimby. While Kan and others hunted down materials—polycarbonate panels, LED lighting, welding tools—Huffman troubleshot the vehicle's engine. The physical engineering challenge was a welcome respite from his typical days managing Hipmunk programmers.

By 2014, Burning Man had become a weeklong creative outlet for outsider artisans everywhere, but for Silicon Valley's tech plutocrats it had become an almost mandatory annual social event, an opportunity to rub sunburned, sand-specked elbows with millionaire and billionaire attendees such as Larry Page, Sergey Brin, and Jeff Bezos. Kan's friends, Huffman included, spent the end of August camping in Black Rock City and roaming it in their massive iceberg on wheels, which had been dubbed "Titanic's End."

Huffman had embraced the Burning Man mantra of "radical self-reliance." Like so many after the 2008 financial meltdown, he had become concerned about the stability of government and the risks associated with large-scale unrest. Certainly, Reddit provided a window into online political dissent, with its communities devoted to anarchy and several little-known subreddits that helped germinate the alt-right movement. "We all collectively take it on faith that our country works, that our currency is valuable, the peaceful transfer of power—that all of these things that we hold dear work," he explained in a 2017 story in the *New Yorker* about "doomsday preppers." Should something upend the order of things, Huffman wanted to be prepared. He'd stockpiled munitions, vehicles, and provisions and made a point of keeping physically fit. He even had a theory as to his fate, should society collapse: "I also have this somewhat egotistical view that I'm a pretty good leader. I will probably be in charge, or at least not a slave, when push comes to shove."

In that same piece, Huffman did not try to shield himself from some measure of blame for the very fears of catastrophic events or societal unraveling that caused him and his friends to ponder buying real estate in New Zealand. "It's easier for people to panic when they're together," he said, noting that "the Internet has made it easier for people to be together."

The possibility of Armageddon aside, the past two years had been full of professional success—Hipmunk was in full growth mode—but private pain. His wife, Katie, had completed her residency and was now a pediatric doctor affiliated with multiple hospitals in the Bay Area. Their relationship never soured, so much as it sort of stagnated. Steve and Katie were nonconfrontational with each other, Huffman said. He later recognized that meant they were also noncommunicative. They didn't fight out their issues, but their romantic love was like the proverbial frog placed in water, then slowly set to boil. It didn't survive.

The divorce process took more than a year, which Huffman described as an agonizing experience. Still, the couple remained something like friends; the day they signed the divorce papers they went home together and watched a Redskins game. Katie continued to live with Huffman's Hipmunk cofounder, Adam Goldstein, in the original home they'd all shared in San Francisco's Mission District. Huffman moved a few blocks away; his car was still parked at Katie's.

Huffman has since despised brief blips of singlehood. He's prone to insecurity when by himself. "I'm really bad at being alone," he said. "I always have friends—or someone—with me."

AMAGEDDON

July 2, 2015, began almost like any other morning for Victoria Taylor, Reddit's blonde-haired AMA chief.

She had prepped one subject for an AMA upcoming that afternoon and was ready to dig into her email. But when Taylor arrived at the office at about 9:30 a.m. Eastern Time, human resources was waiting. Reddit's San Francisco–based HR chief had taken a last-minute red-eye flight. She greeted Taylor and opened a laptop. She dialed in Ohanian on a video call. Taylor saw Ohanian's face pop up on the screen.

Ohanian offered some pleasantries, and then thanked Taylor for the work she'd done at Reddit. He informed her that this would be her last day. She'd need to pack up her desk and take any personal possessions home.

Taylor was shocked. She had planned to go from Reddit's office in the coworking space in WeWork's SoHo location to New Jersey that evening to visit family for the long Fourth of July weekend. Her packed suitcase was by her side. There were multiple AMAs in planning stages—she couldn't abandon the individuals working hard on them. "What?" she stuttered. "How?" Taylor looked around the little glass-walled room; she'd amassed quite a collection of knickknacks and gifts from celebrities whom she'd interviewed. God, she wished she still had Jerry Seinfeld's old coffee cup, which she'd kept for ages but a WeWork cleaning staffer had inadvertently discarded.

Taylor blinked through tears and asked Ohanian: *Why?*

Ohanian messaged Pao over Slack at 6:44 a.m. Pacific Time. "It's done."

"Thanks," Pao wrote back at 6:45.

Twenty-four hours later, Reddit was flickering out to dark.

(• •)

The day Taylor was forced out, many Reddit employees were already beginning their Independence Day weekends. But as word spread about the HR chief's abrupt and mysterious flight east and Ohanian's video call, employees pinged one another over Slack and Gmail chat with questions. *Why? How? Why again?* No one had clear answers. Taylor had managed to immediately tell a couple of her current and former colleagues pieces of what transpired, but almost everyone in the San Francisco office was in the dark.

Over the past year they'd seen plenty of their colleagues called into an HR meeting, or receive a call from an executive, and then vanish. But Taylor? She was almost universally considered hardworking, kind, responsive, and helpful. She bent over backwards for her AMA subjects and the Reddit community. She seemed to embody the site's democratizing spirit, in which the best content bubbles to the top, by treating every AMA subject—from a random user's World War II veteran grandfather to Meryl Streep—with the same respect and admiration. To her colleagues, Taylor would glow, but not boast, about her subjects—she'd say that Sarah McLachlan was the cheeriest person, that Yao Ming was considerate, and a history buff, and that Robin Williams's home smelled like a nineties childhood and that he gave her the best hug she'd ever had.

On Reddit.com, word spread fast. Far-flung moderators of subreddits of all sizes, from the large, polished "default" subreddits like r/science to tiny niche ones, were confused and enraged. To hundreds of volunteer moderators who'd regularly corresponded with Taylor about AMAs and general site questions, she had been their sole conduit to the company. It appeared to them that Reddit had no system in place for conducting AMAs going forward.

Moderator u/karmanaut posted on r/OutOfTheLoop, "We all had the rug ripped out from us and we felt betrayed." He explained in a post that Taylor handled the vast majority of scheduling AMAs, prepping subjects with expectations of the process, and providing proof of their identity—a key part of AMAs. "Without her filling this role, we will be utterly overwhelmed."

At about 1 p.m. on Thursday the second, during the AMA of a Berkeley mathematician named Edward Frenkel, the entire subreddit r/IAmA suddenly went dark. Its moderators turned the forum, which had amassed 8.6 million subscribers, private.

Inside Reddit's office at 101 Montgomery, the small community management team at first only raised an eyebrow at the AMA hub shutting its doors. They began following comments on sections prone to discussing internal Reddit politics, such as r/SubredditDrama, as they lit up with comments about Taylor (a.k.a. u/chooter). Moderator chat rooms and private subreddits, too, were becoming discussion forums. Moderators of r/IAmA and r/books posted that they weren't warned about the firing and had no way to contact the individuals with AMAs scheduled.

Dell Frost, a community manager at the time, said it initially wasn't clear to his colleagues whether the reaction among users and moderators to Taylor's firing would fizzle or snowball. "Community managers were so used to the community being upset at us," he said, "that we didn't take it that seriously at first." The small community team, now led by Moreno, who was out of town and who later said she had no warning as to Taylor's dismissal, hustled to answer moderator emails asking for an explanation. They tried to calm the power moderators of default subreddits—but before long the momentum seemed to have tipped toward avalanche.

"It only took a matter of hours before we were like, 'Oh wait, this is really getting out of control,'" Frost said.

Within hours, three hundred subreddits—from r/science to r/ skrillex, from r/Calligraphy to r/cameltoe—were participating in a protest of Taylor's dismissal. Within one day, Reddit was in full revolt. Twelve hundred subreddits were essentially turned off. The term "AMAgeddon" had been coined to describe the event, and the press took to it. The Daily Dot, a website that reported frequently on the machinations of Reddit, wrote, "The great Reddit meltdown has begun."

Former community manager David Croach gave an AMA about his sudden termination from Reddit after recovering from two battles with cancer, further intensifying anti-Reddit vitriol. The site, used to seeing 160 million users a month, was being crippled by the very volunteers who'd kept it churning for years.

The portions of Reddit still online and accessible to visitors obsessed over the situation. The front page was being taken over by posts about Taylor and the blackout. At one point on July 3, every single one of the top hundred posts in r/all were about AMAgeddon. There were photos of Taylor posing with the celebrity guests she'd interviewed, such as David Duchovny and Gillian Anderson of *The X-Files*, and photos of pitchforks and torches. There were memes poking fun at Reddit's management, and a link to Google Trends' report on the sudden rise of the search term "Reddit alternatives." Meanwhile, a brand-new subreddit, r/Blackout2015, received more than ten thousand subscribers in less than eleven hours.

Taylor wrote in a brief comment on Reddit that she was "dazed" by her termination. She nodded to the fact that she appreciated the community's support. Then she went silent. She, like most other Reddit staffers, had signed a strict nondisparagement agreement, which made her fearful of speaking to the press. Her silence didn't stop the tech press and Reddit from reporting and opining on the matter.

This was it: This was the big one. This was what Reddit's community team had feared. It was why they'd been handling even absurd or baseless moderator complaints with kid gloves for years.

To moderators, this wasn't just about Taylor; this was a rebellion in which Taylor was a catalyst, but which was rooted in years of what some moderators saw as haphazard policymaking, years without the company releasing well-functioning moderator tools, even as the site grew beyond two hundred million monthly users.

In the midst of the blackout, Pao posted a defense of Reddit, a plea to moderators that stated, "We do value moderators; they allow reddit to function," and said that while new moderator tools were in the works, "Our infrastructure is monolithic, and it is going to take some time." The post inspired a host of questions from Reddit users, which went unanswered. Pao had left the thread.

To the vast majority of Redditors, Ohanian, too, was eerily quiet. The community he'd nurtured for the greater part of a decade was in full mutiny, and he'd flown to London to watch Williams compete in Wimbledon and to visit his godson. Ohanian "was suddenly nowhere to be found, via cell, text, Slack, or email," Pao wrote in her book.

Ohanian says that despite his travels, he worked tirelessly on Reddit that weekend, focusing his efforts on redistributing, and himself taking over a lot of what had been Taylor's work, and responding to AMA requests as well as to angry individuals who'd been left in the lurch. He was on Slack with Pao and the community team for hours both Saturday and Sunday, and says he spoke to multiple reporters at major media outlets while paying a visit to his godson.

Live on Reddit, he spent what he estimated to have been five or six hours responding to enraged moderators in two prominent subreddits where moderators hung out, r/defaultmods and r/modnews. He felt like he'd helped placate them and given the media something new to digest.

He was wrong: Those subreddits were private. Only moderators could view them. That meant his hours of work, all his comments he considered thoughtful, could only be viewed by a select group, the moderators who'd already subscribed.

The information that did get out immediately wasn't good. A

leaked chat log showed that Ohanian also engaged in a mostly tone-deaf exchange with the moderators of r/science, who'd hit walls in trying to solidify an AMA with Stephen Hawking, for which Taylor had been Reddit's point person. Ohanian claimed he would dig into her mailbox to find the contact information and handle it but repeated over and over that moderators with questions should email a general message box. "You managed to burn through years of goodwill in an afternoon here," one commented. "Asking us to 'just send an email' is de facto telling us to get bent."

In the meantime, Ohanian also typed some words into what happened to be a public subreddit. To him, it was just one of many comments. To the rest of the world, it was the first thing he, or any other member of Reddit's leadership, had said recently regarding the firing of a woman whose name all of a sudden was not just all over Reddit and the tech press but also in the pages of the *New York Times* and other mainstream publications. Ohanian wrote a classic Reddit in-joke line meaning, *I'm standing by watching this drama unfold*: "Popcorn tastes good."

(• •)

What actually precipitated Taylor's dismissal remains a matter of great speculation, something that the Reddit community blamed largely on Pao—and that the press pinned, though more lightly, on Ohanian as well.

Both Ohanian and Pao have apologized for it; Ohanian actually performed the act of telling Taylor the news. To this day, neither readily admits the decision as their own. Pao, as interim CEO, took the brunt of the Reddit community's vitriol. She weathered a tremendous amount of online and offline abuse. It seemed to add up: She had been trying to reshape Reddit, and had been known to dismiss employees. Former employees have said that she had displayed no significant degree of respect for Taylor.

But Pao blamed Ohanian. She wrote matter-of-factly in her book that he not only made the call but also "flubbed" the "involuntary departure." He "botched so much of the process," she wrote. "Alexis thought the job was easy and so didn't understand how motivated I was to keep Victoria. I felt that he didn't appreciate the skill and finesse that went into these conversations or the value of relationships with the AMA moderators."

Ohanian maintains that Pao's account is flawed. On multiple occasions, when speaking about this period in which Taylor was terminated, he has said that he deferred to Pao on staffing matters; that the board, by making her chief executive, gave her control over hiring and firing.

He later said that he was called in to meet with Pao and human resources the prior afternoon, July 1, and that Pao brought up the matter of Taylor's employment. "I had the impression she saw Victoria as one of the last holdovers from the Yishan era. She'd floated firing her to me previously," he said. Pao then asked the human resources director to fly to New York, in order to make sure Taylor's termination was completed before the company's next all-hands meeting, which was scheduled for not long after the long Fourth of July weekend, Ohanian recalled.

Ohanian respected Taylor and had attended her small wedding in Wisconsin roughly six weeks earlier. "I volunteered to call and tell her," he said, so she wouldn't be alone with the human resources employee when she got the news. "It was the right thing to do."

Ohanian did have a different vision for AMAs than did Taylor. He wanted to modernize them, enlisting an outside transcription service rather than relying on Taylor's quick fingers to type out AMA subjects' responses on the fly. He had hired a crew to work on video AMAs. He'd helped bring his personal publicist and friend, Ashley Dawkins, into Reddit's fold; within months of Taylor's dismissal, Dawkins would assume a new position at Reddit, head of entertainment, which managed celebrity engagement—including the top-billed celebrity AMAs.

In her book, *Reset*, Pao noted that a condition of her resignation was that Ohanian would "take ownership of his failures publicly."

On July 10, 2015, the very day Pao resigned, Ohanian says he was sent a statement to post online. He later admitted he was frustrated by the request, but that he complied. He posted: "Ellen is a class act...I have admired her fearlessness and calm...It was my decision to change how we work with AMAs and the transition was my failure and I hope we can keep moving forward from that lesson."

Immediately after Taylor's dismissal, the press speculated that Taylor had been unwilling to work with Ohanian's new vision for AMAs—more hands-off from the team, a more automated process for regular Joes, more celebrities and notable individuals interacting with Reddit on their own. This was precisely what Taylor did not want this process to become, and it is precisely what it evolved into after her departure.

(• •)

By Friday night, July 3, Huffman was on edge seeing Reddit in revolt. His phone was blowing up with texts with messages like "Now is the time!" "You have to go back!" "Save Reddit!" There were dozens upon dozens of messages. Still, Huffman wasn't certain what to do. On some level, he knew he had a duty. When Chris Slowe texted him to ask whether he'd make the leap, Huffman responded, tellingly, "Stand by."

He spent Saturday the Fourth in Sonoma, celebrating the thirtieth birthday of Jamie Quint, a fellow Y Combinator alum. His friends, mostly from the Y Scraper days, had rented a house just outside Napa Valley, and as they sipped wine and soaked in the sunshine, they speculated about whether Reddit could survive this massive moderator revolt.

To Kan, Huffman seemed torn about his next move. Huffman felt responsible for keeping Hipmunk afloat and did not want to let down Goldstein by jumping ship. But he also felt beholden to Reddit: He was just thirty-one, but it had been his life's work, and now it was being flushed down the toilet. Kan told Huffman he thought he should and—possibly—could do both. The return of a company's founder was a familiar storyline in Silicon Valley; Steve Jobs had returned in Apple's darkest hour; likewise, Mark Pincus had recently reassumed the chief executive role at his floundering creation, Zynga.

Huffman and his peers were guided more by trying to build a remarkable life than by personal joy. "Among our friend group, a lot of what you should or shouldn't do isn't really based on what we think will make you happiest," Kan explained. Instead, it's more about building a body of work—a legacy. Kan said he entered the discussion under the framework of: "Is it the right thing for him to do for his legacy, him being in a position to build something really great?" So his answer to whether Huffman should return to Reddit was: "Definitely." To Seibel, it was a risk, but perhaps a necessary one. He locked eyes with Huffman and told him, "You're running into a burning building."

Huffman figured Sam Altman, one of Reddit's major financial backers, had been back-channeling through his friends, in an attempt to positively influence him, so he tried to take encouraging counsel with a grain of salt. Regardless, the advice—*go back!*—hit him from all angles. He knew what he had to do. He found a spot on the property with decent cell phone reception and dialed Condé Nast president Bob Sauerberg.

No answer. Huffman tucked his iPhone back in his pocket. Altman called him soon thereafter. He started to launch into a full-tilt pitch for Huffman to return to Reddit as CEO. Huffman cut him off.

"Dude, stop it," Huffman said. He'd heard this all too many times. And he'd made up his mind.

"I'll do it," he said.

Sunday, July 5, Huffman finally got hold of Sauerberg, who attempted to hammer out the contract. Huffman wasn't in the mood to negotiate, and just said, "Fine, fine," to the words streaming from Sauerberg's end of the line. He couldn't listen straight; he couldn't yet fully grasp to what he was agreeing. But he knew it would irrevocably shape the rest of his days. Still, he'd do it: He'd run into the burning building. He told Sauerberg, "I'll get it done."

(• •)

Erik Martin, the longtime community manager and former general manager of Reddit, watched Reddit's blackout continue from afar, from his apartment in Red Hook, Brooklyn, and from his new job in Manhattan at WeWork. The massive moderator revolt didn't shock him. "I mean, that's what we trained them to do—sort of," he said. "You can't do what we did, organizing against SOPA and against doxing and then say, 'Oh, don't use these organizing skills when it's about *us*.'" Some facets of the blackout were strangely validating to former employees. Alex Angel recognized that even the calendar-year timing was prime for revolt: She'd made a mental note that late summer was always when "the shit hit the fan."

The community's ability to revolt—and potentially affect the decisions that come down from corporate on high, away from the powerless users—was more broadly satisfying to underdogs everywhere. One post that rose to the front page of Reddit from r/Showerthoughts read, "Victoria is living the dream we all have when we get fired—that the company that fired us will instantly and fantastically fall apart."

(• •)

Whether indeed Reddit had brought this AMAgeddon upon itself, within days it turned from a nonviolent protest of silence by hundreds of subreddits into a furious, hate-fueled witch hunt.

A Change.org petition called for Pao to step down as the chief executive of Reddit, stating that she'd ushered in a "new era of censorship" on the site. It was weeks old, but picked up one hundred thousand fresh signatures in a day.

As posts on Reddit encouraged more community members to join the revolt, signatures to the petition swelled, as did the widespread harassment of Pao. Some of the Hitler imagery reemerged. Threads on r/Blackout2015 associated every four-letter word with her name; the posts were sexist and racist. Her in-box was again jammed with insults, slurs, and overt threats.

The community managers, who under normal circumstances would have been tasked with mediating disputes and resolving tensions, had spent months nurturing grievances with Pao's leadership. Most of them had been close friends with Taylor. Plus, just weeks earlier, McComas, Reddit's head of product, had been suddenly let go. He was also the husband of the woman in charge of enforcing content policies at Reddit, Jessica Moreno. Regardless of motivation, Moreno's attention was divided; also she was traveling that holiday weekend when the blackout ignited.

At the office during the week following the blackout, Pao maintained a steadfast, hardened demeanor. Employees at the time say she was a beacon of calm. "Ellen was getting attacked from all angles on the Internet, and in person she had the strongest face, and never showed any signs of vulnerability," one young female employee later recalled. Pao religiously kept mum to press and employees on the matter of Taylor's employment, stating, "We do not discuss personnel issues," but when employees asked about the company's stability, she maintained, all week, as the petition for her removal grew to more than two hundred thousand signatures, "I am not resigning. I am committed to staying here."

It wasn't the truth, though. Pao had already met with two members of the board, who she later claimed made it clear that she should step down. They said she was unwilling to commit to their growth plan, which she wrote, one board member said, was half a billion users. "The number was not possible unless we brought back stolen celebrity pictures," she later wrote.

She called her executive coach and told him she was about to be fired. The next day, according to Pao, a board observer called her and told her she'd need to resign right away, or "They said they'll go to Plan B!" (The board observer at the time, Alfred Lin, said he was a friend of Pao and denied making such a phone call. Altman, who had previously had a nonvoting board seat, making his role for a time similar to that of an observer, recalls having been the board member who spoke most often with her during this time. He denies saying it, and noted that it was not a phrase he would use, nor his style of doing business.)

Pao, in the end, resigned. She later wrote that she didn't want to learn what "Plan B" might entail. She'd already been through the wringer with Kleiner Perkins. Her family did not deserve to endure more of this. She continued, "My joints and ego ached, I was physically and emotionally exhausted, and I had no idea what would come next."

(• •)

Ellen Pao posted her resignation on Reddit on July 10, 2015.

> In my eight months as Reddit's CEO, I've seen the good, the bad and the ugly on Reddit. The good has been off-the-wall inspiring, and the ugly made me doubt humanity.
>
> I just want to remind everyone that I am just another human; I have a family, and I have feelings. Everyone attacked on Reddit is just another person like you and me. When people make something up to attack me or someone else, it spreads, and we eventually will see it. And we will feel bad, not just about what was said. Also because it undercuts the authenticity of Reddit and shakes our faith in humanity.

Pao, the woman who'd been harassed and threatened for her attempts to clean up Reddit and grow it as a company, urged users to "remember the human." For this, she was gilded with Reddit Gold a remarkable 107 times. She thanked Redditors on the thread profusely.

When a user responded to her post, "Time to grab some popcorn," Pao commented back: "Popcorn tastes good."

U/taario replied: "Make this woman CEO already! Oh wait."

U/ahampster commented: "maybe she'd want to mod r/IAmA," to which u/Kip_Hackman_ wrote: "Aaaaand scene."

THE RETURN OF STEVE

On Friday, July 10, the same day Ellen Pao posted her resignation letter, Steve Huffman and Alexis Ohanian met for an early lunch at Super Duper Burgers on San Francisco's Market Street. It was going to be a hell of a day, so they each had a locally sourced, organic burger. They were to meet Altman outside the front door of 101 New Montgomery at noon.

Huffman had been given the decision by the board over the past week about what role Ohanian would play in the future of Reddit. "If you want to work with Alexis, that's awesome. I'm perfectly comfortable if you say no," Keith Rabois, a board member, recalled to Wired.com that he'd told Huffman. Altman knew the pair had been working through their past issues, but said a few weeks later that things between them had been resolved "enough that things weren't going to blow up. It's probably still not sorted out, honestly."

Once in front of the Reddit office, the three men shook hands, and Ohanian and Altman ushered Huffman past the doorman and into an elevator to the fifth floor, where the three went straight to a small conference room and shut the door. Pao was already inside. She had a list of journalists' names and numbers they were to dial.

Within minutes, a handful of reporters, including Laurie Segall of CNN, Mike Isaac from the *New York Times*, and Kara Swisher of Recode, fired questions at the incoming—and former—CEOs of Reddit. Altman did a lot of the talking. It was easy for him to hype Huffman to the journalists on the phone, since he had long respected him both as a programmer and a leader. Plus, the magic of the comeback story was not lost on Altman. "He actually built Reddit, he wrote the code," Altman said into the speaker at the center of the table. "The chance to get that back was so special."

It was professional, clean, and cool. Somehow, everyone managed to keep their answers to the questions about Pao's departure positive. "She did an incredible job," breezed Altman. "She stepped into a really messy situation." When Swisher cut in and asked Pao directly whether she was fired, Pao managed to force out a laugh. "Thanks for getting right to the point," she said, reiterating that she had resigned due to the board's aggressive growth goals. She said that her departure was a "mutual decision" between herself and the board. She didn't mention the threat of "Plan B."

Across the table, Huffman's skin was crawling. "I was just thinking, *God, this is very awkward*," he recalled later. "It's kind of like being in a room with your ex *and* your new girlfriend or something."

His heart was racing. The panic wasn't just a response to the reporters on the phone, nor simply being in the same room as Pao. Rather, it was in anticipation of the moments that would come once the phone had been hung up, once they, together, would take the elevator one floor down. In just moments, he'd need to stand up in front of nearly the entire staff of Reddit, only a tiny handful of whom he'd ever met before, and address them en masse. He'd need to begin to build these individuals' trust. He'd need to inspire them.

He felt moisture begin to accumulate on the surface of his skin as he stood in the elevator with Altman, Ohanian, and Pao. When the doors opened on the fourth floor, he was a deer in headlights: The entire staff was already gathered. He stood and breathed deeply for a couple minutes as Pao spoke first, delivering prepared remarks. Her words were a shock to many junior staffers, who'd heard her repeat over and over in the past ten days that she would not resign.

To Huffman, her words were a blur. He told himself, *This is almost over.* He told himself in order to cope, *Someday, this will just be a memory.*

Huffman had told Goldstein, his Hipmunk cofounder, that previous Monday—and despite objections from the Reddit board, had told most of Hipmunk's staff on Tuesday. He knew they were loyal, and although they were teary-eyed and disappointed, they wouldn't leak the news. All week he was poised to walk over to Reddit's office and take the reins; the fact that it took the full week to solidify Pao's resignation meant he'd already gone through five days of racing adrenaline and uneven sleep by the time he stood facing employees at 101 New Montgomery.

Huffman panned the crowd of unsmiling faces and realized that each of these people had been through a week of hell, too. Heck, a year of purgatory for some. He'd be their third CEO in nine months. He'd prepared a speech but didn't want to read from a paper. So he ad-libbed, introducing himself, his history, and what he wanted to see out of Reddit. It was not a slam dunk. He came across as enthusiastic—if a little terrified.

Some employees were nonplussed by his actual words, which included multiple notes on issues that needed imminent fixing: Reddit should be shipping product; Reddit should get a handle on users. To others, they felt critical, arrogant: the Ultimate Creator of this thing telling everyone in the room they were screwing it up. "It just rubbed a lot of people the wrong way," a former staffer said. "They were like, *fuck this guy.*"

To Huffman, the crossed arms and dour expressions were a shock. He'd just left Hipmunk, where his longtime employees offered up encouragement and hugs. "That was not what I got at Reddit," he said.

Other employees saw in Huffman's words and tone a laser focus on product, a specific set of goals in mind. "You could tell there was motivation, you could tell he was very intent on being back, and had the confidence that he was ready to do it," said Stephen Greenwood, a video producer hired by Ohanian.

Huffman took a few questions from the gathered staffers, including: So, are we allowed to drink now? Sure, Huffman said. "I'm not gonna work at a company where we're gonna treat you like children. We're gonna treat you like adults, and in exchange, I want you to act like adults and look out for one another."

By the time Huffman was done introducing himself and making a feeble attempt to rally the team, Pao had already left the building. Despite having announced to the press that she'd stay on as an adviser, she would not be seen at 101 New Montgomery again. While Huffman spoke, Altman's prepared post revealing to the world that Huffman was again chief executive of Reddit, titled "An old team at Reddit," posted to r/announcements. It was official. It was only 1:15 p.m. Huffman had more work to do.

He grabbed his laptop and logged in as u/spez, his longtime primary account. He pulled up Altman's post and read in. Already, questions were waiting for him. He typed an initial greeting response into the comment box, and answered Redditors' questions for the next fifteen minutes.

Huffman realized he wanted to immediately make good on his goals, to meet the team, to make all that was wrong right. He swiveled his chair around and introduced himself to the first staffer he saw. "Hey, I'm Steve." The employee looked at him and grunted, "Hmm." Huffman stared for a moment, then turned back around to his computer. It took every ounce of restraint he could muster not to fire the guy on the spot. Instead, he tried again. He turned to the next computer over. "Hey, I'm Steve." It worked. "I'm Jack," said an engineering team leader, Jack Lawson. They struck up a friendly conversation. That afternoon, Huffman shook hands and introduced himself to about half of the sixty-five staffers.

At 2 p.m., Huffman convened a meeting of department heads. He asked them to simply go around and tell him their names, what they were working on, and note any pressing issues they were having. Simple enough, he thought. He knew this was a team that hadn't, in Silicon Valley parlance, been adept at "shipping product," so he suspected there were issues—deeper issues, perhaps, than any of the surface-level content scandals of the past year.

What he received was an absolute deluge of problems: interpersonal issues on teams, upcoming projects that had fallen off schedule. "It was one kind of crisis after another." He said he left the room shell-shocked, thinking, "What the fuck? What are you doing? Like what the . . . this is insane."

But he also left the room knowing who could be his major allies in the forthcoming battle for the future of Reddit. First, there was Melissa Tidwell, who went by Missy, and who was Reddit's highly capable general counsel, a veteran Googler who'd been hired by Pao and helped shepherd through some of the controversial content policies. She possessed a sense of humor and yet held a firm grasp on reality; she had a clear-eyed comprehension of the issues that dogged Reddit. There was also Blount, the head of engineering. She'd not only capably explained her own small team's situation but helpfully interjected to give context on other issues throughout the company. "Okay, here's somebody who I can lean on," Huffman thought.

Huffman pulled Blount aside after the meeting. But when she countered by immediately asking, "Can we talk?" Huffman's heart sank. He knew what she was going to say. She was quitting. She said she'd been through chaos before and didn't have the appetite for this. This was not what she signed up for.

Huffman implored her to think about it over the weekend. She agreed. It was a moment of relief amid a dispiriting day. Huffman realized the company was plagued by low morale, deeply in technical debt, and low on ability to correct course. It had just one iOS engineer, one Android engineer, and one and a half mobile web engineers. Bleary-eyed and daunted, he made his way down to the café area, where he found a few staffers had cracked open beers. Soon thereafter, a group departed the office for John Colins, a brick-walled bar not a block away from the office.

At the bar, a couple employees approached Huffman to chat, noting that they'd met him at the ten-year party.

"Did you know then?" they asked. He said no way, no. Obviously not.

"We knew," they said.

(• •)

The following day, a Saturday, Huffman and Ohanian went into the office to work, side by side, nearly alone, for the first time in five years. Huffman had a hundred questions; he needed to absorb a new lifetime of the company he'd begun. He'd also built up five years of ideas; now he needed to figure out how to begin to make them reality. Huffman also had an AMA to complete beginning promptly at 10 a.m.

On the thread begun by Sam Altman, "An old team at reddit," and on his AMA, "I am Steve Huffman, the new CEO of Reddit. AMA," he promptly stuck his foot in his mouth.

U/kickme444 asked on the former, "I wonder if you have any intention of keeping redditgifts around in the future?" Huffman responded, "Not sure. I'm just starting to get to know everyone here and getting a lay of the land." He later recalled having read it too quickly, typed too quickly, and didn't recognize the username of Dan McComas, the creator of Reddit Gifts who'd very recently been suddenly let go. McComas was the one asking that question.

Some users gave Huffman the benefit of the doubt. But then two dozen others explained the beautiful phenomenon of mass giving that is Reddit Gifts. Some claimed it was their entry point into Reddit and begged him to keep it going. Others entreated him to rehire McComas. McComas's wife, Jessica Moreno, who'd remained at Reddit after he'd been let go, chimed in on the thread, too, to explain that awkward arrangement.

Between that AMA and commenting on Altman's post from the previous day, Huffman created some trouble for himself. When a user asked if he'd be hiring Victoria back, he wrote "no," and said she'd been let go for specific reasons. He later explained, "I didn't realize we weren't even allowed to say her name."

Huffman knew these words for "the community" of 150 million Redditors, whose hearts he was pursuing, were of paramount importance. So perhaps his most significant question to tackle that morning was not about upholding Pao's bans on controversial Reddit communities. Perhaps it was this: Would you rather fight 1,000 duck-sized horses or one horse-sized duck?

He wrote that he would rather fight "1,000 duck-sized horses. Since they can't climb stairs, you can easily get away from them long enough to figure out how to drown them." It garnered more than fourteen hundred upvotes.

While Huffman endured his stressful AMA, the background soundtrack was the *plunk*, pause, *plunk*, pause, *plunk*, applause of a televised tennis match. Ohanian had flown back from Wimbledon for all of this change at Reddit, but he wouldn't miss watching his girlfriend's matches. At one point, Huffman saw the flicker of Ohanian's cell phone screen lighting up, and a text come in with a lines-long string of kissy-face emojis.

Huffman glanced up at the television and watched Serena Williams entering the tennis court for a match. She was just putting down her cell phone.

"Did I just watch Serena Williams text you a wall of kissy emojis?" he said to Ohanian.

"Yeah bro," Ohanian replied.

FUZZY APPROACH

How did Reddit grow into a community with hundreds of millions of users that could snuff itself out in a single day? How does a single employee's dismissal lead an entire company valued at half a billion dollars to almost implode?

When Yishan Wong had referred to Reddit as a hivemind, he hadn't been entirely wrong. He had reason to fear it, but the trepidation with which he approached Reddit's community ended up undercutting it. He granted the hive too much power to perceive its own reality. Users regarded Reddit as a playground for pushing and testing the limits of free speech, and where pseudonymous users could be the masters of their own strange online domains. When Pao told staffers to "remember the human" in their work and their decisions, it didn't even resonate. The set of rules that governed Reddit were considered one thing—but executed as another. The belief system was incongruent. The center could not hold.

Chris Slowe, Reddit's first employee, had a different—and more deft—metaphor to examine this gap in perception. He said, "Things that should be treated as case law started getting turned into the Constitution." What he meant was that standalone, and often poor, decisions to allow certain behavior or content ended up being elevated to govern everything that happened on Reddit. That incoherent and disjointed constitution then dictated that when completely immoral content, say, a photo of Jennifer Lawrence naked in a bubble bath, which invaded her privacy and had been stolen from her, showed up on the site, it was considered fine.

Never was this tension more apparent than when Huffman stepped back into the CEO role. Huffman wasn't just the new CEO; he was Reddit's James Madison. As Reddit's "creator," the author of most of the site's initial codebase, he was imbued with the power to rewrite its constitution.

He didn't waste time. On his fifth day as CEO, he posted an announcement that Reddit was reevaluating its policy on the most "offensive and obscene content." "Neither Alexis nor I created Reddit to be a bastion of free speech, but rather as a place where open and honest discussion can happen." Commenters went wild.

Yishan Wong, from his personal computer, watched thousands of comments come back at Huffman, and chimed in on the thread: "AYYYYYY LMAO. How's everyone doing? This is AWESOME!"

On his seventh day as CEO, Huffman posted on Reddit, "Let's talk content, AMA." He laid out a brief history of free speech on Reddit, with himself at the center of it. "As we grew, I became increasingly uncomfortable projecting my worldview on others. More practically, I didn't have time to pass judgment on everything, so I decided to judge nothing." He dubbed the ensuing era "Don't Ask, Don't Tell," and said it didn't go well. It led to inconsistent reasoning and policy stagnation.

Huffman on that day, July 16, 2015, announced a new set of "additional restrictions," which would ban content on Reddit that was deemed to incite harm or violence against an individual or group, anything that harassed, bullied, or harmed an individual or group, or that included sexually suggestive content featuring minors.

This new set of restrictions essentially gave Huffman and his teams the power to cut off a handful of the worst offenders. Bans on individuals grew into a tiered warning system; they could be automatically instituted for one, three, or seven days. Truly egregious policy violations resulted in permanent username bans. Similarly, Huffman introduced a new quarantine system under which legal but generally offensive subreddits could only be viewed by subscribers who had specifically requested to sign up for them—and those subscribers needed to do that through a verified email address. Quarantining a subreddit in this fashion also meant that Reddit's most important ads would be removed from it, and the pages' posts wouldn't show up in search or on r/popular. The move allowed certain problematic subreddits, such as r/SexWith-Dogs, to go on existing, while Reddit stunted their growth and shielded them from Google, advertiser offense, and the eyes of unsuspecting newbies.

Enacting the changes was a slog at first. Huffman said he and the community staff decided to quarantine the overtly racist subreddit r/CoonTown and then debated its existence for weeks. Not long after, he described the back-and-forth as "This is free speech. This is racist. This is bad for the community, this and that. There's a lot of ways you can argue it." During the debate, Reddit continued to be criticized in the press for not taking action—that the site was essentially subsidizing white supremacist behavior by continuing to host r/CoonTown, with its two hundred thousand page views a day.

Just weeks later, in August 2015, Reddit finally banned r/CoonTown. Not for being overtly racist or harboring a group of white supremacists that rivaled the traffic of Stormfront, the decades-old and notorious white supremacist website. Instead, Reddit said it did so only as part of a group of communities that Huffman wrote "exist solely to annoy other redditors, prevent us from improving Reddit, and generally make Reddit worse for everyone else." Also included in the list of bans that day were communities dedicated to animated child pornography and a subreddit called r/WatchN---ersDie. Even if he wouldn't admit it at the time, Huffman had applied case law.

A few months later, Huffman was happy with the result of the bans and the new subreddit quarantine system. "We quarantined a couple nasty ones yesterday and nobody even noticed. No press picked up on it," he said. "We just found a shitty community and took action." (The community in question was a new attempt at r/CoonTown. "They basically replaced the n-word with 'Google,'" Huffman said. "They're trying to be cute, but they're fucking idiots. We're not stupid.")

The process of cutting off noxious communities and users had become an actual process, a streamlined system in which user-reported comments and threads would reach moderators and the community team. A new team dubbed "trust and safety" would perform an analysis. Legal would sign off on the ban or quarantine. The subreddit's moderator team would have been warned multiple times before the ban, either by a member of the community team, whose identities are public, or by a username from the trust and safety team, whose identities are entirely shielded.

Still, despite a cleaner line being drawn, Reddit continued to rest on claims that a community had violated the site's policies, rather than, say, violating human decency, morals, or ethics.

(• •)

Blount, who ran engineering, ended up leaving within days of Huffman's return. Her departure was widely seen as a move made in protest of Pao's ouster; she told media outlets at the time that Victoria Taylor "wasn't on a glass cliff. But it's hard for me to see it any other way than Ellen was." Blount insisted at the time that it wasn't a matter of protest; she said Huffman simply couldn't convince her the mission going forward was sound.

Moreno, too, resigned. She was the fourth woman in a highly visible role at the company to depart in a month. Two members of the existing executive team stayed: Zubair Jandali, the advertising chief, and Melissa Tidwell, general counsel.

In seeking to find engineering talent, Huffman would be

laughed at, or worse. "Laughing would be generous," he said later. "Some people were offended that we would ask." In light of this, he was extremely proud to within months bring on Marty Weiner from Pinterest to lead engineering; soon they'd put teams in place to hatch plans for developing and launching products, analytics, and moderator tools. He also made quick additions to the now-shattered community team. He'd heard from a community manager that there'd been a drawn-out HR failing he might want to revisit. Two avid Reddit moderators had applied for jobs way back in 2014; they'd had their offer letters pulled after Wong stopped showing up. Then, under Pao, their hiring process had gotten restarted—but chugged to a stop again. One of them, Bill Cline, u/sodypop, had quit his steady job in Illinois and packed up a moving truck before the second offer had been rescinded. Reddit's staff wasn't sure what came of him. But Huffman figured it would be worth a shot to get these two, Cline and Susie Vass, back.

For the past several months, Cline had been essentially homeless. He'd been driving around in his car, camping at national and state parks. He'd sold most of his possessions. "It was pretty devastating to think, 'Well, now I'm never going to get a job at Reddit,'" he said.

Cline was more than four months into his vision quest when he got a call from Huffman. He hiked out from his campsite, drove through glacial ridges of pine bluffs sweeping along lakes near the Canadian border, and pulled into a visitor center in North Cascades National Park to find a land line. He conducted the best interview with Huffman he could muster.

Huffman hired him. Cline drove to Utah to pick up some possessions he'd stored there, and about a week later reported for duty at the San Francisco office.

Vass was a harder sell: She'd settled in the Pacific Northwest, and was unwilling to move. Huffman told her it wasn't a deal-breaker for him anymore. Huffman also brought in a former community manager from the Wikimedia Foundation, Philippe Beaudette, as the group's leader. A capable community team was coming together.

(• •)

Steve Huffman woke on December 1, 2015, in New York City. He rubbed his eyes. He squinted. He could see a little better now, he thought. Or could he?

He had just undergone a vision correction surgery. He'd been a –6 prescription—significantly nearsighted. By December 1, he was perhaps –3, growing clearer every day, though preparing for his second board meeting as CEO, for which he was in New York, without being able to see his screen "was really annoying." He later said he'd gone in for the surgery in relation to his doomsday preparation. "If the world ends—and not even if the world ends, but if we have trouble—getting contacts or glasses is going to be a huge pain in the ass."

He had spent much of the past quarter trying to staff up Reddit. Before he stepped in as chief executive, the company hadn't brought on a new engineer in nine months, he said he learned. The fourth quarter of the year for executives usually entails a lot of plotting goals for the following year, but for the staffing changes and other reasons, Huffman didn't have a thorough plan to present to the board for 2016: Like his own vision, Huffman said Reddit's was "a little fuzzier" than he'd have liked at this point.

Still, Huffman was confident. He later admitted that the board didn't have any questions for him he couldn't easily answer. There'd been just one comment of which he felt he had to read between the lines. A board member said, "You're in a honeymoon period with the press. That should last until about April." Huffman interpreted that as, "You're in a honeymoon period with *us*, and that should last until about April."

Not that the board hadn't already, along with Ohanian, set him an extraordinarily steep goal: Get Reddit to one billion users.

Huffman chose to believe that meeting that audacious goal would be possible. It was double the number of users that Pao wouldn't agree to overseeing the growth toward. Later, a year into his tenure as chief executive, when asked whether he still believed it was possible for Reddit to have a billion monthly users, he said with a laugh, "It better be!" Altman, a board member, later explained Huffman's confidence by noting that Huffman proactively chose to link his future compensation to meeting that goal.

Instead of viewing the billion-user mark as one to dart toward as quickly as possible using typical strategies of bolstering search engine optimization and pouring dollars into online marketing, which Pao had attempted, Huffman decided to first try to gain control over the very concept of growth at Reddit. When he started, he still saw Reddit as something of an unruly hydra. "We're not fully in control," he had said. "Reddit grows, traffic goes up. Sometimes a little, sometimes a lot. We don't really know why; we don't really have any control over it."

What would control look like? Launching a mobile app, and being expressly focused as a company toward growth on mobile, would be one way, Huffman proposed. Getting a better grasp on metrics, another. "Without them, we are flying blind," he said. One of the first steps toward growing Reddit to a billion-user company would be to accurately chart progress and identify its roots. Then lay out a vision for achieving more. Reddit ditched the costly and (it thought) inaccurate Google Analytics and created its own internal traffic-tracking tools.

What else did Huffman want to fix about Reddit? "Oh my God," he said. "Everything."

(• •)

Repairing Reddit's culture was crucial to Huffman's ambitions. In January 2016, he hired a head of human resources, Katelin Holloway, through an executive search so secretive she didn't know the company with which she'd be interviewing until she received a cell phone call halfway through her Uber ride to Reddit's headquarters to meet with Huffman. Holloway has the air of a modern superhero in a black leather jacket and bright-blonde blunt cut. She's the type of woman who can casually mention she's worked in advertising, law enforcement, hedge funds, and public education. She can fly planes and has a book deal. Despite this, she's ridiculously likable, and her former and current colleagues believe she is one of the world's best at her job.

Upon starting at Reddit, Holloway set out to interview every single employee—at the time, about seventy-five individuals. She hosted small group chats, asking questions like "What was the last time the company laughed together, you know, a laugh-so-hard-you-cry moment?" Once, upon asking that question, she was met with minutes of silence. She says she thought, "Wow, there really is nothing here. Where do we go from nothing?"

In aim of establishing some semblance of culture in the void, Huffman revamped a Reddit tradition of "Friday fundays," where after 4 p.m., employees could gather and have a beer and play board or video games or just hang out. It was informal, and sometimes awkward. So Huffman added a structure most employees took to immediately: team demonstrations. It would rotate from project to project, but each team could occasionally show off what they'd been working on. It had a side effect of opening up cross-team communication and spreading enthusiasm for projects, such as a new app launch, which was planned for that coming April. Even a sales-team demo was met with oohs and aahs from staffers in other departments. One longtime staffer later said that during one of these Friday gatherings she had an epiphany. "Oh, yeah. This is what working at a Silicon Valley tech company is supposed to feel like."

(• •)

Over the calendar year 2016, Reddit would double its staff, growing from approximately 75 to 150 employees. There were stumbles and mistakes that predated Huffman and Holloway, which they'd be left to mop up. Fresh problems arose almost immediately.

In the months following Huffman's return to Reddit, about fifty staffers resigned or were terminated. It was a near-complete changing of the guard, leaving only about twenty longer-time employees. The process took months. "Some people just wanted the status quo; some people wanted to monetize. Some people wanted to grow users," Huffman said. There was no clarity. And there was still a palpable fear of users. "The company was operating scared, scared of the community and afraid to make changes," he said, echoing a longtime sentiment. Fear would not fly.

Huffman had, starting his first day, made an effort to meet every employee, to shake hands and keep an open-door policy. He made many allies this way. That doesn't mean others weren't lost in the shuffle.

One of these was Dell Frost, Reddit's only African American community staffer. Frost didn't have particularly warm feelings for Huffman when the leadership change happened; he said Huffman made no detectable effort to connect with him. Jessica Moreno, his boss, soon departed the company in order to move with her family back to Utah. The community team as he saw it was crumbling. He recalls that one day, without warning, he was called in to speak with his manager and a human resources staffer. They told him it wasn't working out. "Oh my God, you can't be serious," Frost remembered thinking.

Frost said being terminated was devastating and sent him into a spiral of depression that lasted months. He couldn't stop turning over in his head a strange thing that had happened about six weeks prior to his dismissal. Shortly after Huffman's return to Reddit, as the debate heated up over shutting down the hate-speech-filled subreddit r/CoonTown, Frost heard there would be a meeting about it, which was set to include Ohanian and Huffman.

Frost recalls one day he looked around his seating area and saw that his team members were away from their desks. He realized that they were in the meeting with Huffman and Ohanian, and that he—the only African American community team member—had not been invited. "I remember that day so vividly," he said later. "I just left the office. I was hurt, I was angry."

A representative of Reddit described Frost's account as flawed. The company confirmed that two content policy meetings involving Ohanian and Huffman occurred during that time period. But those meetings were comprised only of department managers—individuals such as Jandali, who is Muslim, and Melissa Tidwell, who is African American—and would not have included Frost, who both held a junior position and was new to the company, according to Reddit. Moreno remembered it differently. She recalled such meetings, but said they included a range of staff of varying seniority, including most of the community team. She said she neither called the meeting nor set its attendance list. She said Frost's exclusion from a meeting is possible, but was not planned.

Frost said one of his biggest regrets professionally is never bringing up his complaint to managers. "I never really said anything about it because that job really meant a lot to me. I loved Reddit." He later explained that he'd decided he didn't want to be the black person complaining about race. "I didn't want to be that guy; I just wanted to do my job."

He said he did not receive a formal warning before being dismissed from his job. Reddit representatives said the company does not comment on former employees' employment history.

Many former employees, as well as current ones, recall Huffman generally having had an open ear in the early days of his return; he met with employees with specific concerns about diversity and in-office harassment. No new formal diversity initiatives were immediately put in place. Huffman has said he's satisfied with Reddit's diversity and doesn't want what he feels is a significant effort toward making Reddit's staff inclusive and diverse to become a "numbers game"; it shouldn't end when a certain quota is reached. Reddit has refused to release its diversity numbers, not unlike other tech companies of its size, but it is fairly typical in its composition: The staff skews male and white.

Pao, in her book, painted a picture of Reddit being a place at times uncomfortable to women and wrote that one account of a sexual harassment complaint, a groping incident at Huffman's return party, subsequent to her tenure, got back to her. According to multiple individuals who worked at Reddit during the incident, it did not occur as Pao wrote she'd heard. However, an incident of inappropriate behavior did occur later, the week after Huffman's return. It was perpetrated not by an employee, but rather by a guest of an employee, according to those with knowledge of the situation. Reddit's office manager had been present, and asked the man making others uncomfortable to leave. By the end of the month, the employee whose friend was accused of inappropriate behavior was no longer employed by Reddit. Before long, the longtime human resources manager wasn't either.

(• •)

In the weeks following Huffman's return to Reddit, photographers from *New York* magazine, *Wired*, and others had hauled their gear through Reddit's office. They set up lighting and tripods and staged portraits of Huffman, lounging among stuffed Snoos with his laptop, generally looking like a fresh-faced hacker-in-chief.

Huffman had spent hours in person and on the phone with journalists, including Benjamin Wallace of *New York* magazine and Jessi Hempel of *Wired*. The long features that resulted would not be the deer-in-headlights Huffman who faced staff on his first day back at Reddit in almost six years. This would be a comeback story, fresh and encouraging and—unlike the Reddit of the past—distinctly mainstream. In interviews, Huffman spoke to the reporters with the blithe confidence of a more seasoned leader, even wishing well new competitors such as Voat.co (a Reddit clone that billed itself as a place where no topic was too controversial for its fundamentalist free-speech ethos). He claimed to be undaunted by the need for Reddit to find new ways to make money in aim of delivering a profit to its investors. He hypothesized that Reddit could easily lure in celebrity users and become ten times larger.

Before long, Huffman coined a new tagline for the site. "Reddit: come for the cats, stay for the empathy." It wasn't all kittens and rainbows, though. *Bloomberg Businessweek*'s feature dubbed the pre-Huffman-return period as "A Nine-Year Case Study in Absentee Management." Each of the articles painfully rehashed Taylor's firing and the ugly user revolt and online petition against Pao. Some delved into the rift that had grown over the years between Ohanian and Huffman; others noted the theory, propagated online by Wong, that Huffman and Ohanian had been plotting for years to return. (Wong later laughed that anyone had taken his "theory" seriously, saying his post was a troll.) One article included a sizable infographic of the site's most heinous subreddits, sorted by their level of accessibility on the site.

Still, this media push, this effort to let Huffman be a tech-elite debutant and speak his story, was a way to control the narrative. It was an attempt to set this new era of Reddit apart from all its prior humiliations.

To that end, Reddit's public relations offered reporters access to Huffman's friends, such as Kan and Slowe, and one interviewed his girlfriend at the time, Adrienne Plaskett, who had not been extensively media trained. Plaskett revealed to a reporter that Huffman had vomited from stress several times since returning to Reddit. She told *New York* magazine, about Huffman, "To say he has thick skin—absolutely not."

"SERENDIPITY" AND "BULLSHIT"

B ut what does Alexis *do*?
     As a Reddit board member whose title was only "co-founder," Ohanian did not merely attend quarterly meetings. He'd long harbored other ambitions, and since Huffman's return, he'd already set his plans back in motion. In October 2015, Reddit announced it was launching a media arm. It would be called Upvoted, and on a new website, Upvoted.com, a small team of young journalists would distill and craft newslike stories out of the best content on Reddit.

The decision to create an internal editorial team seemed logical to Ohanian. News sites such as BuzzFeed and Gawker had long made a habit of pillaging Reddit's content troves, courtesy of the site's 205 million monthly viewers—and Ohanian had long been attempting to own the traffic generated by Reddit's golden material rather than let mainstream sites have it.

Ohanian hired a handful of just-out-of-college journalists to write articles such as "Can Insects Experience Orgasms?" and "What Happens When a Black Hole Is Formed in Your Pocket?" courtesy of popular recent discussions on r/science and r/askscience respectively.

He also recruited two video freelancers to produce high-production-quality videos and to revive, yet again, video AMAs. Upvoted.com would be a natural home for these videos. But there would be, well, no upvoting. There would be no commenting. It was like Reddit—only clean, pretty, and immune to user tinkering. Another resemblance to some mainstream media: There would be sponsored content. (On the first day of Upvoted's existence there was a story called "The United Franks of America," about hot dogs, which had been sponsored by Goldbely, a regional-specialty-food delivery startup in which Y Combinator had invested and of which Ohanian was an adviser.)

Still, at the site's launch, the mainstream media was impressed. Several outlets, including the *New York Daily News* and the *Los Angeles Times*, ran articles acclaiming Reddit's foray into journalistic online publishing, citing Upvoted as a "no-troll zone" and a potential "bright spot" on the site. Regarding video AMAs, *Adweek* had already opined that "there's every reason to think that Reddit's engaging content could bring in new users, and generate revenue."

Some Redditors were less impressed. Just a month into the Reddit sister site's existence, on November 5, 2015, a user who went by the handle u/Hedgehog_sandwich submitted a post to the subreddit r/CorporateFacepalm titled "Reddit's 'Upvoted' blog is literally everything redditers hate about reddit." It received eighteen hundred upvotes in two weeks. Commenters called the site "clickbait," compared it condescendingly to BuzzFeed, and saw through it as a way to bifurcate Reddit's most mainstream discussions from the rest of the site.

(• •)

Two months later, Josh Wardle posted on the Reddit changelog that reddit.tv, a video-hosting component of Upvoted.com, would be shut down in order to "focus more on core Reddit improvements." By January 2016, it was clear within Reddit that Upvoted wouldn't stick around either. By July, the team was laid off. The experiment had lasted just seven months. "We were trying to build a media business inside of this company that did not need to build a media business," video producer Stephen Greenwood said. He was let go in June 2016, but he wasn't bitter: Huffman had candidly discussed with him how the video projects were not core to Reddit's goals; Greenwood was happy he'd been able to stay and experiment with them as long as he did. He admits they were slow to gain traction.

Ohanian's media dreams, again, were crushed, and again, it was Huffman's decision. But Huffman let Ohanian down gently this time. Later, Ohanian explained the decision that came from Huffman to stop devoting Reddit's resources to traditional media. "It came down to the question: What is Reddit going to be?" Reddit needed to hire engineers and to ship product. These departments Ohanian had created were not core to that vision. So Huffman shut them down.

Another project did work. Within months of his return, Huffman kick-started an initiative to upgrade Reddit's mobile app. After six months of development, on April 6, 2016, a Facebook post teased, "Reddit for your thumbs. Coming soon to iOS and Android."

Some users complained that the app was a tidied-up, simplified Reddit—and sure, it was. Images on the official app, which is just called Reddit, are displayed in-line, so the appearance is initially just an up-to-the-minute meme reader. And it included "serendipity" mode, a blast from iReddit past, which allowed a user to shake their device for a random post. But by fall, mobile users were 10 percent of Reddit's audience while accounting for 40 percent of the total time-on-screen for all 250 million monthly users. A year later, roughly 20 percent of users were mobile, and they spent 50 percent of the total time all users spent on the Reddit platform.

"Reddit hasn't been known for high-quality product work in a long time," Huffman said. "I'm really excited to get back there."

(• •)

Late in January 2016, Huffman posted an admin thread announcing only positive changes—including the tidbit that Chris Slowe was returning to Reddit. Slowe had matured a lot over the past six years. He was thirty-seven years old and the father of two young children, a boy and a girl. He and Kristen were moving their family to a new home in Marin, north of San Francisco. She'd by this time upgraded his wardrobe: button-down shirts, expensive, well-fitting jeans, and suede Asics.

The last time Slowe had worked at Reddit, he was one of six people; now there were ninety. But once he dug into the site's codebase, he found it jarring how little the fundamental product had matured. "Problems I encounter are familiar, because to a large extent we created them in the first place," Slowe said. He found not only kludgy old code—some of which he'd written and which embarrassed the experienced programmer he'd become—but also that big concepts he'd once envisioned hadn't been tackled over the past six years.

Slowe was given a Reddit hoodie, black with subtle orange-red accents, and began working on managing the effort to update the site's very infrastructure, update the homepage algorithm, modernize anticheating measures, and keep users' data safe.

It wasn't long before a handful of other Hipmunk engineers also joined Reddit. Some rejoined, including early Reddit employees David King and Jason Harvey. Later, once Reddit started furiously hiring programmers, more than a half dozen former Hipmunk data scientists and engineers would join their ranks. (Hires of his trusted team weren't limited to engineering; Huffman later hired Hipmunk's marketing executive, Roxy Young, as VP of marketing.) Ricky Ramirez and Neil Williams had never left Reddit. Combining the forces from essentially all eras of Huffman's career made it feel like he'd created a reunion show of star employees.

Keith Mitchell, a back-in-the-day Reddit engineer, chimed in on a code deploy post made by Williams, another longtime engineer, which had turned into an old-time-Redditor in-joke fest. There was everyone there: Huffman, Slowe, Ramirez, King; even Mike Schiraldi was commenting on the history of code deploys at Reddit.

Upon seeing Mitchell's handle, u/kemitche, in the thread, Slowe commented, "*cough* don't know if you saw the *hiring* thing. *nudge nudge wink wink know-what-I-mean.* You get a punch card when you come back. Free small sundae on third rehire!"

Huffman's long-standing trust in Slowe was so deep that when Slowe returned to Reddit, Huffman said his mandate was simply: "Go do stuff, Chris." Slowe dug into how Reddit's homepage functions for various users, dubbing the project "Relevance." Updating the homepage algorithm led him to revisit the recommendation engine project they'd worked on eleven years before. Soon, he added another major project to his plate: overseeing a department that would be dubbed "anti-evil." It would build specific tools for use by the secretive trust and safety team, and essentially be its programming counterpart. As new engineers were hired, more were handed over to Slowe to build robust antispam systems.

As Slowe's team grew, he proved an adept manager and was handed an even larger team—eighty engineers—leading the group in charge of maintaining and developing the full Reddit site's architecture. Before long, data science was spun out as its own team and also placed under Slowe's purview. By September 2016, he had four teams of engineers reporting to him. They'd put in motion a longer-term customization of Reddit's homepage, busted spam by 90 percent, and hired like mad—giving Reddit the future capability not just to maintain the status quo, but rather to build well-functioning systems on top of the site's old code, rendering the last version Slowe had touched so many years earlier, at long last, mostly useless.

In March 2016, in lieu of a quarterly three-hour slideshow presentation in the cafeteria, Reddit's staff decamped to Lake Tahoe. Although they stayed at a Harrah's casino, which was almost universally viewed by the staff as cheesy, Huffman was impressed by the social bonding he witnessed. Various groups skied together; he himself hit the slopes with a group of recent hires he didn't know well. The company organized some team-building-style activities. Board games were played, trails were hiked, hot tubs enjoyed—so much, well, fun, happened. Half the staffers were green to the team, and even they were being included.

"This is new Reddit," Huffman thought. This could work.

(• •)

For much of Huffman's first year running Reddit, he had also tried to hold multiple fingers in multiple leaks at Hipmunk. The travel-search site was hemorrhaging money and having trouble assembling a new financing round. These circumstances meant he also had an increasingly skeptical board of directors to mollify. Huffman spent many Friday afternoons working with Hipmunk CEO Adam Goldstein. He told skeptics at the time, "Well, if Jack Dorsey can run both Twitter and Square, well, I can do both, too." Later, he'd confess the truth: "That's total bullshit."

The pressure was on: Huffman knew that if Hipmunk couldn't find new investors, or a serious acquirer, and soon, Goldstein risked being ousted. It would mean the employees he'd taken so much pride in hiring that he'd told them the old Joel Spolsky line, "You'll never have to write a résumé again," would get nothing—and, well, might have to go job hunting. He concentrated his efforts on the one thing that could tie up all his loose ends: getting Hipmunk acquired.

By September 2016, after countless calls and dinners, Goldstein and Huffman had their deal. Concur Technologies, the corporate travel giant that had itself been acquired by German multinational software corporation SAP two years earlier, agreed to acquire Hipmunk for more than $60 million. Goldstein and the Hipmunk employees made nice little sums of money in the deal. Huffman says he made little in the deal, but he smiles at its mention, because with it, he finally regained his long-lost ability to focus fully on Reddit.

R/THE_DONALD

S teve Huffman and his friends celebrated that fall, at the wedding of Justin Kan and his longtime girlfriend, Kristine Oh. Two weeks later, they would have another celebration, at what had been dubbed Camp Reddit. It was part quarterly presentation, part team building, part raucous fun. Roughly 100 of the 140 staffers attended; 60 planned to spend the night. Everyone drove out from San Francisco to a campsite in the woods, breaking into groups for hiking or cooking. Huffman instructed everyone, even those not planning to camp out, to bring a change of clothing. "I will peer-pressure them into hanging out more," he said, "and I think some of them will fall for it."

They needed the respite: The bruising 2016 election cycle was almost at its end, and although Huffman and his teams had made some attempts at cracking down on the hate speech that Reddit had become associated with, new gates that enclosed the worst content on Reddit barely masked the reality: There was still a lot of awful stuff.

There were lightly veiled white supremacist subreddits, such as r/european, with a distinctly anti-Muslim sentiment. Others were dedicated to spreading a strain of ultra-right-wing, pro–"Western culture" misogyny, such as r/PussyPass, which tallied allegations of women receiving preferential treatment, and a small universe of subreddits dedicated to "taking the Red Pill," a reference to *The Matrix*, which in the movie signaled becoming indoctrinated with an uncomfortable, unpopular truth. More recently, the term had been appropriated by the "manosphere" to describe the epiphany one would undergo once coming to see their viewpoint on gender inequality against men, or men's rights. R/TheRedPill and r/Incels were particularly sexist and overlapped with the alt-right and neoreactionary communities, with which they shared a vocabulary. (Redpilling was simultaneously becoming used online as a description of the conversion of an individual to far-right or alt-right beliefs, and as slang "redpilled" was at times the conservative version of liberals' "woke.") They were places where women were treated as submissive, stupid possessions who should be trained to bow down to their "king" or "alpha" and where disgruntled young white men ranted about perceived ills. R/hitler still existed, though Huffman, when confronted with that fact, shrugged. He said he was confident that if that subreddit became popular or grew, his teams would cut it off.

None of these, however, attained the level of notoriety or popularity that did r/The_Donald.

R/The_Donald began as a straightforward, if slightly tongue-in-cheek forum dedicated to news about and advocacy for the presidential campaign of Donald Trump. It was created in June 2015 after Trump announced his candidacy, and immediately, posts mimicked his blunt, hyperbolic speech patterns. Due perhaps to Poe's law of online ambiguity, there was no telling whether this content was mocking or earnest (one Reddit community manager believed it was begun as the former and quickly transformed to a den only welcoming to ardent Trump supporters). Growth was slow initially, which made sense—Bernie Sanders had seemed to be Reddit's candidate of choice early in the 2016 election cycle.

In December 2015, r/The_Donald was still a mostly mild place, though infused with some of the wall-building rhetoric spouted by the candidate himself. Its extensive set of rules, maintained by the moderators, forbade most bigotry and racism, with the exception of Islamophobia, which it expressly permitted. Then the brigading and memetic warfare started.

Brigading is the invasion of a topic, thread, or entire message board by a group of individuals who have organized themselves online with the purpose of manipulating content or its visibility. This sort of plotting happens in massive private-message threads on Twitter, in Facebook groups, on private chat servers such as Discord, and, very overtly, on 4chan's /pol, a "politically incorrect" board that had been created by 4chan's founder in 2011 to siphon off and contain the overtly xenophobic and racist comments and memes from other wings of 4chan. This mostly off-Reddit organizing then plays out on Reddit as vote brigading, or attempting to silence individual voices by downvoting them into oblivion. Other products were meme generation and dissemination, harassment campaigns, and propagation of disinformation, largely aiming to disseminate far-right viewpoints. Brigading had long been against the site's rules, but this activity was difficult to track, and almost impossible to differentiate from regular Reddit activity due to the fact that it looked an awful lot like normal Reddit activity: Those taking part were coming from disparate IP addresses, mostly domestic, and most of which otherwise interacted typically with the site.

The_Donald's subscriber list grew in fits and lurches—and examining its growth patterns helps explain both its constituency and why it became both an outsized force on Reddit and Trump's most active and vocal base of support on the entire Internet.

Early on, an influx of brigaders came from 4chan's /pol board, and its Reddit counterpart, r/pol. There was more crossover of /pol users to Reddit after 4chan was abandoned by its creator, Chris Poole, in January 2015, after he'd lost any semblance of ability to control the sprawling, vile communities it harbored. Over the following year, Reddit's political boards, most prominently r/The_Donald, experienced a substantial influx of traffic from former channers. They brought with them some of what became The_Donald's signature vernacular, as well as meme-proficiency and lots of keks, which is 4chan slang for laughs and possibly a reference to the frog, sometimes Pepe the Frog, an image that thanks to memetic strategizing on 4chan and 8chan had been infused with anti-Semitic meaning and that the Anti-Defamation League subsequently declared a hate symbol.

Each of Trump's primary wins brought to The_Donald a fresh wave of subscribers. Another reliable driver of new subscribers—whom The_Donald began collectively to describe as "high energy individuals," or "centipedes" ("'pedes" for short—both a rallying cry and a penis joke)—was every time some piece of content from The_Donald became popular on r/politics, the long-standing politics subreddit, or r/all, an unfiltered version of the homepage favored by many longtime and avid Redditors.

A wave of likely racists had also joined in the late summer of 2015, after Huffman and his teams shuttered r/CoonTown. Its constituency subsequently migrated to other subreddits "where racist behavior has either been noted or is prevalent," a study by six researchers associated with the Georgia Institute of Technology, Emory University, and the University of Michigan found. One of the top places it was discovered that these users migrated to during their time on Reddit was The_Donald. (A later semantic analysis by FiveThirtyEight confirmed that the nonpolitics subreddits on Reddit most closely related to The_Donald were r/fatpeoplehate, r/TheRedPill, and r/CoonTown.)

Milo Yiannopoulos of Breitbart, who'd seen his star rise while chiming in on Gamergate, a campaign of harassment against female programmers and game designers (of which Reddit was one hub), had developed a flair for drawing young gaming and programming types into the alt-right movement. He tweeted his support of The_Donald subreddit and mentioned it in his articles. His cross-platform evangelism created a sort of alt-right synergy that seemed to translate to an increased following for r/The_Donald. (Yiannopoulos also later teamed up with r/The_Donald to participate in a Reddit AMA, which was headlined "I AM MILO YIANNOPOULOS, AND DONALD TRUMP IS MY DADDY. AMA." In it, he mostly delivered one-liners in his flamboyantly brash style about his love for "daddy." He also called Ted Cruz a "weird amphibian loser" and referred to feminists as "obese.")

Another constituency growing around this time, it would later become known, was Russian propagandists, apparently in an effort to sow disinformation and discord among the American electorate. Reddit later identified 944 user accounts associated with a Kremlin-tied troll farm; the largest posters were active on The_Donald, using upvoting schemes to make their posts more popular. While most of the accounts' efforts were ineffective, a few were successful; one posted a sex video that falsely claimed to include Hillary Clinton, and it received more than one hundred thousand upvotes.

As the 2016 campaign season wore on, Donald Trump's big tent on Reddit was his largest online supporter group, and it included a constituency of: racists; the 4chan migrants, largely in it for the keks; alt-righters; Gamergaters contributing sexism and conspiracy theories; some former Bernie Sanders supporters; Russian propagandists; and anyone lured by the promise of a place that tolerated Islamophobia. R/The_Donald was their clubhouse, a thriving "safe space" that blossomed into one of the most absurdist and influential communities in all of Reddit. With all this in mind, perhaps it makes sense that by mid-2016, The_Donald had become a two-hundred-thousand-strong community producing a steady stream of far-right talking points, coded racism, casual misogyny, Islamophobia, and the now-well-established alt-right "free speech" and hatred of the mainstream media.

Since its inception, Reddit's community team had flagged T_D (for short) as problematic and devoted regular resources to monitoring it. But as T_D devolved into a place with its own rapidly evolving vernacular in part to code its extremism, and shitposting became a norm, the forum's moderators and the Reddit admins keeping an eye on them together slipped into stranger and stranger territory.

The limits of free speech were indeed being stretched here—deftly and deliberately. Plenty of content and thousands of users were banned by T_D's rotating cast of thirty-some volunteer moderators—users with usernames such as sublimeinslime, ivaginaryfriend, and pm_me_yo_doggos, whose profile photo was a cartoon hybrid of Donald Trump and Pepe the Frog aiming an automatic rifle. Here on T_D, MAGA was the rallying cry, and epithets abounded. Former secretary of state Hillary Clinton was simply "Crooked Hillary." Anchor Megyn Kelly, "Dopey Megyn." Little frog icons and centipede flair (to decorate their usernames when posting) were designed for top users; posts featured extra tags reading "HIGH ENERGY" or "Praise Kek." "News" from questionable sources such as Infowars and Breitbart abounded; many of the far-right's messages were honed here, and primed for appearance on Twitter and other social media where major news outlets might pick them up.

The rash of iconography created and disseminated by the pro-Trump battalions earned a name: the Great Meme War. And its decentralized troops were at work on symbols that were individually absurd, but collectively as poignant to their audience as was the Obama "Hope" poster eight years earlier. This election season's "grassroots" activity was now entirely online, masterminded by savvy, subversive trolls who engineered pro-Trump and anti-Clinton supermemes, designed to be spread on Reddit and through networks of Twitter accounts, and designed content that played upon sensational and tawdry accusations, such as conspiracy theories about Hillary Clinton's health. The wide dissemination of such wildly extremist content at times even forced mainstream media to address bizarre falsehoods that it might otherwise have ignored.

As memes, slang, and acronyms metastasized, the subreddit's lingua franca evolved so far from what others might recognize as common usage—daily, even hourly—that it became onerous to track its lightning-fast online etymological evolution. This language was a key part of their defiance of the mainstream: "If you're using the left's buzzwords like 'racist' and 'sexist' then you're gonna find yourself following leftist thought patterns," one moderator wrote. "However, it's very hard to accidentally align with SJWs by using words like 'cuckold' or 'faggot.' Our culture exists for a reason and we're gonna cherish it, and enjoy the power it gives us."

The massive effort, in all its extremism, wasn't lost on Donald Trump's campaign. In the lead-up to the election, Donald Trump on his Twitter account reposted memes and videos that bubbled up on T_D, including, as far back as 2015, an image of Pepe that had been altered to resemble Trump. Former campaign staffers have admitted that from the war room that had been set up in Trump Tower in New York, they relentlessly monitored the huge forum for content to push out to Trump's followers online. Before long, though, the subreddit's moderators were directly in touch with campaign staffers, and, according to Reddit staffers, together they arranged for Trump to participate in an Ask Me Anything in July 2016.

Other portions of Reddit were apoplectic. Posts on r/TheoryOfReddit, a forum dedicated to meta-examination of on-site phenomena, had long pondered The_Donald's meteoric rise, with posts ranging from "is it a cult?" to "is it an anti-muslim, anti-immigration subreddit?" On one day in late April 2016, as Trump moved toward securing the Republican nomination, ninety-three of the top one hundred posts on r/all originated from The_Donald. Even r/TheoryOfReddit gave up. It had just four moderators and said they didn't have the bandwidth to deal with the backlash to every post that mentioned T_D. "It's not worth the drama or political sniping for us as mods," one wrote on April 29, 2016. The subreddit banned any mention of The_Donald. This was just one of hundreds of micro-dramas that played out across Reddit at the hands of the 'pedes.

By mid-2016, T_D was the most active community on Reddit, and therefore, among the site's most influential. But the extreme engagement of its various factions was far from organic. When a post from T_D rocketed to the top of r/all, often it was the intentional result of an orchestrated campaign. The extensive slate of The_Donald moderators had developed an intricate and highly regimented structure, one that members of Reddit's community team have referred to as "bureaucratic," "coordinated," and "militaristic." It was very unusual for Reddit, on which serendipity and natural virality is championed—and it was born in part because it was mandatory for the forum's survival. The_Donald was a tough-to-manage community full of bigotry and, at times, rule-breaking hate speech and doxing, which they knew put them at risk of being shut down by Reddit. Simultaneously, it was also constantly under fire from the rest of Reddit, which would brigade the forum and organize targeted campaigns against it. "It's defensive in a way," said Bill Cline, a community manager, who explained that the moderators needed "to present themselves as a unified front" to the forum's various constituencies of subscribers—and to their vast opposition.

While most subreddits' mod teams operate as volunteers—each dabbling in their free time in reading modmail and flagging spam—on The_Donald, moderators developed a communication system and hierarchy, wherein tasks were more cleanly divided; everyone had their role. Over IRC, Discord, other message boards, and on in-depth documents, editorial calendars of sorts, they developed a new system for ensuring that their content could gain steam in a controlled fashion.

Moderators of T_D harnessed and manipulated simple Reddit site customizations, using them in unorthodox ways to disseminate T_D content far beyond its pages. First, the typical Reddit downvoting function was cut off throughout T_D—meaning a post could only gain, not lose, traction. To gain subscribers, at times the moderators created a large Trump pop-up that visitors had to click on to make it disappear—but by clicking, they became subscribed to the forum, meaning they would regularly encounter its content on their custom homepage. At one point, the most problematic subsite hack T_D moderators utilized was locking a post of their choosing on the top spot on the site, where typically the subreddit's current most popular post is found. Moderators referred to this as "stickying" a post; it is akin to "pinning" a tweet to the top of a Twitter feed. Typically, moderators of other subreddits would use it to promote straightforward announcements. On T_D, it was the splashiest, most anti-Clinton or pro-Trump headline of the day. Stickying a post on T_D became a rallying cry for upvotes and comments, and subscribers complied, often propelling the chosen content to the front of r/all. T_D had gamed the sacred algorithm. They had unlocked a way to disseminate content handpicked by moderators.

Philippe Beaudette led Reddit's community team at the time. He and his colleagues got to know the moderators of T_D well; opposing subreddits, such as r/EnoughTrumpSpam, were also familiar, as they frequently barraged Reddit staff with questions and complaints. Beaudette said that over time, T_D became not only one of the most extreme examples of subculture development on a forum he'd ever witnessed, but also one of the most highly organized. New moderators came on board frequently, and they were heavily trained by veteran mods, all volunteers themselves. The documents they'd created for newbies to read in on the multitude of rules and philosophies of the subreddit were intense—as was the wiki it hosted full of policy papers and guides for newcomers to the subreddit, such as "Understanding Trump's Border Wall."

Particularly admirable, said Beaudette, was the moderator team's playbook for the Democratic National Convention in Philadelphia in late July, which he'd viewed. "They had it scheduled out in fifteen-minute increments for the entire week what they were going to be posting and taking action on, timed to the speakers," Beaudette said. He'd never seen such balletic coordination on a subreddit. "I found that to be absolutely splendid to watch."

That precision was almost entirely undetectable to the community, though—to a casual viewer T_D was visual chaos. Even regular readers felt the whole thing was organic. "Weirdly, the rest of the community isn't aware they are being organized," Beaudette said. "They aren't realizing how closely tied to the actions the moderators are."

On June 12, 2016, T_D recruited more than eleven thousand

new subscribers through exposure on r/all. Moderators of r/news had made a bizarre decision in the wake of a deadly attack on a gay nightclub in Orlando to disallow posts and comments about the attack, compiling all information into a single "megathread." It resulted in a dearth of news about the attack on Reddit's front pages, which are usually dominated by the day's top news headlines. T_D swooped in to fill the void. With what amounted to planned brigades of upvotes, it propelled several posts to the home page. T_D had found a weak spot and used it to grow, again. "Of course, the subreddit was already well-versed in Islamophobia, so it was a particularly apt place to wildly speculate about [the shooter's] motives, involvement with the Islamic State, and what should eventually happen with all Muslims in this country," Vice News wrote at the time.

Huffman attempted to engage the broader Reddit community about the handling of the release of news after the nightclub shooting, on Reddit's blog. In it, he made a tweak to how "stickied" posts could be employed, now dubbing them "announcement" posts and requiring they be text-based and created by a moderator. That brought the direct ire of The_Donald, which retaliated with the Internet equivalent of a raised middle finger: a bunch of swastikas in the headline of a post that contained nothing other than a subtle ask for upvotes from others who wanted to retaliate against u/spez. The_Donald subscribers gamely upvoted it—and it soared to the top spot on r/all. It read: "(⌐͡° ͜ʖ ͡°)ノ_卐卐卐卐 Don't mind me, just taking my admins for a walk. Dear cucked admins, stop lying to people on the internet."

Swastikas on the front page was unambiguously not a good look for Reddit. Angry, Huffman decided to double down. On June 16, he posted to r/announcements that over the past day Reddit had tweaked the algorithm that determined hotness on r/all. Now, rather than competing against one another for popularity, each given community would be judged against itself and its own recent viral activity in order to achieve front-page status. "Our specific goal being to prevent any one community from dominating," Huffman wrote. "This undermines Reddit, and we are not going to allow it." It was a direct move to limit the reach of T_D. Later, to further rein in T_D, Huffman specifically banned posts stickied by T_D from r/all, calling the subreddit's tactics "antagonistic to the rest of the community."

But by that time, T_D had more than three hundred thousand subscribers. It would soon thereafter begin to use stickied posts as organizational memos of sorts, highlighting the top Trump-centric news and its objectives for the day. There was no stopping it. Not that Huffman actually wanted to.

(• •)

Donald J. Trump was elected forty-fifth president of the United States on November 8, 2016.

Huffman said he should have seen it coming.

When asked at the end of November whether he believed Reddit had a role in the election's outcome, Huffman was open to the possibility, saying, "It's hard to say." He said The_Donald, specifically, was a reflection of the conversation that was happening nationwide—only amplified, thanks to the nature of the see-what-you-want-to-see social web. "I think that's one of the challenges you see when you democratize media and news consumption," he said. "The feedback loop gets louder and louder and louder."

Within a week of the election, both Facebook and Google came under intense scrutiny for having allowed the propagation of blatantly false articles, videos, and stories about political candidates and polarizing issues that may have influenced how the American electorate voted. Facebook took the brunt of the accusations for spreading misinformation and allowing blatantly fake stories to be treated as factual news. Employees of the social network were concerned not only about the false or misleading articles, but also about the rampant spread of the The_Donald–style racist memes. As early as election night, a group of Facebook vice presidents asked one another in a private online chat what role their company had played in this outcome. They called a meeting with the company's policy team, pledging also to address the issue at an all-hands meeting.

Twitter, too, was embarking on a soul search. As the election results were coming in, one former Twitter engineer asked online, "What did we build?" Another replied, "A machine that turns polarization into $." Reddit investor Dave McClure had a near meltdown onstage at the Web Summit in Lisbon the day after the election, saying that social networks built by Silicon Valley are "a propaganda medium" that "assholes like Trump" use to get into office. "We provide communication platforms for the rest of the fucking country and we are allowing shit to happen just like the cable news networks, just like talk radio." Later that day, McClure lamented, "Sometimes I feel like we're just a bunch of nerds who don't know how to play the game."

A few weeks later, onstage at a conference in Brooklyn, Huffman was confronted with the question of whether Facebook's longtime defense—that it was not a publisher of content, which would require editorial control, but rather merely a technology platform, useful for distribution of individuals' content—was valid. The "neutral platform" defense had become a common one not just for Facebook, but also for tech companies of all stripes. Its core concept, that a platform merely connects buyers with sellers of a service, was one that allowed Uber to pay its drivers as independent contractors and therefore not provide them costly employment benefits, one that Airbnb had used at times to throw up its hands when rental listings broke local laws or when users behaved inappropriately.

Reddit itself had been here before, in dealing with the dissemination of copyrighted material, and in arguing the fundamentals of the SOPA and PIPA legislation that could have held Internet companies responsible for the content they disseminated. Online, a platform's role was a little more subtle and less overtly transactional; Facebook and Twitter and Imgur connect advertisers with users, users with one another, users to interesting content. Now Huffman had to answer to this same "platform" question regarding Reddit—when what had been at stake was a presidential election.

"They are filtering what we see," the interviewer said of Facebook. "If you look at Reddit, do you see yourself becoming a social network or as a publisher, or—what *is* Reddit?"

Huffman gave a standard line, that Reddit is home to thousands of communities, which each choose what they see and discuss. He said that Reddit is a reflection of humanity in that way, but noted that like Facebook, what Reddit had done was open up communications between individuals to a before-unseen level, which meant a hugely greater breadth of conversation than the world had ever known. "I see our role as a communications platform, primarily, bringing people together." It put the responsibility for content on the royal *them*, not the *us*.

Afterward, in a private discussion, Huffman opened up a bit more. He said he did not believe that Facebook has a moral obligation to exert a sweeping hand of editorial judgment over what its users posted. "Right now what I see is a lot of self-righteous 'Somebody's to blame for this,'" he said. "They're looking for a scapegoat."

Yet Huffman said he believed that due to the scrutiny, Facebook would take a harder stand on fake news. Reddit had already banned many "suspicious domains" in the lead-up to the election, Huffman disclosed, but it wouldn't become clear for months to the broader world that these were Russian propagandists, intent on posting and disseminating divisive content.

To Huffman, at the time, the existence of T_D and its divisive, uncivil, often conspiracy-theory-minded discourse was a matter of free speech—on which his once-absolutist thinking had begun to evolve. He and Reddit had begun to treat different types of content differently. Noxious communities aimed at antagonizing Reddit were subject to banning by Huffman and his team. So was content of the crying-"fire"-in-a-crowded-theater stripe: Anything inciting violence or harm, regardless of its validity or intent, he'd empowered his teams of administrators to cut off. But political speech: This, to Huffman, was at least somewhat separate. It was what the First Amendment at its core was contrived to protect.

But it would not be simple to protect—nor even comprehend. "Political speech" had been redefined by savvy, aggressive trolls. And that left Huffman in the wake of the election a bit flabbergasted. "Do I force equal time to candidates during election season? Do we ban communities? No, no, no," he said. "It just doesn't make sense." But he knew that what was unfolding on Reddit was consequential. He didn't agree with it, but he was pretty sure he should protect it. "I mean, Trump won, right? Fifty percent of people voted for him, let's not pretend that this is some aberration, that The_Donald is some freak occurrence."

SPEZGIVING

In the fall of 2016, Lisa Liebig usually went to bed around 5 a.m. and woke up a little after noon. From her home in Sunnyvale, California, partway between the Googleplex and Apple Park, she logged on to Reddit and its staff communications systems in the afternoon, and through the evening and early morning hours was sometimes the sole community team member managing all communications between Reddit and its thousands of moderators. She read and responded to modmail (handling "tickets," in modern Reddit-employee speak) and put out fires on the site. The night shift meant that the afternoons were her mornings, and the afternoon of November 23, 2016, was looking like it was going to be a flaming garbage can.

As a former crime scene technician from Indianapolis, Liebig wasn't easily ruffled. On Reddit, she'd been trolled and harassed, but seeing the heartwarming interactions that Reddit enables—the gifts, the charitable giving, the micro-moments of humans sharing brutally honest thoughts with one another—helped even out the bad.

Waking up on November 23, 2016, Liebig glanced at her phone and saw a voicemail from her boss as well as dozens of Slack alerts.

It was a quantity of urgent messages she hadn't seen in her two and a half years at Reddit. Something bizarre had happened on the site. It wasn't a raid, or moderator infighting, though it did seem to have begun on r/The_Donald, which regularly required a lot of attention from herself and her fellow site administrators.

She opened Slack. She saw members of the community team brainstorming on a dedicated channel, trying to figure out what the hell was going on. Liebig scrolled up to read their earlier comments. First, her team had gotten emails from moderators of The_Donald with links to a post, saying they thought comments to it had been slightly modified. It didn't appear the original posters were doing the editing, which the site allows.

More than six hundred miles north, community manager Susie Vass was also at home on Slack. She and Bill Cline had emerged within the team as particularly adept at managing the political communities on Reddit, and they typically dealt with moderators of The_Donald. They'd managed to build a solid working relationship with the chiefs of this controversial community. Vass hadn't seen a complaint of this specific variety before, and, bizarrely enough, it appeared to be legit—which meant it was also inexplicable. She messaged her boss about it, and texted Chris Slowe, the always responsive head of the "anti-evil" team, asking for help.

"Somebody hacked the site," Vass wrote. Cline and Cassidy Good, a young community moderator who specialized in AMAs, were on Slack, too—and they quickly came to share Vass's alarm. A developer let their team know that the comments appeared to have been edited in an unusual way—from inside their system. "Oh my God did somebody compromise the site somehow?" Good said. They'd been hacked. And they were freaking out.

It was the day before Thanksgiving, and the office was sparsely populated. The community team pinged every developer they could find. Slowe's teams had built robust systems to avoid this sort of thing. How, and why, would an attack like this, so random, so subtle, have even happened?

Vass noticed that Huffman had joined the Slack channel. He

asked some of the community team, "Where are you guys?" He told them he was in their area of the office. Some explained they were working from home.

At 3:25 p.m., Huffman posted on Slack.

"I did it."

The full-tilt discussion skidded to a stop. Minutes passed in extremely awkward digital silence. Was he kidding? They hoped he was kidding. The chief executive couldn't—he wouldn't—go on the site and edit comments. Surely he didn't even have the capability. Although—just maybe he did. After all, Huffman had written the site's original code; it wasn't beyond the realm of possibility that he could get in.

Vass couldn't fathom it. "I thought he was making a bad, bad joke." On Slack, she broke the silence. "Are you kidding right now?"

Huffman wasn't kidding. He'd done it: He'd edited a handful of comments mentioning his username, spez, and changed "spez" in multiple places to usernames of top moderators of The_Donald.

The community team revered Huffman, and many of them had gotten to know him personally over the past sixteen months. They knew what he'd been dealing with on the site recently, namely all the harassment that had accumulated thanks to Pizzagate.

The r/pizzagate subreddit was only two weeks old, but it had become the all-time fastest-growing in terms of subscriber numbers. It had launched on November 7, the day before the U.S. presidential election, and some of its roots can be traced in part to a highly organized effort among subscribers of The_Donald to comb through and disseminate information from the Wikileaks files of emails from Hillary Clinton's campaign. Upon its launch r/pizzagate was dedicated to discussing the bizarre theory that attempted to link the Clinton Foundation to a pedophilia ring based in the basement of a pizza joint that had no basement.

The whole concept, from its inception, was identified by the more reputable media as a conspiracy theory—and a wild one at that. At its center was a pizza-pie-and-Ping-Pong joint located in Maryland outside Washington, D.C., that was being accused of being a hub of international child trafficking and tied to Hillary Clinton, Barack Obama, satanism, triangular symbols, and punk bands. Breaking down how the Pizzagate theory emerged is an exercise in absurdity, but essentially a message board on 4chan attempted to link mentions of the word "pizza," and other foods, such as "hot dogs" and "cheese," in the leaked emails of Clinton campaign chairman John Podesta—apparently he's a foodie—to child sex trafficking. (What was seen by conspiracy subscribers as a linchpin was that Podesta was once invited over email to a dinner by a nonprofit organization's government relations head who'd noted that her stepgrandchildren would likely be playing in the pool.) Soon it was being spread around in the ecosystem of fake news, including Infowars, and even was tweeted by soon-to-be national security adviser Mike Flynn. On Reddit, members of conspiracy-theory-heavy subreddits piled onto r/pizzagate.

R/pizzagate's problems were not limited to disseminating fake news and wild theories, as well as spoofs of these theories, provided by lulz-seeking trolls. The Reddit community team noted instances of doxing—and warned moderators their community could be subject to a ban. Five days later, personal information was still flying. Reddit admin Susie Vass sent Pizzagate's moderators a note, midday on the twenty-second: "We recognize that you feel this is an important investigation, however as it has become clear that this community is unable to stay within our sitewide rules we will be banning the subreddit at 4:00 PM PST."

On r/pizzagate, as hours ticked down to 4 p.m, a mass effort to archive "important threads" began. So did the name-calling—primarily aimed at u/spez. "Fuck u/spez" was the most common refrain, but he was also being looped into the subreddit's conspiracy echo chamber, and being inexplicably called out as a pedophile. After the 4 p.m. shutdown, that wrath moved to the more popular, and thus more visible, The_Donald.

Huffman had publicly ignored instances of harassment toward him, just as Pao had done in the past. General name-calling on Reddit wasn't against the site rules. While posting sexualized images of minors was banned, discussion of pedophilia definitively was not. So even the CEO was open to being called a ped. In theory, at least.

The community team was well aware by this point that Huffman himself identified as a bit of a troll—and he seemed to understand portions of the Reddit universe as only a troll could. A few knew that back in 2009, he had admitted that previously he'd trolled his own site, tweaking appearances on Reddit of the slur "fag" to "fog." But they didn't realize that by that time, Huffman had developed a long mental list of ways he very badly wanted to troll the trolls back He had a small library of methods in his mind; he'd previously joked with some staffers, confidants, about this specific method.

On that Wednesday afternoon before Thanksgiving, Huffman was both frustrated and bored. He sat alone at his desk, looking at all the nasty comments about him and shaking his head.

"The worst thing is a CEO with an hour of free time," Huffman said later. "I was like, 'You know, I haven't written any code in a while. These guys are annoying me; I've got an idea.'"

He stared at his screen, thinking, "These are children. They are acting like children." Huffman had grown up with his sister, a peer, but also with four younger half brothers. "How do you deal with children? You push 'em over. You're deliberately obtuse," he said. It was the stuff of his childhood, lightly trolling his little half brothers.

Because these users were repeatedly calling him a pedophile, and posting over and over again "fuck u/spez," Huffman's Reddit in-box was piled full of these on-site mentions. Plus, he didn't like that they propagated a vibe on T_D and Pizzagate that he was out to get them. Huffman knew the reality was the opposite: While he despised these users' posts, their attitude, and their politics, he'd been the one defending their right to exist on the platform. At times he'd specifically defended The_Donald's existence to staff who disagreed. Just maybe, he thought, he could relate to them, or push them to relate to him, on the level they were operating. Level: troll.

So Huffman went into the site's code, and navigated to The_Donald's front page, where a thread about r/pizzagate being banned was taking off. In the thread, he saw a line reading,

"'Member when reddit thought u/spez would completely revamp this shitty website, but then he just ended up doing the same old shit as the other admins?" Huffman changed "u/spez" to "u/mivvan," a top The_Donald mod.

It didn't work. He almost gave up. But he'd made up his mind. He called over an engineer, who gamely complied when asked to help his account obtain permissions to edit comments. Then Huffman went back into the comments, changing that one permanently, and an instance of "FUCK u/spez" to "FUCK u/Trumpshaker." He refreshed the page and saw his edits were live on the site. Then . . . nothing. No new comments appeared. No one seemed to notice. The whole point was for T_D to notice, so he continued waiting. Nothing. He went into a meeting.

When he got out, he saw that his community team's Slack channel was rolling a mile a minute, and among community managers the tone was confusion and concern for the site's security. All hands were on deck—on the eve of a long holiday weekend. Huffman saw everyone concerned and dismayed, and knew his revenge had backfired. He'd done this to his own staff. He'd fucked up.

After fessing up on Slack, he told them, "All right. Sorry. I'll fix it. I'll own up to it." He went back to r/The_Donald and posted, admitting that he'd edited comments. He wrote:

Hey Everyone,

Yep. I messed with the "fuck u/spez" comments, replacing "spez" with r/the_donald mods for about an hour. It's been a long week here trying to unwind the r/pizzagate stuff. As much as we try to maintain a good relationship with you all, it does get old getting called a pedophile constantly. As the CEO, I shouldn't play such games, and it's all fixed now. Our community team is pretty pissed at me, so I most assuredly won't do this again.

Fuck u/spez.

Later that day, Huffman recalls, he sent an email to the company's board of directors giving them a heads-up, saying approximately,

"In case you're getting demands for my resignation, here's what happened."

It blew over fairly quickly. But within the whole situation, which has since been dubbed "Spezgiving," there are several things Huffman regrets. He regrets wasting his community team's time. That feeling, he said, was "devastating." He regrets making Reddit, as a company, feel embarrassment. "It threatened the company," he said. A significant part of his strategy for almost a year and a half had been to make Reddit "stop looking like idiots," he said. "I spend so much time trying to make Reddit not look like buffoons." But now he'd gone and done it himself.

For all of Huffman's confidence in stating his opinions, he is eminently flexible and recognizant. He revisits his own reasoning often, and can navigate pathways to different logic—and thus his opinions frequently evolve. While even a year later, Huffman still regretted distracting his team by essentially hacking his own site, another thing he regrets is posting on T_D his very responsible, straightforward apology.

"In hindsight, I probably should have said, 'You mad bro?' I should've really leaned into it," he said, straightening his posture with self-satisfaction. "I don't have an ounce of regret trolling that community."

WHAT'S GOOD FOR THE UNITED STATES

Even months after the election, Steve Huffman continued to believe that r/The_Donald should, without doubt and with only a few qualifications, be allowed to exist.

To be clear, Huffman despised r/The_Donald. He didn't like its viewpoints, its vernacular, or those of its moderators. There have been many legitimate reasons why Reddit could ban r/The_Donald. It has broken many, if not all, of the site's rules by some interpretation. But to shut down The_Donald would be bad for Reddit, Huffman believed. Moreover, it would be bad for the United States.

"Now, I don't always factor in 'what's good for the United States' into my decisions," Huffman said. "But Reddit's getting to a point where our actions do have an impact." Reddit's own estimates show that one-third of all Americans view at least something on the site every month.

As of early 2017, Huffman believed that the most likely end for The_Donald would simply be its petering out, like so many political and trend-based subreddits before it. It—like Trump himself—was no longer the underdog. Huffman and the community team, though, planned to keep r/The_Donald online. Over time, he figured, it would fracture. He didn't rule out the opposite scenario, though: "And if that doesn't happen, if they continue to grow and thrive, well, maybe that says something about our country right now."

For all its limit-pushing inflammatory content meant to rile up, or, in alt-right speak, "trigger" liberals, The_Donald continued into 2017 to be a well-oiled meme machine, according to Reddit. Its moderators were very responsive to requests by Reddit community managers, and the community abided by the specific and additional rules Reddit laid on them. "When they get close to the line, which they love to do, we step 'em back and they'll stay back," Huffman said. "They back off. 'Cause they know they're on borrowed time."

So, rather than pushing this vibrant community out—this community that had become the epicenter of pro-Trump fervor online—perhaps pushing them closer to the outright alt-right and allowing them to migrate elsewhere online, where they also might thrive, Huffman said, "We're gonna watch it play out right there on the bottom. Am I going to let them, in the meantime, antagonize the rest of the community and be really annoying and ruin r/all, something I love? No."

(• •)

By the turn of the new year, community team members would openly talk about Spezgiving, joking about the long hours they pulled that long Thanksgiving weekend huddled over laptops in corners while friends enjoyed their Crock-Pots of stuffing and carved turkey. The camaraderie they gained in handling that crisis together was called by one the "great gift Spez gave us for Spezgiving." In the somewhat public-facing act of living the company's value of openness and to "keep Reddit real," employees occasionally referred to Huffman, their boss, as a troll.

Spezgiving had been transformed from embarrassment to inside joke. It was a new chapter in Reddit-the-company's official story, so much so that when designers created sheets of Snoo-the-mascot stickers to give to visitors, they included a couple tiny stamplike circles that read, "Edited by u/spez."

For an organization that deals with so much daily strain, it's perhaps understandable to take this sort of media-highlighted incident and rally around it. Spezgiving began to be seen by staff as a turning point in the company's recent history. It helped the various teams execute at the drop of a dime; the new, much larger trust and safety and community teams hadn't recently honed their muscle memories in a crisis.

Those reflexes would be tested again soon. Following the election of Donald Trump, the subreddit r/altright doubled down on its activity and behaved more aggressively.

By the time Huffman was ready to take action on it, he had planned to make the case for a ban and nudge an entire new, sizable team in that direction. He understood that it could take weeks. First, he casually pinged the head of trust and safety to ask whether he'd considered cutting off r/altright.

"Yeah, we're banning them," Huffman recalls the manager said. Trust and safety had already met; Tidwell, the general counsel, had already signed off on their proposal. They were ahead of Huffman on it. It was straightforward, due to the community's violations of Reddit's content policy. "Like, by the book, no drama," Huffman said. "Cool."

Just a year earlier, Huffman considered his greatest challenges regarding the Reddit community to be differentiating the good trolls from the bad ones, and trying to navigate the conversation between free expression and hate. Drawing lines wasn't possible, he had said. But by now, he'd begun to see things differently. He'd learned that just because he had a thick skin (to a point) when it came to harassment online, that didn't mean other people did. Bullying and harassment were no longer tolerated on Reddit. "That's a big change in the philosophy that I think has made the company better," he said. The community team, along with trust and safety and legal, would come over the next year to rethink what constituted "illegal" behavior on Reddit—primarily content that could fall under the umbrella of "inciting violence." Huffman explained, "Just like the line is fuzzy, our approaches need to be fuzzy, right?" This was a distinct change. He'd continue to embrace the fuzziness.

At the dawn of 2017, Huffman posted a sort of State of Reddit post on the site, in which he wrote that Reddit is "a completely different company than we were a year ago, having improved in just about every dimension." Among the company's achievements were reducing spam by 90 percent, the new apps, which he called "the fastest and best way to browse Reddit," new moderator mail, and new blocking tools for users. He hinted at a forthcoming site redesign.

Traffic, too, had continued its climb—though this was not something Huffman publicized. Reddit had at this point more than eight billion monthly page views, with almost fifty thousand active subreddits, and Ohanian would soon boast that three hundred thousand individuals viewed Reddit every month. Perhaps most incredibly, though, Reddit itself was now run by a company of 150 people, mostly in San Francisco, with a few sales and business-development staffers in a sizable office with water views at One World Trade Center in New York, and a couple employees in Los Angeles. Every department Reddit's management and board needed to function was in place, at least structurally. They had a master plan to fill out that structure: Reddit would continue hiring and planned to double in size the following year, to three hundred employees.

Growing the userbase further was a separate challenge. Living up to his billion-user mandate consumed a chunk of Huffman's mental energy. Despite the enthusiastic tone of his post, he had spent the end of 2016 in a funk that had descended on him in the wake of Spezgiving. In the past, he had gone through periods of happy contentment, followed by periods of terrified anxiety in which he felt like "everything is going wrong." He'd be up a month, down a month, up a month. The end of 2016 was down.

He was also beginning to realize that to meet his aggressive hiring and growth goals, Reddit needed more money. A lot more money. And that was going to be on him.

THIS IS MY WHOLE LIFE

Serena Williams, too, was looking to put 2016 behind her. She'd won Wimbledon, but only after smashing a racket there in a burst of fury, for which she was fined $10,000. For much of the year she'd been hampered by injuries to her shoulder, knee, and thigh muscle. So she had a long mental list of goals in mind for 2017. She'd win the Australian Open, and then she'd go on to win Wimbledon once again.

Her life outside of tennis was all roses. She'd starred in one of Beyoncé's music videos from *Lemonade* and appeared in ads for Beats by Dre and the lingerie company Berlei. In December, Ohanian had conspired with Williams's agent to make her take a break; they whisked her off to Rome on a surprise trip. There, she'd meet Ohanian at the very same hotel at which they first laid eyes on each other. A thick trail of rose petals led her way out to a poolside table. Later, on December 29, she made her very first post on Reddit to mark the occasion. It read:

> I came home
> A little late

Someone had a bag packed for me
And a carriage awaited
Destination: Rome
To escort me to my very own "charming"
Back to where our stars first collided
And now it was full circle
At the same table we first met by chance
This time he made it not by chance
But by choice
Down on one knee
He said 4 words
And
r/isaidyes

Ohanian helped her post it to a new subreddit called r/isaidyes, which they had created, earning a place in every nerd's heart—and Ohanian added flair to her moderator handle, a little tag that said "Verified GOAT," as if to note that, yes, this really was the Greatest of All Time tennis champion posting herself on Reddit. As further verification, or perhaps just to be adorable, she attached a cartoon of herself and Ohanian that he'd drawn of them, with red Snoo eyes and little alien antennae.

She may not have posted it herself, but Williams—who likes writing in her spare time—said she wrote it herself. In part inspired by Miranda Kerr and Evan Spiegel's engagement announcement via the platform he'd created, Snapchat, Williams says she floated to Ohanian the possibility of letting the world in on their engagement on Reddit. She'd been wanting to make an effort to be more involved with her fiancé's work, so one day she said, of their engagement: "Wouldn't it be really cool to do a blog on Reddit?" Ohanian told her it would be amazing.

When on tour, Williams often traveled with a cohort of publicists, coaches, physiotherapists, agents, family members, and advisers. There were friends, too: Zane Haupt, the Australian, and, at times in the past, Canadian actor-rapper Drake. Fiancé Alexis

Ohanian often joined them in Williams's player's box, as did a rotating cast of celebrities, such as Olympian Allyson Felix, *Vogue* editor Anna Wintour, and musician-moguls Jay-Z and Beyoncé. At one point, the U.S. Tennis Association's media outlet estimated that there were forty people in Williams's entourage.

Her insanely full schedule meant that when Ohanian wasn't along for the tour, they had to rely on video chat. Williams would prop a laptop by her bed and would sometimes doze off to sleep while still talking with Ohanian.

She was already in Auckland competing when she posted a photo to r/Sneakers: "Engagement shoe game," the post said. In the image, she's posing with Ohanian in the evening in a cobblestoned alley, outside a charmingly Italian restaurant, wearing a dark skirt and kicking back one foot, clad in a white-soled black Nike. It was as if to say, "Never mind the ring game," which some have estimated to be a $2 million diamond solitaire.

What no one, Williams included, knew was that back in December when they'd gotten engaged, Williams was already pregnant—or would be within days. Her friend and Hollywood agent Jessica Steindorff soon noticed symptoms that Williams had been experiencing, and came in with a bag from a local pharmacy containing a pregnancy test. To prove her friend wrong, and for a laugh, Williams gamely took it.

Seeing the result, she was in disbelief. "I was terrified," she recalled later. "And Alexis wasn't there." She tried five more tests, thinking the result impossible. She had the Australian Open next to win! And then Wimbledon. "I was thinking, this is insane. What do I do now, where do I go from here?" she recalled later. She called Ohanian and told him to come to Melbourne right away. She didn't give him a reason, but when he arrived, she handed him a paper bag containing the six positive pregnancy tests.

A doctor confirmed the results, and told Williams there'd be absolutely no harm in playing. When she won seven matches in the Australian Open tournament, including the final, her twenty-third Grand Slam singles title, this one against her sister, Venus, only a loose handful of people close to her and Ohanian knew that she was carrying their baby.

(• •)

Huffman always despised the Reddit office at 101 New Montgomery. Although its desirable open floor plan meant it was a broad space surrounded by windows, he found it dark and depressing. The only way to move between floors was to wait in a queue for stodgy old elevators. The company's two floors also harbored for Huffman ghosts of Reddit past. This was where he'd had that unbearably awkward press call alongside Ellen Pao; where more than half of the company had resigned or been dismissed before it began to rebuild its teams. This was a new company, in Huffman's mind. He wanted a new office.

By mid-2016, he'd found one. The location was just decent: at the intersection of one of the toniest neighborhoods in all of San Francisco, the tourist-hotel-and-department-store-saturated Union Square, and one of the worst, the Tenderloin, dotted with methadone clinics and single-room-occupancy flophouses. Walking out of the front door in either direction—toward Neiman Marcus with its $400 toddler dresses, or south through makeshift street camps of homeless individuals—could make you doubt your faith in humanity.

The building, at 420 Taylor Street, was gorgeous, though: It was an art deco–style commercial space, built in 1941 as NBC's West Coast Radio City. Its façade featured an impressively vibrant mural on tile, barely noticeable from bustling Taylor Street unless you really crane your neck, but gorgeous to behold: It depicts a broad hand, grasping a dial and surrounded by various instruments and meters, from which appear to emanate a visual depiction of sound waves traveling to both sides, and up, up, through layers of people. They are people of eras past, whose garb—some indigenous costumes, a headdress or loincloth, some in regal uniforms—looks more than a little archaic now, but they are of an impressive diversity, from many walks of life, with several skin hues, young and old.

NBC had constructed one of the most impressive broadcast facilities of the golden age of radio; it was never fully utilized, as NBC moved most of its West Coast presence to Los Angeles shortly thereafter. The former tenant, Chartboost, had moved to a smaller space in SoMa. But perhaps here, now, behind this mural to modern communications, in this building with functioning elevators, was precisely where Reddit should be.

When employees began moving in at the start of 2017, they took the stairs up to the second, main, floor, and were greeted by a massive stream of light pouring down from a skylight three floors above. It created the effect of a giant atrium, like the one at Y Combinator's original Garden Street office—only twenty times larger.

Huffman cut out a lot of the flourishes typical to startups that Chartboost had integrated: No longer would there be a twelve-foot dinosaur statue greeting guests upon their entering the main floor. Where there was little room for opulence inside, save a kombucha kegerator in an airy, ample kitchen and high-tech conference rooms named after subreddits, a couple floors up there eventually would be. Surrounding the skylight-atrium atop the building would be a sprawling roof deck accessible from the top floor of the office. It would be outfitted with a row of cushioned chaises and adorned with murals by Reddit's resident artist, Dante Orpilla. He painted in graffiti style a bunch of tiny horses, and, not to leave out the joke, a massive duck.

(• •)

As Redditors were moving into their still unfinished offices, Reddit the website was fittingly rolling out new digs for its users as well. The morning of March 21, 2017, Reddit announced it was "testing a new profile experience that allows a handful of users, content creators, and brands to post directly to their profile, rather than to a community." A group of beta testers had been granted souped-up profile pages that appeared when one clicked on their usernames. These pages, replete with a customizable profile photo (yes, it could be a photo, or almost any user-uploaded image, instead of a custom Snoo) and image background, similar to Twitter or Facebook profiles, were a full generation of Internet development from the rest of the user pages and subreddits, which simply looked like a Verdana list of words upon words. They were distinctly un-Reddit. They seemed to encourage being a real person, with a photo, rather than an anonymous individual with a username.

So were the new abilities owning one of these profile pages allowed: to be "followed," just as one would subscribe to a community. Now in addition to r/science or r/The_Donald, users could follow a "brand" or a "personal brand," just like other social media. User pages included a bit of history—which subreddits an individual frequented. There was also the ability to post directly to one's profile—thus essentially becoming one's own subreddit. It allowed users or brands to "build a following" independent of existing communities on Reddit.

The news made some loyal Redditors cringe. Dozens of comments in response to the announcement compared it to Facebook. Unfavorably. Others sneeringly compared it to LinkedIn. One compared it to a move by Yik Yak, a social media company that made an anonymous-comment app and whose efforts to be more brand-friendly proved fatal. U/Oxxide wrote, "I don't understand this feature, why it was implemented, or what kind of show Spez is running over there, but this is laughably incompetent and makes me wonder how out of touch the admins really are. You guys Digg that hole a little deeper with each new announcement. ;)"

Huffman stepped in to answer questions on the blog post, but that didn't go well, either. "Instead of the total destruction of Reddit," he wrote, "what we'd like to accomplish is to make it easier for folks to find a place to share on Reddit." The comment got downvoted to obscurity, with −863 points, but not before some longtime users chimed in, explaining that they felt this move "changes the core, fundamental ideology that underlies the site," that it would lead to "signal-to-noise denigration," and be a "step away from anonymity."

At the end of the day, Huffman shuffled up to General Counsel Melissa Tidwell's desk. He mentioned the poor reception to the new profile rollout and said he was getting in-box fatigue. Users were in outcry mode, and just looking at his screen that afternoon had been an onslaught. "Users don't get it," he said about the new pages.

Huffman seemed a bit distraught. He noted that his Reddit mail showed all comments that mention his u/spez handle, and did so blindly, without context, so it could be difficult to discern exactly what was being criticized, and from what angle. It almost perfectly mirrored what Yishan Wong believed led to his "particular strain" of PTSD.

Tidwell cut in and asked her desk-row mate to lighten the mood by showing Huffman something else they had been monitoring that day. They pulled up a clip from the congressional confirmation hearing of Supreme Court nominee Judge Neil Gorsuch.

"My family has been texting me throughout this process asking me to ask questions that they would ask," Senator Jeff Flake, a Republican from Arizona, leaned over his microphone and said to Gorsuch. "My son . . . a teenager, said to ask him whether he'd rather fight 100 duck-sized horses or one horse-sized duck." There was laughter throughout the chamber at the Reddit-ism. Gorsuch blinked multiple times and shook his head in exasperation. "You can tell him I'm very rarely at a loss for words, but you've got me."

(• •)

What the post on March 21 didn't mention explicitly was that the user profile change was not just Reddit simply trying to be like Twitter, Facebook, or Medium. It was Reddit actively attempting to encroach on the big social sites' territories—to literally give individuals, companies, and brands the ability to put their own content of any stripe on Reddit.

But just hours into it, Huffman confessed that the launch didn't go well, and he wished he'd written the introductory post himself. "Nobody gets it," he said. For a site mostly comprised of pseudonymous users, some faction of whom posted intimate relationship or private financial advice, or shared kink porn without fear of their fetish being Google able, giving users "about me" pages was understandably seen as strange.

But the profile pages were an integral part of Huffman's larger effort to make Reddit easier for new users to grasp. He didn't subscribe to the age-old Reddit philosophy that one should have to ingratiate oneself into a community before posting one's thoughts, one's *content*. "They think this process of finding the community and learning the rules and learning the norms is somehow what makes Reddit great," he said. "I think that's actually held it back."

Another fact the product launch skirted was that this move was essentially a welcome sign to brands. A profile page is an automatic stake in the dirt for them, an easily understandable way to have a presence on Reddit, an alternative to either spending considerable time and employee bandwidth ingratiating itself with relevant communities or buying advertising. Historically, this sort of move was exactly what drew ire from Redditors. "They're like, 'Oh, this is really bad. No self-promotion,'" Huffman said, pointing out that there already was a lot of self-promotion on Reddit, and he didn't see that as a bad thing. "Are you kidding me? You're a little self-righteous if you think nobody's marketing to you right now."

The concept of a user page, and the ability to essentially blog live on Reddit, actually dated back twelve years, to the days when Huffman and Swartz would take long walks and mull tactics for integrating their nascent Y Combinator companies. They'd eventually hoped to give users Infogami's platform for writing anything, anytime, and then cross-posting it to subreddits. They hadn't gotten there. More than a decade later, though, a portion of the young hackers' theory had been back on Huffman's mind. He recalled that his and Aaron Swartz's idea that their genre of Internet company was comprised of "lists"—lists of ideas, articles, songs, images, podcasts, anything—had incepted Huffman with the idea that Reddit users should ultimately be able to define for themselves their own "list."

In June 2016, Reddit had rolled out Reddit-hosted images. Then in August 2017, video. These were two types of posts. Huffman rattled off others, including *audio, question, poll, chats, events.* He noted that image posts already utilized a programming language called Markdown, which allowed for the simple in-line addition of multimedia. He described any of these theoretical changes as concepts that would only take Reddit a week to launch. They are all eminently possible.

By Huffman's estimation, half of all images on Reddit in 2017 were hosted by Reddit. That was a massive change from a year earlier, when Imgur hosted the majority of images one would encounter on the site.

Imgur was still run by Alan Schaaf in its own sprawling San Francisco office with its own massive roof deck. Huffman became irked at Schaaf when he heard that a few years earlier his fund-raising pitch to venture capitalists included, "We're going to destroy Reddit." Huffman said, "That does not ingratiate one to me." (Around that time, in 2013, Imgur also boasted having more traffic than all of Reddit: one hundred million monthly views, to Reddit's roughly seventy-three million.) Imgur raised $40 million in 2014.

Months into 2017, Huffman said he liked where Reddit was in terms of executing, and building new things. "Shipping product" was the aim, and Reddit had become much better versed at it. User numbers were growing; hiring a team to build new products was working, too. The company was well on track to reach three hundred employees by the end of the year.

But when Huffman was asked how he liked being a full-time CEO, he tucked his hands into his sides and stiffened. "This is my life. This is my whole life. Well, this is one-third of my *life*. But it's my entire reputation and sense of self and purpose. So yeah. I enjoy it," he said flatly. "Most days, but not every day. Most days."

REDDIT 4.0

For April Fools' Day 2017, senior project manager Josh Wardle proposed building out an idea that'd been worming around in his head for more than a decade. Wardle was the third-longest-tenured employee at Reddit, and the only nonprogrammer holdover from the early days of Reddit. He'd been through three different offices and four different executives.

He'd been thinking back to 2005, when as a way to avoid taking on student debt, a British university student launched a website comprised of one million pixels on a 1,000-by-1,000-pixel grid. He set out to sell the pixels for $1 each, in blocks of 100, which he'd fill with the buyer's image and a hotlink to their service. It became a hypercolored Times Square of the Internet, jammed with tiny ads for porn, poker, psychics, and bottles of liquor. It looked horrendous, this snapshot of the capitalist Internet's land rush. And that stuck with Wardle as somehow magical.

Remove the money, keep the land rush, and crowdsource the project—now, that would be interesting, Wardle thought. What if Redditors were allowed to choose their pixels, draw images, and create words?

Wardle had managed April Fools' projects for years, including an extremely popular one two years prior called "The Button." It was a massive multiplayer online game that only allowed each Reddit account holder to click once, before bestowing a colored-dot flair label on them based on how much time had expired on the Button's communal clock before they'd clicked. It appealed to two primal human impulses: channeling boredom and status competition. By introducing labels, the Button opened up the potential for groups, however haphazardly formed, to take their given labels seriously. Entire tribes, organized through new subreddits, cohered. Greens formed the r/Emerald_Council, which despised the impulsive r/ThePurpleConclave, and which in turn envied those who'd displayed the most patience, who'd seen the Button run down close to zero and had segregated themselves in the subreddit r/TheRedguard. The gaming website Kotaku called it the "Internet-est thing to happen on the Internet."

Reddit was a different, larger company now. Wardle knew that another project of that scale—or larger—would be a substantial risk. He ran it by peers before bringing a formal proposal to his boss, Alex Le. Wardle envisioned his April Fools' wide-open pixel canvas he'd dubbed "Place" as a collaborative project, in which any given participating individual would only be able to place one individual colored pixel on the canvas every so often. Communities of individuals—likely, subreddits—would have to work in concert to see any meaningful images emerge.

As with so much else on Reddit, Huffman and the other executives decided that the community could likely moderate itself here: For every one person who'd want to draw a swastika, there'd be ten thousand others wanting to turn the hate symbol into a flower, or a cat with a Pop-Tart for a body flying through space on a rainbow. Engineers across multiple teams, including front end, back end, and mobile, set out to build Place. They used mostly existing technology at Reddit, and tested it among staff only, which was unusual.

In the past, Reddit Gold subscribers had been used to test potential features, and by 2017 Reddit relied on a set of loyal users to beta-test each new product launch, rolling them out to some fraction of 1 percent of Redditors first to test both their efficacy and strength. Then, to test the load of a new feature on servers, Reddit would deploy it to, say, 2 percent of users.

Place was not such a project. It would launch the morning of April first to all users and be subject to an immediate traffic swarm, putting immense strain on Reddit's servers and, potentially, on its developers.

On the morning of April 1, it went live with just four mysterious lines of instruction.

There is an empty canvas.

You may place a tile upon it, but you must wait to place another.

Individually you can create something.

Together you can create something more.

Immediately, the blank 1,000-by-1,000-pixel canvas became a color battlefield, with swaths at the center and corners immediately populated by blips of color. The northwestern and southeastern corners of the canvas turned blue... and the blue spread rapidly, thanks to individuals who'd created a subreddit supporting the proliferation of blue pixels at r/TheBlueCorner. The upper right corner, red, bled toward the center, too, though efforts of r/RedCorner were soon decimated due to the organizational strength and manpower of r/TheBlueCorner. Soon, white space on Place was sparse, with images, mostly tiny, popping up all over, a brigade of hearts here (r/placehearts), a small clan of Pokemon there (r/TheSilphRoad). One group, The Darth Plagueis Project, created a massive red square and began filling in black text, most letters five pixels high, creating the dialogue from Chancellor Palpatine in *Star Wars: Episode III—Revenge of the Sith*. To maintain it, it created a megathread on r/PrequelMemes, a three-hundred-thousand-strong community of individuals enthused by memes inspired by the *Star Wars* prequels. A live chat on Discord offered tips for participating in Darth Plagueis, and a Google sheet provided joiners with the precise pattern to follow.

By twelve hours into the existence of Place, significant turf battles erupted. Most notably, a white blob wouldn't seem to leave the very center of the canvas—it was spawned by r/EraseThePlace. Soon, darkness fell. Dubbed "The Void," a mass of rapidly spreading black pixels, streaming out like an oozing lava flow, began dominating the canvas center. Just below it, a war erupted between France and Germany—or, well, their flags. Germany was strong: Its flag, once completed, continued extending to the right, longer than a normal flag. A French one popped up to stop it—but was overtaken by the Germans, who'd organized on r/de and forced the French to retreat to the north, where they found a permanent settlement.

After seventy-two hours of obsessively watching the million-pixel canvas become filled, and then morph, Wardle and his team felt it had run its course. He closed r/place to further edits.

What was left was a garish digital quilt of extremely detailed images, mostly in bold, primary colors, cross-cut with rainbow lines at forty-five-degree angles, and smattered with dozens of national flags: Brazil, Sweden, Germany. (There were also some less commonly flown flags, such as the flag that represents polyamory.) By this endpoint, an American flag had emerged where The Void had been, and stood at center, a great victory of multiple subreddits, including r/The_Donald. Where the German and French flags had fought their battle and briefly overlapped was now an EU flag. There was a depiction of Leonardo da Vinci's *Mona Lisa* (thanks to r/MonaLisaClan), and, utilizing the black background created by The Void, which had been fought off collectively by a cohort of Redditors, a crystal pyramid refracting light into a rainbow, à la Pink Floyd's *Dark Side of the Moon*. The only remnant of the formerly quarter-canvas sprawl that was The Blue Corner was now a tiny framed and labeled rectangle, the tiniest violin of a tribute to what had once been a great blue-pixel-covered empire that could not beat back a thousand tiny warring tribes.

More than a million individuals had placed 16.5 million colored tiles on pixels, creating a garish masterpiece of Internet culture. Wardle's experiment had tapped into something incredible that Reddit, as a mass of individuals, loosely connected through common interests, could accomplish. In the end the canvas mirrored the project's own fruit-fly-duration life. It was fractured and weird, and really, really cool.

(• •)

Despite that by the spring of 2017 most Reddit employees had moved into 420 Taylor Street, its top floor was still unfinished and mostly deserted. It was all beams of sunlight and eerie silence. But there, on the walls of a small conference room tucked in next to the elevator, was the story of Reddit.com's future.

Tacked up were high-resolution mock-ups for a full website re-design. There were massive title banners and huge video-game logos. Entire subreddits had been redesigned in visually appealing fonts, such as Helvetica Neue, with varying sizes and a diversity of spacings. On these pages there were evolved iterations of the Reddit alien, Snoo: It finally looked like it had abandoned its MS Paint prototype shell and stepped into its own gorgeously animated Pixar film. Other mock-ups showed streamlined subreddit pages for users, games, and sports teams—with multiple configurations for on-page elements, which could in the future be moved by subreddit moderators using web-design tiles.

Reddit would be shedding some of its decade-old skin that had earned it a nickname for its lack of design savvy: *Craigslist for links.* The site would be undergoing a comprehensive redesign over the course of the following year.

It would not be a massive, all-at-once unveiling: Elements of the redesign were being deployed to a handful of users and communities at a time. Subreddits such as r/Overwatch, which was dedicated to the hit video game of the same name and had more than one million subscribers, was an early tester of the visually over-hauled version of Reddit. As of March 2017, most of the site was still its plain old sans serif font list of headlines, which internally was called R2.

To reach one billion users, Huffman knew that Reddit would need to erase its perception debt. "Reddit feels old," he said. "We don't want to be associated with 'old.'"

The site redesign project had been dubbed "Reddit 4.0," an in-joke on Digg 4.0, the version that led to a massive user exodus, which led to its demise as a vibrant site. Even though Digg 4.0 happened almost seven years earlier, it still loomed over Reddit as a cautionary tale.

Heading up the redesign project was Diego Perez, a former Microsoft employee, who brought in with him Benjamin Rush. They are smart young men, working as part of a mostly new, sixteen-person design team. Neither had been an avid Redditor before applying for positions.

By mid-2017, they'd put together a sleek presentation of their work, all bullet points, vision-plan goals, and underlying design principles. In what's now a staple of even Reddit's most corporate presentations, it opened with self-deprecating humor. "So, Reddit has designers?"

The team focused on three primary areas: visual and brand design, which includes the site's logo and Snoo's look; user experience research, which figures out how a variety of individuals navigate Reddit's site and app; and user experience design, which seeks to make the experience of using Reddit more intuitive.

Old was out, except when it came to users. The design team couldn't risk pissing off old users. In designer speak, this is called "preserving the spirit," and as Rush explained, when it came to Reddit, it mandated that the designers not touch the comment structure or left-hand-side voting. Some of the spirit of Reddit was tied to its cluttered pages and its distinctly undesigned aesthetic.

Reddit pages have always been crowded with information, links, and cascades of text. Throughout the redesign process, "visual density" was a matter of significant debate, right up to Huffman, who was vocal about avoiding renderings that appeared "too clean." "Just take a chisel to this and distress it a little bit," he recalled telling his design team when presented with pristine site mock-ups. Their ultimate objective, then, was to try to create something better, yet still imperfect; still crowded and dense and a little bit raw.

As for the brand itself, that's a different story. "We want people to feel like Reddit is an approachable brand, just because it's something that we've struggled with in the past," Perez said. While the "brand" of Reddit had always sort of faded away once a user was deep into a subreddit, with its own intensely customizable design and unique use cases, in the new iteration of the site, a portion of the brand would remain consistent to guide new users through it. Its name is Snoo.

Snoo's makeover was tasked to Dante Orpilla, a longtime favorite artist of Redditors, who had found a community there and built a following as an artist and thinker while serving a prison sentence. New Snoo is a cuddlier version of the old alien; he has more expressive facial features and three-dimensionality due to newly added shadows. He appears to have a range of motion, and looks squishy and plump. His little antenna appears floppy, tilting under the weight of its bulbous tip. There's a casual nature to the sketchy, uneven outline of his body. "It's emblematic of who we are as humans," Rush said. "It's rough around the edges, it's not perfect. It's not clean-cut."

After the initial uproar over Reddit user profile pages, hundreds of users requested early access to the redesign, and, gradually, permissions were granted widely. Within months, thousands of users around the globe had access to spiffed-up websites of their own within Reddit, which they were customizing and maintaining via new user and moderator tools, all of which had been built by Reddit over the past year and a half. Sometime in 2018, all of Reddit would have the option to exist in this new, slightly cleaner, far more customizable iteration. Unlike Digg 4.0, this would not be the end of Reddit. It would be a new beginning.

SALESMAN EMERITUS

Every June, the worlds of advertising and publishing converge upon Cannes, France, to party, honor themselves with awards, and ostensibly do a little business. In other words, it was a perfect scene for Alexis Ohanian. One evening at the 2017 Cannes Lions event, as he was seated for an alfresco dinner at a bunch of pushed-together tables filled with drinks, bread, friends, colleagues, and hopeful business partners, Ohanian hit "Start Live Video" on the Instagram app on his phone. He panned the phone screen around the table flotilla: It was a dimly lit affair, but boisterous, especially when the food started coming out. Ohanian spoke to the phone a bit, to hundreds of individuals who'd tuned in through Instagram. Little hearts flew up the screen, displaying their fleeting approval in flutters. Messages, too, started to appear. He attempted to read them while keeping the camera steady.

Commenters asked for shout-outs to Armenia, from where Ohanian's paternal great-grandparents hailed. He indulged them. He also obliged when a commenter expressed adoration for the flowy red dress worn by his assistant, Lissie Garvin, and asked for a full-body view of the whole outfit. Garvin gamely stood up and performed a pirouette.

In Cannes, Ohanian was filling a new part of his role at Reddit: salesman emeritus, in which he fostered new client relationships and tried to seal deals. It was Reddit's second year of making any sort of appearance on the French Riviera for this massive advertising-world conference, which included four awards ceremonies, an opening and a closing gala, and hundreds of brand-sponsored parties in between. Reddit itself had an event, and an apartment suite just for client meetings. This was, of course, nothing compared to some other digital companies, who were taking over parts of the city. Facebook had its own beach, Pinterest had a full pier, and Snap sponsored a giant yellow Ferris wheel. But Reddit now belonged in Cannes, too. The company was up for an award, for a campaign it had executed for FedEx. Reddit's sales team held meetings at their apartment, and mingled with brand representatives over frosé on patios decorated with logo-laden banners.

By mid-2017, Reddit was in the throes of altering much about the way it catered to advertisers. It had revamped its now-aging self-serve advertising platform. Ohanian touted it during his Cannes press spree, and proudly proclaimed to be rolling out lucrative and in-demand video ads.

Inside Reddit, the sales operation had been entirely transformed over the past two years by Zubair Jandali. He'd arrived from Google, hired by Pao right before Wong resigned, and taken the helm of a team that had been pitching Reddit to major companies in a way he described as one "that would only work on Reddit." The pitch deck had contained slides of memes of cats and unicorns. When companies bit, Reddit didn't have the metrics to prove a campaign was meaningful, so they often wouldn't come back.

Within months, most of the old team had been replaced—and so had the pitch deck. Jandali tailored its content and language, removing cutesy wording and innocuous mentions of "porn" (as in the ultra-popular r/EarthPorn, featuring beautiful images of our planet). The new pitch specified for brands that communities that loved them—ones dedicated to cars, makeup application, Audi, Xbox, virtual reality—already existed on the site, and were primed for sponsorship and brand integration through natural-feeling campaigns. These specified pitches were often met with wide-eyed surprise by corporate marketing departments. "Like, 'Oh. My brand's being discussed. Is it being shat on?'" Jandali said. His team showed them real examples, that generally showed no, the commentary was neutral or slightly positive.

Two years later, Reddit was equipped with the tools to provide advertisers not only with a custom on-site experience, but also more of the metrics to back up that the brand could get a boost from interactions with Reddit users. It had executed campaigns for Coca-Cola, to boost excitement about its Super Bowl ad, and direct-to-consumer brands such as Duracell.

Jandali and his team had found particular success working with the largest brand marketers in spaces already super-popular on Reddit, namely technology, movies and television, and gaming. Universal Studios was a big advertiser; gaming studios, too, were natural sells. Maintaining these relationships, though, considering the nature of Reddit's pseudonymous users, far-flung communities, and diversity of voices, meant alerting brands to new mentions across thousands of communities—positive and negative. This was, simply put, a lot of work. A handful of U.S. companies by this time had employees whose full- or part-time job was to manage their Reddit presence, though Jandali was already looking forward to the day when advertisers or their agencies trained up on doing this themselves. He was prepared for third-party ad vendors to pop up to design and sell Reddit ads, the way several had emerged to specialize in selling Snapchat ads and creating product placements there.

If Jandali was the calm and steady leader inside Reddit, all dark-rimmed glasses and cashmere sweaters, Ohanian, in flashy sneakers and T-shirts, had begun to serve as a jet-setting hype man. After Huffman shut down Ohanian's pet project, Upvoted, he helped shift Ohanian's priorities to include meeting with potential corporate clients.

"He likes to travel, he likes to speak, he likes to talk about

Reddit. I think there's 70 percent of the population that just really falls for his charms, and many of them are CMOs," Huffman joked, with a little grin. "That works out great."

Jandali informally dubbed Ohanian "chief bullhorn." One of his big successes was working with the producers of the sci-fi tech dystopia show *Mr. Robot*. During its third season, which aired in 2017, they pulled off an elaborate integration in which there were nods to Reddit on the show itself, and, simultaneously, clues from the show unfolded in subreddits online.

Months later, Ohanian would visit Samsung in New York, the very morning after his pregnant fiancée was featured wearing only thong underwear and a silver belly chain on the cover of *Vanity Fair*.

"Oh, that," Ohanian said when the *Vanity Fair* cover was mentioned in the lobby of Samsung in Manhattan's tony Meatpacking District. It was a long and glowing cover story focusing solely on his courtship and pregnancy with Serena Williams. The pregnancy had come to light the past April when Williams set public what appeared to be intended as a private Snapchat pic of herself in a swimsuit with a tiny midsection bulge labeled "20 weeks." Ohanian has said he'd been reluctant to participate in big, splashy, overtly personal press, but was game to do whatever Williams wanted—and she had already become convinced to participate in the story.

"You'll always be her assistant," Garvin, Ohanian's assistant, joked.

Ohanian threw Garvin an almost undetectable side-eye, and joked about the magazine photographs: "It killed a couple birds with one stone. I'd been meaning to schedule both engagement and maternity photo shoots for her. Now we have both—taken by Annie Leibovitz."

After a little desktop robot took Ohanian's and Garvin's pictures, they were greeted by Paul Leys, Samsung's marketing head of an entity dubbed "creator partnerships." They were waiting on Casey Neistat, a prolific maker of short films, a vlogger, and now

Samsung's "brand ambassador," something of its answer to AOL's Shingy. After a few minutes, Neistat rode up on a $1,500 battery-powered skateboard.

The Bluetooth-remote-controlled skateboard was designed by San Francisco startup Boosted Boards, a company Ohanian had invested in. It was later revealed that Neistat owned six. By the time they returned to Leys's glass-walled office, Leys had already loaded Ohanian's—Reddit's—pitch presentation on a three-foot-wide freestanding computer monitor. "Generation Create," read the first slide. Ohanian issued a disclaimer: "That's just our two-second idea for a name."

"I like that," Leys said, nodding.

Ohanian launched into a sturdy pitch for a collaboration between Reddit and Samsung that would scout for and enlist a to-be-determined number of up-and-coming *creators*—ostensibly the future Casey Neistats of the world—into a web-savvy artist's version of a tech incubator. It would be a short, months-long YC of sorts for the creative class, for whom online tools and hardware for creatives (provided, of course, by Samsung) were becoming gateways to a livelihood. Corporations such as Samsung were keen to empower more of these people who might self-identify as graffiti artists or fashion designers to become, in addition, prolific *content creators*, whose content could populate their platforms.

Leys's boss, Marc Mathieu, the chief marketing officer of Samsung Electronics America, had introduced him to Ohanian. Ohanian says he encountered Mathieu for the first time at a dinner in Austin during South by Southwest. They'd also met up in Cannes.

In the Meatpacking District tower, Ohanian began to wrap up his pitch by drawing parallels to Paul Graham's original Y Combinator, and explaining the success in building a vast network of powerful company creators that little experiment had attained.

Using a line that had become one of his standbys for sales pitches, he explained that Reddit, while commonly seen as sprawling communities, is really just "word of mouth, at scale." And he said that plenty of Redditors are creators—young people with keyboards and

webcams and cell phones to document their lives. "This is a generation that can default think of themselves as creators. That is a huge
shift. To not harness that...oh my God!" Ohanian said.

Neistat, who at one point in the conversation referred to himself
as "the fucking oracle," proved an admirable hype man for the
project almost immediately. He referred to Ohanian's pitch as
"tremendous for Samsung from a branding perspective," and said,
"This is closer to *American Idol*, where you sing, and at the end of
it you don't get your song recorded—you get a career."

Leys seemed to approve, and asked in what timeline they could
reasonably accomplish an integration into Reddit—definitely featuring a custom subreddit, possibly featuring content by their
burgeoning class of potential content creators. "We could do it at
the speed of Samsung, which is like, in two weeks we have the
space, three weeks we start, and in eight weeks we'll have output,"
said Leys.

Ohanian faltered for a moment. "Jeez. Okay. Wow." He'd be out
on paternity leave in T minus six weeks. And his calendar until then
was jammed.

As artfully as he could, Ohanian explained that the collaboration
should be done in a "thoughtful way." In other words—it would
take more than two weeks for Reddit to get a move on this. Ohanian promised only to coordinate with his team in San Francisco to
set up a larger meeting and more specific deck for Samsung's marketing department. He said he wanted to "get this right" and "get
the right people at the table." If he—and Reddit—could, it would
be Reddit's second-largest marketing package to date. What hinged
on this meeting was a $10 million deal.

(• •)

In summer 2017 came a moment of epic relief for Steve Huffman.
Finally, he had completed a new funding round. The process of
putting together the round—setting terms that could shape the
future of Reddit and its value to both existing shareholders and

employees—had been a slog. At least once during the yearlong process, he'd grown so frustrated that he'd come close to calling off the effort. Now it was done, which meant time for a victory lap.

On July 31, dozens of articles appeared in the tech press, under headlines reading some variation of "Reddit raised $200 million in funding and is now valued at $1.8 billion." Just like that, six years after Advance Publications bestowed upon its little acquisition the power to raise outside funding and grow like a startup, Reddit joined a new echelon of Silicon Valley elite. It was now a "unicorn," a private company valued at $1 billion or more, like Uber or Pinterest. There were only about two hundred of these companies in the world, and one hundred in the United States.

After all these years and this major cash infusion, Advance Publications was still Reddit's majority shareholder. The fact that it was a massive victory for Steve Newhouse's now-years-old vision for an autonomous Reddit, which had been shepherded into life by Yishan Wong and his unorthodox management, was barely noted.

Altman clearly had a hand in this huge funding round; he participated again. Sequoia Capital, unsurprisingly, invested: Its partner Alfred Lin had been a board observer. Andreessen Horowitz, another top-performing Silicon Valley investment powerhouse, joined as well. It was a diverse round; individuals such as investors Ron Conway and Edward Lando, who had a small investment fund, participated. So did more established players known for seeking reliability, such as Fidelity Investments. Huffman clearly wanted to keep the round from being too sprawling, as it contained just eleven investors, but he'd also had to search far and wide over the past year: Two Dubai-based firms were also on the roster.

Reddit's board remained steady, and exceedingly friendly to Huffman. It was composed of himself; two longtime friends, Altman and Ohanian; one independent member, Rabois; and one longtime partner at Advance Publications, Sauerberg.

Something else miraculous happened over the summer of 2017: Reddit's traffic grew to such an extent that it was now considered by the primary site-ranking service, Amazon's web analytics arm Alexa, as the fourth most popular website in the United States, behind only Google, YouTube, and Facebook. It was one of only two in the top twelve that were run by private companies. Imgur, which got its start on Reddit, was number thirteen. Twitch, run by Huffman's old Y Combinator friends, was ranked eighteenth.

As of July, Reddit had 234 million individual visitors to its site, according to Alexa. According to Reddit, this number was much higher: more than 300 million. Reddit's own internal analysis of site traffic is consistently higher than that of Alexa; both founders claim it is as reliable as Google Analytics, which the site formerly used for internal traffic numbers.

Reddit had doubled revenue in 2016, and it climbed again through 2017 to five times what it was when Huffman joined, as the company charted a future in which it could broaden its revenue streams from advertising and Reddit Gold. One significant effort would be enlisting publishers and brands to sign up for profile pages and engage organically with Redditors—and pay to promote their content. Another would be major campaigns with advertisers such as Google or Toyota. Ohanian's pitch to Samsung would not yield a successful partnership for Reddit, but revenue was one of Huffman's three top-line goals going forward. The other two goals were to increase the number of daily active users, and to bolster EDI, the company's engagement, diversity, and inclusion.

The question was: Which path was Reddit the corporation truly on? Advance Publications may have been Reddit's majority owner, but other investors would eventually be looking for a payday, despite that they had little power over the board. There were many paths Reddit could take, but one would be to eventually conduct an initial public offering. Huffman was open to it, potentially, years down the road. As with Hipmunk, he saw it as implicit to having offered stock to employees that eventually, they'd see a payday from their hard work.

Building a strong company, a company that could go public, is just as complex a prospect as the challenge of amassing users. To that aim, one thing Huffman was really proud of was that of the hundreds of employees he'd hired since returning as CEO, only a handful had left. In 2017, Huffman still interviewed most new hires himself. Sometimes, on nice days, he would take a candidate up to the top floor of 420 Taylor, which was no longer empty; it was equipped with communal tables and desks. He'd open the glass doors to the sprawling, sunny rooftop deck and show them to a chaise. He'd kick his feet up, lean back, and maybe rest a hand behind his head.

He was trying to stay balanced. In late August 2017, he took a vacation, out to Burning Man with his girlfriend, Elvie Stephanopoulos. During a windstorm, sand whipping up from the playa, he swooped her up into the air. She wrapped her arms around his shoulders, over which was draped a goofy red Hawaiian shirt, and kicked her dusty black boots up in the air. Under a vintage marquee sign whose letters read "stage your own death," they kissed.

LIVE FROM HOLLYWOOD

August 1, 2017, was a helluva last hurrah for Alexis Ohanian. He'd flown into Los Angeles with a small squad consisting of his assistant, Lissie Garvin, and Jon Swyers, who'd been his buddy since first grade. The following weekend, Ohanian and Williams would host their baby shower in a Florida diner. The place would be decked out in a '50s theme—as would guests: family members, childhood friends, and fellow celebrities. Ciara, Kelly Rowland, and Eva Longoria posed in poodle skirts in front of a gleaming red Mercury M100 pickup truck. After the party, Ohanian planned to decamp to his fiancée's home in West Palm Beach to wait for the baby. Which meant this day in Los Angeles, this hot late-summer Tuesday, would be his last Reddit-centric public appearance before a significant paternity leave.

The day began with a visit to the Los Angeles office of an e-sports company called Cloud9, which manages teams of professional video-game players, and in which Ohanian had invested. Afterward, Swyers and Garvin waited while Ohanian took a few Reddit-related calls, and then a car arrived to drive the three to Hollywood Boulevard, to the old Hollywood Masonic Temple, now called El Capitan Entertainment Centre, where Ohanian would be a guest on *Jimmy Kimmel Live!*

Stepping out of the car on Hollywood Boulevard, the three were escorted into a dressing room, where producers briefed Ohanian about what Kimmel would ask him: about Reddit, about Serena Williams, about imminent fatherhood. Settling in out in the theater audience was Ohanian's cheerleading section, which included a handful of Reddit staffers from its Los Angeles office and longtime Reddit engineer Neil Williams from San Francisco.

Right at 5 p.m., Ohanian began to hear Kimmel's opening monologue, which was piped into the green room. Kimmel introduced Kate Beckinsale, his first guest. In the course of bantering with Kimmel, Beckinsale mentioned that she once had a crush on tennis great Boris Becker. Kimmel said, coincidentally enough, that his next guest, Ohanian, was also in love with a tennis star.

"I know Reddit," Beckinsale replied, deadpanning in her posh London accent. "It's the one where you can sometimes find pictures of porn stars with your own face on it." The audience snickered. Clearly her joke had landed, and so Beckinsale went on with it. "I've been sent a few quite distressing photos of myself. Very *busy*, actually," she said, using a Briticism for sex. She joked that she'd sent the Photoshopped images to her own mother, just to rattle her.

The show's producers ushered Ohanian to the wings during this casual Reddit-bashing. Walking out onto a stage was by now a comfortable act for Ohanian, though he wasn't usually preceded by a celebrity victim of involuntary and fake pornography, disseminated by his own site.

Ohanian sat down in the upholstered chair next to Kimmel's stage desk. Kimmel asked him if there were subreddits he visited regularly. Ohanian mentioned a few that fall into what could be called the "best of silly" Reddit, including the self-explanatory r/ChildrenFallingOver, r/AnimalsBeingJerks, and its countersite, r/AnimalsBeingBros—which contains photos of animals appearing to comfort or assist one another.

Kimmel pulled up the homepage of Reddit.com to show the audience what the site looks like, and began scrolling. "This dog looks like William H. Macy," read one post. "Yep, I'm gonna have to click on that," Kimmel said.

"Would you upvote that?!" Ohanian exclaimed, by means of explanation. The dog did, especially in this particular photographic side-by-side comparison, very much resemble the star of *Fargo* and *Shameless*. Ohanian joked, "Someone get that dog an agent!"

Kimmel, who appeared to be comfortable navigating Reddit, clicked the poster's username, gryff42, and began scrolling through their post history. Ohanian looked at the projected screen, and his face went blank. *Uh-oh.*

Kimmel's eyes scanned the screen while he scrolled. "Well! We could go way down a rabbit hole here." He chuckled, broadcasting his screen on a large projection behind him. "Yeah, there's some filthy stuff on here." He paused, still reading. He appeared to be looking for something funny but appropriate. He opted not to read anything aloud. "Yeah."

Sensing potential disaster, Ohanian opened his mouth. "What's impressive, though, is the fact that, you know, people are spending this time, and, and, you know," he stumbled, emitting a string of mismatched Reddit-related sound bites, barely stopping for breath. "By the wisdom of the crowd, I mean three hundred million people every month are on Reddit, and—some of you all hopefully in the audience, um, thank you, by the way, thank you for all the upvotes!—and, and, and, they're creating this through the wisdom of the crowd."

Ohanian's save was bumbling, but at least the camera had been rehomed on him, and Kimmel had shut down his screen during the twenty seconds. All was recovered, and Kimmel went back to softball questions, asking Ohanian whether he had an all-time favorite Reddit post.

Ohanian selected a fantastic one. It was from December 2010, by u/rhoner. The user had written that once his car had blown a tire, and, stranded on the highway, for four hours he couldn't get anyone to stop to help him. Finally, a car with a full family of Spanish-speaking immigrants pulled over. The father not only loaned the jack he required, but also fashioned a brace for it after sawing a log from a downed tree. The family also fed the Redditor, despite the language barrier.

Ohanian didn't explain the entire content of the post—it's eleven hundred words, and a real tearjerker—but it also included that the Redditor had slipped the mom a $20 bill after the father refused payment. Later, a little girl in the car brought him a tamale and explained to him that the family was there in the United States for a couple weeks picking peaches. U/rhoner had written, "I thank them again and walk back to my car and open the foil on the tamale cause I am starving at this point and what do I find inside? My fucking $20 bill!" He tried again to give it to the family, but was denied.

This story had become known on Reddit as "today you, tomorrow me," for the phrase the migrant worker said in English to the Redditor as he refused to take his $20 bill back.

The story gave Ohanian a window to state what he really wanted to express about Reddit: "In the last twelve years since we've started it, the platform has given me so many more reasons to be hopeful about my fellow humans and less scared about my fellow humans and feel more connected to my fellow humans than any other social network."

Kimmel, of course, also asked about Williams, and Ohanian's soon-to-be status as a father. Did he know the sex of the baby? "We have our hunches," he said, noting that Williams had won the Australian Open while pregnant. "Everything that little baby went through and handled like a champ, only a woman could do that."

"In a way, it's the greatest nerd-makes-good story in history," Kimmel said, of the very fact that Ohanian and Williams were expecting a child together and were engaged to be married. "She might be the greatest athlete in history. It is just amazing that she has chosen to copulate with . . . " He gestured to Ohanian.

(• •)

As the clock ticked up to 9 p.m. on Friday, August 11, about 250 young men and a few women snaked down a dark, long expanse of grass in Charlottesville, Virginia, called Nameless Field. The assembled group was abundantly white, and almost uniformly dressed in pressed khakis and polo shirts. Each held a tiki torch, unlit, filled with kerosene.

They formed a column, lined up two by two. They lit their torches. Organizers, wearing earpieces, paced up and down the line issuing directions, amplified by electric bullhorn. "Now! Now! Go!" the bullhorns ordered. The men marched, and began to chant. "Blood and soil!" they yelled, echoing Nazi ideology. "Jews will not replace us! Jews will not replace us!"

Journalists had been tipped off to the organized white nationalist march. They knew the location, Nameless Field, and the timing, the night before the Unite the Right rally. They didn't know it would be this overtly antiblack and anti-Semitic. The torches, the nighttime setting, the clash with student counterprotesters that ensued at the base of the field's central statue—Thomas Jefferson, who'd founded the University of Virginia—foreshadowed that this would be a weekend of terror. There were alarming echoes of Nazism and the Ku Klux Klan.

This was a physical manifestation of many factions of the alt-right, whose identities were so often masked by online pseudonyms on forums such as 4chan or Reddit or tucked away in private Discord channels. Now they were attempting to prove they were more than an Internet meme machine. These factions of the alt-right had extensively plotted through online messages on alt-right boards the optics of this rally, down to their fitted collared shirts. "We want to look slick and sexy," wrote Andrew Anglin on the Daily Stormer, an alt-right website. Even the lack of chat-board meme symbolism and swastikas was deliberate. "Pepe banners are a non-starter," Anglin wrote. Supporters were instructed to stay at home if they were obese or looked like disheveled trolls.

"We are starting to slowly unveil a little bit of our power level," Robert "Azzmador" Ray, a neo-Nazi writer for the Daily Stormer, told Vice News. "You ain't seen nothin' yet."

Saturday, on the streets of Charlottesville, alt-right-aligning protesters and hundreds of counterdemonstrators—mostly local—flooded the streets. The two sides hurled water bottles and sprayed chemical gases at one another. Journalists were assaulted with urine. Late Saturday morning, the police ordered all protesters to disperse, deeming it an unlawful assembly. Virginia's governor declared a state of emergency. Then a car driven by a twenty-year-old, who'd been photographed hours earlier carrying a hate-group emblem, plowed into a crowd of demonstrators, killing thirty-two-year-old local paralegal Heather Heyer and injuring at least nineteen others.

As Huffman watched this overt display of terror unfold, from small screens on an airplane and then at home in San Francisco, he was heartbroken and incensed. He was angry about the whole rally and display, but also that his city, one of his favorite places on the planet, near where he grew up, where he went to college, where he returned immediately after leaving Reddit in 2009, would be painted by others as a haven for racist vigilantes. Charlottesville to his mind was the perfect mix of a slow and friendly-feeling southern town with a campus and a progressive vibe. The starting point for the march, the main University of Virginia quadrangle, was a field Huffman and Ohanian had traversed often as undergrads. It was a less than five-minute stroll from the UVA dormitory in which they first met.

Huffman got more angry at the alt-right than he'd been before. "I was like, fuck all these people. Ban them all!"

Six months earlier, Huffman's trust and safety team had, with little ceremony, shuttered Reddit's most popular meeting places for the alt-right, r/altright and r/AlternativeRight, of which some fraction was white nationalist. Shadow forums were still popping up, though. While Reddit had caught and closed some similar subsites, others, such as r/NewRight, were continuing to gain steam.

Enraged by the news, Huffman visited a Slack channel of the

trust and safety team and read in. Members had already pinpointed where on Reddit the rally, or the crash, were being applauded. One subreddit, r/Physical_Removal, which advocated for the elimination of liberals from the United States, frequently posted memes featuring an alt-right image dubbed "Pinochet's Helicopter" (a veiled reference to the dictator's regime's reputation for throwing communists out of aircraft into the ocean). It was known for bashing communism and comparing American leftists to ISIS, and on the Saturday of the march featured a large Unite the Right banner and several upvoted discussions of the crash. One moderator posted that the murder of a counterprotester was "ethical."

Trust and safety was already discussing banning r/Physical_Removal. "They were not talking about *if*, but *when*," Huffman said.

To Huffman, the days surrounding the Unite the Right rally were a turning point for Reddit. He said staff rallied together and realized that if they wanted to have a hand in stopping this from happening again, they'd need to be more proactive. It wouldn't be easy. It would mean banning r/Physical_Removal and other subreddits, and again rethinking part of the site's content policy. By the end of the following week, they'd gotten approval from Tidwell's legal department to zap r/Physical_Removal.

Not that these voices have been silenced, by any means. Some of the most inflammatory users migrated to new dens, to networks that specifically catered to extreme "free speech." They were sites such as Voat, a "no censorship" Reddit clone. There was also Gab.ai, founded by onetime Silicon Valley–based Trump supporter Andrew Torba, who'd been kicked out of Y Combinator for violating its harassment policy. When Gab, which uses as its logo a green frog face, raised $1 million in crowdfunding, it boasted with a tweet that read, "FUCK YOU Silicon Valley elitist trash." Others went back to 4chan's /pol board.

The alt-right's prolific memetic warriors and its vigilante white nationalists weren't just Reddit's albatross. Other Internet gatekeepers took note—and Airbnb booted some of the Unite the

Right rally's organizers off of its services even prior to the rally. Facebook removed at least eight pages connected to the white nationalist movement. Spotify removed musicians deemed "hate bands" by the Southern Poverty Law Center, and LinkedIn blocked a profile of the Daily Stormer.

As mainstream sites such as YouTube and Facebook cracked down on high-profile proliferators of hate speech, the alt-right vowed to circumvent their gateways and create their own parallel Internet. More than a dozen alt-tech companies launched bizarro versions of mainstream sites, including PewTube, an alternative YouTube, WrongThink, an alt-Facebook, as well as GoyFundMe and Hatreon, alt-crowdfunding alternatives to GoFundMe and Patreon.

Google booted Gab from its app store a week after the Charlottesville hate rally, and after the neo-Nazi publication the Daily Stormer's domain registration was shuttered by GoDaddy and was reregistered on Google, Google blocked the registration, too. A major financial institution kicked Hatreon off its network. Silicon Valley—along with Wall Street—had, by not wanting to do business with these groups and individuals, put up structural barriers to the sites' functioning. There were work-arounds—Tor, IP masking, Russian domain registration, and simply creating new accounts on sites such as Reddit and participating in an ongoing game of whack-a-mole there.

(• •)

One year after the election of Donald Trump, politics still deeply haunted Reddit. In the fall of 2017, Congress launched a formal investigation into the widespread presence of hyperpoliticized online misinformation, a.k.a. "fake news." It had been known even prior to the election that some sort of Russian meddling, an attempt to influence the American electorate, had taken place: There was the hacking of Democratic Party emails, which U.S. intelligence agencies concluded were leaked by Russians. The Republican National Committee's computer system had also been breached. Then there was a more amorphous problem: all the dubious content swirling around social networks from websites posing as news sources, peddling deliberately false stories.

The U.S. Senate launched an investigation into the dissemination of fake news. In the course of it, Mark Warner, a Democratic senator from Virginia, grew concerned that Reddit may have been used as a tool in the Russian campaign for social media influence over the 2016 presidential election. Considering that Reddit's r/The_Donald was a highly coordinated hub of information analysis and dissemination after the leak of Democratic emails, it was not a far leap. An Oxford University researcher who had studied governmental use of social media to manipulate public opinion told *The Hill* that patterns she'd witnessed on the site pointed to deliberate efforts to distribute fake news.

Twitter executives met with congressional investigators in advance of both a House and a Senate hearing on Russian influence, and disclosed that Twitter had deleted hundreds of Russia-linked accounts. As part of the Senate investigation, Facebook turned over to the government more than three thousand advertisements it had independently linked to Russia. By November 2017, it was clear that content produced by an army of Russian-government-backed individuals on social media had reached 126 million Americans through Facebook posts. Warner called this all "the tip of the iceberg."

Reddit was not called to testify alongside executives at Facebook, Google, and Twitter on October 31 and November 1, 2017. A Reddit spokesperson claimed that no one at Reddit had been contacted by Warner's office or the FBI regarding their investigations into Russian influence on the election. (Warner's office in October 2017 acknowledged it was focusing on Twitter and Facebook, but would not confirm whether it had attempted to contact Reddit.) Reddit launched its own internal investigation into suspicious ads and content. A Reddit representative later said no advertisements connected to the Russian Internet Research Agency were detected. In the midst of all this, Reddit's legal team proactively reached out to Warner's office to introduce themselves.

As part of the internal investigation, Reddit dug into an isolated conspiracy theory, Pizzagate. Its data scientists found no evidence at the time of suspicious Russian domains orchestrating the dissemination or analysis of Pizzagate on the subreddit. That was all regular Redditors.

The spread of political disinformation by regular users wasn't what Congress was investigating—it was primarily looking into easier-to-track and -grasp advertising—but a representative from Warner's office said at the time, "No one denies that Reddit has been a hub of anti-Semitic and white nationalist expression. Much of that was generated by Americans, who certainly have a First Amendment right to do so."

While Reddit was secretly investigating, and keeping mum to the public on its findings, outside researchers determined that during the lead-up to the election, there'd been not just an uptick, but a 1,600 percent increase in links on conservative subreddits to what they'd dubbed "controversial" media—dubious news sources that spread hyperbole, unverified claims, and highly opinionated articles framed as truth. Republican forums had spread fake news at a rate sixteen times higher than prior to the election cycle—or at any other time in the past decade, researchers found. Certain conservative subreddits (such as r/The_Donald and r/Conservative, the two major hubs, and r/HillaryForPrison, an extreme anti-Clinton forum) were home to 80 percent of all fake news on Reddit, during and after the 2016 election cycle, they determined. From the outset of Trump's presidency, instances remained high.

Reddit wouldn't admit anything of this sort publicly until six months later. Huffman would post in April 2018, as Facebook's Mark Zuckerberg testified before Congress, that Reddit had identified 944 accounts that linked to and disseminated Russian propaganda meant to sow discord among Americans. He wrote that the majority of the accounts had been banned in 2015 and 2016. Regardless, thousands of posts in the lead-up to the 2016 election had shared links to phony websites created by the notorious Russian troll hub the Internet Research Agency to spread divisive propaganda. In

February 2018, the U.S. Justice Department had issued a sweeping indictment of thirteen individuals and the Saint Petersburg–based IRA, for their scheme to interfere with the U.S. election by tricking Americans into consuming and promoting divisive propaganda aimed at pushing voters toward Donald Trump.

Huffman noted in a separate announcement on Reddit what was, in his mind, perhaps a more significant problem: These false messages had been "amplified by thousands of Reddit users, and sadly, from everything we can tell, these users are mostly American, and appear to be unwittingly promoting Russian propaganda." In other words, what the Russian trolls had set out to do had worked to trick Americans. Huffman wrote that "the biggest risk we face as Americans is our own ability to discern reality from nonsense, and this is a burden we all bear." Banning propaganda would not be enough. Huffman admitted in a comment in an April post on Reddit that he was glad he wasn't in Mark Zuckerberg's shoes testifying before Congress. (Reddit said it had turned over its findings to congressional investigators.)

Such issues as requests from federal investigators would not be easily solved for Reddit. Back in October 2017, Reddit had filed a federal disclosure that in July it had hired a lobbying firm called the Franklin Square Group, which works with Alphabet, Apple, Dropbox, and Uber, among many other public and private tech companies. The disclosure stated that the lobbying would be for general "Internet issues, including net neutrality and liability protections for online platforms," but clearly a nod was being made to Reddit having a presence and a voice connected to Congress.

Before the turn of 2018, r/The_Donald had reached half a million subscribers. Brad Parscale, the Trump campaign's digital director, had claimed social media was the reason "we won this thing." He wrote on Reddit that "members here provided considerable growth and reach to our campaign." The_Donald again celebrated Trump's win with a thread cataloging its greatest hits of viral imagery and boasted, "'Member when we memed a man into the White House?"

ALL TOGETHER NOW

Two years after those awkward dinners between Steve Huffman and Alexis Ohanian, the men said they had come to accept one another for the people they had become. Ohanian deferred to Huffman on business matters—he'd gone from a mandate of "let Alexis be Alexis," which led to the unsuccessful media sites and video products, to a more clear-cut role in helping solidify business deals, closing ad buys, and speaking about Reddit to audiences on college campuses, in tech companies, and on the occasional talk show. Ohanian grew to appreciate his new position: Making money and converting traffic to money were clear goals that could be measured, something he'd never had before. (Exceptions include his personal investments and the portfolio managed by his investment company, Initialized Capital. They appeared promising, with some big names such as HubSpot and Evernote, but Ohanian said none of his investments were yet liquid.) Huffman had come to accept Ohanian's wildly jet-setting lifestyle, and had even become prone to smile at his consistent appearances on magazine covers and talk shows, which had only accelerated thanks to his extraordinarily famous fiancée.

Perhaps most encouragingly for their relationship, the pair had again begun to banter like brothers. They were not together in the office an awful lot, but when Huffman was asked how working side by side was going, he was so comfortable that he went straight for a joke: "Smells so good, I can't concentrate." Ohanian laughed, too: "People have given me really great feedback on that."

Ohanian was traveling much of 2017, and took a two-month paternity leave through September and October. He'd catch up with Huffman over the phone once a week, but they didn't see much of each other. They're not best friends, and they are perfectly fine with that. They had, after all, lived together on and off for eight years. They had their finances intertwined for years. Their legacies were still tied together, in Reddit.

"There's a level of trust there that he'll always be number one in," Huffman said of Ohanian. "I think that will always color our relationship. It did even when we didn't really get along, and it does even when we're not really spending a lot of time with each other."

Ohanian had switched therapists so he wouldn't be working with Huffman's coach; both men still met with their coaches and therapists regularly. Huffman had even picked up management tactics from his. He realized it one day in the office when he made a statement to a colleague that he knew wasn't going to be received well. Instead of just letting it sink in and walking away to avoid the conflict, he followed up with, "I see you're bristling right now. Can you tell me how what I just said landed for you?" Huffman said the interaction turned into a productive conversation that cut to the core of the issue. Only afterward did he realize it was a page from his own shrink's playbook.

Huffman also began meeting regularly with a new executive coach, Marcy Swenson. She was less focused on helping him home in on relationship skills, and more "quit your bitchin'," Huffman explained. Swenson is the coach Huffman leans on when he needs to consider what's best for business, and "stop taking it so personally."

In the future, making decisions that are good for business is perhaps the biggest change Reddit faces—though Huffman was poised to walk into that wind. Reddit had improbably survived a decade of management lax enough that its communities spiraled out of control—and now everything, down to specific content and communities, was under the microscopes of multiple teams at Reddit, the friendly, interactive community team, the secretive, ban-enacting trust and safety team, its engineering counterpart, anti-evil, as well as policy and legal groups.

August and September 2017 went by without a single major community flare-up—the first time a late summer and autumn had passed in five years without Reddit nearly strangling itself out of existence. By winter, and the dawn of 2018, Huffman's past cycles of self-doubt seemed to have lifted. To people close to him, the funding round seemed to promote a new sense of calm. To employees and others, it also seemed to result in a new strength.

There was joy for Huffman in experiencing the daily rhythm of 420 Taylor Street, the flow of more than two hundred in-office employees pausing to chat with one another on their way to their workstations in the mornings. He could often be found with his laptop at a couch in front of the elevators on the third and central floor of the building, his feet in scruffy Adidas soccer shoes, propped up, greeting anyone who walked by.

He particularly relished working so closely with his buddy Chris Slowe, who had been promoted to chief technology officer. Slowe described post-funding Huffman as "happy and content," and said the only complaint Huffman had voiced to him was that he attended too many meetings and he didn't get to write enough code. Huffman had joked to Slowe that he'd like to write a software project (hackers know this particular sort of program as a "chaos monkey") that would randomly nuke 5 percent of all meetings from calendars office-wide—just to see if anyone would notice. He figured that if a meeting was truly important, someone would regenerate it.

As Huffman's staff zeroed in on hate speech and other noxious content on Reddit, the company was also looking inward, at diversity among its own staff. Reddit's hiring tear had brought the company to almost three hundred people; the efforts to hire diversely, Huffman admitted, were a work in progress—though one of importance that was not lost on Huffman. "To build a product that appeals to the world, you need to have that sort of diversity and broadness reflected in your company," he said.

The company has refused to release its hiring or diversity statistics. Likewise, it has not disclosed its full organization chart, despite repeated requests. Reddit appears to be on par with other large technology companies in terms of hiring a diverse staff (which is to say, not great), though significantly better than average in hiring a diverse leadership team. Of Reddit's nine senior executives, five were women or people of color, or both. The general vibe in the office is relaxed and open-minded. For example, one Tuesday afternoon in late 2017, a male employee wore a T-shirt, a khaki kilt, and sandals.

By late October, Huffman's policy team, along with trust and safety and legal, had solidified their tougher policy on violent posts. The new rule: "Do not post content that encourages, glorifies, incites, or calls for violence or physical harm against an individual or a group of people; likewise, do not post content that glorifies or encourages the abuse of animals." It opened the door for Reddit to ban another extensive list of subreddits. These were mostly far-right-leaning and Nazi-sympathizing forums and those that glorified harm or death, such as r/selfharmpics and r/PicsOfDeadKids. Most were small forums, with fewer than a thousand subscribers each, but the list was extensive. It included seventy different communities that violated the updated rule.

Among the subreddits banned or quarantined was r/pol, a carryover from 4chan's main discussion board, which, in lieu of rules typically noted on a subreddit's right-hand rail, simply said, "This is not a safe space. Do not report posts you disagree with or that hurt your feelies—we won't remove them." Also banned were r/europeannationalism, r/nazi, and r/killthejews, and a few sites that mocked, parodied, or stemmed from r/CoonTown. Animal abuse, harm, or bestiality comprised another significant subset of the list. Among those cut off was a subreddit dedicated to images of horse vaginas. The company made clear in its post to moderators that this wasn't limited to strictly text: On-site styling, names of subreddits, usernames—and the flair given to them—would all be subject to scrutiny and removal.

If Reddit had made such a move any time in its past, the results could have been catastrophic. This was a mere blip. The press made note of it, but neither users nor moderators revolted.

Huffman was relieved by the lack of attention. "This was kind of the last of the big wave of communities that caused me angst," he said, leaning back in satisfaction. A few moments later he amended that thought: "Oh, gun sales. Never mind, we probably will still look into gun sales," he said, referencing another albatross the site bore since back in 2014, when *Mother Jones* published an examination of how certain subreddits had become popular online gun marketplaces, and how Reddit had even allowed its alien logo to be used on AR-15s. (Reddit would ban all sales of guns and controlled substances through its site five months later.)

The tide of backlash had turned. Many top comments the day after the violent-content ban called for more, rather than less, action by Reddit. Many users demanded that Reddit ban r/The_Donald. Users listed extensive, hand-compiled instances of posts on the subreddit that appeared to violate site rules. While Huffman's personal opinion of the subreddit was still low, he saw value in keeping it both online and tightly managed. There's the democracy, for one, as he'd noted in the past. Protecting political speech, which is almost universally seen as being the purpose of the First Amendment, was important to him—even though he had come to recognize potential danger in that, because an individual's soapbox had the amplifying power of the social Internet, and that allowed their voice to reverberate far further than ever before. Two, the forum's moderators were making reasonable efforts to walk the line Reddit was drawing, and sometimes redrawing, for them. Reddit's community team, and Huffman, gave them a measure of credit for that. Three (and here, it seemed, Huffman's opinion was evolving), there was wisdom, he thought, in keeping his enemies close. "I think there's some value to the United States to having Donald Trump's most vociferous supporters constantly make fools of themselves," he said. "Why turn them into martyrs when we can let them say racist stuff and be idiots and they can really own that reputation of being a bunch of asshole idiots?"

With a shrug, Huffman said perhaps he'd prefer that not to play out on Reddit. But he noted that he also sees it playing out on Twitter, and in the president of the United States' own speeches. With a congressional investigation under way into the influence of divisive content aiming to sway geopolitics that had been planted on Reddit and other social sites—by a group and individuals who'd soon be indicted by the FBI on charges of conspiracy to defraud the United States—there was no going back. There would be repercussions for Reddit and the entire social sphere in the vast reckoning over the proliferation of hate speech, fake news, and foreign influence online.

It was wishful thinking, he knew, and a lark from an earlier, simpler time, but Huffman admitted he'd already schemed up several new ways he wished he could troll r/The_Donald. It would not pass. His colleagues had already plotted ways to lock down Huffman's computers and exile him from the office on the anniversary of Spezgiving.

(• •)

Late in 2017, in some of the now-purged darkest trenches of Reddit, hints of new life had begun to generate. The subreddit r/WhitePolitics, formerly exactly the modern-Nazi content one would expect, came back online, with posts titled "White power" and "why whites must be separated from blacks." Noxious it was not. The former post featured a photograph of a massive power generator painted white. The latter was a post about properly washing laundry. A user, Ianna Urquhart, had filed a request to Reddit and had taken over other formerly hate-speech-filled subreddits with the aim of pun-fueled goading. When asked her motivation, she said, "It's hilarious. What's not to like?"

There was also r/Trannys, discussion about, and close-up photographs of, car transmissions. R/stormfront is meteorology. R/whites is dedicated to conversation about "shades of whites, off-whites, and light grays." R/faggots—which far-right Internet provocateur Milo Yiannopoulos seemed to have wanted to moderate (his speaking tour was called the "Dangerous Faggot Tour")—was handed to a Redditor who said she'd use her mod powers for "good instead of evil." R/faggots became a forum that hosts mostly photos of elaborate bundles of branches.

It's tempting to view this witty do-gooding as a sign—maybe all those years of hate speech and uncivil discourse, masked by rallying cries of "free speech," were all a blip, a painful, multiyear blip—that maybe, just maybe, the Internet will indeed return to its happier, blithely egalitarian roots. It's unlikely. It wouldn't be Reddit—or the modern Internet—if elsewhere on the site some critical faction wasn't enraged that subreddits such as r/punchablefaces had been taken over by people they called SJWs.

Bill Cline and Susie Vass, the community team members who dealt most frequently with politics moderators, including those of The_Donald, are on chat with each other most of the day, and, despite being separated by almost a generation and hundreds of miles, are kindred spirits. They sometimes reminisce about back in the day, back before they were Reddit employees, before they were even made the multiple job offers, and before Cline went on his spirit quest. Those were simpler days, when they were just screen names who'd notice each other chiming in with complaints to Reddit's bare-bones staff of four programmers, back when Cline helped build up and moderate the forum for women on Reddit, r/TwoXChromosomes, and Vass started the r/stopsmoking subreddit. These days, she's still proud of that forum she'd created on a whim: Thousands of individuals around the world have gained help through the whole ecosystem of addiction-related subreddits it spawned. Many users have as flair next to usernames little timers of how many days they've been clean—a highly effective digital positive reinforcement. Vass created those digital symbols. At least one user got a tattoo of her virtual achievement badge; the pixels

Vass had arranged at her home computer, as a volunteer, are now ink on skin. That thought brings her a sentimental smile.

"You forgot the most important subreddit of all, Bill," Vass said to Cline one day over video chat, ribbing her longtime online acquaintance and years-long colleague. She squinted in jest and said that one of Cline's past creations, which he still moderates, was— tongue-in-cheek—up for consideration in the most recent ban of subreddits.

It wasn't r/crepeshots, Cline's forum for lovers of thin pancakes. No, Vass was referencing another of his subreddits, r/onionhate, on which some ten thousand people who dislike the taste and texture of onions post their grievances. "Ahh." Cline laughed and said, "The people in R/OnionLovers call us the *Alt-Root*."

(• •)

In August 2017, Ohanian decamped to West Palm Beach, where Williams would give birth not far from her tennis training facilities and family. There, he and Williams were finally together for three weeks, and assembled the baby's shiny rose-gold crib, arranged baby books and stuffed animals on shelves, and waited. They plotted the future: a wedding in November, comfortably after the baby arrived. Williams pledged to get back on the tennis circuit come January. Ohanian would stay in West Palm Beach at least six weeks after the baby's birth, then resume some measure of his typical flight-hopping back and forth from San Francisco to wherever in the world Williams would be.

In the meantime, Ohanian waited for the next episode of his life to begin. He lived, for a moment, a normal suburban life of painting a baby's room and sitting on the lawn, watching Williams's tiny dogs, Chip and Laura, frolic in the grass. He broadcasted video Snapchat of the dogs, or of his late-night grocery store runs. "I was told there would be cravings," he said into his cell phone camera.

Then, on a Friday, it happened. Ohanian and Williams drove to the local hospital, St. Mary's Medical Center, and a full floor was cleared. Extra security was added. Ohanian and Williams emerged six days later with a healthy baby with wide brown eyes and a shock of espresso hair.

The baby's name was Alexis. She was a girl.

(• •)

Two months later, on November 15 in New Orleans, wedding vendors hoisted a massive arch into the Contemporary Arts Center. Soon they would arrange on it hundreds upon hundreds of antique-gold-hued roses. They placed rows of sofas and loveseats for guests to perch on the following day, when Ohanian and Williams would walk down the aisle. Staff draped black lamé tablecloths, and hung chandeliers ensconced in faux bird cages to fit the "vintage Parisian fairy tale" theme, which was, more or less, *Beauty and the Beast*, while Ohanian and Williams rehearsed their first dance nearby. Pieces of a vintage merry-go-round were hauled in and reassembled in the middle of a cavernous warehouse space for the afterparty.

That evening, those closest to the Ohanians and the Williamses gathered for a private dinner cooked by celebrity chef Emeril Lagasse. It was a complete commingling of Silicon Valley, Hollywood, and professional sports. Chris and Kristen Slowe sat next to tennis great Caroline Wozniacki and also chatted with Sheryl Sandberg.

A long slate of toasts brought laughter and tears—particularly those by Williams, and by Ohanian's dad, Chris. Huffman was present, but didn't give a toast; he'd decided too late—that very day. He was told it didn't fit the schedule. The party extended late into the evening and morphed into a welcome party as more guests arrived in New Orleans for the ceremony the following day.

On the morning of November 16—a date chosen because it had been Ohanian's mother's birthday, and the couple wanted to find a way to infuse the wedding with her presence—Ohanian had his coffee while his closest friends milled about the stately Victorian home where they'd all slept, assembling their groomsmen essentials: shoes, ties, and where were the rings? Ohanian's dad had them. By afternoon, the men, including Jon Swyers, Ohanian's friend since first grade, Michael Pope, his longtime employee, and Huffman, gathered in the second-floor living room to toast Ohanian. Lissie Garvin repeatedly shooed the men away from the windows, mindful of the paparazzi swarming the street downstairs.

Indoors, the wedding parties had their own photographers to capture the moment. The men joked around and poured champagne and whiskey. They tried to act natural; the photographers wanted to take candid shots. Ohanian fastened a pair of Gucci cuff links onto the sleeves of his crisp, made-to-measure Armani shirt. He squared his shoulders to a mirror on the wall, and slipped a black bow tie under his starched white collar before fumbling with the ends. He made a cursory knot—and stopped. "I don't really know how to tie a bow tie," he admitted to the room. Huffman stood up and said, "I do."

Huffman had already managed to fasten his own bow tie, and was wearing his shirt and vest. He came over to Ohanian and leaned in close. He instructed Ohanian: Perhaps it was time to learn this small skill? They laughed. A photographer snapped a photo.

Two days later, Ohanian would post the first photo from the whole incredible wedding event on Reddit, and across his social media streams. It wasn't any of the lavishly staged photographs taken on a velvet couch by *Vogue*'s multiple photographers and assistants, who attended and captured the family and celebrities for its website. The photo Ohanian would post was the candid snap of Steve Huffman stepping up to fasten Ohanian's bow tie. Light pours in from the window behind them. Huffman is focused on the task at his hands, the bow tie. Ohanian is catching his own reflection in a mirror. Both men are beaming.

Shortly before 5 p.m. the groomsmen piled into a Sprinter van parked just outside the door, and were shuttled to the back entrance of the arts center, more or less across the street. The paparazzi presence was too much to handle. The men were ushered to the building's top floor, all glass and overlooking the

Mississippi River. Soon, they'd head downstairs to the ceremony, where they'd walk down an aisle lined with celebrities perched on couches: Beyoncé, Jay-Z, Kim Kardashian, and Anna Wintour, who'd been the one to suggest that Williams be married in a Sarah Burton for Alexander McQueen dress and cape. Steve Newhouse, from Advance Publications, was present. Ohanian's dad, the travel agent from Maryland, beamed and clutched the rings. He would deliver them to the couple during the ceremony. While Ohanian and Williams exchanged vows, baby Alexis Olympia Ohanian Jr. would be snuggled in the arms of Serena Williams's mother, Oracene Price.

After the ceremony, a marching band ushered guests to dinner. Ohanian and Williams ducked away to pose for the *Vogue* photographers, but before long, the couple entered dramatically. Williams had changed into her second of three dresses for the evening, a beaded, feathered Versace number, which took five embroiderers fifteen hundred hours to create. The couple perched on gold thrones.

After dinner, guests were invited to the afterparty—for a surprise performance by New Edition, and to take rides on the full carousel, as a post-midnight present from the groom to his new wife. Near the door, staff had assembled miniature reproductions of Grand Slam trophies that had served as place cards, so guests could take theirs home as tokens to remember the evening.

As it came time to leave, Huffman approached the table. He scanned the trophies for his name for a few moments before pocketing a memento. The nameplate on the tiny trophy read "Kim Kardashian."

ACKNOWLEDGMENTS

This is my first book. Reporting and writing it was an immersive adventure, at times messy and trying. Many, many individuals in my life have given me gracious guidance, support, encouragement, and love during the course of its making.

I would like to thank my editor, Paul Whitlatch, who believed in and was fascinated by this story from his first introduction to it, and whose adept questions and edits made this work better at every turn. Everyone at Hachette has been a joy to work with, and everyone up to Mauro DiPreta *got it*, right away. I'd particularly like to thank Lauren Hummel, Michelle Aielli, and Joanna Pinsker.

I'm extremely grateful to have my agent, Howard Yoon, and his colleagues at Ross Yoon in my life. Howard went above and beyond at every step of the process of turning my concept and years of interviews I had into a book. He always believed it would be a vibrant story. His courtesy and grace are infectious, and I think bettered the process at every juncture. I'm extremely lucky to count him also as an adviser and friend.

The very first believer in this book—at least he was game to come along on the journey—was Alexis Ohanian. Steve Huffman was the second believer. They agreed separately to speak with me exclusively for the purpose of a book, though none of us had any way of knowing that more than five years later, an absolute eternity in "iterate fast" Silicon Valley, it would still be part of their lives. Over the years, both were generous with their time, as well as that of their families and the company they had built, and to which they later returned. I'd like to thank Reddit for giving me, and readers, glimpses inside how, precisely, they built this unique, remarkable institution. This is not to say every request I made of them or of Reddit was met with a yes, or an answer of any stripe; plenty were met with frustrating silence. Anna Soellner is good at her job.

So many people spent more time with me than I probably deserved, but Chris and Kristen Slowe stand out the most. I'm grateful for their tremendous memories and willingness over the years to pick up the phone and tell their personal stories. I'm also extremely thankful for the time, energy, and dedication of dozens of current and former Reddit employees, some of whom were reluctant to speak to me at first, and many of whom I cannot thank by name. Their willingness to take a risk and share hundreds of documents and a multitude of experiences helped make this book rich and true.

I am lucky in so many ways; professionally, I am fortunate to have a home at *Inc.*, where I was given the encouragement and space to write this book. I'm grateful to Eric Schurenberg, for his support and kindness, to James Ledbetter, for his mentorship and encouragement—he makes it all look easy—and to Jon Fine, for giving me a glimpse into the struggles of book creation, always infused with humor. Thanks also to Leigh Buchanan, Danielle Sacks, Laura Lorber, Kimberly Weisul, Allison Fass, Kris Frieswick, Diana Ransom, Stephanie Meyers, and Maria Aspan, for inspiring me every day.

Many people helped me get over the finish line. April Joyner and Zoe Henry did tremendous research and had an unflinching willingness to delve into some of the Internet's darkest corners. Jason Rothauser contributed his sharp eye and snappy work. And Joel Froude was a secret weapon, jumping in to consult on a range of photographic, technological, and aesthetic challenges.

It's an honor to note that the first person who read this book from start to finish was David Lidsky. I owe him a great deal of gratitude. His swift and thorough read of the book improved it vastly.

To the mentors, friends, neighbors, and colleagues I turned to along the way for advice specific and broad, I'm extremely grateful. To name a few: Andy Hall of the Wisconsin Center for Investigative Journalism, Burt Helm, Jessica Pressler, Dawn and Andrew Siff, Jess Weit and Bob Martus, Tom Robbins, Jane Berentson, and danah boyd's outstanding crew at Data & Society. Jill Schwartzman guided me in so many ways, and she and her family were there for my family at so many junctures, she cannot properly be thanked here. I'm grateful to no end for Wayne Barrett, who was my very first believer in the New York journalism community, and who became my longtime mentor. We lost him in 2017. While he has left holes in many hearts, he has also left far more than a lifetime of inspiration with all those who were lucky enough to be close to him.

This book would not exist without the loving support of my family, who endured many confusing phone calls in which I talked about the Internet and who forgave my absence and frequent absentmindedness. Shire Chafkin and Laurie Peek were there for me with tireless support, interest, and encouragement. Anne Cassidy served up inspiration, care, and many meals. Mom and Dad, Carla and Andy, you know this, but I love you.

The littlest people whose lives were affected by the writing and reporting of this book are Solomon and Alice Chafkin. Their budding patience, constantly uplifting joyful spirits, and love helped ease this book into the world. A big network of loving caretakers, local friends, and teachers have over the past three years helped introduce Alice and Sol to the wonders of the world. I could not have made this book without them.

This book is dedicated to Max Chafkin, my husband and the greatest love. His encouragement, advice, and love made this book possible. He has been generous with his time in helping me in so many ways over these past few years, but also provided inspiration to me in matters of reporting, writing, patience, wit, running, and reading of bedtime stories to toddlers. He does all the voices. I love him.

SOURCES

This book is based primarily on the author's firsthand reporting. Unless otherwise noted, material originates from hundreds of hours of interviews conducted by the author, or materials, such as photographs, videos, chat logs, emails, or records gathered by the author. Reporting and research for this book was conducted over the course of more than five years; the author was present at many of the scenes as they unfolded. Others are rendered truthfully due to copious reporting, and have been constructed with help from multiple sources. That's not to say sources are necessarily firsthand for each scene.

Most, but not all, individuals who appear in the book consented to be interviewed. There were exceptions, one of whom was Ellen Pao, who responded only to a couple of the allegations and questions the author presented to her, and who denied interview requests multiple times by saying her recent book, *Reset*, should speak for itself. It is treated here as a primary source that at times informs the narrative. Most of Pao's perspective here originates in *Reset*. Points of particular interest are sourced below, with page numbers from the Kindle edition.

The Internet Archive was an invaluable source of old, now-defunct, updated, or since-censored content. Where current or easily accessible webpages are unavailable, they are often referenced through the "Wayback Machine," as it's known. Reddit itself, of course, was also invaluable; so was its blog, which took at least four iterations over the years. Reddit posts themselves are usually quoted when referenced in the text, and despite the common refrain that Reddit's search function is lackluster, it does the job in most cases here, so references to most Reddit posts, threads, and blog announcements are omitted. Media and other online sources quoted and well referenced in the text, and which are easily located, are also omitted here. A web address is provided only when a basic search may be insufficient. A visual timeline of additional sources can be found at WeAreTheNerds.com.

NOTES

PART I

This Guy Has No Shame

"There is hope!": "2005 Reddit Interview" (video interview of Paul Graham, Steve Huffman, and Alexis Ohanian), YouTube, July 14, 2015, https://www.youtube.com/watch?v=6kzhtIuh1qQ. Likely source: outtakes from *Aardvark'd: 12 Weeks with Geeks*, Boondoggle Films, 2005.

"I will probably have rocket-high sales": Fifth-grade yearbook, Thunder Hill Elementary School, Columbia, Maryland, 1994, courtesy of Alexis Ohanian.

Rejected by girls: Alexis Ohanian, *Without Their Permission: How the 21st Century Will Be Made, Not Managed* (New York: Business Plus, 2013), 21–22.

How to Start a Startup

an eighty-page thesis: "Our Y Combinator Summer 05 Application," posted by Alexis Ohanian on November 29, 2010, AlexisOhanian.com.

Swartz was pondering: Aaron Swartz, "The Case Against Lawrence Summers," aaronsw.com, March 9, 2005.

"If you want to do it": Paul Graham, "How to Start a Startup," essay delivered before the Harvard Computer Society, posted online March 2005.

Not Your Standard Fixed-Point Combinator

Graham snapped a photo: Paul Graham, "How Y Combinator Started," blog post on Y Combinator's former website, March 15, 2012.

"How do we even tell people": Jessica Livingston, *Founders at Work: Stories of Startups' Early Days* (New York: Apress, 2007), 448.

"You better quit your job": Ibid.

"You know, Sam": Ibid., 449.

When the meeting ended: Aaron Swartz, "SFP: Come see us," aaronsw.com, April 16, 2005.

Modern frat-life touches: Sarah Maslin Nir, "Are Finals Clubs Too Exclusive for Harvard?," *New York Times*, August 2, 2016.

eight they had selected: In *Founders at Work*, Livingston notes that seven teams were accepted initially—before Huffman and Ohanian's team was accepted. Graham, in a separate video interview, says that nine were, and one of the companies "imploded before the summer started." Their memories on this are now unclear.

Front Page of the Internet

owned by a domain squatter: Comment by Paul Graham (username: pg), "Guy Who Copied Digg Slams Digg for Copying Twitter," Hacker News, May 30, 2010.

"If you're attached to the little bug guy": Ohanian, *Without Their Permission*, 60.

It's Online

"Hollaback Girl": Ohanian, *Without Their Permission*, 61.

He even designed stickers: Alexis Ohanian, "Time Machine," Reddit's blog, December 5, 2006.

Their lives, home and work: Paul Graham, "Jessica Livingston," paulgraham.com, November 2015.

"The relationship between hackers": *Aardvark'd: 12 Weeks with Geeks*.

"VCs: soulless agents of Satan": Tad Friend, "Sam Altman's Manifest Destiny," *New Yorker*, October 10, 2016.

"Paul in one person": *Aardvark'd: 12 Weeks with Geeks*.

Hell Summer

Within months, twelve thousand people: Richard Adams, "Innovations: Reddit.com," *Guardian*, December 7, 2005.

"Having that kind of grounding": Interview with Alexis Ohanian, *Real Biz with Rebecca Jarvis*, ABC News, accessed March 15, 2018, http://abcnews.go.com/Business/video/reddit-founder-alexis-ohanian-real-biz-rebecca-jarvis-40771917.

How to Act Like a Real Adult

had thrown up his hands: Justin Peters, *The Idealist: Aaron Swartz and the Rise of Free Culture on the Internet* (New York: Scribner, 2016), 148.

"fake world of school": *Aardvark'd: 12 Weeks with Geeks*.

"I found myself stuck": Aaron Swartz, "Introducing Infogami," Infogami.com, accessed through Internet Archive, https://web.archive.org/web/20070308114441/http://infogami.com/blog/introduction.

Rounding Error

"Together, we felt unstoppable": Swartz, "Introducing Infogami."

The Algorithm and the Cupboard

"just a list of links": Aaron Swartz, "The Aftermath," *Raw Thought* (blog), November 1, 2006.

when Arrington phoned Delicious's founder: Michael Arrington, "Yahoo.icio.us?—Yahoo Acquires Del.icio.us," TechCrunch, December 9, 2005.

You Are Making Us Sound Stupid

"We all started getting touchy": Aaron Swartz, "How to Get a Job Like Mine," speech, as prepared, for the Tathva 2007 computer conference at NIT Calicut.

He wrote a program: Aaron Swartz, "Some Announcements," *Raw Thought* (blog), January 5, 2006.

He built and released: Aaron Swartz, "Wassup?," *Raw Thought*, March 27, 2006.

"You'd think, this is a kid": *The Internet's Own Boy: The Story of Aaron Swartz*, documentary film by Brian Knappenberger, 2014.

"The situation was so toxic": Peters, *The Idealist*, 157.

We Are the Nerds

"Suits...are the physical evidence": Aaron Swartz, "The Anti-Suit Movement," *Raw Thought*, March 16, 2010.

The Deal

"The other year": Aaron Swartz, "A Night at the Coop," *Raw Thought*, October 24, 2006.

PART II

Chasing That Moment

Swartz whiled away a portion: Aaron Swartz, "The Aftermath," *Raw Thought*, November 1, 2006.

On the phone a little later: Audio recording, Michael Arrington, "Talk Crunch," episode 17, "Wired Acquires Reddit," http://web .archive.org/web/20070723115645/http://talkcrunch.com/wp -content/TalkCrunch-EP017-WiredAcquiresReddit.mp3.

Millionaires' Ball

"I looked them straight in the eye": Aaron Swartz, "The Afterparty," *Raw Thought*, November 2, 2006.

The opening price: "Web Startup for Sale on Ebay," Bloomberg News, August 24, 2006.

a final price tag of $258,100: Jeff Yang, "Man with a Cam," *San Francisco Chronicle*, March 27, 2007.

"Wired has tried to make": Aaron Swartz, "Office Space," *Raw Thought*, November 15, 2006.

A Moment Before Dying

"Heh. I bet the first time": "A Chat with Aaron Swartz," transcript of interview by Philipp Lenssen, Blogoscoped.com, May 7, 2007.

"I know exactly what to do": Aaron Swartz, "Last Day of Summer Camp," *Raw Thought*, January 22, 2007, accessed through Internet Archive, https://web.archive.org/web/20070127190324 /http://www.aaronsw.com:80/weblog/.

"He was freed of all": Larissa MacFarquhar, "Requiem for a Dream," *New Yorker*, March 11, 2013.

"She never says": Swartz, "Last Day of Summer Camp."

The Physicist, the Information Cowboy, the Hacker, and the Troll

"So I have my own justification": Aaron Swartz, "Free Speech: Because We Can," *Raw Thought*, November 23, 2006.

"I fight laws that restrict": Aaron Swartz, "Bits are not a bug," NotaBug.com, accessed through Internet Archive, https://web.archive.org/web /20060105054203/http://bits.are.notabug.com/.

Mister Splashy Pants and the Large Hadron Collider

with 4,329 votes, or 3 percent: "Mister Splashy Pants the whale—you named him, now save him," Greenpeace.org, December 10, 2007.

had brought in $3.2 billion: Nat Ives, "Conde Nast Media Group Preps for Layoffs," AdAge.com, March 17, 2009.

Tools, Yo

they went into a moderator IRC: Jeremy Edberg, "We had some bugs, and it hurt us," Reddit's blog, September 29, 2009.

PART III

Take Me Home

As a teen and young adult: Biographical details of Dan McComas from Mike Isaac, "Imzy Is a Kinder, Gentler Reddit. If It Can Stay That Way," *New York Times*, June 9, 2016.

"really big community": "It's All About the Giving: Dan McComas at TedxDePaulU," YouTube, May 13, 2013, https://www.youtube.com /watch?v=phoUVH05kEg.

17,079 participants from 102 countries: "Over 17,000 reddit Secret Santas spread a world record setting amount of clandestine holiday cheer," Reddit's blog, December 13, 2010.

less than $10,000 in U.S. dollars: "The Informal Sector and Informal Employment in Armenia," National Statistical Service of the Republic of Armenia, 2011.

fund-raising Reddit had begun: Alexis Ohanian, "You asked, DirectRelief answered—learn how your dollars are helping Haiti," Reddit's blog, January 26, 2010.

The Ones That Got Away

what he called "late-night colors": "Alien Blue App Developer Speaks," interview transcript posted on TheAppleGoogle.com, October 10, 2010.

Geek Woodstock

Fans of the idea sent emails: Mike Isaac, "The Tech Behind the Rally to Restore Sanity: How Social Media Sparked a Parodic Revolution," *Forbes*, October 29, 2010.

Within weeks, more than $100,000: Megan Friedman, "Reddit Campaign for Colbert Rally Breaks Donation Record," Time.com, September 14, 2010.

more than two hundred thousand showed up: Brian Montopoli, "Jon Stewart Rally Attracts Estimated 215,000," CBSNews.com, October 31, 2010.

Exodus and Ill Will

Users were highly skeptical: Rachel Metz, "Why Did Reddit Succeed Where Digg Failed?," *MIT Technology Review*, July 18, 2012.

served more than four hundred million page views: Stan Schroeder, "Reddit: We Have More Traffic Than You Think," Mashable.com, July 16, 2010.

A quarter million Digg visitors: "Everything Went Better Than Expected," Reddit's blog, August 31, 2010.

Free-Speech Sandbox

"I wrote out my experience": Joe Coscarelli, "The Dangers of Going Viral: Kidney Donor Attacked by Reddit for Plugging Charity," *Village Voice*, December 18, 2010.

His phone rang: Ibid.

By 2012, Reddit had one hundred thousand communities: "2 Billion and Beyond," Reddit's blog, January 5, 2012.

more than $80,000 to build a massive wall: "Attack on Kenya orphanage yields $80k in donations," Associated Press, February 2, 2012.

pro-pot nonprofit: Fernando Alfonso III, "Reddit pot nonprofit goes up in smoke," Daily Dot, January 15, 2012.

"jailbait" was the search term: Adrian Chen, "Unmasking Reddit's Violentacrez, the Biggest Troll on the Web," Gawker, October 12, 2012.

second most used search: Alexa data, portions of 2017 (representative page: https://web.archive.org/web/20170711140628/https://www.alexa.com/siteinfo/reddit.com).

Violentacrez himself moderated: Kevin Morris, "Banned subreddit sparks debate on censorship," Daily Dot, August 17, 2011.

Blackout

The bill would have authorized: S. 3804—111th Congress: Combating On-line Infringement and Counterfeits Act, www.GovTrack.us, 2010.

"This bill would allow the government": "Aaron Swartz: How We Stopped SOPA," YouTube, August 17, 2012, https://www.youtube.com/watch?v=gl0vHBsapBc.

"a battle to define everything": Ibid.

"bunker-buster bomb": Grant Gross, "Senator Threatens to Block Online Copyright Bill," IDG News Service/PCWorld.com, November 19, 2010.

Some, including Sony and Nintendo: Data from the Center for Responsive Politics lobbying database (example: www.opensecrets.org/lobby/clientbills.php?id=D000042273&year=2011).

"without bringing in the nerds": "Rep. Jason Chaffetz (R-Utah) on SOPA: 'Bring in the Nerds,'" YouTube, December 20, 2011, http://www.youtube.com/watch?v=xrrj9Wc2L84.

More than 350,000 emails: Chenda Ngak, "SOPA and PIPA Internet blackout aftermath, staggering numbers," CBSNews.com, December 19, 2012.

"It was stopped by the people": Swartz, "How We Stopped SOPA."

"The Voice of His Generation," "He represents the idea," and *"hugely helpful in winning"*: Michelle Koidin Jaffee, "The Voice of His Generation," *Virginia* magazine, Fall 2014.

"The spirit of Reddit": "Alexis Ohanian (Reddit) at SOPA/PIPA Protest @ 780 3rd Ave. in New York City UNEDITED & RAW FOOTAGE!," YouTube, January 18, 2012, https://www.youtube.com/watch?v=s3G26V9H26k.

Meet Your New CEO

a billion a month: "reddit: billions served," Reddit's blog, February 2, 2011.

that much traffic every fifteen minutes: Erik Martin, "Independence," Reddit's blog, September 6, 2011.

NOT BAD!

"We'd call up press secretaries on the Hill": Alexis C. Madrigal, "AMA: How a Weird Internet Thing Became a Mainstream Delight," *Atlantic*, January 7, 2014.

Goff suggested an AMA: Michael Hastings, "How Obama Won the Internet," BuzzFeed, January 8, 2013.

"POTUS is doing an AMA": Peter Kafka, "How Reddit Got Obama: 'There Are Quite a Few Redditors at 1600 Pennsylvania Ave.,'"

AllThingsD.com, August 29, 2012; Hastings, "How Obama Won the Internet."

Barack Obama spoke to students: Hayley Tsukayama, "President Obama hits Reddit on 'Ask Me Anything,'" *Washington Post*, August 29, 2012.

"No. I have no idea": Hastings, "How Obama Won the Internet."

yes, this indeed was the chief of state: "I am Barack Obama, President of the United States—AMA," Reddit, August 29, 2012.

Within ten minutes, there were 278 comments: "POTUS IAMA Stats," Reddit's blog, August 31, 2012.

At one point Reddit was receiving: Ibid.

Many individuals were only seeing: Peter Delevett, "How Reddit landed Obama interview—and stole the GOP's thunder," *San Jose Mercury News*, August 30, 2012.

"Chaos over here": Adrianne Jeffries, "Reddit has its biggest day ever thanks to President Obama's AMA," The Verge, August 29, 2012.

The Wall Street Journal *published*: Sam Favate, "Obama Supports Constitutional Amendment on Campaign Finance 'If Necessary,'" *Wall Street Journal*, February 7, 2012.

"a staple of digital life": David Carr, "Left Alone by Its Owner, Reddit Soars," *New York Times*, September 2, 2012.

"Did it go perfectly smooth?": "POTUS IAMA Stats," Reddit's blog, 2012.

The Id

"visioning retreat": Peters, *The Idealist*, 173.

"It genuinely opened his eyes": Noam Scheiber, "The Inside Story of Why Aaron Swartz Broke Into MIT and JSTOR," *New Republic*, February 13, 2003.

It was titled the Guerilla Open Access Manifesto: Aaron Swartz, "Guerilla Open Access Manifesto," July 2008.

"get bossed around": Aaron Swartz, "Aaron's Patented Demotivational Seminar," *Raw Thought*, March 27, 2007.

"What was so striking about Aaron": "Sir Tim Berners-Lee pays tribute to Aaron Swartz," *Telegraph*, January 14, 2013.

Brewster Kahle of the Internet Archive: Brewster Kahle, speaking at a memorial to Aaron Swartz, January 24, 2013.

Malamud emailed him back: Carl Malamud archives, Aaron Swartz email message 299, https://public.resource.org/aaron/pub/msg00299.html.

"You definitely went over the line": Carl Malamud archives, Aaron Swartz email message 319, https://public.resource.org/aaron/pub/msg00319.html.

federal agents were conducting: John Schwartz, "An Effort to Upgrade a Court Archive System to Free and Easy," *New York Times*, February 12, 2009.

The file was closed: Aaron Swartz FBI File #1, 2009, http://www
.aaronsw.com/weblog/fbifile.

He had set up a website: "Content Liberation Front," contentliberation.com,
accessed through Internet Archive, https://web.archive.org/web
/20090102192453/http://contentliberation.com:80/.

At dinner, the activists bemoaned: Scheiber, "The Inside Story of Why
Aaron Swartz Broke Into MIT and JSTOR."

The conference ended on September 22: Peters, *The Idealist*, 201.

It violated JSTOR's terms of service: "JSTOR Evidence in United States vs.
Aaron Swartz"; see document cache at https://docs.jstor.org/.

downloaded some two million JSTOR articles: Connor Kirschbaum, "Swartz
indicted for JSTOR theft," *The Tech* (MIT), August 3, 2011.

MIT estimated to police: According to a Cambridge police report:
http://www.emptywheel.net/wp-content/uploads/2013/01/gov
.uscourts.mad_.137971.81.19.pdf.

Minutes later, MIT police captain Albert Pierce: Harold Abelson, Peter A.
Diamond, Andrew Grosso, and Douglas W. Pfeiffer, "Report to the
President: MIT and the Prosecution of Aaron Swartz," Cambridge:
Massachusetts Institute of Technology, July 26, 2013.

He and another local officer: Cambridge police report.

had with him a thumb drive: Kirschbaum, "Swartz indicted for JSTOR
theft."

Swartz was charged: Cambridge police report.

the New York Times *dubbed Swartz*: John Schwartz, "Open-Access Advocate
Is Arrested for Huge Download," *New York Times*, July 19, 2011.

"makes no sense": Ibid.

The Secret Service searched: FBI File, Aaron Swartz, p. 12, https://www
.bibliotecapleyades.net/archivos_pdf/aaron-swartz-first-release.pdf.

Investigators searched for a motive: David Kravets, "Feds Used Aaron Swartz's
Political Manifesto Against Him," *Wired*, February 22, 2013.

It was a direct call to action: Swartz, "Guerilla Open Access Manifesto."

"Most people, it seems": Aaron Swartz, "Stanford: Mr. Unincredible,"
aaronsw.com, March 26, 2005.

"the bad thing": Eulogy to Aaron Swartz, delivered by Taren Stinebrickner-
Kauffman, January 24, 2013.

"Am I always going to feel like this?": Peters, *The Idealist*, 258.

"were more interested in making": Eulogy to Aaron Swartz, delivered by
Taren Stinebrickner-Kauffman.

a massive memorial service: Susan Berger, "Family, Web Celebs Mourn Internet Activist," *Chicago Tribune*, January 16, 2013.

"Aaron Swartz this is for you": Larissa MacFarquhar, "Requiem for a
Dream," *New Yorker*, March 11, 2013.

Anonymous also hacked: "Hackers take over gov't website to avenge
Swartz," CBS News, January 26, 2013.

PART IV

Omniscient Guardians of the Depths

Every weekday morning: Adrian Chen, "Unmasking Reddit's Violentacrez, the Biggest Troll on the Web," Gawker, October 12, 2012.

Brutsch was a programmer: Michael Brutsch résumé, www.mbrutsch.com.

Brutsch's family depended: Chen, "Unmasking Reddit's Violentacrez."

he picked up in the Air Force: Michael Brutsch résumé.

There were occasionally new posts: Chen, "Unmasking Reddit's Violentacrez."

"It seems like you're not super careful": Ibid.

As Yishan Wong settled: "IAm Yishan Wong, the Reddit CEO," Reddit, April 20, 2012, https://www.reddit.com/r/IAmA/comments/sk1ut/iam_yishan_wong_the_reddit_ceo/c4en2w6/.

When asked about revenue: "IAm Yishan Wong, the Reddit CEO."

He proposed a hypothetical advertising model: Ibid.

an ample $20 million: Reddit's incorporation papers, newly refiled at the time, showed that Advance Publications had purchased $20 million in convertible preferred stock from Reddit. George Anders, "Today I Learned: Reddit Could Be Worth $240 Million," Forbes, October 31, 2012.

she'd recommend women altogether avoid: Kevin Morris, "Reddit's enemy within," Daily Dot, December 11, 2015.

a victim of sexual assault: Kevin Morris, "Alleged sexual assault victim questioned by skeptics," Daily Dot, September 12, 2011.

a fifteen-year-old posted: Rebecca Watson, "Reddit Makes Me Hate Atheists," Skepchick, December 27, 2011.

r/ShitRedditSays, or SRS: Más Wired, "On Reddit, racism, sexism still thrive," MasWired.com, October 9, 2012.

"Crush the Redditors with your Dildz": Morris, "Reddit's enemy within."

"I love not knowing": "IAMA reddit General Manager. AMA," Reddit, July 20, 2011.

"We just stayed out of there": Chen, "Unmasking Reddit's Violentacrez."

"People take things way too seriously": Fernando Alfonso III, "A free-speech haven wrestles with violent images," Daily Dot, August 11, 2011.

His boss called him: Adrian Chen, "Reddit's Biggest Troll Fired from His Real-World Job; Reddit Continues to Censor Gawker Articles," Gawker, October 15, 2012.

soon word circulated: "The real reason why Violentacrez deleted his account: Adrian Chen, Gawker Media, Creepshots, PM's and real-life doxing," Reddit, October 10, 2012.

a "scummy journalist": Ibid.

"Without assurances of anonymity": Chat logs: https://pastebin.com

/ibG6LSzD. Two participants in this chat, u/sodypop and u/redtaboo, were both well-established moderators at the time, and went on to be Reddit employees. Their opinion has evolved on this matter; they believed at the time of this book's publication that Reddit's policy need not apply outside of Reddit. They have described the time period detailed here as an uncertain one, in which new content rules were being established.

Wong posted a long-winded explainer: Adrian Chen, "Reddit CEO Speaks Out on Violentacrez in Leaked Memo: 'We Stand for Free Speech,'" Gawker, October 16, 2012.

"They're constantly under attack": Dave Thier, "Reddit General Manager Erik Martin on Violentacrez and the Gawker Bans," *Forbes*, October 17, 2012.

"Reddit users' [sic] and administrators": Chen, "Reddit's Biggest Troll Fired from His Real-World Job."

"We stand for free speech": Chen, "Reddit CEO Speaks Out on Violentacrez."

The Internet Bus

launched an Indiegogo campaign: "Internet 2012 Bus Tour," Indiegogo.com.

the very same bus: Charlie Warzel, "Inside Reddit's Internet 2012 Bus," *Adweek*, October 5, 2012.

they'd forgotten to wire: Charlie Warzel, "Reddit Hits the Road," *Adweek*, October 15, 2012.

had reached out to Wong: Ellen Pao, *Reset: My Fight for Inclusion and Lasting Change* (New York: Spiegel & Grau, 2017), 157.

In May 2012 she filed: Ellen Pao vs. Kleiner Perkins Caufield & Byers LLC et al., Superior Court of California, County of San Francisco, May 10, 2012, available at https://www.scribd.com/document/94428235/KP.

"worst of both worlds": Pao, *Reset*, 160.

"How about you?": Ibid., 161.

The 117th Boston Marathon

a twenty-three-year-old professional poker player: John Herrman, "The Man Behind the Internet's Hunt for the Boston Bomber," BuzzFeed, April 17, 2013.

created the subreddit r/findbostonbombers: Ibid.

in 2012, one gearhead: "Car part left at hit and run scene, any idea what it belongs to? It's a right front headlight," Reddit, December 18, 2012.

"Does anyone remember Richard Jewell?": "Does anyone remember Richard Jewell?," Reddit, April 17, 2013, accessed through Internet Archive,

http://web.archive.org/web/20130419234150/http://www.reddit
.com/r/findbostonbombers/comments/1civf6/does_anyone_remem
ber_richard_jewell/.

"basically every brown person wearing a backpack": Adrian Chen, "Your
Guide to the Boston Marathon Bombing Amateur Internet Crowd-
Sleuthing," Gawker, April 17, 2013.

An acquaintance noted: "Blue Tracksuit Guy Identified...ends up being a
local kid," Reddit, April 18, 2013, accessed through Internet Archive,
https://web.archive.org/web/20130420030905/http://www.red
dit.com/r/findbostonbombers/comments/1cl3cj/blue_tracksuit_g
uy_identifiedends_up_being_a/.

"Bag men: Feds seek these two": Larry Celona, "Authorities circulate photos
of two men spotted carrying bags near site of Boston bombings,"
New York Post, April 18, 2013.

deeply fearful of appearing in public: "Blue Tracksuit Guy Identified," Reddit.

It included an email link: r/findbostonbombers subreddit, accessed
through Internet Archive, http://web.archive.org/web/201304
18155254/http://www.reddit.com/r/findbostonbombers/.

"At one point I was banning": "I was one of the moderators of
r/findbostonbombers," Reddit, February 24, 2014.

"Reddit users are hosting": Ian Steadman, "Reddit users are hosting a witch-
hunt for the Boston Marathon bomber," Wired.co.uk, April 17, 2013,
accessed through Internet Archive, http://web.archive.org/web
/20130419231714/http://www.wired.co.uk:80/news/archive/201
3-04/17/reddit-solve-boston-bombings.

The special agent in charge: Remarks of Special Agent in Charge Richard
DesLauriers at Press Conference on Bombing Investigation, FBI
Boston, April 18, 2013.

The Washington Post *later clarified*: David Montgomery, Sari Horwitz,
and Marc Fisher, "Police, citizens and technology factor into Boston
bombing probe," *Washington Post*, April 20, 2013.

Reddit turned up a real: Ravi Somaiya and Jeremy Zilar, "New, Higher-
Resolution Image of Boston Marathon Suspect Emerges," *New York
Times*, April 18, 2013; Craig Kanalley, "Photo Of Suspect 2 in
Boston Marathon Bombing Emerges on Facebook," *Huffington Post*,
April 19, 2013.

His name was Sunil Tripathi: "Is missing student Sunil Tripathi Marathon
Bomber #2?," Reddit, April 19, 2013, accessed through Internet
Archive, http://web.archive.org/web/20130419090359/http://
www.reddit.com/r/boston/comments/1cn9ga/is_missing_student
_sunil_tripathi_marathon_bomber/.

NBC reported that Tripathi: Jay Caspian Kang, "Should Reddit Be Blamed
for the Spreading of a Smear?," *New York Times Magazine*, July 25,
2013.

Dzhokhar Tsarnaev was apprehended: "Jury Documents Sought in Boston Marathon Bomber's Appeal," *U.S. News and World Report*, May 20, 2017.

Money on the Mind

"Their strategy": Felix Gillette and Gerry Smith, "Reddit: A Nine-Year Case Study in Absentee Management," *Bloomberg Businessweek*, August 6, 2015.
sixty thousand individuals from 125 countries: Katie Rogers, "Reddit's secret Santa harnesses site's power for annual gift exchange," *Guardian*, December 12, 2012.
$3.85 million twenty-third-floor apartment: Suzanna Andrews, "Sex, Lies, and Lawsuits," *Vanity Fair*, March 1, 2013.
ten Reddit employees: Mike Isaac, "Reddit Execs Ellen Pao and Jena Donlin Get Serious About the Site's Business (Q&A)," Recode, April 8, 2014.
Graham had approached him in 2012: Colleen Taylor, "Sam Altman Taking Over as President of Y Combinator, Replacing Paul Graham at the Helm," TechCrunch, February 21, 2014.

Every Man Is Responsible for His Own Soul

141 million people visited the site: Andy Greenberg, "Hacked Celeb Pics Made Reddit Enough Cash to Run Its Servers for a Month," *Wired*, September 10, 2014.
servers for twenty-seven days: Ibid. Wong says the number was a vast exaggeration, but could not provide one more accurate.

Tiny Boxes

"shit sandwich": David Heinemeier Hansson, "Reddit's crappy ultimatum to remote workers and offices," *Short Logic*, accessed through Internet Archive, https://web.archive.org/web/20141004175215/http://shortlogic.tumblr.com/post/99014759324/reddits-crappy-ultimatum.

Unbelievable Because It's So Weird

"unbelievable because" and *"If the job had been an energizing one"*: Post on Quora by Yishan Wong in response to "Why did Yishan Wong resign as Reddit CEO?," January 23, 2016.

Closer to Yes

He wasn't a strong manager: Pao, *Reset*, 165.

The Poltergeist

"striking statement": Helen Popkin, "Reddit Interim CEO Ellen Pao: A Rare Instance of a Woman Running a Tech Company," ReadWrite.com, November 14, 2014.
"poltergeist": Pao, *Reset*, 174.
At a recent company-wide meeting: Ibid., 180.
Pao made staffing decisions: Ibid., 176.
gone through chemotherapy: Matthew Fleischer, "Incoming Reddit Community Manager Has Leukemia, Needs Bone Marrow Donor," *Adweek*, March 22, 2012.
"They all wound up leaving": Pao, *Reset*, 159.

PART V

Revenge and Revenge Porn

"Are we comfortable becoming 4chan?": Pao, *Reset*, 194.
but her lawyers advised her: Pao, *Reset*, 206.
"shrewd, and cagey": Dan Raile, "The Chart of Resentment: Dispatches from the Pao vs Kleiner Courtroom, Pt 5," PandoDaily, March 13, 2015.
Reddit hired a full-time security guard: Pao, *Reset*, 225.
the only post they removed: Ibid.
"The reason for the influx": "Reddit's 'CoonTown' Thriving Under New Harassment Policy," SPLCenter.org, July 5, 2015.
"Starting to crack down on harassment": Jay Hathaway, "Reddit Removes 'FatPeopleHate,' 'CoonTown' Still Cool Though," Gawker, June 10, 2015.

Fame and Its Inverse

"Aye, mate!" and other details from this chapter: Buzz Bissinger, "Serena Williams's Love Match," *Vanity Fair*, June 2017.
"I also have this": Evan Osnos, "Doomsday Prep for the Super-Rich," *New Yorker*, January 30, 2017.

AMAgeddon

"was suddenly nowhere to be found": Pao, *Reset*, 229.

"botched so much of the process": Ibid., 228.

A Change.org petition: James Titcomb, "Petition calling for Reddit boss Ellen Pao to resign hits 200,000 as she admits 'we screwed up'," *Telegraph*, July 7, 2015.

"They said they'll go to Plan B!": Pao, *Reset*, 230–31.

The Return of Steve

"enough that things weren't": Benjamin Wallace, "Reddit Redux," *New York*, October 6, 2015.

"He actually built Reddit": Laurie Segall, "Reddit CEO Ellen Pao steps down," CNNMoney.com, July 10, 2017.

"Thanks for getting right to the point": Kara Swisher, "Pao Out as Reddit CEO; Co-Founder Huffman Takes Over," Recode, July 10, 2015.

"Did I just watch": Guy Raz, interview with Steve Huffman and Alexis Ohanian, *How I Built This* podcast, August 31, 2017.

Fuzzy Approach

"Things that should be treated": Wallace, "Reddit Redux."

"wasn't on a glass cliff": Noah Kulwin, "Reddit Chief Engineer Bethanye Blount Quits After Less Than Two Months on the Job," Recode, July 13, 2015.

"If the world ends": Osnos, "Doomsday Prep for the Super-Rich."

"Serendipity" and "Bullshit"

"Reddit hasn't been known": "Behind the Scenes: Reddit's New Mobile App" (Reddit), YouTube, April 7, 2016, https://www.youtube.com/watch?time_continue=196&v=6IWMbdAuy1M.

r/The_Donald

they shared a vocabulary: Alice Marwick and Rebecca Lewis, "Media Manipulation and Disinformation Online," Data & Society, 2017.

massive private-message threads on Twitter: Shawn Musgrave, "The secret Twitter rooms of Trump nation," Politico, August 9, 2017.

an influx of brigaders: Jason Koebler, "How r/the_donald Became a Melting Pot of Frustration and Hate," Vice Motherboard, July 12, 2016.

Its constituency subsequently migrated: Eshwar Chandrasekharan et al., "You Can't Stay Here: The Efficacy of Reddit's 2015 Ban Examined Through Hate Speech," (Proceedings of the ACM on Human-Computer Interaction vol.1) November 2017.

A later semantic analysis: Trevor Martin, "Dissecting Trump's Most Rabid Online Following," FiveThirtyEight.com, March 23, 2017.

alt-right synergy: Joshua Green, *Devil's Bargain: Steve Bannon, Donald Trump, and the Storming of the Presidency* (New York: Penguin, 2017).

messages were honed here: Savvas Zannettou et al., "The Web Centipede: Understanding How Web Communities Influence Each Other Through the Lens of Mainstream and Alternative News Sources," September 30, 2017.

Former campaign staffers have admitted: Ben Schreckinger, "World War Meme," *Politico Magazine*, March/April 2017.

Facebook and Google came under intense scrutiny: John Herrman, "Inside Facebook's (Totally Insane, Unintentionally Gigantic, Hyperpartisan) Political-Media Machine," *New York Times Magazine*, August 24, 2016.

As early as election night: Mike Isaac, "Facebook, in Cross Hairs After Election, Is Said to Question Its Influence," *New York Times*, November 14, 2016.

"Sometimes I feel like": Nitasha Tiku "After Trump, Soul-Searching in Silicon Valley," BuzzFeed, November 10, 2016.

Spezgiving

national security adviser Mike Flynn: Bryan Bender and Andrew Hanna, "Flynn under fire for fake news," Politico, December 5, 2016.

"The worst thing": Kara Swisher, *Recode Decode* podcast interview with Steve Huffman, transcript posted January 18, 2017, as "Full Transcript: Reddit's Steve Huffman says he's really sorry for trolling Trump supporters."

What's Good for the United States

epicenter of pro-Trump fervor: Martin, "Dissecting Trump's Most Rabid Online Following."

This Is My Whole Life

containing a pregnancy test: Buzz Bissinger, "Serena Williams's Love Match."

"My family has been texting me": "Question to Gorsuch: 'Would you rather fight 100 duck-sized horses, or 1 horse-sized duck?' (C-SPAN)," YouTube, March 21, 2017, https://www.youtube.com/watch?v=UQBYX_GsXX8.

Imgur also boasted: John Herrman, "Imgur Is Now Bigger Than Reddit," BuzzFeed, September 26, 2013.

Reddit 4.0

"Reddit feels old": Kurt Wagner, "Reddit raised $200 million in funding and is now valued at $1.8 billion," Recode, July 31, 2017.
built a following as an artist: "The Story of /u/youngluck," *Upvoted* podcast, episode 0, transcript at https://www.reddit.com/r/Upvoted /wiki/transcripts-0-the-story-of-youngluck-english.

Salesman Emeritus

a campaign it had executed for FedEx: Lauren Johnson, "Reddit Is Pitching Brands at Cannes on Why It's Ripe for Advertisers," *Adweek*, June 22, 2017.
in-demand video ads: Lara O'Reilly, "Reddit Looks to Lure Advertisers with Video and Redesign," *Wall Street Journal*, June 22, 2017.
about two hundred of these companies: "The Global Unicorn Club," data compiled by CB Insights.

Live from Hollywood

"We are starting to slowly unveil": "Charlottesville: Race and Terror," Vice News, originally aired August 14, 2017, on HBO.
Facebook removed at least eight pages: Ali Breland, "Facebook removes pages for racist groups after Charlottesville," *The Hill*, August 15, 2017.
Spotify removed and *LinkedIn blocked*: David Ingram and Joseph Menn, "Internet firms shift stance, move to exile white supremacists," Reuters, August 16, 2017.
An Oxford University researcher: Ali Breland, "Warner sees Reddit as potential target for Russian influence," *The Hill*, September 27, 2017.
"the tip of the iceberg": Kurt Wagner and Tony Romm, "Live updates: Facebook, Google and Twitter testified before Congress again," Recode, November 1, 2017.
outside researchers determined: Rishab Nithyanand, Brian Schaffner, and Phillipa Gill, "Online Political Discourse in the Trump Era," November 14, 2017.
issued a sweeping indictment: United States of America v. Internet Research Agency LLC, U.S. Department of Justice, February 16, 2018.
works with Alphabet, Apple: Senate individual lobbying data for Kara Calvert Campbell of the Franklin Square Group, courtesy of the Center for Responsive Politics.

The disclosure stated that: Lobbying registration filed to the House and Senate under the Lobbying Disclosure Act of 1995 by the Franklin Square Group, July 24, 2017.

"we won this thing": Issie Lapowsky, "Here's How Facebook *Actually* Won Trump the Presidency," Wired.com, November 15, 2016.

All Together Now

"It's hilarious": Ben Collins, "Trolls Hijack White-Power Sites to Discuss Color Swatches," Daily Dot, August 4, 2017.

Internet provocateur Milo Yiannopoulos: "Requesting /r/faggots—No moderation, creator account gone, no activity," post on Reddit by user yiannopoulos_m, October 30, 2016.

They placed rows of sofas: Alexandra Macon, "Inside Serena Williams's Fairy-Tale Wedding in New Orleans," Vogue.com, November 17, 2017.

Williams had changed: Ibid.

INDEX